AEROFILMS GUIDES

Dartmoor and Exmoor

Des Hannigan

Ian Allan
Publishing

First published 1993

ISBN 0 7110 2044 2

Photographs © Aerofilms (unless otherwise
credited) 1993

Text © Ian Allan Ltd 1993

Published by Ian Allan Ltd, Shepperton, Surrey; and
printed by Craft Print PTE Ltd, Singapore.

Title page: Lydford Gorge

*Above: Haytor Rocks, a well-known landmark on
Dartmoor*

The publishers gratefully acknowledge the following
for the use of photographs. AA Photo Library: pages
72, 86, 132. Nature Photographers Ltd: pages 8, 20,
46, 58, 73, 87, 102, 103, 120, 121, 133, 156.

Contents

Other titles in this series:
The Yorkshire Dales

Other Aerofilms Guides:

The Cotswold Way

The South Downs Way

The South Devon Coast Path

The Thames Path

Using the Book

The book has two parts, covering Exmoor and Dartmoor, and each one is divided into chapters which follow the main river valleys as shown on pages 6 and 7. Each chapter consists of consecutive spreads like the one shown here.

In general, the right-hand edge of the photo-map joins the left-hand edge of the map in the next spread. However, to make the direction of the route absolutely clear, arrows indicate how the maps link together.

The vertical photography used in the photo-maps is taken from an average height above sea level. This means that the scale of the photography will alter slightly as the contours of the ground vary. The photo-maps are constructed by piecing together a series of photographs to make each page. They are intended to give a pictorial representation of the ground and strict accuracy of scale throughout cannot be guaranteed. There may also be a mis-match in areas of extreme relief - ie where the land is steepest.

Scale for Photo-maps
The scale-bar represents a distance of 0.310 miles (0.5km).

Vertical Photo-maps
Vertical photographs using a scale of 1:10,000 (0.6 miles:3.9ins, 1km:10cm) have been used to plot roads, footpaths, villages and features of interest.

Several footpaths lead to Hurlstone Point with its now redundant coastguard lookout. It marks the eastern end of Porlock Bay.

34

Exmoor

THE MAIN COAST road leads east from Porlock to Minehead, but a detour to the north of Porlock will take you to Bossington, one of Somerset's most attractive villages. Bossington consists of a straggle of colour-washed cottages with deeply thatched roofs, tall external chimneys and flower-bedecked porches. It retains the form of its Saxon origins and although the village is now less of a traditional farming community and more of a holiday attraction, there are still thatched cow-sheds by the roadside recalling its true pedigree. Bossington Green at the entrance to the village is shaded by walnut trees, while graceful willows fringe the banks of the Horner Water. There is a National Trust car park from where a number of paths offer pleasant walks.

A track leads from Bossington down to the great pebble beach fringing Porlock Bay that runs for 2 miles (3.2km) along a grey escarpment of polished boulders and pebbles seamed with thin quartz veins. The sea shuffles noisily along the tide line and the Horner Water filters through the banks from retaining ponds. In times of flood, however, the pent-up river may burst through the pebble beach and allow the sea to flood into the inland ponds before the pebbles build up again. The coast path leads west from the mouth of the Horner Water to Porlock and makes for a refreshing, open walk with exhilarating views of

Exmoor's wide embracing hills. The marshes and sea shore of Porlock Bay play host to a number of wild duck including shelduck, mallard, wigeon and teal, and are important winter feeding grounds for such migrant birds as curlew, lapwing, sandpiper, whimbrel and godwit.

From the car park at Bossington the Horner Water can be crossed to the east and a path followed out to Hurlstone Point, which has an impressive natural archway in its cliffs and an ornate and now redundant coastguard lookout on its highest point. Just before the Point, the coast path leads sharply uphill via the very steep Hurlstone Combe and on to an old military road leading over Selworthy Beacon. The top of Bossington Hill is easily reached from the path (A) up Hurlstone Combe.

Adjoining Bossington, and on the road to Allerford, is Lynch, a hamlet with strong traditions and surviving buildings to support them. On the side of the road opposite the Aller Water stands the small chapel-of-ease, built in the early 16th century and connected with the manor house of Bossington which survives, at least in part, alongside. The chapel is a peaceful, enduring place with several strong features including a wagon roof which has some original carved bosses. The Somerset Farm Park at Lynch offers a host of fascinating attractions for all the family.

The great sweep of Porlock Bay, with its flat coastal plain, provides delightful and easier walking for those not keen on the gradients inland.

Ilfracombe to Minehead

35

General Text
Information covering relevant places of interest, history, wildlife, the landscape, and routes both by road and footpath accompanies every photo-map.

Oblique Photographs
These photographs bring a new perspective to the landscape and its buildings. All the subjects chosen fall within the areas covered by the vertical photo-maps, or lie within easy reach of them.

Compass Point
Every photo-map is accompanied by a compass point for ease of orientation.

Key Map

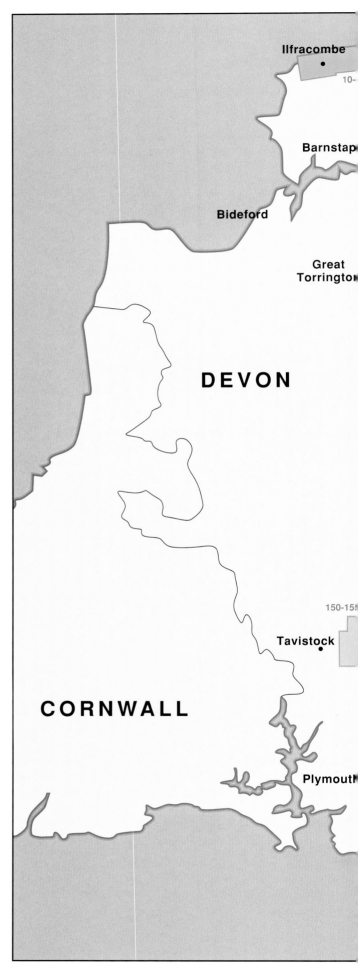

Lynmouth

Minehead

ombe Martin

48-51

Parracombe

52-57

Dunster

42-45

Exford

60-65

74-85

66-71

Exton

South Molton

Dulverton

SOMERSET

R.Exe

Chulmleigh

Tiverton

R.Taw

Crediton

ehampton

Exeter

DORSET

3

Chagford

R.Teign

94-101

R.Dart

Moretonhampstead

stbridge

Bovey
Tracey

104-109

Exmouth

2-131

Two Bridges

Teignmouth

Dartmeet

Princetown

Newton Abbot

49

110-119

Ashburton

Torquay

Paignton

34-141

Totnes

Dartmouth

Exmoor

EXMOOR NATIONAL PARK is a complex and beautiful landscape of tawny moorland and smooth-browed coastal hills, of wooded river valleys and green fields. Within this landscape lies a wonderful variety of towns and villages and an ancient pattern of hamlets and farmsteads. Within the 265 square miles (686 sq km) of the National Park lies an astonishing mix of coast and country shared between North Devon and West Somerset.

The boundary of the park follows the coast for 30 miles (48 km) from Combe Martin in the west to Minehead in the east. Spectacular coastal features like the Valley of Rocks are matched by the sylvan lovliness of Woody Bay and the quiet beauty of Culbone. Towering coastal hills like Hangman Point and Foreland Point slope steeply seaward to a final dramatic fall to lonely pebble beaches. This unrelenting coast is breached at rare intervals; rivers like the Heddon and the West and East Lyn tumble down their deeply wooded valleys to the sea at, respectively, Heddon's Mouth and Lynmouth. East of here the great sheltering heights of

Winsford

A red deer stag

Hurlstone Point and North Hill rise to seaward of such lovely villages as Allerford, Luccombe and Selworthy to run on towards Minehead and the low-lying shores of Bridgwater Bay.

Inland from the spectacular coast the northern moors rise dramatically through the heights of Challacombe, Brendon Common and Dunkery to merge with the rich, green farmland and islanded heaths of the southern moor. This is the country of the red deer and the sturdy Exmoor pony, the river-haunting dipper and the soaring buzzard. East from Dunkery, the flat-topped ridge of the Brendon Hills runs to where the National Park boundary falls short of the Quantocks. Exmoor's high country is drained by rivers like the Barle, the Exe, the Badgworthy

Valley of Rocks

Water of the famous Doone Country and Horner Water, all of which cut deeply into the massif. The name Exe derives from the ancient word for water, *isca,* which fits the moor's water-borne character and its containment between rivers and sea. Inland Exmoor is crossed by some excellent roads and is overlaid by numerous narrow lanes which require careful and courteous driving.

Walking opportunities on the coast and the high country are outstanding. Exmoor's towns and villages are delightful and its coastal resorts offer a lively contrast to the more reflective pleasures of the moorland interior. There are many fine old properties, gardens and nature reserves open to the public, and there is a wealth of handsome buildings including hospitable old inns, and numerous village churches of great antiquity. Accommodation is particularly plentiful around coastal resorts and there are excellent hotels, guesthouses, bed and breakfast establishments, and camping and caravanning throughout the whole area.

Exmoor offers a compelling experience for the discerning visitor who recognises its subtle and at times fragile beauty. Its resident community works with the National Park Authority to ensure that Exmoor thrives as a living, working environment rather than a scenic museum.

ILFRACOMBE TO MINEHEAD

38 miles (61km)

THE FIRST – or last – miles of the South West Coast Path follow the coastline between Ilfracombe and Minehead and it is a section with its own character and interest. Unlike many other stretches of this 515 mile (830km) national trail, a town or village is never far away.

Ilfracombe, North Devon's leading resort, lies about 9 miles (14.4km) north of Barnstaple within a sheltered inlet where the sea breached the valley of the East Wilder Brook. It has been a fishing port from earliest times with a robust seafaring tradition which also embraced shipbuilding and the cargo trade. Today the port still has a busy fishing fleet and there is a lifeboat station. The Napoleonic Wars of the early 19th century made France less attractive to fashionable English travellers, who began looking for home-grown watering places, and Ilfracombe was one of several West Country resorts which, as a result, flourished during the Victorian era and its architecture reflects that Golden Age. The town is a good shopping centre and is well supplied with car parks and all main facilities. Entertainment for all the family is extremely well-catered for; facilities include a museum, theatre, cinema, indoor swimming pool, tennis courts, bowling green, golf club and a host of children's attractions including the Rolling Falls model village off Torrs Walk Avenue. The tourist information centre is on the

The town of Ilfracombe lies protected in a dip in the cliffs, its buildings — many of them hotels and guesthouses — sprawling up the hillsides.

Promenade, and there are several gardens and parks including Bicclescombe Park, off St Brannock's Road, with its restored 18th-century watermill and numerous attractions. Ilfracombe is the base for the splendid paddle steamer *Waverley* and her companion ship *Balmoral,* which conduct cruises from the port throughout the season. There is also a ferry service between Ilfracombe and the island of Lundy.

The coastal area of Ilfracombe is composed of layers of slatey rock known as the Ilfracombe Beds, and the local landscape is typified by high, rounded hills punctuated by deeply eroded valleys. The town is flanked on the east by the grassy heights of Hillsborough where there are numerous walks and family attractions. Between Hillsborough and the town is Capstone Point. To the west lies the matching hill of the Torrs, where there are pleasant paths leading to National Trust property.

Within the heart of the harbour area is Lantern Hill, crowned by the tiny Chapel of St Nicholas which was used as a lighthouse for many years. It is now restored and its guiding light still functions. The building contains an interesting exhibition of old prints of Ilfracombe. On the south side of the town is Cairn Top Hill, where there is a nature reserve. Ilfracombe has several fine beaches including well-known Tunnels Beach, reached via tunnels through the rocky bluff from the eastern end of the Promenade.

Close to the town are the beaches of Wildersmouth, Larkstone and Rapparee Cove, and there are excellent beaches a few miles to the south at Woolacombe, Croyde and Braunton Burrows and to the east at the village of Hele Bay.

About a mile (1.6km) south-east of Ilfracombe and reached from the Combe Martin Road is Chambercombe Manor, the 16th-century manor house of Ilfracombe. The house has been handsomely restored and stands amid lovely gardens.

Chambercombe, south-east of Ilfracombe town centre.

THE A399 LEADS east from Ilfracombe, hugging the coast past Hele Bay and Water Mouth, the small fjord-like inlet tucked into the east of Widmouth Head. An early 16th-century watermill at Hele Mill on the A399 has been renovated and now produces wholemeal flour. It is open to visitors.

Water Mouth is a classic example of a drowned river valley. The sea has broken in at the point where a small stream emerged and is still eroding the valley's seaward wall, which projects in the form of a peninsula and is known as the Warren. The sea has already cut off the point of the Warren to create the small island of Sexton's Burrow. The landward side of the drowned valley terminates in Widmouth Head which in turn may end up as an island one day. There are several impressive caves at Water Mouth and the inlet is a natural harbour where there are always small boats riding at anchor or pulled up on the beach. Water Mouth was used during World War II for invasion training of waterborne troops and as a

Dating from the 19th century, Watermouth Castle has been turned into an entertainment complex with attractions guaranteed to keep children amused all day.

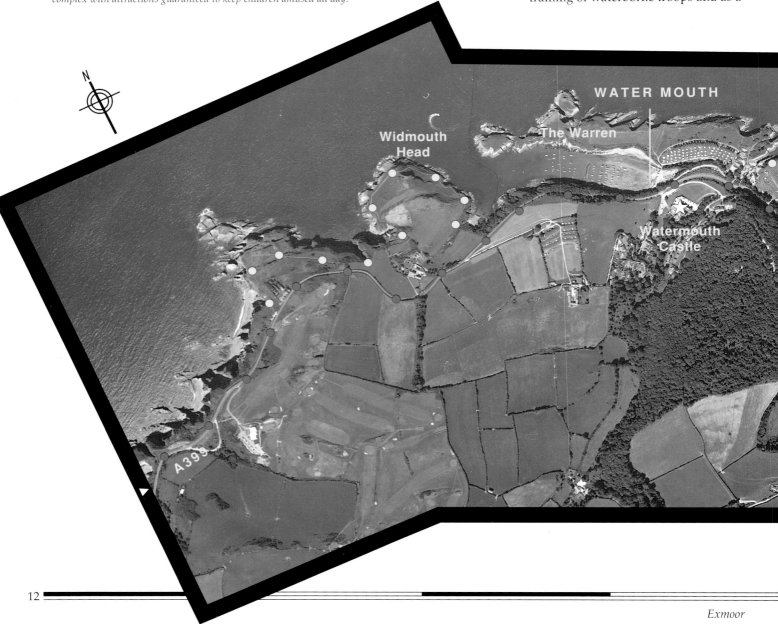

WATER MOUTH

The Warren

Widmouth Head

Watermouth Castle

A399

fuelling point for allied shipping during the Normandy landings.

On the opposite side of the A399 is Gothic Watermouth Castle, built in 1825 and now one of North Devon's liveliest tourist attractions. There are haunted dungeons, illuminated displays, a model railway, collections of memorabilia, children's games and many other features within the building and its landscaped gardens, all guaranteed to entertain the whole family.

Walking opportunities along this section of coast are slight because of proximity to the main road and parking can also be difficult, especially at the height of the season. However, there is a fine walk round Widmouth Head, with rewarding views east over Water Mouth and on to the striking heights of Great Hangman and Little Hangman in the east above Combe Martin. The path starts from the main road about 300yds west of the head of Water Mouth inlet: cross a stile on to the path which leads into woods and on round the Head. A

Water Mouth inlet, just across the road from Watermouth Castle.

path also runs out along the seaward peninsula of the Warren from the head of Water Mouth inlet. A section of the old coast road can be followed on foot from a point on the main road 500yds south of Watermouth Castle. About ½ mile (800m) along the old road a short path loops seaward to reach a viewpoint on the National Trust property of Golden Cove. Just before the start of the loop path a very steep flight of steps, 213 in all, leads down to a shingle beach at Broad Sand. Golden Cove itself is not accessible because of unstable cliff slopes.

The attractive village of Berrynarbor lies just south of the A399 and can be reached down the side road opposite the start of the old coast road. The village has a handsome 15th-century church with a tall sandstone tower. White limestone from Beer Quarry on the South Devon coast is a cool, contrasting feature of the inside of the church, where there are some fine monuments.

COMBE MARTIN EXTENDS for 1½ miles (2.4km) within a long narrow valley that winds down to a pleasant beach. The village developed originally as a mining community as lead, silver, copper and manganese were all mined in the area from medieval times. Iron ore was a later product and was shipped from Combe Martin to the smelting works of South Wales until about 1875, after which the village faced post-industrial decline. However, market gardening had long been a feature of Combe Martin's sheltered valley and this, together with the developing Victorian tourist industry, saved the village.

With its generous beach and splendid coastline Combe Martin still commands a large part of the North Devon holiday trade. There are numerous guesthouses and hotels, caravan and camping parks, and self-catering facilities. It is a good shopping centre and there are several

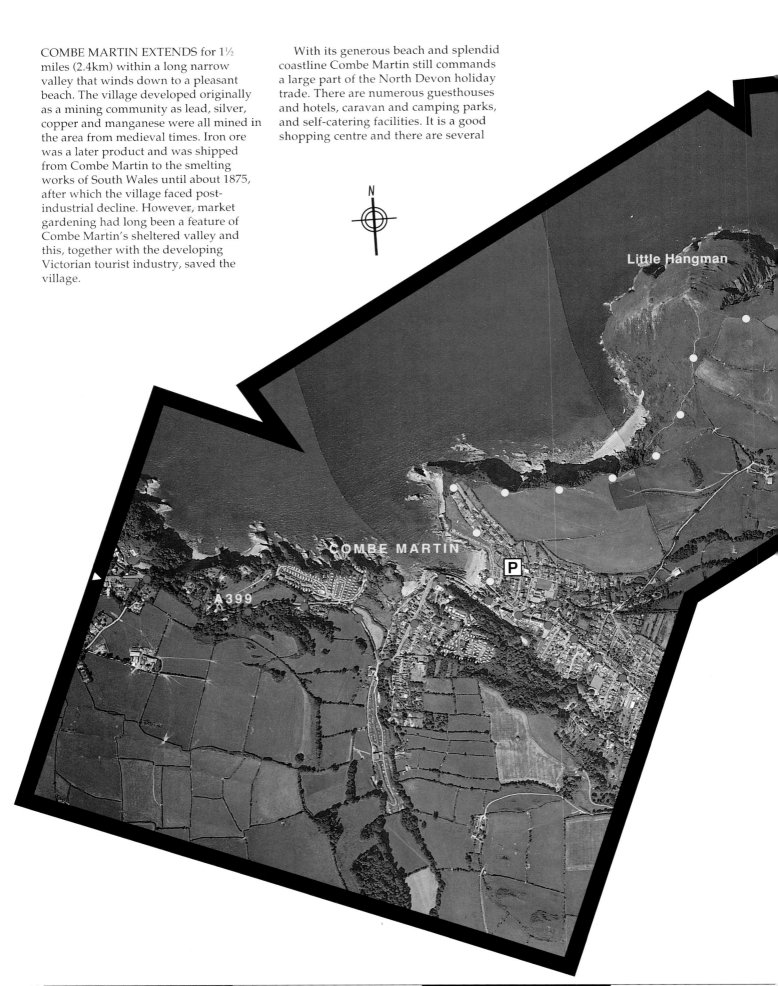

full spectacle is only visible from the sea. A path leads down Sherrycombe but the lower reaches of the combe should not be explored too far. The main coast path passes through a small copse of beech and birch trees then crosses the stream and winds steeply up the opposite slope. Ahead lies Holdstone Down, a bulky hill that offers a steady but reasonable climb. The summit is an excellent viewpoint. A late-Victorian speculator planned bungalow development on the hillside and even laid out two rough tracks with the names Seaview Road and Beach Road. The scheme failed, however, probably through a combination of hard times and even harder weather.

Holdstone Down can be reached more conveniently from the road which winds round its eastern flank. To reach this from Combe Martin, drive along the continuation of Shute Lane past the first car park (see page 16) to reach Stony Corner. Turn left at Stony Corner and then immediately left again to reach a car park by a large modern house. A broad path (B) leads due west from the road to the summit of Holdstone Hill.

Little Hangman and Great Hangman are two distinctive features of this stretch of coast. Although it is not as high as Great Hangman, Little Hangman is steeper and reaching the top is a much more strenuous exercise.

Ilfracombe to Minehead

Tiny, isolated Trentishoe is just a stone's throw away from popular Hunter's Inn to the south-east.

THE HEDDON VALLEY and famous Hunter's Inn can be reached from the car park at Holdstone Down by driving east along a narrow road that eventually leads steeply downhill through lovely woodland. For the walker the coast path from Holdstone Down continues along the breezy cliff edge skirting Bosley Gut. The path is narrow in places. At a junction above Heddon's Mouth the left-hand path offers a detour via Peter Rock. The right branch leads inland and then zig-zags steeply down into Heddon's Mouth Cleave.

The small hamlet of Trentishoe stands amid lonely moorland above a deeply wooded combe and is reached by turning off to seaward down a narrow lane from the road to Hunter's Inn at Holdstone Down Cross. The Church of St Peter is the main feature of Trentishoe, with only a scattering of houses to keep it company. Carefully sited in a protective hollow, it has a cool, dark interior, although Victorian restoration has rendered it rather bland. The old minstrels' gallery is a fine feature, however. It dates from the 1730s and sports a rough hole in one panel which accommodated the strokes of the bow of the bass-viol.

To reach Hunter's Inn from Trentishoe it is best to drive back to Holdstone Down Cross from where a left turn leads down through Parsonage Wood to the inn. The more direct route leading due south from Trentishoe is the old pre-19th-century road, but this is extremely steep and narrow and

Lime Kiln

Heddon's Mouth

TRENTISHOE

Ⓐ

Hunter's Inn

Ⓟ

should be avoided by motorists.

The valley of the River Heddon is one of the most striking features on this spectacular coast. It is thickly wooded, predominantly with sessile oak. Nearer the coast the great slopes of the cleave are littered with frost-shattered scree known geologically as Hangman Grits. The Heddon valley is best explored to seaward from Hunter's Inn, where there is parking, toilets, refreshments and craftshops. The immediate area is extremely busy during the height of the season but can feel remote in winter.

The stony beach of Heddon's Mouth can only be reached on foot, either from Hunter's Inn further up the valley or along the cliffs from Woody Bay to the east.

Most of the surrounding woodland is owned by the National Trust and there are numerous excellent paths throughout the area. It is possible to walk the mile (1.6km) down to Heddon's Mouth from Hunter's Inn via riverside tracks (A) and wooden bridges.

Heddon's Mouth is a fresh, open place, in perfect counterpoint to the wooded river valley. An old lime kiln stands above the stony beach as a reminder that limestone and coal were shipped into Heddon's Mouth from Wales until the early part of this century. The mix was burned in the kiln and the resulting lime used as fertiliser on the acidic soils of the area. The beach at Heddon's Mouth is stony and although interesting it is tidal and care should be taken. The surrounding cliffs are unstable. The coast path leads steeply up the eastern side of the Heddon valley from the halfway bridge on the track leading down to Heddon's Mouth and follows a magnificent stretch of coast to Woody Bay.

From Hunter's Inn the steep and narrow King's Lane leads due east for just under a mile (1.6km) to Mannacott Lane Head. Turn left here for the hamlet of Martinhoe where there is a sturdy little church. On the cliff-top north of Martinhoe lie the remains of a Roman fort which was established in AD58 to keep watch on the Welsh coast from where warring tribes threatened Roman colonisation.

The Moors in Prehistory

EXMOOR AND DARTMOOR were colonised and quite vigorously exploited during prehistoric times. The evidence of this is most emphatic on Dartmoor where granite artefacts endure. Exmoor with its dearth of surface stone has less to show of its prehistory.

The earliest humans on Exmoor and Dartmoor were the hunter-gatherers of the Mesolithic and Neolithic 'Stone Age' period (*c.*6000-2300 BC) whose tentative foraging into the high ground followed the ending of the last Ice Age. They left only meagre traces of their passage in the form of chert and flint weapons and crude tools. The Neolithic peoples probably used timber for their houses which further accounts for the dearth of remains dating from this time. Exmoor has two possible earthen ritual sites dating from this period, one being near

Below: Bury Castle, an Iron Age hillfort near Selworthy, Exmoor

Above: Spinster's Rock, at Drewstaignton, Dartmoor

Parracombe, while Dartmoor has several vestigial Neolithic chambered tombs like the impressive quoit of Drewsteignton's Spinster's Rock, which represents the inner core of a burial mound.

It was during the Early Bronze Age (*c.*2300-1300 BC) that more substantial stone monuments were established on both Moors. The Bronze Age peoples led a more settled existence which expressed itself in their use of ritual sites and artefacts. They cleared the primeval forests and then established settlements using chiefly timber. The ritualistic customs of these Bronze Age people have left a wealth of fascinating remains, especially on Dartmoor, including the massive burial mounds or barrows like

those at Brightworthy on Exmoor and at Three Barrows on Dartmoor.

But it is the stone monuments which are the most impressive. These include rows, circles and single stones. Again, Dartmoor has the better examples. There are about 70 stone rows on Dartmoor including the impressive row on Erme Plains which is 2 miles (3.2 km) long. Exmoor has a double row of small stones known as Whiteladder on the ridgeway south-east of Simonsbath and there is an impressive stone row in Culbone Woods. Stone circles survive at Withypool Common on Exmoor and at Little Hound Tor on Dartmoor. Both moors have several single standing stones like Exmoor's Long Stone on Challacombe Common and Dartmoor's

Drizzlecombe. The purpose of all of these remarkable monuments may have been religious and ritualistic or associated with astrological calculations.

Human settlement patterns of the Bronze Age and Iron Age periods can be seen in the form of hut circles. There are few such remains on Exmoor but Dartmoor has some striking examples, like those within the great enclosures of Grimspound and on Erme Plains. The great hilltop forts like Exmoor's Cow Castle on the River Barle and Dartmoor's Prestonbury Castle above Fingle Bridge reflected a more sophisticated though dangerous world which was moving rapidly from prehistory towards the imperialism and militarism of Roman, Saxon and Norman Britain.

Cow Castle by the River Barle, Exmoor

Woody Bay

TO THE EAST OF Martinhoe lies one of the loveliest stretches of coast within the Exmoor National Park. May Brothers car park, which lies just under ½ mile (800m) east of Martinhoe at the junction with a road going south to Martinhoe Cross and the A39, affords a splendid view in clear weather: wooded coastal hills to the east crowd the horizon, while the eye is drawn across the birch and oak woods of the bay to the rocky shores below Crock Point and on to Duty Point with its folly tower. Beyond lies the hazy summit of Castle Rock at the famous Valley of Rocks.

From May Brothers car park the road leads straight ahead for a short distance to where a left turn leads through a sharp right-hand bend and down to Inkerman Bridge. Woody Bay can only be reached on foot from the National Trust car park

which is about 150yds before the bridge. From the car park a very steep and often muddy path (A) leads down through sessile oak woods interspersed with birch, beech and red-berried rowan trees. The path then runs above Martinhoe Manor House and down to the beach (B).

At the west side of the beach the stubby remains of an old latticework pier mark the site of an ambitious Victorian tourism project aimed at turning Woody Bay into a major resort. However, the scheme eventually collapsed along with the storm-battered pier. Care should be taken as the beach is tidal and the cliffs are unstable. The road leading east from Woody Bay can be reached by continuing past Inkerman Bridge and the Woody Bay Hotel. Alternatively, the upper road can be regained by returning uphill from the National Trust car park and then turning

left. It should be borne in mind that the minor coastal roads throughout the area can become extremely congested during the high season. For the walker, the coast path joins the road by the Woody Bay Hotel and the route is road-bound until the Valley of Rocks, although the walker avoids paying the toll-fee required from drivers for the stretch from Lee Abbey to the Valley of Rocks. Lee Abbey is a Victorian neo-Gothic building. Its name is fanciful, since there never was an abbey on the site. There is parking, a picnic site, toilets and a seasonal café here.

One theory for the formation of the Valley of Rocks relates to possible erosion during the last Ice Age when the southern edge of the Polar ice cap is believed to have lain along the line of the present coast. The precipitous streams from the high moor had to cut their way to the

Valley of Rocks

Lee Bay

west because of the damming effect of the ice. When the ice retreated, the rivers flowed to the north once more leaving behind a dry valley with a high seaward ridge. A simpler theory suggests that the rivers once flowed to the west but eventually altered course because of easier access to the sea as a result of the natural erosion of Lynmouth Bay. The dramatic sandstone pinnacles of the Valley of Rocks have been further eroded and exposed by frost action and weathering and the scree slopes of the ridge are typical results of such erosion.

There is a large car park at the Valley of Rocks, from where footpaths lead over the strange, baselisk formations. The road leads steeply uphill from here to reach Lynton. Walkers can follow the coast path which leads from the roundabout towards the sea.

It is easy to see why Valley of Rocks is so named. With easy access and plenty of parking, it inevitably becomes a tourist honey pot during the holiday season.

Lynmouth sits at the mouth of the East and West Lyn rivers while its sister town, Lynton, is situated higher up on Hollerday Hill. A steep road, very steep paths and a cliff railway link the two.

ALTHOUGH LYNTON IS irrevocably linked to Lynmouth 600ft (183m) below, not least by a famous cliff railway, the two have distinct identities. Lynton is an unassuming little town, pleasantly compact in style, with a busy tourist centre and a good selection of shops, a number of hotels and guesthouses in the town and a youth hostel. The tourist information centre is at the impressive, though eccentrically-designed, town hall in Lee Road. Lynton's Church of St Mary the Virgin has an unremarkable exterior, but inside the church has many pleasing features such as the splendid altar façade of copper repousse in the Lady Chapel, the Romanesque chancel with its fine east

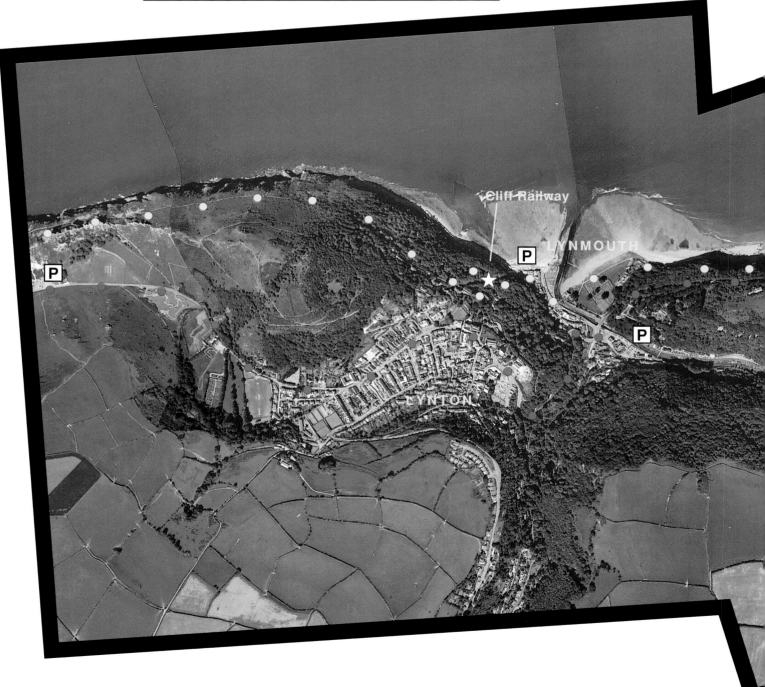

window, and the striking tracery of the west window. The Lyn and Exmoor Museum, tucked away in Market Street, has an excellent collection of exhibits about Exmoor life and history. There is a brass-rubbing centre in Queen's Street and a small museum at the old smithy at the foot of Church Hill.

From the heart of Lynton the delightful North Walk starts between the church and the Valley of the Rocks Hotel. It leads through the public park of Hollerday Hill to the Valley of Rocks and can be linked to several other paths to give excellent circular walks. Another fine walk starts to the right of the town hall and leads through the Hollerday Hill park. The lovely harbourside village of Lynmouth is linked to its sister by a steep downhill road or by the hair-raising cliff railway, opened in 1890 and still a wonder to behold.

Lynmouth is forever associated with the catastrophic flood of 15 August 1952 in which 34 people lost their lives and the heart of the village was torn apart. The events of that August night were stupendous. Millions of gallons of rainwater poured off the impermeable surface of the Chains on the moorland heights and cascaded into the steep northern river valleys with explosive force. The East and West Lyn Rivers funnelled a hurtling mass of water, trees and huge boulders into the unsuspecting village in the dark of the night and with devastating effect. Yet Lynmouth has survived and has retained much of its former beauty as an ancient port and fishing harbour, matched by its eastern outlook across Sillery Sands to the towering western flanks of the Foreland.

The village is a major tourist centre, as it has been since the early years of last century, in harness with Lynton. There are numerous gift and craft shops, several hotels and guesthouses, restaurants and cafés. Of the several fine old buildings in Lynmouth, the deeply thatched Rising Sun hotel is particularly striking. On the quayside stands the famous Rhenish Tower, destroyed in the 1952 floods but rebuilt soon after. The original building dates from the mid-18th century and was used for storing sea water for a wealthy resident's salt baths.

About 1½ miles (2.4km) from Lynmouth along the A39 lie the wooded delights of Watersmeet, where the National Trust has a seasonal shop and restaurant and many woodland walks can be enjoyed.

The A39 road leading due east from Lynmouth climbs the steep Countisbury Hill and offers fine seaward views. Near the top of the hill the road passes through a massive Iron Age defensive embankment (c.600BC-AD43) which extended to the coast and down into the East Lyn valley, thus protecting the tongue of land to the east of modern Lynmouth.

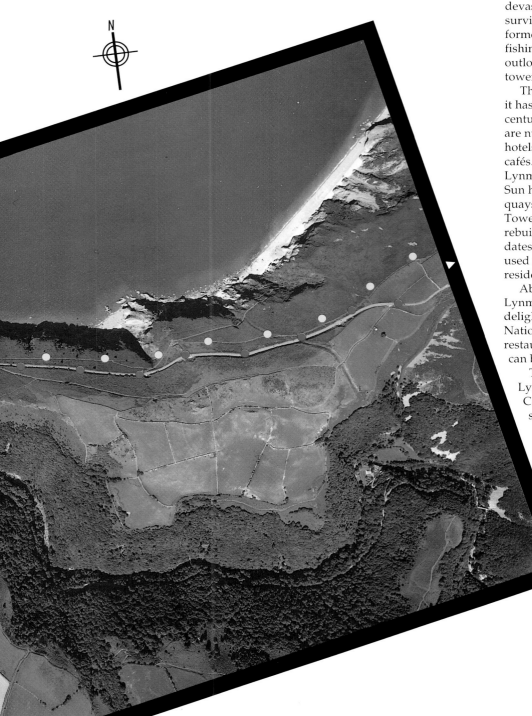

WHERE THE A39 levels off at the top of its steep climb out of Lynmouth lies the hamlet of Countisbury, with its church, its old inn and its row of handsome colour-washed buildings featuring tall Exmoor chimneys. To seaward lies the great headland of the Foreland Point, Devon's most northerly point. To the east the hog's back shapes of the coastal hills increase in steepness and size. Countisbury has an ancient pedigree. Its name means the camp or fort on the hill and relates to the great Iron Age fortification ½ mile (800m) to the west. The hamlet's position between high and low ground would always have made it an important site regardless of its windswept nature. There was a coaching stop for many years at Countisbury, and its Church of St John the Evangelist is still the parish church of Lynmouth. This sturdy little building has been well restored and cherished by its parishioners over the centuries. Dark yew trees line the approach to the building to match the pleasing lines of its tower. A number of gravestones in the churchyard pay tribute to most of the 1899 crew of the Lynmouth lifeboat, *Louisa,* not because of some dark tragedy but in memory of a famous incident when the lifeboat was called out to stand by a distressed vessel. Conditions ruled out launching the *Louisa* from Lynmouth, so instead, the crewmen and scores of helpers pushed and hauled the lifeboat on its wagon up Countisbury Hill and along the rough cliff-top road and down Porlock Hill's notoriously steep descent to be launched from Porlock Weir. The 14 mile (22.6km) journey took 11 hours and included some ad hoc realignment of the road to accommodate *Louisa's* passing. The ship's crew were saved and the lifeboat returned to Lynmouth intact.

The massive bulk of the Foreland represents the northern remains of an ancient range of hills which projected from the main line of the coast. Composed of a hard rock, the Foreland Grits, the highest points are at Barna Barrow, 1,059ft (323m), and Butter Hill, 993ft (302m). Most of the Foreland is in the care of the National Trust and can be explored by a number of paths, though care should be taken near cliff-edges. Access is from near Countisbury Church or from the car park at Barna Barrow, ¼ mile (400m) east of Countisbury.

On the summit of Butter Hill is an old signal station now converted to a television relay point. Part of the building is left open as a welcome shelter for walkers, who share it with nesting swallows! A path descends to the north (A) of the shelter to pass the huge landslip rift of Great Red. Beyond here the path turns east and joins the access road as it winds spectacularly down the scree-covered Caddow Combe to Foreland Point lighthouse, which is open most afternoons subject to working conditions. From Countisbury the A39 continues past the bulk of Kipscombe Hill. For those on foot, the coast path leads east from the lighthouse road and on through the coppiced oak woods at Kipscombe.

At Desolation Point, below Wingate Combe, a seaward diversion down a short path (B) offers exhilarating views of the stream as it plunges in a double waterfall over a series of ledges to the beach.

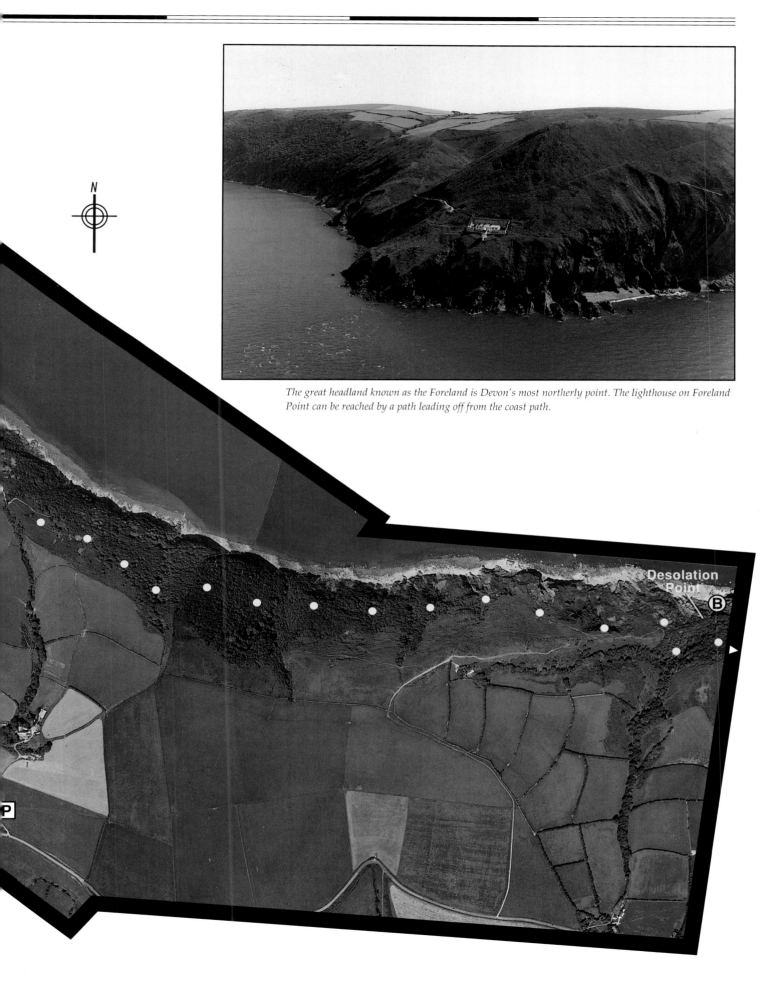

The great headland known as the Foreland is Devon's most northerly point. The lighthouse on Foreland Point can be reached by a path leading off from the coast path.

Desolation Point

Ilfracombe to Minehead

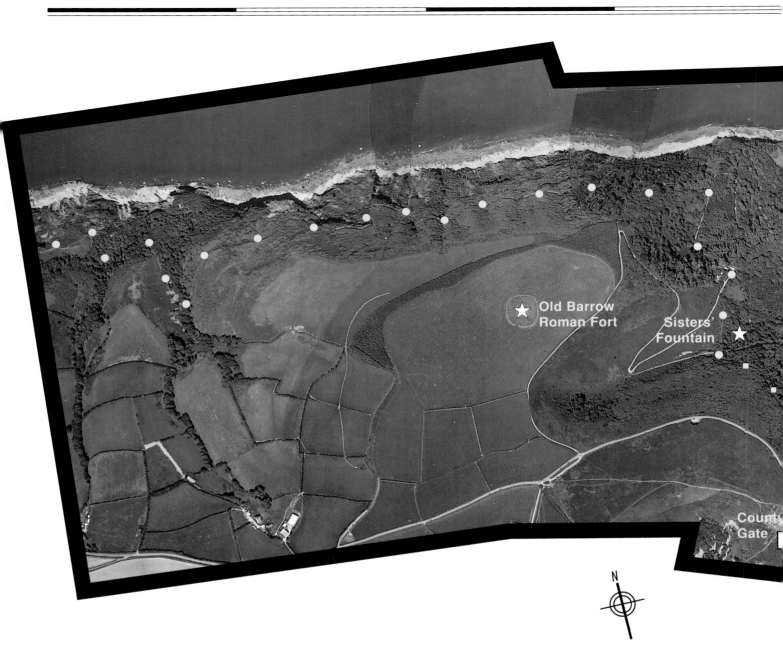

Old Barrow
Roman Fort

Sisters'
Fountain

County
Gate

N

THIS NEXT SECTION of coast includes the Glenthorne Estate, a private property with permitted access agreed between the owner and the National Park authority. The walking opportunities are outstanding although strenuous, as the wooded property drops steeply for 1,000ft (305m) from the A39 to sea level. There is car parking and toilets, and a seasonal information centre at County Gate, which is just over 3 miles (4.8km) east of Countisbury along the A39. The Devon-Somerset border runs inland from the Glenthorne coast through County Gate and on through the famous Doone Country of Badgworthy Water. The cliff slopes above Glenthorne are so steep that, from the road, nothing can be seen of the wooded combe that plunges

dramatically to the sea. Once the impregnable haunt of smugglers and charcoal burners, the estate was created by the remarkable Victorian cleric Walter Halliday, who bought over 6,000 acres (2.430 hectares) of combe and cliff early last century. The land was acquired piecemeal and became Halliday's life's work. He designed and completed Glenthorne House in 1832, on a splendid site just above the shoreline.

The Glenthorne Estate is a mix of old oak wood and conifer plantations, including whole stands of sitka spruce. But conifers are best seen at the delightful Pinetum on the eastern side of the estate just above Glenthorne House, where Halliday planted dozens of seeds of exotic conifers including Grecian fir, incense cedar, Monterey

pine, Dawn redwood, and the intriguingly-named Chinese cow's tail pine. They are now mature trees, of great size in some cases. Other features of the Estate are a Gothic water grotto built for Halliday's four nieces and called Sisters' Fountain, a Victorian ice-house built into the stream bank just above the beach, and the remote stony beach itself reached down a dark ravine by a gushing stream. There is an excellent network of paths across the Glenthorne Estate, all easily reached from County Gate car park.

To the west, above the private drive to Glenthorne House, lie the distinctive remains of the Roman fort of Old Barrow, a lookout post which, like Martinhoe, kept watch on the unruly Welsh tribes. A special feature of the drive in May are the masses of red and

B3225

P

PORLOCK

P

during subsequent restorations. Local legend has it that the tiny spirelet of Culbone Church was 'stolen' from the spire at Porlock. St Dubricius' has an impressive interior with some fine features, not least the outstanding 15th-century Harington monument, a time-worn but still intricate and lovely work in alabaster depicting the 4th Lord Harington and his wife Elizabeth. Vestigial gilding and colouring survives, while graffiti on the monument dates from as early as 1690.

Porlock has many shops and craft galleries, and a number of hotels and pubs, including the handsome 18th-century Ship Inn. There is a tourist information centre and small museum at 15th-century Doverhay Court, near the car park in High Street.

Porlock Weir is a charming dead-end community that developed later than its better-known neighbour, Porlock, at the top of the hill.

Several footpaths lead to Hurlstone Point with its now redundant coastguard lookout. It marks the eastern end of Porlock Bay.

Hurlstone Point

Bossington Hill

Ⓐ

P

BOSSINGTON

LYNCH

Somerset Farm Park

THE MAIN COAST road leads east from Porlock to Minehead, but a detour to the north of Porlock will take you to Bossington, one of Somerset's most attractive villages. Bossington consists of a straggle of colour-washed cottages with deeply thatched roofs, tall external chimneys and flower-bedecked porches. It retains the form of its Saxon origins and although the village is now less of a traditional farming community and more of a holiday attraction, there are still thatched cow-sheds by the roadside recalling its true pedigree. Bossington Green at the entrance to the village is shaded by walnut trees, while graceful willows fringe the banks of the Horner Water. There is a National Trust car park from where a number of paths offer pleasant walks.

A track leads from Bossington down to the great pebble beach fringing Porlock Bay that runs for 2 miles (3.2km) along a grey escarpment of polished boulders and pebbles seamed with thin quartz veins. The sea shuffles noisily along the tide line and the Horner Water filters through the banks from retaining ponds. In times of flood, however, the pent-up river may burst through the pebble beach and allow the sea to flood into the inland ponds before the pebbles build up again. The coast path leads west from the mouth of the Horner Water to Porlock and makes for a refreshing, open walk with exhilarating views of

Exmoor's wide embracing hills. The marshes and sea shore of Porlock Bay play host to a number of wild duck including shelduck, mallard, wigeon and teal, and are important winter feeding grounds for such migrant birds as curlew, lapwing, sandpiper, whimbrel and godwit.

From the car park at Bossington the Horner Water can be crossed to the east and a path followed out to Hurlstone Point, which has an impressive natural archway in its cliffs and an ornate and now redundant coastguard lookout on its highest point. Just before the Point, the coast path leads sharply uphill via the very steep Hurlstone Combe and on to an old military road leading over Selworthy Beacon. The top of Bossington Hill is easily reached from the path (A) up Hurlstone Combe.

Adjoining Bossington, and on the road to Allerford, is Lynch, a hamlet with strong traditions and surviving buildings to support them. On the side of the road opposite the Aller Water stands the small chapel-of-ease, built in the early 16th century and connected with the manor house of Bossington which survives, at least in part, alongside. The chapel is a peaceful, enduring place with several strong features including a wagon roof which has some original carved bosses. The Somerset Farm Park at Lynch offers a host of fascinating attractions for all the family.

The great sweep of Porlock Bay, with its flat coastal plain, provides delightful and easier walking for those not keen on the gradients inland.

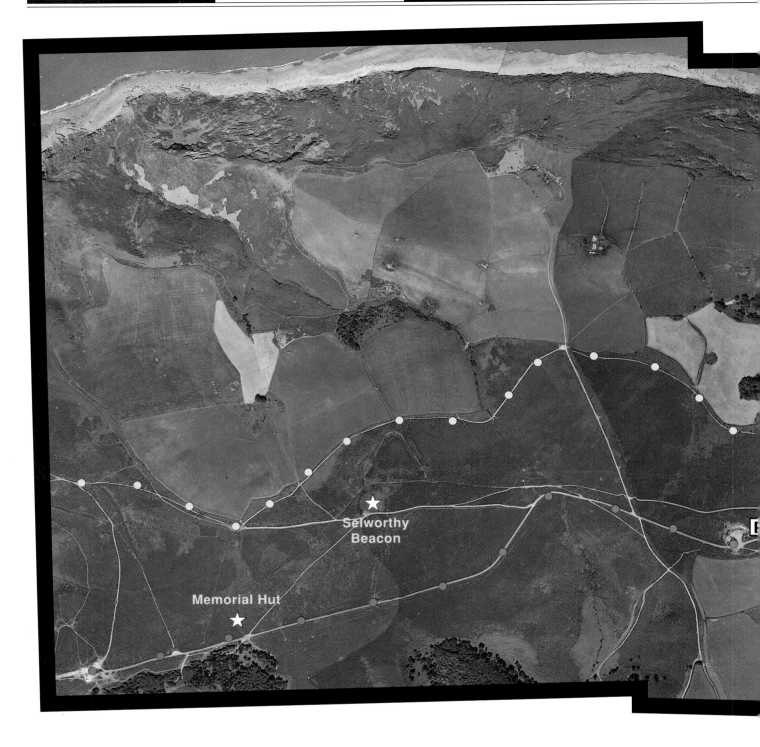

Selworthy
Beacon

Memorial Hut

FROM HURLSTONE POINT to Minehead the great broad-topped ridge of the Selworthy Hills runs through the high points of Selworthy Beacon, Bratton Ball and North Hill. You can reach this area on foot from Bossington and Selworthy, but the only public road which crosses it starts from Minehead, ending at a car park and viewpoint just below the summit of Selworthy Beacon.

The Beacon affords one of the finest views in Exmoor, as befits its purpose as a signal hill, embracing a panoramic sweep of inland hills from the Brendons through Dunkery's brooding heights and on to the high ground of Porlock Common and the hog's back cliffs of Yearnor and Culbone. To the south lies the lovely hamlet of Selworthy amid deeply wooded slopes. These southern slopes were owned by the Acland family for centuries and it was the 10th baronet, Sir Thomas, who created the present woods by planting over 800,000 trees during the early years of the last century. The legacy is a delightful woodland of holm oak, cherry, laurel and conifers.

About ½ mile (800m) back along the road from the car park there is a charming memorial hut among the trees. It was erected in 1878 by the family of Sir Thomas Acland as a 'wind and weather' hut and as a lasting memorial to the baronet who walked regularly to this spot up Holnicote Combe with his children and grandchildren. The east and west walls of the hut bear pieces of religious poetry by Heber and Keble. From the hut the path down Holnicote Combe leads to Selworthy. Another route leads south-east to link with Selworthy Combe. Just south of the memorial hut is the site of Bury Castle, an Iron Age (c.600BC-AD43) hill slope enclosure with an adjoining wedge-shaped rampart of about 3 acres (1.2 hectares) which may have been used for keeping animals.

Burgundy
Chapel

Bratton Ball

The free-wheeling expanse of North Hill is typical coastal heathland with a mix of bell heather and western gorse creating a mosaic of brilliant yellow and red, interspersed with the flaxen sweep of bent grass. The alien-looking bindweed parasite, the dodder, is quite widespread on North Hill in some years. It covers gorse and heather in soft swathes of red, hair-like strands and produces tiny clusters of pink bell-shaped flowers. Skylarks sing and rise above the heath on hot summer days and meadow-pipits and stonechats nest among the deeper cover of the combes. The usurping cuckoo is also a spring and early summer visitor.

Much of North Hill was used as a tank training ground during the later years of World War II and a network of military roads, tracks and raised emplacements for guns was established. Some of the concrete military tracks still survive throughout the area; the public road to the westerly viewpoint was a one-time military road. There is a good viewpoint at Bratton Ball summit close to the road. A circular path (A) leads round the lower slopes of Bratton Ball to the south and can be linked to Bratton village with its 15th-century manor house of Bratton Court.

N

Ilfracombe to Minehead

Harbour

A39

Minehead has all that you might expect from a busy holiday seaside town. It lies just outside the National Park boundary.

MINEHEAD IS A LIVELY, good-natured town as befits Somerset's leading holiday resort. Named from the Welsh *mynydd*, meaning hill or mountain, it was a busy medieval port and was still engaged in brisk trade late into the 19th century. There are restored cannons at the harbour dating from the early 17th century when Minehead was still considered to be second in importance to Bristol as a Severn port and needed defending from privateers and Mediterranean pirates. Quay Town at the western end of the town still has traditional cottages, as does Higher Town, which rises above the harbour area to the handsome 15th-century Church of St Michael. Modern Minehead, however, is more expansive with wide airy streets, long stretches of bathing beach and a handsome esplanade with all the attractions of an ideal family resort. The extensive Somerwest World holiday and leisure centre is situated at the eastern end of Warren Road which leads on from the esplanade. Somerwest World is residential but its many attractions are open to day visitors. There is an indoor leisure pool in Seaward Way and a sports centre in Alexandra Road. The town is a busy shopping centre and has a full range of all types of holiday accommodation, including a youth hostel. It is also the terminus for the West Somerset Steam Railway. The tourist information centre is at the town hall in the Parade.

From the Quay West car park, just to the west of Minehead harbour, a path (A) leads steeply at first through Culver Cliff Wood and on to Greenaleigh Farm and the ruins of the medieval Burgundy Chapel. From the chapel a steep path heads inland to link with the coast path leading back to Minehead. Another pleasant walk can be taken through Moor Wood, reached from the Parade at the centre of Minehead by following Martlett Road, turning left in to St Michael's Road past the church and then along Hill Road to a car park just beyond a camp site. The continuation of this road leads along North Hill's scenic drive to the road-end and viewpoint below Selworthy Beacon.

Minehead was the port for the historic town of Dunster, which lies 2 miles (3.2km) to the south-east along the A39 (see page 40-41).

Dunster Castle

THE ANCESTRAL HOME of the Luttrell family, Dunster castle was imaginatively restored last century to its medieval form and is now in the care of the National Trust. Other notable buildings in Dunster include the octagonal Yarn Market dating from the 16th century, the slate-hung 15th-century Nunnery and the Church of St George. The town's overall appeal makes it a very busy place during the summer.

Dunster Castle

HUNTER'S INN TO PARRACOMBE

2½ miles (4km)

THE RIVER HEDDON

The River Heddon is fairly short-lived, like most of Exmoor's north-flowing streams. Yet within its 6-mile (9.6km) valley there is a fascinating mix of features in an ever-changing landscape.

AT THE HEART of the Heddon valley lies Hunter's Inn, where the river begins its last headlong rush down the oak-shrouded cleave that leads to Heddon's Mouth and the sea. Hunter's Inn is reached from the A39 North Devon coast road via Martinhoe Cross, if approaching from Lynton, or via Stony Corner if approaching from Combe Martin. There is good parking here, although the car park is very busy during the summer season when there is also a café and attendant gift shops. There are public toilets opposite the car park.

The Inn is everything expected of its setting. It was famous for many years as

Below: *Looking north along the Heddon valley: Hunter's Inn, with its hotel, car parks, and road access, can be seen in the foreground.*

The Heddon valley, seen here snaking away from the village of Parracombe.

a centre of stag-hunting, with the Heddon valley itself being a famed woodland refuge for stags. Several delightful woodland walks begin at Hunter's Inn and lead through National Trust property (see page 18). From the Inn a narrow, wood-fringed road climbs inland along the east bank of the River Heddon. The road is bordered on its landward side by the elegant green tracery of male fern while primroses and clumps of yellow flag iris add fresh bursts of colour during spring and summer. The immediate river bank is under siege from Japanese knotweed, reflecting an unsympathetic change in the landscape of white-crested, boulder-strewn river and ancient woodland. The wood to the east is called Mill Wood after the old tuckingmill that once stood in the valley near the 15th-century Mill Farm. Tuckingmills were fairly common on Exmoor until the early 19th century. They operated heavy wooden mallets which pounded short-fibred wool in a

Parks are completely separate organisations although the aims of both often coincide. Trust land is often within a National Park and having the DNPA headquarters at Parke is itself a happy coincidence.

Nutscale Reservoir, Exmoor

establish car parks, picnic areas and information centres. There are continuing programmes of helpful but discreet waymarking and management of paths. Other services include the publishing of useful books and leaflets, the organisation of guided walks, the encouragement of mutually beneficial conservation work with residents, and the running of field courses. Park wardens and rangers are a friendly and helpful link between the public and the Authority.

Exmoor is one of England's smallest National Parks and was designated in 1954. Of its 265 square miles (686 sq km) 80% is privately owned, yet there are 600 miles (965 km) of public footpaths and bridleways criss-crossing Exmoor as well as agreed sections of permissive paths across private land. The Exmoor National Park Authority is a department within Somerset County Council; its headquarters is at Exmoor House, Dulverton.

Dartmoor National Park comprises an area of 365 square miles (945 sq km) of which 87% is farmed; there are also large areas of grazing moorland. Dartmoor was designated as a National Park in 1951 and since 1974 has had a full time management staff. Devon County Council is the National Park Authority, although management is delegated to a National Park Committee; administration is based at the National Trust property of Parke House at Bovey Tracey.

The National Trust and the National

MALMSMEAD TO BADGWORTHY HILL

3 miles (4.8km)

mellow, crowded by wooded hills to the north and with the challenging presence of the great moor to the south. The road crosses Badgworthy Water by an ancient bridge which is just wide enough for modern cars but is flanked by a more amenable ford. The white-walled Malmsmead Farm, now called Lorna Doone Farm, stands close by. Refreshments are available and there is a well-stocked gift shop, a car park and picnic site.

A short walk along the narrow road running south from Malmsmead leads to a gate by a right-hand bend. Beyond the gate, with its sentinel oak and ash trees, a broad track signposted Doone Valley leads into the enchanted combe of Badgworthy above the foaming, rock-studded river. Stout footwear is needed from now on. The track snakes along the side of the combe as Badgworthy takes on its moorland character and the feeling that this is true Doone Country is further emphasised where the track passes a riverside memorial stone to Blackmore.

BADGWORTHY WATER

The lovely valley of Badgworthy Water, which marks the boundary between Devon and Somerset, has become famous as the setting for R D Blackmore's Victorian romance, Lorna Doone. It is best approached by turning off the A39 North Devon coast road about 400yds east of County Gate at New Road Gate. From here a narrow road winds down to Oare, the definitive shrine of Doone Country.

IT WAS IN THE little Church of St Mary The Virgin at Oare that the wedding of Blackmore's eponymous heroine and her sweetheart Jan Ridd was brutally interrupted when Lorna in her white wedding dress 'clouded with faint lavender' was shot and wounded by the robber chief Carver Doone. Drama apart, the church is modest but pleasingly dark and simple with 18th-century box pews, an impressive memorial tablet to R D Blackmore and some rather sombre wooden plaques outlining the ten commandments.

Just over a mile (1.6km) east of Oare along a narrow road lies the picturesque Robber's Bridge, another Doone landmark. West of Oare lies Malmsmead and the true gateway to Doone Country. Between Oare and Malmsmead and opposite the gateway to Cloud Farm is

the Field Centre of the Exmoor Natural History Society where there is an exhibition. The Centre is open on certain weekdays from May onwards.

The name Malmsmead sounds like its riverside surroundings; peaceful and

Malmsmead, on the west bank of Badgworthy Water. Plenty of car parking is available for those wishing to explore the Doone valley from here on foot.

Malmsmead to Badgworthy Hill

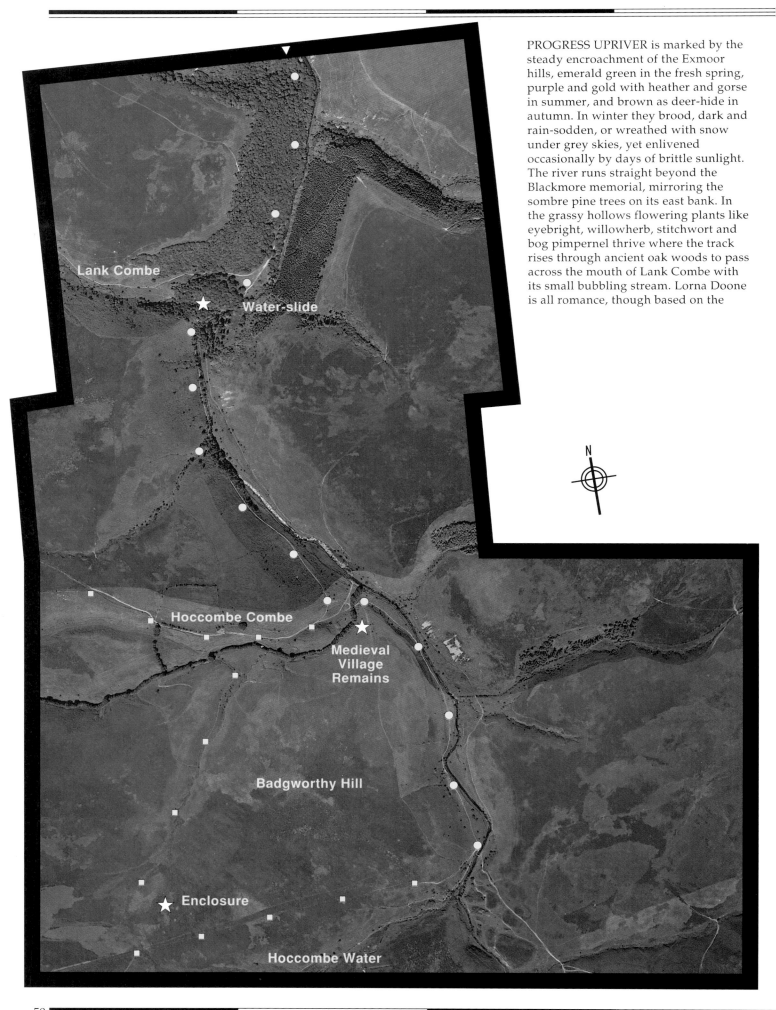

PROGRESS UPRIVER is marked by the steady encroachment of the Exmoor hills, emerald green in the fresh spring, purple and gold with heather and gorse in summer, and brown as deer-hide in autumn. In winter they brood, dark and rain-sodden, or wreathed with snow under grey skies, yet enlivened occasionally by days of brittle sunlight. The river runs straight beyond the Blackmore memorial, mirroring the sombre pine trees on its east bank. In the grassy hollows flowering plants like eyebright, willowherb, stitchwort and bog pimpernel thrive where the track rises through ancient oak woods to pass across the mouth of Lank Combe with its small bubbling stream. Lorna Doone is all romance, though based on the

Lank Combe

Water-slide

Hoccombe Combe

Medieval
Village
Remains

Badgworthy Hill

Enclosure

Hoccombe Water

shadowy reality of a 17th-century band of robbers who were said to live in a secret hideaway deep within the moor, but so powerful is Blackmore's tale that fact has merged seamlessly with fiction. It was in Lank Combe's mossy depths that Jan Ridd and Lorna Doone first met at the famous water-slide, a feature greatly exaggerated by Blackmore. Some enthusiasts claim that the upper reaches of Lank Combe held the Doones' village and that the robber band rode out on its wicked raids via Doone Gate, a desolate meeting of waters on Brendon Common to the west. But a more likely inspiration for the Doone village lies a bare ½ mile (800m) further up Badgworthy Water at the mouth of Hoccombe Combe where a

line of beech trees runs down to the main river and to a wooden footbridge over the tributary stream. A short distance up Hoccombe Combe, beyond a green mound, lie the low-walled but distinctive remains of a medieval village. This was Baga Wordia, the Saxon 'settlement of Baga' abandoned in the 14th century, which may well have inspired Blackmore. Whatever the argument, most theories place the robbers' hideout on the Devon side of the river, which may or may not please Somerset! The ruins are easily found by following the broad track up Hoccombe Combe for a short distance, then going left through grassy mounds towards the tree-lined wall.

Badgworthy Water itself can be

followed deeper into the moor by crossing the small footbridge described above. Beyond here the valley opens out below the high hills until the Hoccombe Water merges with a lively stream to form Badgworthy Water at the moorland's heart.

The Doone valley canal can be reached by an exhilarating walk from the car park at Middle Hill on the B3223 Lynmouth-to-Simonsbath road. The walk can be linked through Malmsmead and back to the Middle Hill car park. It is stressed that this is open moorland and while the tracks and paths are good and usually well-signposted, map, compass, weatherproof clothing and stout footwear should be taken, even in summer.

Badgworthy Water makes its way down to the sea from the high moorland of Exmoor Forest.

Malmsmead to Badgworthy Hill

ALLERFORD TO DUNKERY BEACON

2½ miles (4km)

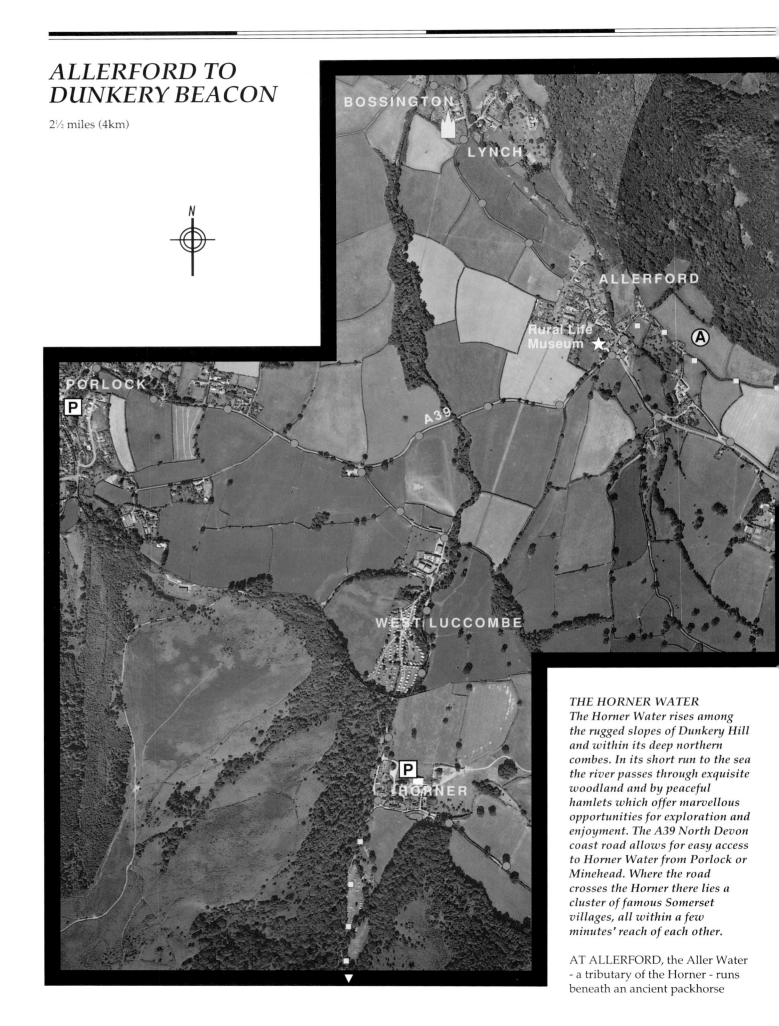

N

BOSSINGTON

LYNCH

ALLERFORD

Rural Life
Museum ★

Ⓐ

PORLOCK
🅿

A39

WEST LUCCOMBE

🅿 HORNER

THE HORNER WATER
The Horner Water rises among the rugged slopes of Dunkery Hill and within its deep northern combes. In its short run to the sea the river passes through exquisite woodland and by peaceful hamlets which offer marvellous opportunities for exploration and enjoyment. The A39 North Devon coast road allows for easy access to Horner Water from Porlock or Minehead. Where the road crosses the Horner there lies a cluster of famous Somerset villages, all within a few minutes' reach of each other.

AT ALLERFORD, the Aller Water - a tributary of the Horner - runs beneath an ancient packhorse

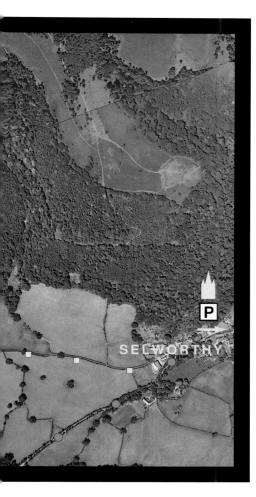

Allerford, with its famous packhorse bridge just visible in the centre of the picture.

bridge adjoining a ford. The building on the south side of the ford was once the Packhorse Inn and on the opposite side of the bridge is a typical Somerset cottage in warm red sandstone with lichened slate roof, tall chimneys and an east portico. A short distance along the main street there is a Rural Life Museum with nearby parking and toilets.

About a mile (1.6km) east of Allerford is Selworthy, easily reached from the A39 or by walking from Allerford along a lane (A) that runs to the right just beyond the packhorse bridge. The hamlet lies at the heart of the Acland Estate, where wide-ranging improvements over the years included the story-book cluster of thatched and colour-washed cottages at Selworthy Green built in 1810 for retired estate servants. The charming complex survives amid oak, chestnut and walnut trees and a mosaic of cropped grass and cottage gardens. It is an architectural gem, though lacking the true character of a community. Selworthy Green is now in the care of the National Trust and there is a Trust information centre and shop in the hamlet, and seasonal refreshments

The picture postcard village of Selworthy, which forms part of the 12,400-acre Holnicote Estate, is cared for by the National Trust.

are available. There is parking higher uphill in front of the Church of All Saints which boasts an exceptional gallery dating from the mid-18th century, while the wagon roofs with their splendid bosses are very fine. But it is the church's setting and its exhilarating outlook across the Vale of Porlock to the brooding heights of Dunkery Hill that distinguish it.

The small hamlet of West Luccombe with its thatched cottages and tiny packhorse bridge over Horner Water lies opposite Allerford, north of the A39. A short distance upriver is Horner, the true gateway to the deep combes and high moor. Here there is a car park with toilets and seasonal refreshments and a gift shop. The few houses are splendid examples of good vernacular architecture with warm red sandstone, steeply pitched tiled roofs and tall chimneys, and the surviving 19th-century corn mill with its 18-ft (5.4m) diameter wheel has been restored. Horner, which stands at the northern apex of magnificent oak woods, is ideally placed for exploring the upper reaches of Horner Water.

Horner Wood, just to the west of Luccombe, is one of the densest woodlands on Exmoor and the haunt of red deer.

Horner Wood

Webber's Post

THE 900 ACRE (364 hectare) Horner Wood is a famous deer refuge and the largest surviving ancient woodland on Exmoor; it dates from at least medieval times. The wood, now owned mainly by the National Trust, is a compelling place, haunted by the largely unseen presence of the deer yet holding out the tantalising chance of a glimpse of these lovely creatures. During the rutting season in October the stags roar challengingly from the misty covers. Horner's mix of sessile oak, ash, hazel, beech and holly, all watered by the stream, creates a green paradise in spring and summer and an autumn portrait in russet and gold. The shady depths of this complex wood limit its flora but there is a wealth of ferns and lichen, and the bird life is brisk, with green woodpecker, chaffinch, warbler, grey wagtail, dipper, goldfinch and goldcrest among the residents and summer visitors. From Horner a leafy track (B) runs upriver alongside the west bank. It can be followed for about a mile (1.6km) to the junction of Horner Water with East Water, where the west bank continuation (C) leads on to the tiny hamlet of Stoke Pero. Alternatively, footbridges give access to the east bank of East Water, from where paths (D) lead up to Webber's Post or (E) past the great rounded hill of Cloutsham Ball to Cloutsham Watersplash and footbridge on the narrow road that dips across the valleys (see page 57). The woodland paths can also be followed pleasantly at will, and retraced, provided one has a good sense of direction.

From the hamlet of Horner the road can be followed a short distance to the east to reach Luccombe, an Exmoor charmer of a village. There is some roadside parking at the entrance to the village where there is a small post office and shop. The main street is lined with cream colour-washed houses with roofs of thatch or dark ochrous tiles and the theme is extended into the adjoining Stony Street with its flanking stream, while the elegant tower of the Church of St Mary the Virgin draws the eye. The church is partly 13th-century with 15th-century additions like the south aisle. There is a fine tomb brass set into the floor in front of the chancel and some lovely medieval glass in the eastern end of the south aisle. A memorial to Dr Henry Byam, a 17th-century vicar, makes fascinating reading, revealing a courageous and adventurous life.

A short distance west of Luccombe the moorland road across Dunkery Hill branches off to the south. About ½ mile (800m) along this road a right-hand branch leads to Webber's Post where there is a car park and access to Horner Wood.

LUCCOMBE

Unspoilt Luccombe has much to recommend it and it is worth taking a look inside the Church of St Mary.

THE NARROW ROAD beyond Webber's Post can be followed to where it descends into the valley of East Water, a main tributary of Horner Water. Across the valley is Cloutsham Ball, a distinctive dome-shaped hill, tree-covered yet maintaining its smooth outline. The road runs in close consort with the bubbling stream and splashes through it by an ancient footbridge where the riverside paths from Horner emerge then climb steeply to pass the impressive old farmhouse at Cloutsham itself. The house was built as a hunting lodge by the Acland family and is still a focus of modern stag hunting in country where the deer congregate between the Horner sanctuary and the great open spaces of Dunkery and Tarr Ball. Steep driving leads on past Cloutsham to a turning to the right at Cloutsham Gate. From here, a backward glance reveals the massive bulk of Dunkery Hill with its graceful summits of Robin How, Kit Barrows, the Beacon and Great Rowbarrow, their dark and ancient slopes soaring above the green combes.

Half a mile (800m) west of Cloutsham Gate lies the tiny church of Stoke Pero, crouched like a brooding stag in its hidden fold of the moor 1,000ft (305m) above Porlock Vale. This individual building was restored in the late 19th century but retains its naturalistic atmosphere, right down to the spleenwort ferns flourishing in a damp alcove of the tower.

The Horner Water and its wooded valleys are dominated by Dunkery Beacon, Exmoor's most famous landmark, and the airy summit of Dunkery Hill. The Beacon reaches 1,705ft (519m) in height and though not of rocky shape, nor crowned with natural tors, it has an impressive grandeur and was used as a signal beacon from the earliest times. The hill's dark heights discourage many people from making the steady uphill tramp despite ease of access from the moorland road between Webber's Post and Dunkery Gate. This is perhaps just as well because the National Trust and the National Park authority discourage

Dunkery Beacon

Above and right: paths radiate out in all directions from the cairn on Dunkery Beacon, the highest point on Exmoor; the climb up is well repaid with panoramic views.

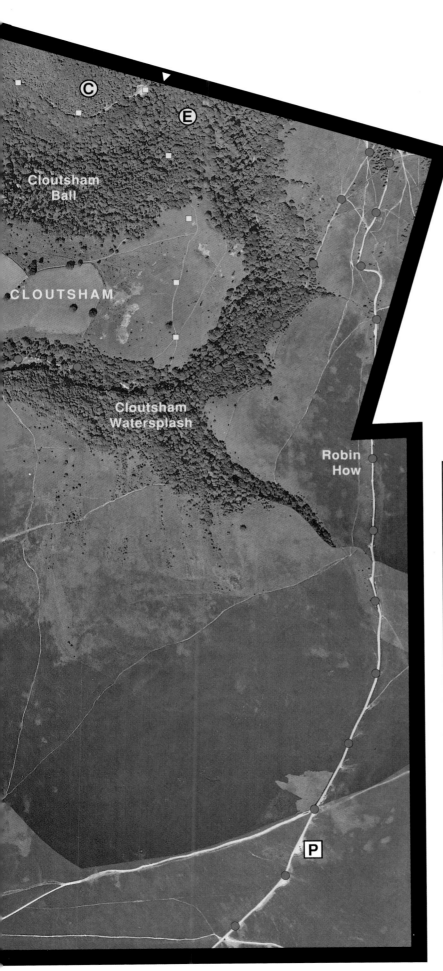

Cloutsham
Ball

CLOUTSHAM

Cloutsham
Watersplash

Robin
How

P

too much foot traffic across the fragile skin of the moor and visitors are requested to stay on the designated paths. For those that do make the climb the rewards are worth the effort as views from the Beacon draw the eye out to Wales across the wooded northern combes and the wide sweep of Porlock Bay. To the east lie the Croydon and Brendon Hills and the high ridge of the Quantocks; west lie the heather and bracken-clad moors and the airy wilderness of the Pinfords and the Chains. To the south the green swell of the southern moor hides the deep valleys of the Exe and the Barle with the prominent skyline of Winsford Hill and the Wambarrows between. In ideal visibility, the tors of Dartmoor can be seen to the south-west as can Brown Willy on Cornwall's Bodmin Moor.

A rocky path leads west from the large cairn on Dunkery Beacon to the Bronze Age Rowbarrows amid a classic moorland landscape of ling, purple moor grass and bracken. Moorland flowers include the tiny yellow-starred tormentil, the bog pimpernel with its bell-like pink flowers and the dark-blue heath milkwort.

Allerford to Dunkery Beacon

Walking on Dartmoor & Exmoor

EXMOOR AND DARTMOOR provide some of the finest walking in England along a network of footpaths and tracks that cross exhilarating moors and wind through farmland, river valleys and deep woods. Exmoor has the bonus of a spectacular coastal footpath which is a part of the South West Way. Public footpaths on both moors are well maintained, signposted and waymarked by the National Park Authorities, often using the colour codes of yellow for footpaths and blue for bridleways. On

Heddon valley, near Trentishoe, Exmoor

moorland, waymarking is minimised to avoid intruding on the open landscape.

All of Exmoor and Dartmoor is owned by individuals or by public or private organisations. Public footpaths mean exactly that; they are routes across country which have been established for generations, usually as links between isolated communities. Many were important thoroughfares in the past. Today the public have the right to walk along these paths, a right which is protected under law and which is fiercely defended against obstruction or illegal diversion.

Common Land

Some of the finest walking on Exmoor and Dartmoor is across open country. Much of the open moor is common land over which neighbouring farmers and others share common grazing rights. People have walked on this land for centuries, by custom though not by right. This holds good today, subject to conservation or other needs. On Dartmoor, the Dartmoor Commons Act of 1985 legalized public access to nearly all parts of the Dartmoor commons subject to byelaws regulating public behaviour. They are:

Do not drive on to moorland or park further than 15 metres from the road.

No overnight camping in vehicles, caravans or large tents.

Do not block water courses.

Do not light fires.

Do not feed ponies or other animals.

Burrator Reservoir, Dartmoor

flood. Stepping stones should be negotiated with care at all times and should not be used if they are submerged.

- Always use stiles and please do not not clamber over walls or fences. Gates should be closed after use unless they are open for an obvious purpose.
- Dogs can be an innocent hazard to livestock and should be kept under strict control in areas where stock are grazing.
- Litter in any form is a contradiction of the countryside ethos and should never be left behind. Walkers are requested to take care not to create fire risks especially in woodland areas.

Enclosed Land

Large areas of land on the moorland edges were taken over and enclosed early last century. The public has legal access only along rights of way across such land. However, in certain cases access agreements and permitted paths have been negotiated by the National Park Authorities. Such permissive paths are indicated and explained on signposts and noticeboards.

Military Land

Large areas of the high ground of Dartmoor are leased to the Ministry of Defence for military training which includes the use of live ammunition. These areas are subject to restricted public access on certain firing days. Some areas described in this book adjoin firing ranges and this is mentioned in the text.

Walkers wishing to venture into MoD areas should check at National Park Information Centres (see page 157) for full details of firing programmes.

Advice to Walkers

- Walkers should be well-equipped at all times of the year with warm and waterproof clothing, stout footwear, food and drink. Emergency rations, first-aid kit, torch and whistle should be carried.
- Paths and bridleways can often be very wet and muddy. River crossings can be hazardous at any time but especially after heavy rain when rivers are in

Countisbury Common, Exmoor

WASHFORD

A39

Cleeve Abbey

P

White Horse Inn

N

Well cared for by English Heritage, the monastic site of Cleeve Abbey is renowned for the completeness of its cloister buildings.

60

Exmoor

WASHFORD TO LUXBOROUGH

6½ miles (10.5km)

THE WASHFORD RIVER

The Brendon Hills run east from Exmoor, bridging the gap to the Quantocks and lying parallel with the Channel coast. The western area enclosed by these boundaries is drained by the Washford River flowing from its source below Luxborough, down past Cleeve Abbey to Washford and on to the ancient port of Watchet. The Washford is not a river that is easily explored on foot but its course is tracked by narrow roads and lanes through a countryside of great charm and interest.

THE WASHFORD RIVER is crossed by the A39 just south of Washford village where there are several shops, an inn and an interesting railway museum. The West Somerset Railway runs through the village on its delightful route between Minehead and Watchet. From Washford a pleasant path (A) runs north between river and railway to Watchet, a working port with traditions as old as Coleridge's Ancient Mariner who set sail from here in the poet's imagination. The town has a

fine little museum detailing its great sea-going past and its connections with the mining and quarrying industries of the Brendon Hills.

A short distance north-west of Washford is the village of Old Cleeve whose 16th-century church is worth a visit. Old Cleeve owed much of its stature to the famous Cleeve Abbey which stands on the banks of the Washford River just south of Washford and the A39, but the village is of greater antiquity than the 12th-century abbey which borrowed its name. Cleeve Abbey was founded during the great expansion of the Cistercian monastic order as a daughter house of Revesby Abbey in Lincolnshire. Dedicated to the Virgin Mary, it was first known as Vallis Florida in respect of the Washford valley's sylvan character. The abbey survived until the Dissolution of the Monasteries when, in a dreadful act of vandalism, the abbey church was demolished. The other buildings remained fairly intact and were used variously as private dwellings and farm buildings. Late

19th-century owners, the Luttrell family, carried out enlightened preservation and Cleeve Abbey now has much to interest and delight the visitor. The foundations of the church embedded in the grass alongside the walls of the cloister add a poignant note to this impressive monument which is open throughout the year and is in the care of English Heritage.

The road south from Cleeve Abbey runs alongside the Washford River for a short distance to a junction by the attractive White Horse Inn. The road leading to the right stays with the river valley as it climbs to Roadwater and Luxborough. The main road continues for ½ mile (800m) to Fair Cross, from where the B3190 leads south to Ralegh's Cross Inn and to Clatworthy Reservoir where there is parking, a picnic site and nature trail. Permit fishing for brown and rainbow trout is available at Clatworthy.

Alternatively, from Fair Cross the B3188 leads to Monksilver and the Elizabethan manor house of Combe Sydenham which has a great deal to interest all the family.

Roadwater is a pleasant village of cottages and small houses which line the northern side of road and stream. The buildings seem held together by a chain of garden flowers: roses, fuchsias, saxifrage and other seasonal species run through the village in counterpoint to the grassy riverbank and its ribbon of trees. The village inn is called the Valiant Soldier and there is a pleasant public space running down to the river, while at Watersmeet a cluster of handsome 18th-century cottages stands round the confluence of the Washford with its southern tributary.

An interesting walk can be made along the lane (A) which leads up the right bank of the tributary stream from Watersmeet to link with the old railway track and the Incline at Comberow where ore wagons were raised and lowered using their own counterbalanced weight. (The fascinating mechanics of the Incline are fully explained at the Watchet Museum.) A narrow road runs north from Roadwater to Rodhuish, an attractive little hamlet with its little Church of St Bartholomew and its atmosphere of isolation and

The Brendon Hills, on the eastern fringes of Exmoor, to the south of the Washford River, offer a different sort of landscape to the moors further west. They are gentler and more pastoral, with much arable land.

THE WASHFORD RIVER was closely linked with the now defunct iron ore industry of the Brendon Hills which flourished here for centuries. There are records of Roman and Elizabethan workings but the industrial heyday was from the mid 19th century when iron mines and slate quarries were established along the crest of the hills and in the surrounding valleys. Until World War 1 local mines supplied the busy smelting works of South Wales and for some distance below Roadwater the river is shadowed by the track of the dismantled mineral railway that carried ore down to Watchet, from where it was shipped across the Bristol Channel.

On the high land to the south stands Ralegh's Cross Inn, a living memorial to the miners and quarrymen, many of them Welsh, who lived throughout the area. Most of the miners lived at the long-abandoned village of Brendon Hill just west of Ralegh's Cross and at the top of the famous Comberow Incline. The village was run by the mine owners who tried to impose sobriety on their workforce by refusing to establish an inn, but thirsty miners simply trecked east to Ralegh's Cross Inn where generations of travellers, drovers and landworkers had taken their ease, and where modern travellers still do. A famous sheep fair is held near Ralegh's Cross in August. The

peaceful, wooded river valley of today belies past activity when mining took precedence over the landscape, yet the industry contributed in many ways to preserving the fabric of the community through maintaining and improving buildings and churches.

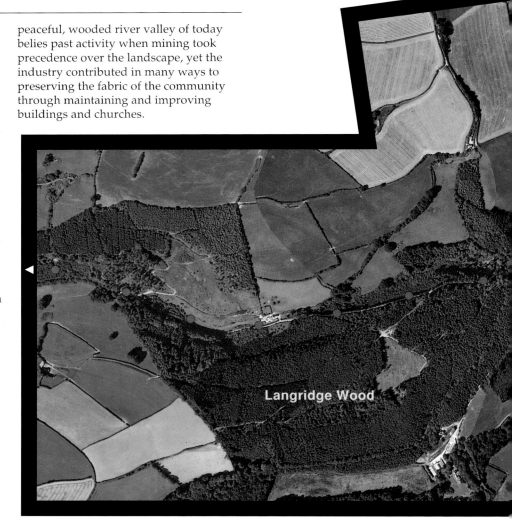

Langridge Wood

antiquity. The main valley road through Roadwater continues alongside the Washford River to Glasses Farm from where a lane (B) branches off left to a fork. From here the left branch can be followed to Leighland with its old miners' church, while the right branch leads to the exposed village of Treborough where slate quarrying was carried out. The main valley road follows the Washford River beyond Glasses Farm, and continues by an impressive line of roadside larches at Langridge Wood.

Washford to Luxborough

The area around the church in Luxborough is known as Churchtown: to the east is Kingsbridge (by the pub) and further south Pooltown.

THE UPPER REACHES of the Washford valley have been greatly changed by modern forestry. For centuries the countryside remained intact but eventually the great conifer plantations overpowered the original woodland slopes and stream banks, affecting the flora and fauna and touching upon the natural rythmn of people's lives. Yet where stream and narrow road run through Druid's Combe, there is still an atmosphere of timelessness. The name of this combe sparks the imagination but early maps show it as 'Drucombe', with a more prosaic meaning of black or dark combe. In spring the river banks and hedgerows are dense with flowering plants like the butter-yellow celandine and primrose, while in summer campion, willowherb and herb robert mix their rose-pink hues with the snowy-white of cow parsley, coltsfoot and stitchwort. Though land use may change, the pattern of settlement is enduring. At Luxborough and Kingsbridge the manner in which this countryside was first colonised from Saxon times is evident in the arrangement of the scattered hamlets, the thatched cottages lining the river, and the concentration of services at Kingsbridge at the junction of incoming roads.

However, most of the old rural services such as blacksmith and sawyer are now gone, their buildings converted to homes. On the slopes of Croydon Hill stands Luxborough Churchtown with its Church of St Mary, ringed with farms which at one time would have comprised several smaller units before being amalgamated. There is a fine old inn, the Royal Oak, at Kingsbridge, as well as a post office and shop. Luxborough Church can be reached by following the steep road leading right from the T-junction at Kingsbridge but parking outside the church is difficult. St Mary's has a particularly lonely atmosphere that sits well with its long history. In the southern part of the churchyard is a fragment of an ancient sandstone cross which may pre-date the Norman foundation, while the rock basin and water spout by the narrow entrance way to the churchyard add to the fine atmosphere of antiquity. The church tower has an uncommon saddle-back roof.

N

There are miles of footpaths throughout the countryside around Luxborough and although much of the land is currently owned by the Forestry Commission access is assured subject to forestry activities. There is a pleasant walk, by drives lined with cedars and rhododendrons, round the old fish ponds below Chargot House which can be reached by going south from Kingsbridge for 400yds and turning right at the T-junction at Pooltown. After 300yds a left turn (A) leads to the ponds. From the ponds walks can be extended uphill through Kennisham Hill and Chargot Wood. Walkers should bear in mind that mining was carried out in this area and that although the mining sites are now covered in conifers and the old engine houses and stacks have been demolished, the mouths of old shafts lie hidden in the woods and it is not advisable to wander off tracks and paths.

North of Kingsbridge and Luxborough the forested slopes of Slowley Wood, Monkham Hill and Croydon Hill offer a number of walks through a network of paths and tracks. From Luxborough Churchtown the road can be followed north along the wooded flanks of Croydon Hill and on down to Dunster (see page 39).

Intriguingly named Druid's Combe follows the river east from Luxborough.

Druid's Combe

Washford to Luxborough

EXFORD TO EXTON

8 miles (13km)

THE RIVER EXE

The River Exe is the longest river in the West Country. It rises at a height of 1,450ft (442m) from the sodden morass of the Chains at Exe Head, then drains the purple moor grass of Exe Plain before gathering pace through the steep-sided Prayway Meads and on down to Exford.

EXFORD IS THE 'capital' of Exmoor. It lies at the heart of the moor by a strategically placed river crossing and is easily reached from the A396 by driving west along the B3224 from Wheddon Cross. A pleasant aproach can also be made across the high northern moors from the A39 south of Lynton, passing through Simonsbath on the way. There is a car park at Exford down a side road opposite the Crown Hotel, a famous hunting venue with its own stabling at the western entrance to the village. The stables and kennels of the Devon and Somerset staghounds have been based at Exford since 1876 and horses are an

Located at the heart of the National Park, and well served by roads, Exford is a good base for exploring the area.

South-east of Exton is the large, irregularly shaped expanse of Wimbleball Lake. Built in the 1970s, the reservoir has integrated well with the landscape and has footpaths around much of its shore.

where the latter begins its emphatic southern course through the last of Somerset and into the heart of Devon. To continue along the river bank on foot, turn right immediately on reaching the road and carry on in the direction of Winsford for about 100yds, crossing Week Bridge. Join a track that starts from the opposite side of the road, signposted Bridgetown. The track runs alongside the river for just over ½ mile (800m) to emerge on to a narrow road by Bridgewater Mill. A left turn over a narrow hump-backed, single-arched bridge leads to the main road and the nearby Badgers Holt Inn.

Bridgewater Mill, one of the biggest and busiest on Exmoor, stands in a lower valley position where the Exe runs wide, fast and deep. The village of Bridgewater boasts a beautifully situated riverside cricket ground with a thatched pavilion.

The village of Exton lifts body and spirit on to the high ground once more. It stands airily on the steep slopes of Exton Hill above the wooded Exe valley and is often snowbound in winter. The eye is drawn to the north as far as Dunkery Beacon and to deer-haunted Winsford Hill in the west. The Church of St Peter

stands proud of its green hill, its sturdy rough-hewn tower four-square to the moorland winds. The church interior is surprisingly spacious, an effect heightened by the absence of pews from the 16th-century north aisle where the graceful proportions of the window tracery add to the charm. There are memorial tablets to the local Everard family, several of whose menfolk died during two World Wars.

North-east of Exton the flat ridge of the Brendon Hills draws Somerset towards the Quantocks and carries the modern road along the line of an ancient highway. Just over 2 miles (3.2km) to the south-east of Exton is the charming village of Brompton Regis with, beyond it, the great reservoir of Wimbleball Lake drowning the heart of the Haddeo valley below gorse-scented Haddon Hill. There is car parking, toilets and picnic areas on the west bank of the lake and at its northern end. There is also an information centre on the west bank, and several waymarked walks. A lovely walk leads down the west bank of the Haddeo River from Hartford at the southern end of the lake to Bury with its four-arched packhorse bridge and ford.

Exford to Exton

The Landscape

DURING EARLY DEVONIAN to late Carboniferous times (400-290 million years ago) Exmoor and Dartmoor were originally submerged beneath a shallow sea which covered south west England. Great rivers flowing from the high land to the north spread sediments across the floor of this sea building layer upon layer.

At the end of the late Carboniferous period great upheaval caused by massive pressure from land movement resulted in an upthrust of the sea bed to produce the Cornubian Mountains.

Exmoor's underlying geology remained substantially intact after this period although a further submergance left other deposits which were eventually eroded. Erosion by wind and rain, the sea and rivers and by powerful frost action has created Exmoor's present structure of a high central plateau of heather and grass moorland surrounded by wooded slopes and deeply incised river valleys. There are few rock outcrops on Exmoor and the open moorland is an exposed and

Hound Tor, Dartmoor

The River Tavy, east of Mary Tavy, Dartmoor

empty wilderness of peat and purple moor grass resting in places on an impermeable sub-soil layer.

The moor bulks large to the north where the characteristic hog's back coastal hills descend steeply to the sea and then precipitously for the final 200ft (61m) or so. All of this makes northern Exmoor a land of fast-flowing and often destructive rivers which have cut dramatically deep valleys through the coastal hills. The flood-swollen West and East Lyn Rivers devastated Lynmouth in 1952, an example of how heavy rainfall on Exmoor's impermeable 'iron-pan' moorland cascades in torrents into the steep-sided northern river valleys. The longer south-flowing rivers like the Exe and the Barle are less precipitous; they flow through an exquisite valley landscape of meadows and broad-leaved woods, where a softer and more workable soil has produced the farming landscape of the southern moor which merges imperceptibly into central Devon and Somerset.

Dartmoor underwent an additional geological change of massive proportions

in late Carboniferous times when molten magma was injected into the base of the Cornubian Mountains. The magma thrust upwards from the south and produced prominent domes of granite evident in the Isles of Scilly, West Cornwall, Bodmin Moor and Dartmoor. Subsequent erosion of the exposed high points of Dartmoor granite has produced the splendid tors which grace the moor, especially in the east. Like Exmoor, Dartmoor was not glaciated but was subject to the powerful effects of frost action which has created the masses of shattered rock known as clitter found on the high summits. Dartmoor's rivers are not so deeply incised as those of the Exmoor coast, but they can be lively and spectacular like the River Lyd where it pours through Lydford Gorge or the River Bovey at Becka Falls. More substantial rivers like the Teign and the Dart flood serenely to the south through deeply wooded valleys similar to those of the Exe and Barle.

Today, the geological landscapes of Exmoor and Dartmoor are stable, although coastal landslides of quite spectacular proportions occur on the Exmoor coast and water and weather erosion continues.

Watersmeet, Exmoor

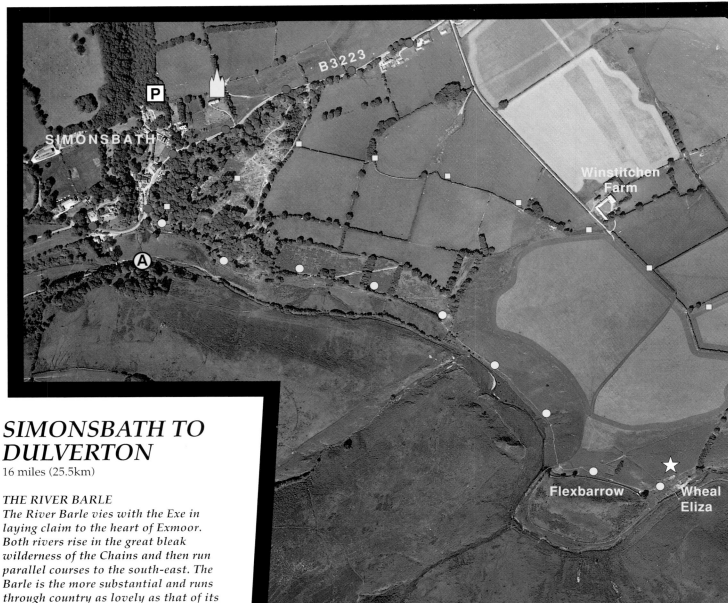

SIMONSBATH TO DULVERTON

16 miles (25.5km)

THE RIVER BARLE

The River Barle vies with the Exe in laying claim to the heart of Exmoor. Both rivers rise in the great bleak wilderness of the Chains and then run parallel courses to the south-east. The Barle is the more substantial and runs through country as lovely as that of its neighbour until the Exe absorbs it south of Dulverton. The source of the Barle is at Pinkery Pond where John Knight, the Worcestershire ironmaster, created his remarkable lake. From here the river winds its way through the combes of Squallacombe to Simonsbath, below where it grows rapidly in stature.

ALTHOUGH A MERE scattering of houses and buildings crouched in a sheltered fold of land, Simonsbath (pronnounced Simmonsbath) is the traditional centre of the Forest of Exmoor and stands at the crossing of the main moorland roads. Parking, toilets and a picnic site are located down a signposted turning just up from the Exmoor Forest Hotel. The name of the settlement was originally 'Simonds Bath'. One derivation relates to a pagan chieftain who was converted to Christianity and baptised in a pool of the Barle. Simonsbath was desolate like much of the high moor until

1651, when the freehold of the Forest was bought by James Boevy, a wealthy Dutch merchant. Boevy built himself a house, the present Simonsbath Lodge, in 1654. Modern Simonsbath has a curious Scottish character heightened by its backdrop of aromatic pine woods and its identity as a deerhunting centre. The rather stark little Church of St Luke is also dourly Scottish. It was built in the 1850s by the Knights, with piety but little artistry. There is an ostentatious memorial to that enterprising family in the graveyard.

A riverside footpath with yellow waymarks follows the east bank of the Barle downstream from Simonsbath. The

path (A) starts at a gate on the south side of the road just down from the Exmoor Forest Hotel and opposite Pound Cottage and continues for a short distance to a junction from where the right branch is taken and followed through Birch Cleave. Though probably ancient, this name is misleading since the trees here are now mainly beeches planted by the Knights in the mid-19th century. Beyond the wood the Barle winds on to the south-east through a wide valley with bracken-covered slopes rising to either side. The river twists and loops round grassy mounds and more substantial hills like Flexbarrow where the path skirts inland to rejoin the river by the ruins of the

The clapper bridge across the River Barle known as Tarr Steps is probably one of the most famous bridges in England. There is some dispute as to exactly how old the great stone slabs are, but it is most likely that they are medieval in origin.

Row Lane

during the medieval period and the present structure has been damaged, repaired and improved through time so its exact age is unknown. The steps have 17 spans in the form of flat slabs resting on buttressed piers. The slabs are 4ft (1.2m) wide and about 7ft (2m) long and the full structure, 180ft (55m) long, stands 3ft (1m) above the river's normal surface, although the slabs can be awash during floods. Motorists should not attempt to drive across the ford at Tarr Steps. There is no path down the west bank of the Barle from Tarr Steps, but walkers can cross the steps and take the uphill road leading west past the Tarr Steps Hotel towards the village of Hawkridge on the exposed heights of Anstey Common. The sturdy little Church of St Giles, with its striking Norman doorway,

matches the honest character of the village, which in spite of its position at nearly 1,000ft (305m) can be a green and pleasant place under blue skies.

Where the road from Tarr Steps enters Hawkridge a track, Row Lane (B), runs off to the east. It is signposted to Dulverton and in turn leads along Hawkridge Ridge and on to a path which regains the river bank at Castle Bridge below the Iron Age fort of Brewers Castle. The river bank can also-be reached without going as far as Hawkridge as there is a permissive path which runs a delightful course along the wooded river bank to Castle Bridge. This path (A) starts about a mile up the road from Tarr Steps and is signposted into a large field then leads through a smaller field before entering the woods by the river.

Row Lane

Brewers
Castle

Mounsey Castle

BELOW TARR STEPS the Barle bites
more deeply into its valley and the
riverside path winds delightfully along
an undulating course amid the trees.
This is an important stretch of ancient
oak woodland with hazel, ash, rowan,
and holly among the other species. Part
of the area is in the care of the Somerset
Trust for Nature Conservation. The
river feeds the surrounding woods with
its moist air and creates a micro-climate
of its own. In deep winter the path
along the river bank is often thick with
mud and the trees are cloaked with
moisture-loving mosses and liverworts.

Mosses, which have no leaves, absorb
water over their entire surface thus
creating an ideal environment for slugs
which can find a warm, damp refuge
beneath the soft green pelt of moss.
From the floor of the wood grow tall
male ferns while the tough little
polypody fern sprouts from the trunks

of old oaks. The strap-like leaves of
Harts tongue fern spill from the shaded
grass. In places the trees thin out at
narrow riverside clearings where
celandines and buttercups shine yellow-
gold in the spring. By early summer the
woodland floor is cloaked with
bluebells and though the shade inhibits

Left: medieval cross near Nattadon

Below: Dartmoor pony

Meavy and Peter Tavy are enhanced by splendid old inns and pubs and fine granite churches.

Dartmoor offers exhilarating moorland walking for the experienced, while its river valleys, woods and lower moorland are criss-crossed with paths and bridleways. There are splendid estates and parks in the care of the National Trust, including the outstanding Castle Drogo and Lydford Gorge, and many special attractions, museums and theme parks, plus a fruitful tradition of art and craft work.

Accommodation within Dartmoor is not as extensive as in other holiday areas but hotels, guesthouses, bed and breakfast, and camping and caravanning are all available in the loveliest of surroundings

Dartmeet

SOUTH ZEAL TO HOUND TOR

6 miles (9.6km)

THE RIVER TAW

Dartmoor's northern wilderness is a landscape of compelling beauty. The River Taw flows from a great free wheeling expanse of high, remote moorland and rocky summits down to the pretty village of South Zeal.

LYING JUST NORTH of the A30 about 3½ miles (5.6km) east of Okehampton, South Zeal is an early example of a planned settlement. It was established as a borough in the 13th century when it straddled the original Okehampton-to-Moretonhampstead road. The hope was that South Zeal would flourish as a commercial and residential centre but the coach road was soon diverted to avoid the village's steep approaches, thus preserving the borough's medieval form which is best seen by looking back uphill from the wide expanse of the lower main street. There has been no tidying up or straightening of the road line and an imaginative eye can reconstruct the image of a dust-covered or muddy road flanked by thatched cottages and outbuildings. The main street is nicely interrupted in mid flow by the little Chapel of St Mary the Virgin and St Thomas of Canterbury who thus share a rather cramped venue. The building is a 15th-century replacement for an original chapel-of-ease. It has a delightfully gnomic tower, complete with battlements and pinnacles and open bell bays. Inside the chapel the

The ruins of Okehampton Castle occupy a small hill in the midst of woodland on the outskirts of the town. The square keep (left) and the great hall and kitchen are all that has survived.

open workings of the clock mechanism add a Heath Robinson touch. Within the chapel compound stands an elegant and very ancient cross. Below the church is the attractive and hospitable Oxenham Arms.

Sticklepath is a busy main-road village with good shops and some fine pubs. It hosts the fascinating Museum of Waterpower at the old Finch Foundry, a 19th-century water-powered factory which produced agricultural tools and continued functioning until the 1960s. Working waterwheels are a good feature.

On the western outskirts of Sticklepath, where the main road rises steeply uphill, a narrow side road leads off left to the village of Belstone. Walkers can follow a good path to Belstone alongside the River Taw, via Skaigh Wood and Belstone Cleave. The start of this path (A) is between houses on the south side of the bridge over the Taw at the eastern entrance to Sticklepath and opposite the road leading to South Zeal.

The main town of Okehampton is only 3 miles (4.8km) west of Sticklepath along the A30. It is an attractive place and has an excellent shopping centre with all modern services and amenities and with ample parking. In Okehampton's West Street the fascinating Museum of Dartmoor Life incorporates a National Park Visitor Centre. Okehampton Castle is a fine medieval building in a woodland setting ½ mile (800m) south-west of the town along the A386 Tavistock road.

South Zeal's linear development along the old coaching route between Okehampton and Moretonhampstead is clearly evident from this photograph.

South Zeal to Hound Tor

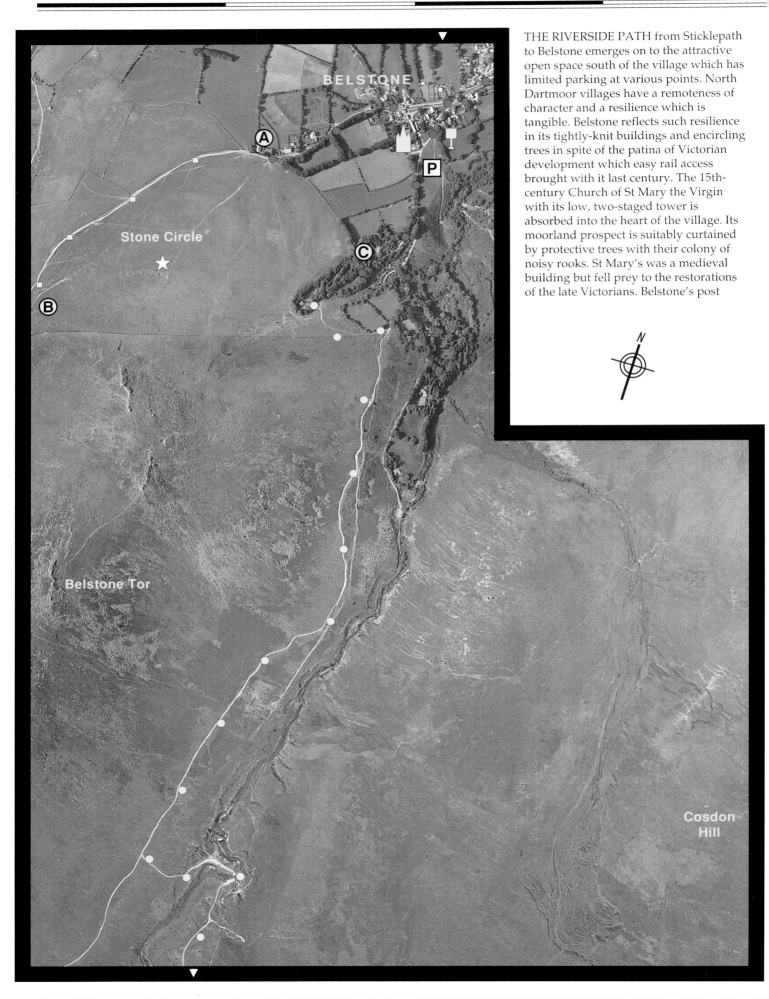

THE RIVERSIDE PATH from Sticklepath to Belstone emerges on to the attractive open space south of the village which has limited parking at various points. North Dartmoor villages have a remoteness of character and a resilience which is tangible. Belstone reflects such resilience in its tightly-knit buildings and encircling trees in spite of the patina of Victorian development which easy rail access brought with it last century. The 15th-century Church of St Mary the Virgin with its low, two-staged tower is absorbed into the heart of the village. Its moorland prospect is suitably curtained by protective trees with their colony of noisy rooks. St Mary's was a medieval building but fell prey to the restorations of the late Victorians. Belstone's post

A view to the north towards the village of Belstone looking along the River Taw: Belstone Common and Belstone Tor with the Nine Maidens stone circle lie slightly to the north-west; Cosdon Hill is further away to the east.

office is housed in a marvellous old building which was once the telegraph office; the Tors licensed hotel and restaurant is just down from the church and the village green with its stocks is flanked to the south by old cottages and the little Methodist church.

Note: Moorland walking from Belstone can be strenuous and challenging, although rewarding. Immediately south of the village lies the emptiness of northern Dartmoor where good walking skills, proper clothing and preparedness for sudden weather changes are essential.

One way to reach the moor from Belstone is to follow the road leading directly uphill in front of the post office. This leads to a moorland access gate (A) from where the summit of Belstone Tor can be reached. A stone circle called Nine Maidens lies about ½ mile (800m) north of Belstone Tor. This access to the moor also leads (B) via Cullever Steps and the East Okement River on to Okehampton Common with its network of military roads. Dartmoor's highest points of Yes Tor, 2,027ft (618m) and High Willhays, 2,039ft (621m) can be reached along this route. The River Taw

can be followed on foot into its moorland fastness. From Belstone a narrow driving road leads south along the edge of Belstone Cleave to a dead-end at a moorland access gate (C). From beyond the gate, rough flagstones lead up onto a stony moorland track. Conifers line the fast-flowing River Taw but these soon thin out and the exhilarating vista of the hills opens up. Across the river is the rock-studded bulk of Cosdon Hill, and rising steeply to the west is the spiny ridge of Belstone Tor. However, it is the southerly view towards the shapely summit of Steeperton Tor that inspires.

South Zeal to Hound Tor

THE UPPER REACHES of the Taw flow through wild country and although there are good paths and tracks throughout the area they can be indistinct in places. Route-finding skills and the use of map and compass are essential.

Note: The southern part of the area described here lies close to the MoD's Okehampton Firing Range. Warning notices, red-and-white posts and hill-top flags mark the boundary lines of the range. Walkers should not go beyond the range boundary on firing days. These are well publicised through the National Park information service and the weekly programme for the Okehampton Range is displayed at Sticklepath post office.

Continue south along the stoney track from the access gate, parallel to the River Taw, to a junction with another track which leads down to where the river makes a distinct U-shaped bend at a concreted ford (see photograph on page 91). This ford is easily waded except in flood conditions. There are stepping stones alongside which can be crossed by the sure-footed but they are often slippery and likely to be awash

The upper reaches of the River Taw flows through exposed and featureless moorland; walkers should be suitably equipped.

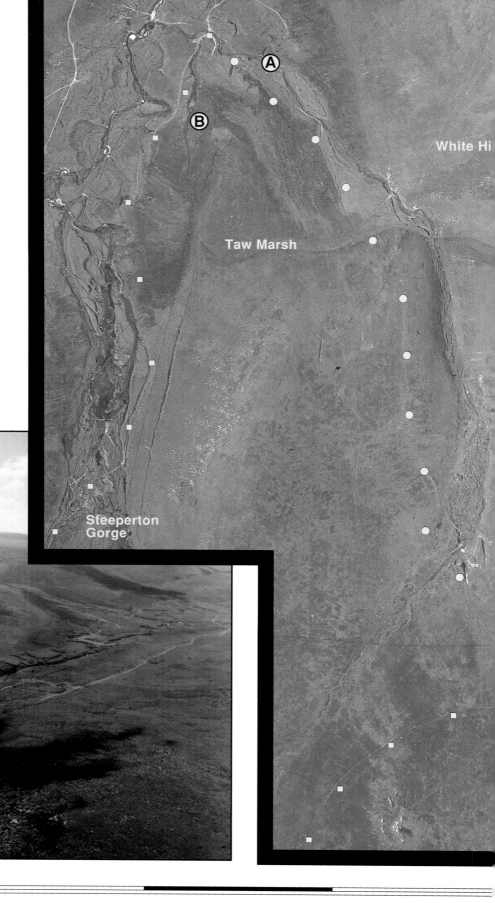

Typical features of Dartmoor are the rocky outcrops known as tors (this is Hound Tor). They are the remnants of granite masses that have been eroded and shaped as a result of millions of years of weathering. Many have very distinctive outlines which act as valuable landmarks to walkers.

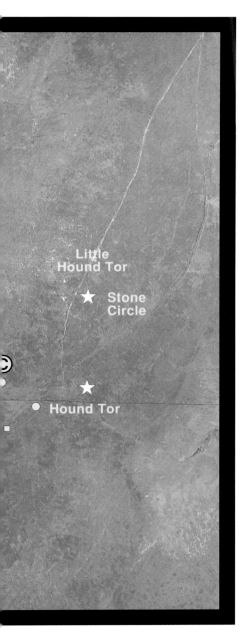

when the river is in flood. Care should be exercised at all times. A track continues alongside the east bank of the Taw but fades out amid the valley bog of Taw Marsh. This river-fed wetland is vibrant with plant life and also supports striking varieties of insects, including dragonflies and damselflies.

To the east lie the rocky slopes of White Hill and Little Hound Tor. It is possible to follow an indistinct path (A) leading south-east and uphill from the river to the summit of Little Hound Tor.

Alternatively, on non-firing days, walkers can continue along the banks of the river (B) towards the shapely peak of Steeperton Tor. The river winds through peat banks and some very wet ground but it is possible to keep to raised banks and drier stretches which lead into the narrowing ravine of Steeperton Gorge. A line of red-and-white poles run up to the summit of the tor and mark the danger boundary of the firing range. A steep climb along the line of the poles leads to the summit of Steeperton Tor where there is an MoD hut and range-warning flagpole.

From Steeperton Tor a path leads almost due south for ½ mile (800m) to the small Steeperton Brook where there are remnants of a tinner's hut and old tin workings. From this point a track and then a path are followed in a north-easterly direction across the side of Hound Tor and on to Little Hound Tor. Just below the summit of Little Hound Tor is a splendid stone circle with 18 stones still standing, although some are very small. Probably dating from the Neolithic-Early Bronze Age period, the circle was restored last century. Just south is White Moor Stone, a boundary stone which may have been part of the original circle. From Little Hound Tor the river bank can be regained by following a path (C) that runs west-north-west from a distinct crossing of paths to the west of the stone circle. The path contours round the western side of Little Hound Tor and when it becomes indistinct it is best to head downhill towards the valley bottom where a small stream joins the River Taw. The river is then followed north to the ford and stepping stones encountered on the outward journey. From here the wide track is followed back to Belstone.

South Zeal to Hound Tor

CHAGFORD TO DUNSFORD

12 miles (19.3km)

THE RIVER TEIGN
The North Teign River rises amid the wastes of Dartmoor's northern wilderness; the South Teign comes ready-made from Fernworthy Reservoir. Both streams meet just west of Chagford at Leigh Bridge, from where the main river flows on towards South Devon through the deeply wooded landscape of the eastern National Park.

CHAGFORD IS THE moorland 'capital' of north-east Dartmoor, a town of surviving medieval style surrounded by woods and streams. It is easily reached

Dogmarsh Bridge

Public Swimming Pool

Rushford Bridge

CHAGFORD

Clifford Cross

Clifford Bridge

(B)

been most vulnerable to attack from the open moor. The woods here are mature conifer plantations of Norway and Sitka spruce, with other species mixed in, including broad-leaved trees. There are magnificent views to the west along the Teign valley from open breaks, and at a clearing alongside Wooston Castle there is a fitting memorial to the local forester who was responsible for management of these woodlands for 44 years. The path

from Wooston Castle reaches a narrow road which can be followed to the left, steeply downhill to Clifford Bridge. Alternatively, if the permissive path from the riverside track to Wooston Castle is not taken, the main track can be followed downstream. Where the river approaches Clifford Bridge the trees thin out and give way to broad open meadows on the north bank. A little farther on the riverside track veers off to

the right and uphill to reach the road where a left turn leads to Clifford Bridge. The route downriver crosses Clifford Bridge and continues up the steep road to Clifford Cross. From the Cross the road continues to the right towards Dunsford. About ⅓ mile (500m) down this road at a sharp left-hand bend, a path (B) leads off alongside the river bank towards Steps Bridge which is just under 2 miles (3.2km) away.

On the eastern edge of Dartmoor, and thus referred to as a gateway to the moors, is Moretonhampstead. Its church tower is a landmark for some miles around.

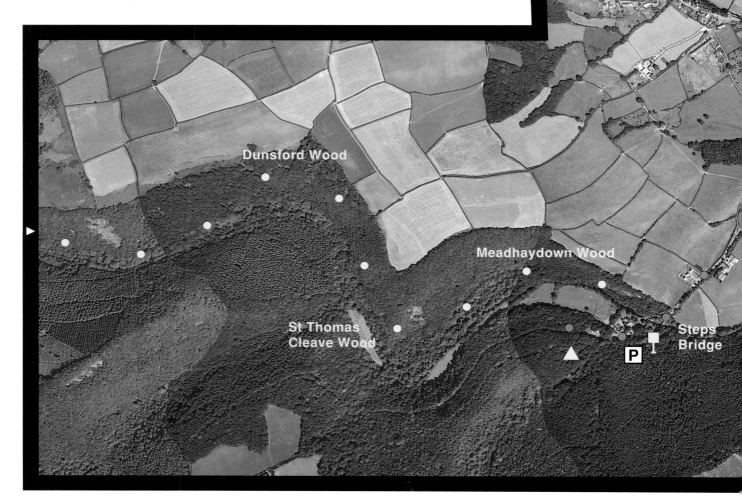

Dunsford Wood

Meadhaydown Wood

St Thomas
Cleave Wood

Steps
Bridge

STEPS BRIDGE CAN be reached by car by continuing east from Clifford Cross to Dunsford, from where a road to the south joins the B3212. It can also be reached independently along the B3212 from Moretonhampstead. The car park above the bridge has seasonal toilets and there is a seasonal information centre. The Steps Bridge Inn has a restaurant and other facilities, and there is an attractive youth hostel near by. The inn sign with its leaping salmon and clumps of daffodils reflects two of the area's most striking features, the great fish itself and the swathes of wild daffodils that transform the river banks in early spring.

There are a number of excellent walks from Steps Bridge. Across the road from the car park a path leads through the National Trust property of Bridford Wood on a circular route affording good views from the southern edge of the wood. Another footpath leads directly west from the car park through the National Trust's St Thomas Cleave Wood. There is access for wheelchair users to this walk. Meadhaydown Wood and Dunsford Wood on the north bank of the Teign comprise the Dunsford Nature Reserve, which is in the care of the Devon Wildlife Trust. This is a precious and fragile habitat and visitors are requested to intrude as little as possible while enjoying its beauty from the paths. The reserve is reached from the north side of the bridge. The path that winds through the mixed oak, beech, ash, sycamore, and hazel woodland is the link to Clifford Bridge (see page 99). From early in the year the woodland flora is a delight, with snowdrops preceding the golden haze of daffodils, followed by bluebells and wild garlic. Bird life is prolific and includes finches, several types of tits, plus goldcrest, wood warbler, greater and lesser-spotted and green woodpeckers. Contented mallards drift to and fro on the

river above the bustle of the weir at Steps Bridge.

Set amid wooded hills and good pasture land, Dunsford stands just within the bounds of the Dartmoor National Park but is emphatically not a moorland village. There are several cob-walled houses and cottages with deeply thatched roofs - even the tops of some garden walls are thatched - and the Royal Oak Inn has all the traditional qualities of a Devon country pub. The Church of St Mary has some fine features, including oak panelling flanking the altar, a stone rood screen, and the striking Fulford tomb with its carvings of grieving children.

The busy market town of Moretonhampstead lies about 4 miles (6.4km) south-west of Steps Bridge along the B3212. It is an excellent shopping centre with all main facilities, several craft centres, and excellent pubs and restaurants. There are some fine buildings, including the 15th-century Church of St Andrew and the 17th-century almshouses in Cross Street. About 3 miles (4.8km) west of the town along the B3212 Princetown road is the Miniature Pony Centre which provides great family entertainment.

Church and thatched cottages form an attractive centre to the village of Dunsford.

Chagford to Dunsford

Living on the Moors

EXMOOR AND DARTMOOR are living communities whose landscapes bear the imprint of thousands of years of human use. A pattern of settlement and communication was laid down in prehistoric times and has been only partly overlaid by the modern road network. On both moors the main roads have followed the lines of least resistance first established by prehistoric settlers and traders.

Exmoor is confined by the Taunton-to-South Molton road in the south and by the coast road in the north, the latter also dividing the narrow strip of coast from the moor. A main road also runs north to south from Minehead to Dulverton and a number of good trans-moorland roads from Combe Martin, Lynton and Dulverton meet at Simonsbath. Within the sectors so defined lies a complex of minor roads and single track lanes which have evolved through centuries of use.

Dartmoor is also well defined within

Right: Brentor Church, Dartmoor

Below: Minehead, Exmoor

main arterial roads to north and south. Two Bridges, at the very heart of the moor, is the crossing place of secondary roads from Tavistock, Yelverton, Moretonhampstead and Bovey Tracey. The moorland wilderness north and south of Two Bridges is free of modern roads, although numerous ancient tracks and paths survive. The MoD has also established a network of surfaced roads across Okehampton Common. East Dartmoor, by contrast, has a complex network of delightful lanes

stands of sessile oak, with occasional hazel, ash, rowan, holly, whitethorn and blackthorn while willow and alder grow in the wetter areas. The river valleys have a wealth of plant life from the brilliant daffodil meadows at Dartmoor's Steps Bridge to the bluebell glades of Exmoor's River Barle below Tarr Steps. Woodland and riverside species like primrose, wood anemone, stitchwort, enchanter's nightshade, pennywort, cow parsley, hard fern and hartstongue fern are abundant. The field edges and hedgerows of the farmland have their own special habitats characterised by such plants as honeysuckle, lesser celandine, pennywort, campion, willowherb, and by shrubs such as elder, blackthorn and whitethorn.

Bird life is sparse on the grudging moors although in summer the skylark sweetens the air with its triumphant song and the meadow pipit maintains a robust survival although frequently imposed upon by the cuckoo. Stonechats frequent the vegetated slopes of moorland combes. The rivers of both moors have resident dippers, grey wagtails and herons, and the broad-leaved woodlands host a variety of birds including green woodpecker, lesser and greater spotted woodpecker, nuthatch, tree-creeper wood pigeon and tawny owl. The formidable buzzard commands the skies above the woods and hunts the moorland edge where the kestrel is also well established.

Exmoor's particular glory is its

indigenous red deer of which there are between 600 and 800, a small number compared to the herds in an average Scottish deer forest. There is a centuries old traditon of deer-hunting with hounds on Exmoor, a practice which survives today although it is under increasing political attack by those who claim that it is a barbaric anachronism. Against this must be balanced the considerable importance of deer-hunting and its lore as part of the social, cultural and practical ethos of the working moorland community.

Exmoor and Dartmoor both support healthy fox and badger populations. There are otters present on Exmoor and Dartmoor rivers but their numbers remain at a critical level. Smaller mammals like grey squirrel are common in the valley woods. The larger rivers have brown trout in plenty and many support breeding salmon. Insect life is prolific in the wetlands and woods with most varieties of hoverflies and butterflies in evidence.

Both Exmoor and Dartmoor have sizeable pony populations which are indigenous and richly symbolic of the moorland spirit. On Exmoor the pure bred moorland pony still survives, although there has been a degree of cross-breeding. The characteristic colours are brown, dun and bay. Tails and mane are black, and true Exmoors have a light mealy muzzle and show no white markings whatsoever. Herds of mares and foals, with a stallion, roam freely across the moor. Two herds are owned by the National Park Authority, one by the National Trust and six are owned privately.

The pure Dartmoor pony is of similar stature as its Exmoor counterpart. Colours are bay, black or brown. However, the pure Dartmoor has been haphazardly cross-bred not least with Shetlands, and there has been a weakening of the stock and a reduction in numbers to a few thousand. Ponies roam freely on the moor but are all privately owned.

Visitors are especially requested not to feed moorland ponies and not to encourage them to roadside locations where they may be endangered by traffic.

Wildlife

TWO BRIDGES TO DARTMEET TO POSTBRIDGE

12 miles (19.3km)

EAST AND WEST DART RIVERS
The River Dart draws its two tributary streams from the moorland wastes to the north of Princetown and Two Bridges. East and West streams unite at Dartmeet after flowing through markedly different moorland settings.

PRINCETOWN, ENGLAND'S highest town at 1,400ft (427m), has been grafted on to a naturally desolate landscape. Dartmoor Prison evolved from the failed ambitions of 19th-century entrepreneur Sir Thomas Tyrwhitt, whose plan for farming vast acres of Dartmoor proved fruitless. Tyrwhitt then came up with the idea of building a prison for French captives of the Napoleonic wars. Built on Duchy of Cornwall land granted to Tyrwhitt by his friend and patron the Prince of Wales, it opened in 1808; conditions proved hard and degrading.

Princetown has car parks and toilets. There are two pubs, the Plume of Feathers and the Devil's Elbow, and there are good shopping facilities, cafés, a post office and a Dartmoor National Park visitor centre. In the windy churchyard of St Michael and All Angels there are lines of small numbered gravestones which record, with bleak poignancy, the deaths of those French and later American prisoners-of-war who helped build both

The Devonport Leat and the West Dart River join at Two Bridges, where there is a hotel and a car park.

prison and church.

The road running north-east from Princetown leads to Two Bridges, where the 15th-century packhorse bridge is part of the medieval route across the moor. The modern bridge was added during road improvements last century. From the small car park on the north side of the road a path (A) leads due north for 1¼ miles (2km) to the ancient oakwood at Wistman's Wood, where wonderfully gnarled and lichen-covered pedunculate oaks rise between moss-covered boulders.

After the 1812-14 war with America, Dartmoor Prison stood empty until 1852 when it was reopened and used to imprison civil offenders.

Note: the boundary of the MoD's Merrivale Firing Range lies to the north and west of Wistman's Wood. Walkers should check whether or not firing is taking place before venturing beyond Wistman's Wood and inside the range boundary.

Just over ½ mile (800m) along the Moretonhampstead road from Two Bridges, a path (B) leads the few hundred yards north from Parson's Cottage to Crockern Tor. This was the site of the ancient Stannary Parliament where the business of tin mining on Dartmoor was conducted from medieval times until about the 18th century. Rough granite seats and a flat 'parlement' table once stood here until Victorian improvers pillaged the stone for their new farms.

THERE ARE NO CONNECTING rights-of-way along the West and East Dart Rivers from Two Bridges to Dartmeet. However, the river can be reached on foot from the Dartmeet road just over a mile (1.6km) from Two Bridges where a conifer plantation runs to the south. From this point, a surfaced road (A), which is a walking right-of-way, leads south to the Prince Hall Hotel and on down to a bridge across the Dart by the Dartmoor Training Centre. Beyond the bridge a track leads up on to open moorland where the sense of distance and space is exhilarating. About ¾ mile (1.2km) across the moor to the south-east, at a sharp left turn by a signpost, a path leads down to Sherberton and the West Dart. The river can be crossed by stepping stones here (B) and followed

From Two Bridges the B3357 can be seen going straight ahead, parallel to the river, towards Dartmeet, as can the road leading left up to Crockern Tor opposite the Two Bridges Hotel and, in the foreground, the B3212.

Dartmoor Training Centre

THE DEWERSTONE, a famous granite cliff towering above the River Plym, can be reached pleasantly from Shaugh Bridge by first crossing the wooden bridge just north of the car park. From this point a broad stony track leads to the right along the river bank. Where the track forks a short distance ahead, the right-hand path leads along the riverbank to the base of the cliffs, but beyond here it becomes a dead end. The left-hand fork gives access to the summit of the Dewerstone, from where other tracks can be explored. Just east of the summit lie the remains of an ancient enclosure and further east still are the remains of an impressive double stone rampart, both likely to have been Early Iron Age. The name Dewerstone probably derives from the Celtic name *dūr* meaning water, although legend attaches it to 'Dewer' or the Devil, who is said to have hunted lost souls across the moors with a pack of hell-hounds, finally driving his quarry over the edge of the cliff. Modern rock-climbers defy both devil and gravity on the many fine climbs that thread their way up the Dewerstone's pinnacles.

The peaceful beauty of the Shaugh Bridge area belies its earlier industrial use. The flanking walls of the car park are made up of the ruins of china clay drying bins, while across the river are the ruins of a Victorian iron mine. A path from the car park leads above the south bank of the Plym along the route of a pipe which once carried waterborne china clay from the Lee Moor clay pits east of Shaugh Prior.

Just north of the Dewerstone's summit are extensive quarry workings where stone-filled wagons were once lowered down a steep incline-railway whose granite sleepers survive. The stone wagons were then carried north by rail to Goodameavy Bridge where they were transferred to the main GWR line, which itself was a feature of the area until closure in the 1950s. All of these points of interest can be reached along paths leading from Shaugh Bridge.

Good views of the craggy face of the Dewerstone Rock can be had from West Down on the other side of the River Plym.

WALKERS CAN CONTINUE north from Shaugh Bridge by crossing the wooden bridge north of the car park and then following a path alongside the River Meavy to the road at Goodameavy Bridge. Cross the bridge to the start of a continuation path along the west bank of the river. This leads on to the road between Clearbrook and Hoo Meavy, running parallel to the Plym Valley Path and Cycle Route which runs along the old railway track. Drivers can continue north from Shaugh Bridge on a narrow road which climbs steeply round a sharp bend and then continues straight ahead past a T-junction and on to the airy moorland. A right turn at another T-junction leads down to the hamlet of Clearbrook. In good weather the view towards Dartmoor is magnificent, taking in wooded valleys and small fields, the graceful summit of Sheeps Tor in the east, and the far northern tors. There is a fine inn, the Skylark, at Clearbrook where the road drops downhill to cross the River Meavy. A sharp left turn at Hoo Meavy just beside some enchanting little 15th-century miners' cottages leads on towards Yelverton.

Walkers can continue on the path beyond the road at Clearbrook which leads alongside the river for a short distance and then continues north towards Yelverton. There is no established path beside the River Meavy beyond the point where it bends to the east towards Meavy village. Drivers can reach Yelverton from Clearbrook via Hoo Meavy.

The strategically placed village of Yelverton is now something of a traffic zone. It lies at the junction of important main roads to Plymouth, Tavistock and across southern Dartmoor to Princetown and beyond. There is ample parking here and several well-stocked shops, pubs and cafés. Yelverton's name is a corruption of the name Elford, the family name of medieval landowners. The village developed rapidly as a desirable residential and holiday town after the opening of a GWR station in the 1850s. During World War II there was an airfield at nearby Harrowbeer from where Halifax bombers, Spitfire and Hurricane fighters operated. The unique Paperweight Centre is situated at Leg O' Mutton Corner between Buckland Road and Tavistock Road. A special feature here is the Broughton Collection of antique and modern glass paperweights numbering over 800. Paperweights can also be purchased.

Two miles (3.2km) west of Yelverton is the charming village of Buckland Monachorum, with Buckland Abbey just south of it. On the eastern outskirts of the village is the Garden House, the grounds of which are open during the season. Buckland Abbey is now owned by the National Trust and houses an interesting naval museum and folk museum where a notable feature is the famous Drake's Drum. An exhibition of farm machinery and carriages is housed in the medieval tithe barn and there is a Trust shop and restaurant.

The village of Meavy is best approached from Yelverton by following signposts along Meavy Lane (A) which runs south-east from the church. A possible meaning of the name Meavy is 'merry', which fits nicely with the liveliness of the river, but the village of Meavy is serene rather than merry. It lies in a peaceful valley between Yennadon Down to the north and Callisham Down to the south with a mixture of characteristic Dartmoor cottages and more substantial 17th-century houses. The heart of Meavy is the village green with its flanking Church of St Peter. The

church is inextricably linked to the village pub, the Royal Oak, which was once the church house and is still owned and administered by the parish authorities. The connection is persuasive; the two are separated simply by the graveyard. St Peter's is mainly early 16th-century and is a compact building with some fine internal features. At the apex of the village green is the Meavy Oak, an aged remnant now cradled for support but not quite in the grave.

The narrow road going north from Meavy to Burrator Reservoir leads to the Yelverton-to-Princetown road via Dousland. Just under ½ mile (800m) from Meavy, a sharp turn to the right leads to Burrator Reservoir. Walkers can reach the reservoir from Meavy by a pleasant woodland path which flanks the river. To find it, walk due east from the village green for 400yds to a T-junction. Just up to the left the path (B) leads alongside the course of an old leat.

The A386 goes through Yelverton making it easily accessible, but it is not one of Devon's most attractive towns. The Paperweight Centre at Leg O' Mutton Corner is interesting, however.

Bickleigh to Burrator Reservoir

The village of Sheepstor lies beneath the summit of Sheeps Tor, after which it was named – or vice versa?

P

THE AREA ROUND Burrator Reservoir and Sheepstor is served by narrow twisting lanes which call for sensible and restrained driving. Man-made lakes often sit uneasily within their surroundings, but Burrator has evolved well and is considered to be one of the loveliest reservoirs in the country. Constructed in 1898 and enlarged to its present 150 acres (60.75 hectares) in 1928, the reservoir can hold over 1,000 million gallons. The west side of the dam with its five arches and its curtain of falling water is impressively Victorian in style. Burrator was further transformed in the 1930s by the planting of mixed conifers. There is car parking at the dam with nearby toilets. Understandably popular, Burrator is deluged with visitors at the height of the season.

North and west of the lake is true Dartmoor country, a landscape of windswept tors and flowing heathland speckled with the frost-shattered clitter of granite. The head of the lake is fringed with tiny fields, many of them submerged by forest rather than lake. It is a landscape which Burrator has drained of its people as well as its pure moorland water, since farmsteads and dwellings were vacated after the building of the reservoir to protect water sources. Beyond all this a scattering of ancient hut circles, settlements and abandoned tin-works indicate the area's long history of human exploitation.

The little village of Sheepstor reflects the stone-hard ground of its surrounding country and there is a pleasing austerity about its buildings. Above the hamlet stands the splendid Yellowmead Down with its granite crown of Sheeps Tor rising above the pattern of ancient fields. Well-proportioned Sheepstor Church was extensively rebuilt during the 16th century. Inside there is an ornate and striking rood screen which is a faithful copy of the original. Sheepstor is famous for its association with the Brookes of Sarawak, a remarkable and peculiarly English dynastic family closely associated with what is now modern Malaysia. The connection began in 1841 when James Brooke was installed as the first Rajah of Sarawak. Four successive Brookes held the title. The family owned a local estate and the first and second Rajahs are buried at Sheepstor. Their monumental gravestones are in the north-east corner of the graveyard and pose a startling contrast, one being red Aberdeen dressed granite and the other a huge rough moorstone.

There are excellent walking opportunities throughout the area and the fine open slopes of Sheeps Tor can be reached along the unmarked lane (A) that leads off to the left just east of the double bend beyond the church. Noseworthy Bridge spans the River Meavy where it enters Burrator and there is a good lane (B) leading on to the moor from near the car park, giving access to a number of paths and tracks and the nearby summit of Leather Tor.

B

P

Noseworthy
Bridge

Burrator
Reservoir

A

SHEEPSTOR

N

Bickleigh to Burrator Reservoir

PETER TAVY TO LANE END

4 miles (6.4km)

THE RIVER TAVY

The A386 Okehampton-to-Tavistock road marks the western edge of Dartmoor. Just east of this lies the valley of the River Tavy which runs from the rocky wilds of Nattor Down and Tavy Cleave south to Tavistock, with the parishes of Mary Tavy and Peter Tavy enclosing it to either side.

THERE ARE no-rights-of-way along parts of the middle reaches of the River Tavy but paths and tracks can be used to link places adjoining the river and a network of narrow lanes runs to either side of it. The villages of Peter Tavy and Mary Tavy are not linked directly by road across the River Tavy but are approached by separate roads on either side of the river. They are, however, linked by a walking route. The Tavy can be followed northwards along the A386 from Tavistock for 2 miles (3.2km) to where a side road leads east to Peter Tavy via Harford Bridge. The river can also be reached at Harford Bridge by turning off north from the Tavistock-to-Princetown road at Moorshop, 2 miles (3.2km) east of Tavistock. About ¾ mile (1.2km) along the Princetown road from Moorshop, a no-through road leads off north round the side of Cox Tor which affords splendid views of the Tavy valley - the pastoral countryside of West Devon - and as far as Cornwall's Kit Hill which dominates the western skyline.

About 1½ miles (2.4km) east along the Princetown road from the Cox Tor road is Dartmoor's only working quarry, established during the 1870s, at Merrivale. The area around Merrivale is rich in prehistoric remains and about ½ mile (800m) east of Merrivale's Dartmoor Inn and just south of the road is a remarkable concentration of artefacts including a double stone row, hut circles, a standing stone, a stone circle and 17th-century guide-stones along the line of an ancient trackway. To the north of the road are numerous remains of medieval tin works. So many ancient remains of separate periods indicate that the area had a special attraction for successive human settlers.

The River Tavy flows quietly under the three-arched Harford Bridge, when it is not in impressive flood. The river is notorious for its fast rise and turbulence after heavy rain. Above the bridge lie the villages of Peter Tavy and Mary Tavy,

N

Dartmoor's only working quarry, at Merrivale. Granite extraction used to be a major industry on Dartmoor, as the many disused sites to be seen testify.

which appear to have developed independently. Both probably claimed the name Tavy for themselves, while ecclesiastical names imposed separate identities. Peter Tavy is a small peaceful village on the east side of the Tavy valley and the close proximity of the high moors enhances its charm. The Church of St Peter is nicely situated under the rocky heights of Smeardon Down. It is mainly 14th-century, with extensive 15th-century additions, including the handsome tower crowned with shapely crocketed pillars. Clear glass windows in the south transept lend a lightness and spaciousness to the interior. Just down from the church is the Peter Tavy Inn with its whitewashed walls. A short distance west of the inn a track (A) going off to the north leads down to the Tavy below Longtimber Tor before crossing the river to reach Mary Tavy.

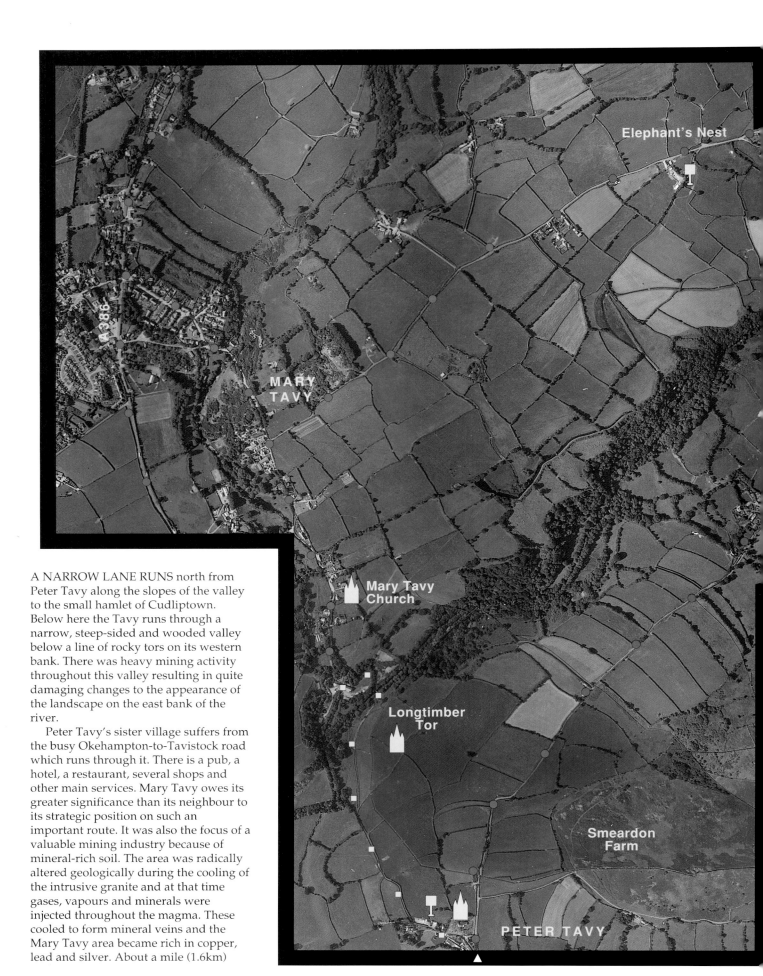

A NARROW LANE RUNS north from Peter Tavy along the slopes of the valley to the small hamlet of Cudliptown. Below here the Tavy runs through a narrow, steep-sided and wooded valley below a line of rocky tors on its western bank. There was heavy mining activity throughout this valley resulting in quite damaging changes to the appearance of the landscape on the east bank of the river.

Peter Tavy's sister village suffers from the busy Okehampton-to-Tavistock road which runs through it. There is a pub, a hotel, a restaurant, several shops and other main services. Mary Tavy owes its greater significance than its neighbour to its strategic position on such an important route. It was also the focus of a valuable mining industry because of mineral-rich soil. The area was radically altered geologically during the cooling of the intrusive granite and at that time gases, vapours and minerals were injected throughout the magma. These cooled to form mineral veins and the Mary Tavy area became rich in copper, lead and silver. About a mile (1.6km)

Dartmoor

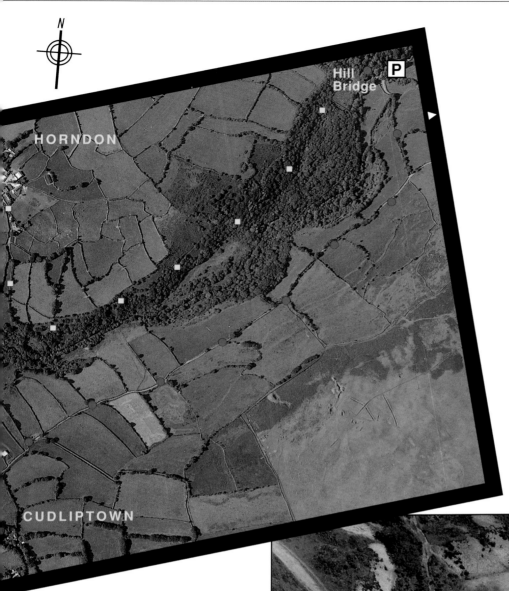

HORNDON

Hill
Bridge

CUDLIPTOWN

humour to match, would always sit on a stool behind the small bar and dispense drinks without having to get up. One night a local wag described him as looking like 'a great elephant on its nest' and the landlord instantly adopted the name for the pub. Horndon is a small hamlet perched between the moorland edge and the more passive valley below. The road north can be followed to Lane End or Hill Bridge from where it continues south to Peter Tavy and the Tavistock-to-Princetown road.

The village of Lydford lies about 3¼ miles (5.2km) north of Mary Tavy and just east of the Okehampton road. Its Church of St Petrock is mainly 15th-century although with an older pedigree. The ruined keep of a Norman castle stands close to the church and once housed the fiercely autocratic Forest and Stannary Courts, with a grim dungeon beneath.

Just south of keep and castle is the famous Lydford Gorge, an outstanding feature now in the care of the National Trust. Riverside walks amidst dramatic river scenery reveal the 100ft (30.5m) White Lady Waterfall and the seething Devil's Cauldron.

Well preserved Wheal Betsy Mine, where lead and silver were extracted.

north of the village and just east of the main road are the remains of the Wheal Betsy Mine, where lead and silver were extracted. The building is Dartmoor's best-preserved engine house and is similar to the famous granite stacks and engine houses of Cornwall. Wheal Betsy is in the care of the National Trust.

The Church of St Mary is a fine match for its rival across the river, although its tower is not as handsome. There is good external stonework in the transept. In the churchyard is the grave of the great Dartmoor writer William Crossing and his wife Emma. Crossing lived in Mary Tavy from the early 1890s. The simplicity of the gravestone is in keeping with Crossing's intense devotion to the great moor.

On the east side of the A386 and just north of the church, a lane runs north-east to Horndon, passing the oddly named Elephant's Nest pub on the way. The pub was known as the New Inn until about 40 years ago. The landlord, a gent of ample proportions with a sense of

Peter Tavy to Lane End

Lydford's castle keep is flanked on each side by the village's church and pub. The keep was built to imprison those who broke the Stannary and Forest laws in force during the 12th century.

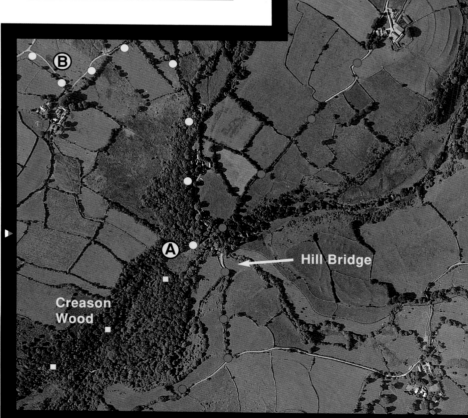

Hill Bridge

Creason Wood

NORTH-EAST OF Horndon and Cudliptown is the lovely Hill Bridge area, reached by bearing left at the road junction which lies about a mile (1.6km) north-east of Cudliptown. It can also be reached from Horndon by following the road north-east and then back to the south. Hill Bridge is a 19th-century structure, a replacement for a previous flood-damaged bridge. There is a stepped weir below the bridge to allow the passage of salmon up river. From the weir a leat with accompanying path (A) runs off along the west bank of the river and this provides a delightful walk that can be incorporated into a circular route via Horndon. The leat can be reached from the south bank of the river by crossing the weir, provided the water is low enough. Otherwise a 10ft (3m) iron ladder has to be descended from the north side of the bridge. The leat is clean and free of vegetation since it is maintained as part of a hydro-electric scheme. It was built last century to carry water to the various mines in the lower reaches of the valley.

Where the path meets a lane, a left turn leads to the pleasant Horndon Bridge while a right turn leads uphill to

The main habitat of the moorland apart from the bare rocky summits is blanket bog. Composed of quite deep peat punctuated by trenches and hollows and dotted with mires, it has limited growth with heathers such as ling and cross-leaved heath on the raised levels, while the wetter levels support white cotton grass, deer grass with its reddish-brown husks and a variety of sedges. Typical moorland plants include the tiny yellow-headed tormentil and the even smaller milkwort with its blue, white or lilac flowers. Bird life is sparse on these moors although in summer the skylark fills the air with its triumphant song. The golden plover and the smaller dunlin breed on the marshy ground and the crow ranges widely.

South of Lydford is its famous gorge, formed by the River Lyd cutting dramatically into the rock. Downriver there are lovely woodland walks.

Horndon itself. The road leading north from Horndon can be followed for about ½ mile (800m) to a lane which leads off right (B) and then goes sharply left on to a rough path down to Hill Bridge.

The road running north from Hill Bridge leads through lonely countryside to a dead-end at Lane End, where there is parking and a firing-range notice board. From here a track (C) leads east towards Nattor Farm and gives access, on non-firing days, to the rugged Tavy Cleave and the high wastes to the north.

Note: this area lies within the Willsworthy Firing Range and should not be entered on firing days.

Peter Tavy to Lane End

Preserving the Moors

THE CONCEPT OF 'conservation' as being an end in itself is a modern one. Yet many would argue that the working practices and the customs of Exmoor and Dartmoor, through time, have preserved the best of the landscape. Others would argue that modernisation and technology threaten that landscape as never before. But the belief that such exquisite moorland areas should be preserved in their wild forms is universal. The reality is how best to do so while satisfying the competing needs of a modern society.

Both moors are in the main privately owned, but are also in the care of a number of 'protective' agencies from the National Park authorities and the National Trust to smaller bodies like local nature conservation trusts. The purpose of National Park designation is to preserve the best of what survives of the moorland landscape and its culture without artificially handicapping a vigorous working community. There are prestigious critics of the current system, not least on Exmoor where many believe that too much moorland has been lost to the plough over the past quarter century.

Other concerns focus on Dartmoor conifer plantations as being intrusive on an essentially broad-leaved woodland environment. Man-made reservoirs also draw criticism and there have been fierce battles over road developments. The continuing use of 33,000 acres (13,355 hectares) of some of Dartmoor's finest wild country by the military, draws criticism from a whole range of individuals and bodies. The National Park Authority's official position on this, as agreed by the Government, is that 'military use is incompatible with the idea of Dartmoor as a National Park'.

Vigorous conservation views are promulgated through distinguished organisations like the Exmoor Society and the Dartmoor Preservation Association which was founded in 1883. The Dartmoor Commoner's Council was established through the Dartmoor Commons Act of 1985 as an arbiter of grazing activities on common land with a brief to promote the best interests of the National Park. Exmoor has recently been designated as an Environmentally Sensitive Area by the Ministry of Agriculture and Fisheries whereby farmers and landowners are invited, on a voluntary basis, to farm traditionally in exchange for annual payments per acre.

One of the greatest modern pressures on Exmoor and Dartmoor is tourism. Both moors are the victims of their own compelling beauty and their suitability for leisure pursuits. Visitors have come to the Exmoor coast and to Dartmoor since early Victorian times and the publicising and extolling of moorland beauty is not a modern development. Yet 20th-century society now comes in greater numbers, armed with polluting technology and increased demands. Traffic throughout both Exmoor and Dartmoor's fragile infrastructure of roads and lanes can be overbearing. The weight of feet across the high moorland's often fragile crust is increasing, and the concentration of large groups of visitors to certain beauty spots is greater than ever.

The dilemma may seem a cruel one. What people come to love they may indeed damage. But the value of Exmoor and Dartmoor for public recreation, in the true sense of the word, is undeniable. Part of the answer may lie in the acceptance that each visitor to the moors is an individual steward of what they have come to enjoy and that each one of us who goes happily through Exmoor and Dartmoor must also go carefully and thoughtfully and so contribute to the conservation of these most lovely of moorland areas.

Farming practices are sometimes at odds with the ideals of conservation.

Trentishoe, on Exmoor

Useful Addresses

Countryside Commission, John Dower House, Crescent Place, Cheltenham, Glos GL50 3RA

Forestry Commission, 231 Corstorphine Road, Edinburgh EH12 7AT

National Trust, 36 Queen Anne's Gate, London SW1H 9AS

English Nature, Northminster House, Peterborough, ,Cambs PE1 1UA

English Heritage, Spur 17, Government Buildings, Hawkenbury, Tunbridge Wells, Kent TN2 5AQ

Long Distance Walkers' Association, 9 Tainters Brook, Hempsted Fields, Uckfield, East Sussex TN22 1UQ

Ramblers' Association, 1/5 Wandsworth Road, London SW8 2LJ

Youth Hostels Association, Trevelyan House, 8 St Stephen's Hill, St Albans, Herts AL1 2DY

Dartmoor National Park Headquarters, Parke Barn, Parke Haytor Road, Bovey Tracey, Devon TQ13 9JQ

Exmoor National Park Information Centre, Exmoor House, Dulverton, Somerset TA22 9HL

EXMOOR

NATIONAL PARK INFORMATION CENTRES

ENP Information Centre, Exmoor House, DULVERTON, Somerset. Tel: Dulverton (0398) 23841.

ENP Visitor Centre, Dunster Steep, DUNSTER, Somerset. Tel: Dunster (0643) 821835.

ENP Information Centre, COUNTY GATE, Countisbury, North Devon. Tel: Brendon (05987) 321.

ENP Information Centre, The Esplanade, LYNMOUTH, North Devon. Tel: Lynton (0598) 52509.

ENP and Combe Martin Information Centre, Seacot, Cross Street. COMBE MARTIN, North Devon. Tel: Combe Martin (027188) 3319.

Note: All postal enquiries should be sent to Exmoor House, DULVERTON. There are tourist and other information centres at Ilfracombe, Lynton, Minehead, Porlock, and Watchet.

DARTMOOR

NATIONAL PARK INFORMATION CENTRES

Parke Barn, Parke, Haytor Road, BOVEY TRACEY. Tel: (0626) 832093.

Postbridge Visitor Centre, POSTBRIDGE. Tel: (0822) 88272.

Princetown Visitor Centre, former Duchy Hotel, PRINCETOWN. Tel: (082289) 414.

Tavistock Information Centre, Town Hall, Bedford Square, TAVISTOCK. Tel: (0822) 612938.

Steps Bridge Caravan Centre, STEPS BRIDGE Car Park. Tel. (0647) 52018.

Newbridge Caravan Centre, NEWBRIDGE car park. Tel: (03643)

Okehampton Information Centre, adj. White Hart Hotel, Main Street. OKEHAMPTON. Tel: (0837) 53020.

When Centres are closed during the winter months, information can be obtained from the National Park Headquarters.

The DNPA has established Village Information Points at a number of localities. These are situated in business premises like shops or pubs and comprise information board and free leaflets. They have signs indicating their location.

Index

CONTENTS

CAR SAFETY

You'll be aware of the major advances in car design over the last decade. The massive rise in popularity of the Multi Purpose Vehicle, which can carry seven people in a car the size of the family saloon. The vast improvement in the quality of diesel engines, which now drive as well, sometimes better, than their petrol equivalents, yet return 50% better economy. The increasing gains in quality which have seen even mundane cars with the reliability of the best ten years ago. But it is in the area of car safety that the biggest gains have been made. The obvious evidence is the proliferation of airbags. Designed originally to protect Americans who could not be compelled to wear a safety belt, it was soon realised that they were of benefit to even belted occupants. Now, in Europe at least, it is rare to see a car without an airbag in the steering wheel, while a second one, facing the front passenger, is becoming increasingly commonplace.

The use of airbags continues to mushroom. Some family cars, like the Beetle, have them built into the sides of the front seats to protect your torso in a side impact. More expensive models get them in the sides of the back seats too and even around the top of the door frame to protect your head.

But it is not just airbags that help save lives, it is the design of the complete car. The bit you don't see is how the designers have made sure that, in an accident, the bodywork crumples in a way that absorbs as much of the energy of the accident as possible. That way the car looks more of a mess but the people inside are injured less.

Choosing a Safer Car

Rely on the car makers and there is no way you can tell which car is safer than the next. As a rough rule of thumb, a brand new car will, probably, be safer than a used one; a heavy car better than a light one, a car that has been designed recently surpassing one that has been around for five years.

But there are independent tests that compare cars and come up with a ranking order of the best and worst. The set of results for European cars can be found on the web site www.euroncap.com

Here are the best cars from each category:

Superminis	Toyota Yaris
Small family	Renault Megane
Family	New Renault Laguna
Executive	Saab 9-5
Mini-MPV	Nissan Almera Tino
MPV	Renault Espace

In the US similar tests have been running for much longer, and the extensive results can be seen on the web site www.nhtsa.dot.gov

COMING SOON

In the ever-changing car industry manufacturers have a constant stream of new models on offer. Some we see years in advance as thinly veiled concept models. Other companies prefer to keep their new models secret until the last possible moment. As such we'd love to bring you pictures of the new Porsche off-roader, the Cayenne, but despite its imminent launch it seems Porsche are keen to keep it under wraps. Despite this we've collected some of the most exciting new models expected in the next year or so. Just think you could be driving one soon!

Mazda RX-8

Heading the forthcoming range of sportier Mazdas is this stunning 280bhp coupe. With four doors – the rear 'suicide' ones are tiny – and a compact Rotary engine, the RX-8 is unique, and should drive even better than its superb RX-7 predecessor. This is a concept, but the production version won't be too dissimilar.

Nissan Z-Car

This sensational V6, 260bhp, rear-wheel-drive coupe looks set to banish Nissan's staid image for good. Similar in concept to the original 240Z, Nissan hopes the new Z-Car will sell just as well; the wide-track looks and modern, simple interior will certainly help. Expect it to be an instant hit when launched in late 2002.

Mercedes Vaneo

Based on the A-Class, the Vaneo will be the first mini-MPV from Mercedes. Small outside, spacious inside, intelligent construction means it is also very safe and efficient. Sliding doors are a sector-first, whilst other features should quickly establish it as one of the most flexible models in this sector.

Toyota Corolla

The world's best-selling family car takes on a far more attractive form in 2002, with a sleek new model that takes on today's popular 'MPV-hatch' style. A 190bhp T Sport version will also be offered, giving the range a sportier image. Reliability is assured, too. The spacious, well-equipped new Corolla goes on sale in early 2002.

Chrysler Viper

500bhp from an 8.3-litre engine? Big is still best in America, and the Viper is the biggest of all. The 2003 model is launched in August 2002, with aggressive new styling and a more focused interior. The RT-10 also offers even more performance than its predecessor, but this time with handling finesse, too.

VW D1

Volkswagen's flagship is said to offer Mercedes-like space, refinement, quality and comfort, for far less money. The new luxury model is built on a special production line, and customers can watch vehicles being built before driving away in their own car; all part of the unique experience. Mercedes should worry.

Renault Vel Satis

Although the Avantime has won the headlines, Renault's equally dramatic Safrane replacement is no less important. Styling is unlike anything seen in the executive class before, while powerful engines and generous equipment should make it good value, too. A brave move by Renault that could just make up for the lack of 'prestige' badge.

Ford Fiesta

Ford hasn't taken any chances with their new Fiesta. Class leading space, safety equipment allied to a new range of engines should ensure the Fiesta's continued success. The Fiesta was always been impressive dynamically, the new car certain to take up where the old car left off. Neat styling may lack the drama of some of the competition but it's unlikely to affect sales - which will be huge.

Mercedes Maybach

For those that find the S-Class too small and basic, Mercedes has the Maybach. Huge, powerful and lavishly equipped and trimmed, it is set to become the world's most luxurious car. It is also very expensive but, at this level, money is rarely an issue. Only the best will do, and the Maybach will be the best of all.

Mercedes-Benz SLR

Engineered by F1 World Championship constructor McLaren Cars, the new SLR will be a technological masterpiece, and developed to the very highest standards. Carbon fibre is used to minimise weight, while the scissor-action doors and F1-style nose add distinction. The 5.5-litre super-charged V8 engine will ensure it performs just as well as it looks.

Mitsubishi Airtrek

Complimenting its existing 4x4s, the Extreme 'crossover' vehicle is designed for those who want road-car handling with 4x4 looks. Its advanced technology, developed with partners DaimlerChrysler, should mean it drives well enough to make it a strong Land Rover Freelander competitor. Good interior flexibility and Mitsubishi's image will certainly help its cause, too.

Cadillac Evoq

It may be Cadillac's first concept car in a decade, but the gorgeous Evoq begs why there haven't been more. The new flagship luxury two-seater should see production in 2002, will be packed with all of GM's considerable technology and powered by a super-charged version of the acclaimed Northstar V8 engine.

Lancia Thesis

This is how Lancia sees its future. Futuristic styling features subtle curves and graceful forms, but it is the interior that is really special. It employs cutting-edge technology, such as advanced climate control and internet-accessible computer, all shrouded in leather, Alcantara and wood; there is little plastic. A promising Jaguar S-Type rival.

Skoda Superb

Skoda continues its growth with this executive saloon model that moves it into a new market. The oddly named Superb features a great deal of shared technology from its VW cousin, the Passat, but will undercut it significantly on the price lists. Engines look likely to follow the traditional VW group line-up - meaning access to an impressive range of diesels.

Hyundai Matrix

Late in the game with its compact MPV, you can be sure that Hyundai's answer will be both good value and well made. Based upon the Elantra, it is the shortest car of its type, which makes parking easy. Engines are promising too, 1.6 and 1.8 petrol options plus a new 1.5 turbo-diesel, but the lack of individually removable back seats is a minus point.

Citroen C3

The C3 slots into the Citroen range between the existing Saxo and Xsara model ranges. A quirky new model it marks a return to Citroen's core values of comfort, style and space. The high driving position gives a great view of the road ahead while the airy interior is full of clever storage ideas making it a practical choice.

VW Polo

Volkswagen's popular Polo will be replaced early this year with this all-new model. Featuring the platform that debuted on the Skoda Fabia, the new Polo is larger than the car it replaces and is certain to become the benchmark for quality by which all its competitors are judged.

GM Omega

This concept vehicle dubbed Signum II gives a clue to how the Omega replacement may look. Based on a front-wheel-drive platform the concept debuts a new direct injection V8 engine from GM. With design cues that will feature on new models, the Signum II represents a move away from the traditional three box saloon - instead offering a more space efficient mono-box design.

Cadillac CTS

The CTS is an exciting new model from the American brand that will reach Europe in 2002. Based on a new rear-drive platform, it utilises two V6 engines of 3.2 and 2.6-litre capacities. Sharp lines promise an exciting drive, the CTS being the first Cadillac to be offered with a manual transmission for around 50 years.

Opel OPC Astra Extreme

Boy racers of the world will be thrilled by this most outrageous creation from the Opel Performance Centre. Originally shown as a concept model at the Geneva Motor Show, interest was sufficient in the racer-based Astra Extreme for GM to consider a limited production run. Shattering performance is a certainty – but such individuality won't come cheap with the expected cost in excess of £300,000.

Smart Roadster

Smart has been showing its roadster model at motor shows around the world for years. Only now does it look likely that it will reach production, with several test cars having been spotted out and about. Neat styling and compact dimensions are certain to make it an enjoyable drive; the Roadster is expected to be available early in 2002.

Saab 9X

This tantalising glimpse of the concept 9X model from Saab shows the future design direction for the Swedish marque. The forthcoming 9-3 will likely feature its stylish front end, though Saab intends to extend its range with a new coupe model - the 9X could be just that car.

Chrysler PT Cruiser Cabriolet

The popular PT cruiser is seen as a figurehead car in the Chrysler range resulting in this expansion of the model range. A 'woody' version is rumoured, as is a three door, though the most exciting is the cabriolet model. Certain to be a hit in the USA, the Cabriolet is not signed off for production yet – but it looks like a mere formality.

Ford Streetka

The Ghia-designed Streetka concept model finally looks likely for production now an agreement between Ghia and Ford has been agreed on the production of future niche models. A wider stance, huge alloys and of course the open topped bodywork should ensure that the Streetka is a hit - expect it to be available in 2003.

Chrysler Crossfire

Chrysler says this small coupe offers 'European proportions with American performance', and is intended to boost the brand's worldwide image. A carbon-fibre body sits on an aluminium frame, and is powered by a 2.7-litre supercharged V6, while inside there is a race car-inspired interior; the two-seater Crossfire even has a 'fastest lap' electronic display.

Toyota RSC

Designed in the US for tomorrow's young sports utility buyers, the RSC establishes an interesting new direction for Toyota. The 4x4 chassis sits on a 2+2 body, thus creating a '4x4 coupe' with considerable appeal. There's a sporty interior too, boasting carbon-fibre seats complete with full racing harnesses. The RAV4 of the future?

Hyundai HCD6

The sixth model in the 'Hyundai Californian Design' series is a mid-engined, rear-driven roadster, with a 215bhp 2.7-litre V6 engine. Styling is futuristic, with advanced details including optical fibre headlights illuminated from a central light source, and colour-changing 'mystic' paintwork. Hyundai hasn't ruled out production – in which case, it could be a bargain.

Lincoln Mk9

The Mk9 concept has been designed by Brit Gerry McGovern, of Land Rover Freelander fame. Said to reveal Lincoln's future direction, it displays plenty of American luxury, including glossy black paintwork and an indulgent red leather interior. 22-inch alloys are impressive, and many of the design features could be seen on forthcoming production cars.

UK BEST SELLERS

It's not as simple as it used to be if you're in the market for a new car. The boundaries between the traditional groupings are blurring and it seems that at every motor show there a new niche category has been created. Take the MPV as an example; it used to be the domain of vehicles like the Ford Galaxy and Renault Espace, but in the past few years more compact MPVs like the GM Zafira and Citroen Picasso have come to the forefront. We've opted to put actual sales figures in this year*, rather than percentages. In addition the top selling diesels and automatics are included - making for some interesting reading. Take the Compact Executive listing and Automatic categories as an example - it tells you a great deal about differences between Mercedes and BMW owners; over 80% of C-Class buyers opting for automatics, while only 26% of 3 Series are specified with an automatic transmission.

More telling though is Ford's domination of the British market. The Ka outsells its nearest opponent by huge numbers, while the Focus, Puma and Mondeo also head their categories. The Fiesta too, despite its imminent replacement, is a close second in the supermini category. Read between the lines and you'll see that the blue oval has a top five car in virtually every category – and more likely top three – if you remember that Ford owns Jaguar, Aston Martin, Land Rover, and Volvo.

*Figures for January-July 2001.

Budget Cars

The KA dominates this category, despite utilising an old platform and engine, its quirky design and keen pricing keeping it popular. The VW Lupo may sell in far fewer numbers, being expensive in this market, but its quality has to be seen to be believed.

Our choice: VW Lupo

Superminis

The British built 206 jumps from third to first this year, its success in the UK being repeated worldwide. The Fiesta is due to be replaced soon - expect it to put up a good fight with the Gallic upstart.

Our choice: Skoda Fabia

Small Family

Justifiably the market leader, the Focus continues to be the benchmark in this class that no manufacturer has managed to beat - yet. They're getting closer, the recently introduced 307 being a worthy adversary, the Honda Civic too being a credible alternative.

Our choice: Ford Focus

Larger Family

The Vectra and Mondeo swap positions this year, the Mondeo being all-new while the Vectra is due to be replaced. Expect it to be the best Vauxhall ever when it arrives - the GM product range is being revitalised – but is it too late?

Our choice: Ford Mondeo

Compact Executive

A recently revised 3 Series is the leader by a significant margin. Quality and driver involvement remain its strongest assets, though the Mercedes C Class and Audi A4 are catching the Bavarian leader with newer, and significantly, more driver orientated models.

Our choice: BMW 3 Series

Large Executive

Interestingly, virtually all the models in this top five are advancing in years, many being second generation versions. All-new competitors are expected soon, the 5 Series likely to be the first – expect it to be good.

Our choice: BMW 5 Series

Luxury

The S-Class will face stiff competition from the new BMW 7 Series when it goes on sale this year. Audi and Jaguar are also due to introduce new models soon, while the Lexus continues to take sales with its incredible LS model.

Our choice: Lexus LS 430

THE UK's BEST SELLING NEW CARS BY SEGMENT JANUARY-JULY 2001

Budget Cars	Cars sold		Super Minis	Cars sold		Small Family	Cars sold
1. Ford Ka	33488		Peugeot 206	60219		Ford Focus	81758
2. Fiat Seicento	6367		Ford Fiesta	56770		GM Astra	59703
3. Daewoo Matiz	6140		GM Corsa	51596		VW Golf	39878
4. GM Agila	4344		Renault Clio	44250		Renault Megane	20768
5. VW Lupo	3725		Fiat Punto	39355		Peugeot 306	19764
Larger Family			**Compact Executive**			**Large Executive**	
1. Ford Mondeo	54968		BMW 3-Series	30693		BMW 5-Series	8795
2. GM Vectra	38814		Merc C-Class	12961		Merc E-Class	7675
3. VW Passat	19986		Audi A4	11645		Volvo S/V/C70	7410
4. Peugeot 406	19361		Volvo S/V40	9719		GM Omega	6806
5. Toyota Avensis	14182		Rover 75	8804		Audi A6	5444
Luxury			**Sportscars**			**Coupés**	
1. Merc S-Class	2061		MGF	4782		Ford Puma	6669
2. Jaguar XJ	1787		Merc SLK	2774		Toyota Celica	3444
3. BMW 7-Series	996		Porsche Boxster	2119		Audi TT	2948
4. Lexus LS400	437		BMW Z3	1829		Hyundai Coupe	2911
5. Audi A8	389		Mazda MX-5	1748		Ford Cougar	1080
Exotics			**MPVs**			**4x4s**	
1. Porsche	3215		Citroen Picasso	26726		LR Freelander	15053
2. Aston Martin	331		Renault Scenic	23931		LR Discovery	6514
3. Ferrari	319		GM Zafira	18175		Toyota RAV4	4810
4. Bentley	233		Ford Galaxy	7824		Honda CR-V	4457
5. Maserati	218		Renault Espace	2598		Suzuki Vitara	4300
Diesels			**Automatics**			**Top Five**	
1. Ford Focus	13026		Merc C-Class	10564		Ford Focus	81758
2. Peugeot 406	12983		BMW 3-Series	7987		Peugeot 206	60219
3. VW Golf	12229		Merc E-Class	7285		GM Astra	59703
4. GM Astra	11099		Ford Focus	7035		Ford Fiesta	56770
5. VW Passat	11059		GM Astra	6239		Ford Mondeo	51596

Sports Cars

Good news for patriots with the MGF heading the sports car sales charts. The opposition may have more prestigious badges but they come at a price. The MX-5 shows a surprise fall, it's position dropping from second to fifth in the past year.

Our choice: Porsche Boxster

Coupes

Ford's dominance continues, the Puma taking top honours here. Cheaper than the majority of the competition, keen drivers won't be disappointed, the Puma offering a cracking drive. The surprise here is the Cougar, which although being a run-out model scrapes in fifth position.

Our choice: Audi TT

Exotics

Selling in tiny numbers, only a few can afford these desirable machines. Those who can have an enviable task, but the Porsche 911 remains the champion. Expect Maserati sales to increase with the introduction of the Spyder later this year.

Our choice: Porsche 911

MPVs

Compact MPV's now dominate this market, outselling bigger, more traditional MPVs in huge numbers. Their popularity lies in their practicality, without van-like proportions, or driving positions. The Picasso is a leader here, though the Zafira is the better all-rounder.

Our choice: GM Zafira

4x4s

Land Rover continues to trounce the competition in this market; even the full-sized Discovery manages to outsell far cheaper more compact competition. Proper off-road ability is on offer - but overall the image is most important - Land Rover has both in equal measure.

Our Choice: Land Rover Discovery

Diesels

The Focus's success in the sales charts is repeated here in the diesel equivalent. Look at the figures, though, and it's clear that as a percentage the Focus diesel models sell in far fewer numbers than the Golf or 406.

Our Choice: VW Golf

Automatics

It's telling that over 80% of Mercedes C-Class customers opt for automatic transmissions. This is despite the company's aim of selling the car to more youthful – and hence sporting – drivers. Mercedes automatics are impressive though, going some way to explaining the public's choice.

Our Choice: Mercedes C-Class

BUYERS GUIDE

We've introduced this new section to increase your awareness of the competition and market segments. Some segments are more obvious than others, family cars being a notable example, but every year the motor manufacturers seem to come up with more variations on a theme to sell more models. This year we've focussed on the major market areas.

The next few pages give a useful insight into various vehicle groupings, listing the best examples and the alternatives worth considering. All this should help your understanding of the various niches that exist, and will guide your purchasing decisions. For 2002 we have concentrated on six categories.

Budget Busters

For those who need transport but are on a strictly limited budget. It's no longer the case that these vehicles are a compromise, with many offering the space, pace and increasingly the specification to make the rest of the competition look outrageously pricey.

MPVs

It used to be full-sized MPVs like the Espace that dominated this market, but the rise of the compact MPV has seen larger vehicles wane in popularity. Offering loads of practicality and novel space-saving features, the compact MPV has had a huge impact on the whole car market.

Junior Executives

Growing in popularity as the buying public demands designer goods. It's no longer enough to have a new car on your drive – it has to say the right things about you. Premium marques are the easiest route to fulfilment.

Estates

With the growth of MPVs, many thought the estate car would fall by the wayside. Quite the contrary - estates as popular as ever. Space is increasingly becoming less of a consideration, for estates are now lifestyle vehicles offering a dash of style and hinting at exciting sporting pursuits.

Sports Cars

What could be more enjoyable than a country road on a sunny afternoon with a sports car? With the resurgence of affordable two seaters we look at the best. Not just the stuff of dreams either; who needs luggage space and rear seats anyway?

Dream Machines

We can't help it can we? They may be impractical, hugely expensive and utterly pointless on our congested roads – but given a lottery win we'd all have one. The stuff of fantasy, this two-page spread should grab the attention of all but the most ardent of car haters. Keep buying those tickets!

There have been a number of changes this year for British car buyers. Firstly the number plates are set to take a new format. The familiar new letter will now be replaced with a code denoting the area and month of registration. Company car taxes are also changing; for more information on both these changes check out the following:

www.smmt.co.uk   www.inlandrevenue.gov.uk/cars   www.vca.gov.uk

BUDGET BUSTERS

Quite simply the cheapest way to get on the road in a new car, these seven can be run on even the tightest of budgets. As a rule they're rather small, their diminutive proportions dictated by cost, though there are some surprises. Watch out for warranty offers, free servicing, strong fuel economy and low insurance ratings. You could run one of these budget specials for a year for less than you might spend on public transport.

Perodua Nippa £4,624

Based on tried and tested Daihatsu mechanicals the Nippa is one of the cheapest cars on the road today. While basic, the Nippa crams a surprising amount of space into its compact dimensions, adding to its practicality. Cheap and honest transport, the Nippa offers group 3 insurance and 53mpg-fuel consumption.

Citroen Saxo First £5,940

Due to be replaced soon, the Saxo range starts with the First. Even as a 'poverty spec' model, the First has most of what you need. The 1.1-litre engine offers 44mpg while like all Saxos it is entertaining to drive. As part of a wider range the First benefits from the halo effect of the sporting VTR and VTS models, thus being quite a cool budget choice.

Daewoo Matiz £5,995

Of all the cars in the Daewoo range the Matiz is undoubtedly the most convincing package. Outselling even Fiat's small cars in Italy, the recently restyled Matiz offers space, if not pace, and cute looks allied to aggressive pricing. A Daewoo that transcends badge snobbery, the Matiz is a great way to get about town.

Hyundai Amica £6,599

Funky looks and "tall and small" proportions make the Amica the idea companion around the city. The willing 1.0-litre engine has the pace to make the odd motorway trip too, while the tidy handling helps when buzzing about the city. Well equipped and spacious, the Amica is a worthwhile competitor in the more-for-less market.

Kia Rio £5,995

Finally available in the UK, the Rio brings with it an amazingly aggressive pricing strategy. A full five-seater, the Rio range is the only car in this class to offer so much space. While its unlikely to turn any heads, the Rio offers value for money that's impossible to ignore.

MCC Smart £5,700

Becoming a common site around city centres, the compact Smart is the most fashionable entry into motoring possible. The wacky styling inside and out means you'll never be missed, but it isn't a case of all style and no substance. As strictly a two-seater its practicality is limited but otherwise it's a great alternative to the bus or train.

Fiat Seicento £5,940

A budget car page wouldn't be complete without a small Fiat, the Seicento being our choice here. While one of the oldest models on this page the Seicento still wins many buyers with its combination of Italian style and low pricing. Fun and compact, it's not as spacious as some of the competition, but you'll be grinning too much to notice.

Also worth considering – Suzuki Swift, Seat Arosa, VW Lupo, Proton Satria, Peugeot 106, MCC Smart, Ford KA, Daihatsu Cuore, Toyota Yaris, Skoda Fabia

ESTATES

In an increasingly fashion-conscious market, the rise of the 'estate' or wagon as a desirable alternative to the executive saloon has been phenomenal. Keen to fulfil the demand, manufacturers have turned their best-selling compact executives into stylish estates. Don't, however, expect much in the way of increased capacity, for the majority of these cars are styling exercises rather than capacious load carriers. Not quite as grown-up as an MPV, the sports estate marks the owner out as someone who spends weekends doing adventure sports, yet remains a serious driver.

Audi A4 Avant from £19,000 est.

The Avant version of Audi saloons has always been a big seller, and has been the basis for two outlandish super estate models, the RS2 and RS4. It's too early to know for certain whether the new A4 Avant will be developed into another supercar-chasing load carrier, but it's quite likely. Until then the option of quattro drive and a wide range of engines should appeal to all with a bonus of, unlike many here, a boot that is actually quite large.

Alfa 156 Sportwagon
from £15,620

Alfa steadfastly refuses to call this car an estate, the preferred name being Sportwagon. Perhaps this is a reflection of the fact that the lengthened roofline makes very little impact on the carrying capacity of the 156 though there's more space to fit a roof-rack for all your sporting paraphernalia. The styling of the Sportwagon actually complements the lines of the stylish 156.

Lexus IS300 SportCross
from £28,450

The newest estate with a sporting badge, the IS300 SportCross went on sale in the British market late in 2001. As with the majority of the competition, don't expect too much in the way of increased capacity, for the IS300 SportCross is yet another 'lifestyle' model. Do expect class-leading levels of specification and extra performance over the saloon with the newly-installed 3.0-litre engine.

BMW 3 Series Touring
from £20,990

Based on the hugely successful 3 Series saloon, the Touring adds even more appeal to the range. An accomplished driver's car, the Touring gains some, but not much, extra space behind the rear seats, but adds some particularly neat new lines. Offering the same range of engines as the saloon, the only omission is an M3 Touring.

Mercedes C-Class
from £22,090

Mercedes has always had a strong tradition of producing competent and practical estate models. Buyers of the C-Class had a year-long wait while this latest derivative was developed, though it's been worth it. With a plunging rear roofline you might be forgiven for thinking the capacity is limited. It isn't, but the shape compromises what you can carry. AMG specials are rapid and refined - the C-Class now has real driver appeal.

MG ZT-T from £20,000 est.

Based on the Rover 75 Touring, the MG ZT-T is the hot version of the newest addition to the Rover range. The base car, largely developed by then parent company BMW, is superb; the MG version promises to be something even better still when it arrives. Pricing will be keen to keep demand high, but nice details throughout will also help convince customers to buy British.

Volvo V70 from £20,500

The only car here to be developed from the outset as an estate and it shows. Clever detailing, a spacious load compartment and stylish lines clothe a very competent chassis. As you might expect safety is paramount, but the V70 is a capable performer when pushed on a demanding road. The T5 is the most powerful but the mid-range 2.4-litre engine is a good performer. The range has recently been expanded with the addition of a new turbo-diesel.

Also worth considering – Skoda Octavia, Volvo V40, Volkswagen Passat, VW Golf, Ford Mondeo, Renault Laguna Sport Tourer

COMPACT MPVs

Traditional MPVs, like the Renault Espace and Ford Galaxy, are increasingly playing second fiddle to smaller, more nimble models. The 'Compact MPV' genre began with the Renault Megane Scenic and has been widely copied. Essentially a tall five-door hatch with versatile seating and lots of clever storage, the Compact MPV has proved to be a boon for families that want space and practicality – without van-like proportions. Now they outsell their bigger relatives, we highlight seven of the best on sale in the UK today.

Vauxhall Zafira from £12,995

While it was Renault that recognised the potential demand for compact MPVs, it was Vauxhall that really shook up the market with its seven-seat Zafira. Placing two passengers in the boot isn't a new concept but the clever Flex-7 under-floor seats gives the Zafira the edge on versatility. Based on the Astra platform the only thing that detracts from the otherwise excellent Zafira was its recent mediocre performance in the Euro-NCAP crash testing initiative.

Mazda Premacy from £13,995

The Premacy follows the Scenic in only offering five-seat capacity, though it lays claim to having one of the largest load spaces in its class. The sharply-styled compact Premacy isn't quite the sales hit Mazda had hoped, but it recently received a re-style and a sporting flagship to boost appeal. Why it hasn't been more of a hit is a mystery.

Fiat Multipla from £12,995

Clever construction makes the Multipla one of the most space-efficient vehicles of its type. Seating six, in two rows, the Multipla has a wide track that makes it an accomplished performer through the twisty bits. Wacky styling is both its strength and weakness, attracting those that appreciate its individual looks, while turning away more conservative buyers.

Citroen Picasso from £12,780

Another five-seater, the Picasso, like the Premacy and Scenic, cannot offer quite the versatility of the Multipla or Zafira. Unlike the Multipla, however, its slightly wacky looks seem to have found favour among British buyers, even though the steeply raked rear windscreen limits outright carrying capacity. Easy to drive, the Picasso isn't perhaps the most practical of its type but is relatively inexpensive.

Honda Stream from £16,395

Until the arrival of the Stream, a compact MPV was always going to be a compromise for the driver who enjoyed getting involved with a car. Honda recognised that the family vehicle won't always be on the school run, and engineered the Stream to provide a more sporting drive than the rest of the competition. Like the Zafira, though, it offers seven-seat capacity that broadens the Honda's appeal even further.

Toyota Avensis Verso from £17,795

The new Toyota Avensis Verso bridges the size gap between compacts MPVs and full-sized models. The Verso name has been seen before on the Yaris range in the UK, and will feature on the Corolla soon; on the Avensis Verso it makes the debut of a the new platform for the forthcoming Avensis hatchback. With up to seven seats the Versos is both roomier and more expensive, than other rivals covered here.

Renault Scenic from £12,285

Grand-daddy of a whole market segment, it's not surprising that newer rivals have surpassed the Scenic in terms of space efficiency and practicality. However it's the only model here that's offered in four-wheel-drive, a niche within a niche if you like, and still sells in impressive numbers. A new model is expected soon, and its certain to be right there - back at the top of the class.

Also worth considering – Citroen Berlingo Multispace, Daewoo Tacuma, Fiat Doblo, Kia Carens, Mercedes A-Class, Mitsubishi Space Star, Nissan Almera Tino, Peugeot Partner, Renault Kangoo.

SPORTS CARS

Given the vast choice of sports cars now available it's amazing that, as recently as ten years ago, they were a relative rarity. Quite how they fell out of favour with manufacturers seems a mystery but today there are few companies that would ignore this image-building market segment. Mazda revived interest with the MX5, now in its third incarnation, with other manufacturers quick to follow with a range of alternatives. Here are just a few. We've concentrated on the cheaper models, so you needn't just dream about them.

Mazda MX5 from £14,995

The car that started it all the MX5 (Miata and Eunos in some markets) has attained quite a following. Superb handling and a slick-shifting gearbox, allied to neat lines at an affordable price still make the MX5 one of the class leaders. Two engines are available, a 1.6 and 1.8; both offer a fun drive but you'll probably want the 1.8. Surprisingly useable, the MX5 has a useful boot and its optional hardtop makes it a real all-year proposition.

Toyota MR2 from £17,890

The third incarnation of the MR2 was not meant to be produced, so goes the marketing speak at Toyota, but they simply couldn't deprive us of their little sports car. A proper roadster this time, previous models being targa topped, the MR2 is an accomplished performance car. Mid-engined, it can be tricky in the wet, but for many that's the appeal. Just don't expect to carry anything except yourself and a passenger – luggage space is almost non-existent.

BMW Z3 from £18,990

First seen at the cinema, being driven by a British agent named Bond, the Z3 was an instant hit when it finally reached the showrooms. The appeal of the blue and white propeller on the bonnet, and its purposeful looks, make it a popular choice. Available with a wide range of engines, from a 1.9-litre unit through to the thundering 3.2-litre engine that also powers the M3, the Z3 appeals to posers and serious drivers alike.

Lotus Elise from £22,995

That this, the second Elise, betters its predecessor so comprehensively gives you some idea of the talent on offer at Lotus. The restyle has still to convince some but anybody who has driven it has been blown away by its abilities. Light weight makes the most of the engine's performance and lets it change direction quite like no other. The sports car by which all others are judged.

Vauxhall VX220 from £22,995

Badged Opel Speedster in Europe, GM liked the Lotus Elise so much it wanted a slice of the action. Who better to produce the interpretation than Lotus themselves, using a similar bonded chassis to the Elise, Lotus developed the VX220/Speedster for GM, building it at its Hethel facility. Slightly more spacious and practical than the Elise the VX220/Speedster is a worthy alternative, but purists opt for the Lotus every time.

MG MGF from £15,500

The MGF has proved to be a popular model, and one of the first to offer a mid-engined format in such a cheap car. Patchy build of early models has now largely been conquered, the MGF forming an important image-builder for the whole new MG sports saloon range. The latest Sport Trophy model develops 160bhp, though is perhaps a bit too firm for rough British roads.

Caterham 7 from £13,245

Its enduring popularity is down to the fact that the Seven, in any incarnation, provides a drive quite like no other. You need to be prepared to put up with a few compromises - okay a lot of compromises - if you're going to own a Caterham. That doesn't seem to put off the majority of buyers, though, and the self-build option makes them surprisingly affordable, though be warned - once you've driven one, all other cars will seem pale in comparison.

Also worth considering – Fiat Barchetta, Westfield, Mercedes SLK, Porsche Boxster, Alfa Romeo Spider, Audi TT roadster, TVR Tamora, Strathcarron

JUNIOR EXECUTIVES

Perhaps the most vibrant market at the moment, the rise of the junior executive model, as opposed to traditional 'rep-mobiles' is significant. Likened to the boom in designer clothing, people now want their cars branded too. The new Ford Mondeo may be able to compete with, and convincingly thrash, a number of these cars, but the blue oval of Ford has little kudos in comparison to these premium badges. Their success, if it continues, should mean greater profits for manufacturers - but in the long run these brands may well become too mainstream, making buyers look elsewhere.

BMW 3 Series from £17,570

The 3 Series is firmly entrenched as the benchmark car in this class. Offering a tremendous range, from the 316 through to the awesome M3, it's available as a saloon, coupe, cabriolet and also an estate. A talented performer, the rear-drive chassis provides one of the best drives in its class. A long-standing benchmark car - that has yet to be beaten.

Lexus IS200 from £18,380

Lexus was late to enter this market but when it arrived it did so in convincing style. While the IS200 may be sold as a Toyota in some markets, there is no doubting its appeal as a premium machine. Neat detailing and sharp lines give the IS200 head turning looks and the interior has some nice touches too. Limited to a 2.0-litre four-cylinder in the UK for too long, a 3.0-litre engine has recently arrived.

Mercedes C-Class from £21,140

Taking the fight directly to the 3 Series, the current C-Class is Mercedes' most accomplished junior executive ever. Less stodgy than its predecessors, the C-Class may not feel as solid as the car it replaced though it offers an enjoyable drive quite new to the marque. The model that's aiming to introduce more younger buyers to the brand, the C-Class is a convincing all-round package.

Audi A4 from £18,640

Audi always managed to take a large chunk of sales in this sector with its combination of neat design, solid build and a brand identity that is uniquely free of stigma. The new A4 builds on this, but now offers the more enthusiastic driver something too. The comprehensive engine and transmissions choice includes superb turbo-diesels and a clever CVT automatic, while the Avant and new Cabrio add practicality and style to the range.

Saab 9-3 from £16,790

Based on ancient mechanicals the Saab 9-3 has always been a choice for the more individually-minded buyer. Stylish and safe, the 9-3 can't compete in the driver stakes though offers everything else you could possibly wish for. The neat interior and sharp exterior lines still look good despite their advancing years, expect a new version soon.

Jaguar X-Type from £22,000

The most important car that Jaguar has ever produced, the X-Type reintroduces the brand into the junior executive market. Based on the Mondeo platform, the X-Type utilises four-wheel drive and a range of V6 engines to good effect. As Jaguar's volume model it needs to sell well - and initial sales look deservedly promising.

Volvo S60 from £19,995

Volvo's executive models used to be poor alternatives to their competition but with the recent revival of the marque it can hold its own in this hotly contested market. The S60 is a stylish contender offering refinement, comfort and a good specification over outright driving ability. Not that the S60 isn't an accomplished driving tool, it's just more suited to a comfortable cruise than a frantic dash.

Also worth considering - Alfa 156, Lancia Lybra, Pontiac Grand Prix, Buick Century, Cadillac Catera, Chrysler Sebring

DREAM MACHINES

The stuff of fantasy, this collection of cars represents the pinnacle of expression of power and performance. How they achieve their goals differs between marques, some going for subtle looks, others screaming about their intentions. Rare and incredibly expensive, many commentators have anticipated the demise of the supercar, suggesting that their existence is unnecessary, expensive and wasteful in these more politically correct, environmentally conscious times. Thankfully this prediction has, so far, proved to be a falsehood - the supercar is in rude health and there's more on the way. A glimpse of any of these cars is special, to get behind the wheel puts you in an exclusive club. Sadly for the majority of us these cars will remain just dreams, but the lucky few who can afford to buy, and run, these machines should be thanked by motoring enthusiasts everywhere. For without their dedication manufacturers wouldn't make them - and the car industry would be a less interesting place.

Pagani Zonda C12

Setting a new supercar benchmark the Pagani Zonda C12 arrived with a huge impact on the supercar world. Here was a car from an unknown manufacturer that took on more established rivals from Ferrari and Lamborghini and taught them a lesson. The C12 comes with a Mercedes-sourced V12, producing between 350bhp and 550+bhp depending on specification, built around a composite chassis tub. The Modena based manufacturer is here to stay too - with firm orders meaning it's sold-out until the end of 2002. Simply awesome.

AC Cobra

Perhaps the first real 'supercar' the AC Cobra has been around for longer than many would wish to remember. AC will still build you a 427 Cobra if you wish - with a mighty 7.0-litre engine producing in excess of 400bhp - though it's not approved for street use. The more 'civilised' models, including the CRS, 212SC and the Superblower won't disappoint however, offering outlandish performance in a package that, while old, reeks of character.

Ferrari 360 Modena

The 360 Modena is about as useable a supercar as you could wish for from the famous Italian manufacturer. The newest car in the range offers an unforgettable driving experience, whether in Coupe or Spider body styles. The 4.0-litre V8 is all the accompaniment you could possibly wish for on your chosen route, giving a tuneful bark and a useful 400bhp at your disposal. The smallest Ferrari in the range is also the newest - until the new F60 megacar hits the streets sometime in 2002.

Lamborghini Diablo

The raging bull from Sant' Agata is perhaps the most widely recognised of the supercar genre. The Diablo, unsurprisingly meaning 'Devil' in Italian, has all the right ingredients to keep it at the top of the supercar pile. A 6.0-litre V12 produces 550bhp - driving the Diablo onto a 208mph maximum - while the styling, with its scissor doors, is as breathtaking as the performance. Getting old, this will be the last time the Diablo will feature in the World Car Guide; its replacement is due very soon. It will, undoubtedly remain a supercar icon.

Porsche Carrera GT

It's still uncertain whether Porsche will go ahead with a production version of this fantastic concept model. Firm orders from enough customers will ensure this, but Porsche learned an expensive lesson with its previous ultra-car - the 959 - that lost it money with every one sold. A mid-mounted V10 will provide the power should it get the go-ahead, the Carrera GT certain to offer a driving experience like no other.

Maserati Spyder

One of the more accessible dream cars, the Maserati Spyder GT is the latest model from the resurgent Italian manufacturer. Looking like the 3200GT Coupe, the Spyder is in fact significantly different from its closed relative. A shorter wheelbase, a new 4.3-litre V8 engine and clever suspension, which will be adopted by the coupe in due course, improve the Spyder dramatically. As an alternative to more common Porsches and Jaguars, the Maserati has serious appeal.

Bentley Continental

Taking a rather different tack to the be-winged monsters available from other manufacturers, the Bentley Continental is an unlikely performance machine. Brick-like styling does nothing for aerodynamics but the Continental has the 6.7-litre V8 muscle to make the big Bentley coupe an incredible performance machine. With over 400bhp under your right foot the Continental is one of the most comfortable ways to travel at speed - though you'll need a lottery win to afford one.

Bugatti Veyron

Over the past few years Bugatti has produced a number of show cars that have all been rumoured for production. This one, the Veyron, is the latest, and despite its track record, it looks like it may finally be produced. A technological and luxury-fest, the Veyron will feature an 8.0-litre W-format 16-cylinder engine producing 1001bhp - enough said.

Mercedes SLR

The first Mercedes to be built in Britain, with F1 partners McLaren, the SLR is a certain hit. Mercedes has collected deposits from eager owners, with deliveries expected late in 2002. Utilising F1 construction techniques, with power coming from an AMG-tuned 5.5-litre V8 the SLR has a 198mph top speed and 0-62 time of 4.2 seconds. The styling hints at the F1 cars with its distinctive nose, while more visual drama is created with the scissor-action doors.

Aston Martin Vanquish

The Vanquish is landmark car for Aston Martin. No longer encumbered with old technology, the Vanquish features a composite and aluminium structure to keep weight down, while increasing rigidity. Powered by a 460bhp V12, performance is shattering, putting it right up there with its rivals. That engine, the paddle gearshift and agility that defies belief ensures its status as one of the greats. That it looks fantastic too is just a bonus.

Chrysler Viper

Certain to offer huge performance from its truck-sourced 8.3-litre engine the Viper features one of the biggest capacity engines in a current production car. With 500bhp available things could get unruly; but the new car comes with a more sophisticated chassis than the old car giving it handling to match its awesome straight-line capability. The new Viper may not look as outrageous as its predecessor - but its performance is sure to be even more so.

THE WORLD'S CAR GUIDE

The world car market is not just about the cars. Behind the scenes, where cars are built and why, is sometimes just as interesting as the models themselves. It seems that nowadays, you have to think big to survive. No longer can manufacturers rely on a single market for success; the only way to succeed is to stake a stronghold on the world-wide scene, which is leading to some increasingly remarkable developments.

A look at just where cars are made confirms that heritage no longer decides locations. That job is left to accountants, global strategists and willing Governments offering the sweetest incentives. The consummate example of this is the US, the world's largest market for luxurious off-roaders. Vehicles with a strong image sell particularly well, so in a masterstroke, both BMW and Mercedes-Benz set up factories in the southern states of America to build the X5 and M-Class, benefiting from huge reductions in both

labour and transport costs. The only thing that needed to be maintained was build quality – standards need to be the same right across the board. Will we see more and more car production moved to different countries, to benefit from far lower overheads than in the West?

It is already beginning to happen. 20% of all right-hand-drive BMW 3-Series and Volkswagen Golfs – and all right-hand-drive Mercedes C-Class saloons - are built in South

Africa, and Audi has set up a facility in Hungary to build the ultra-desirable TT. The associated savings result in increased profitability – and really, how many buyers mind where their car is built, or what it is based upon? The idea can only mushroom.

These policies have been especially beneficial to the UK, for, odd as it seems, it has actually rarely been easier to buy British. "Foreign" manufacturers like Honda, Nissan, Peugeot and Toyota, all assemble

Ford's Mondeo can not be a successful world car...

cars here, supporting the UK economy as well that of their home country. The problems faced by the British industry in the past are well-documented, but it is encouraging that the UK is still attractive to the world's industry.

In recent years it has been the Japanese car companies that have been busiest setting up those foreign factories, initially to bypass restrictive but now-superseded 'block exemption' rules in the UK. This placed a cap on the number of cars that could be imported from Japan, so the manufacturers built facilities over here instead. Nissan was the first, with Toyota and Honda soon following. Nowadays these factories are viewed as increasingly important 'satellite' facilities, offering savings in transportation costs, and also allowing the manufacturers to react faster to local market influences – essential if they are to maintain their sales drive. Honda is, for example, building a new factory in France to produce its new European supermini. Where better to optimise a supermin, than in the small-car heartland of Europe?

So, there are two main reasons for setting up factories outside a manufacturer's home country: to benefit from reduced labour and to build unique cars for the specific region

where they are sold. But this is not the only way manufacturers make significant savings that are hidden from the customer. 'Platform sharing' offers tremendous opportunities. in development and mass-production costs. Take the Volkswagen Golf - it forms the basis of seven other cars, including Skodas, Audis and SEATs. This means that not only can different styles of cars be produced to cover a huge range of markets, but very different cars can also be developed comparatively cheaply. Combined with very large world-wide sales, profits are up for smaller investments.

Really, the only true 'world cars' – that's cars that are both visually and mechanically almost identical in many different continents – are prestige and low-volume brands, where image and desirability overrule any other compromises. Witness the success of the Mazda MX-5, BMW 3-Series and Porsche 911. In contrast, a Ford Mondeo can not be a successful world car, for a European version will be too small for the US, too large for Japan, and lack overriding desirability in all three. This is why Honda produces three different versions of the Accord for these markets – and why the flexible platform-sharing strategy is of such prime importance.

Mind you, not only are cars not made where you'd expect, and not based upon what you'd predict, but the actual structure of some of those companies is also not as clear-cut as you'd think. The late 1990s was the era of take-overs, which left that most American of companies, Chrysler, in German hands, Swedish Volvo owned by the Americans, and even our very own sports car specialist, Lotus, under Malaysian control. Indeed, a role-call of who owns who is fascinating; who'd have predicted Renault taking a controlling stake in Nissan, Lamborghini owned by Audi, or Mitsubishi falling under German DaimlerChrysler control? The big companies are getting bigger, widening the gap between them and the smaller brands. The days of there being just five or six main manufacturers owning the world's car companies is predicted.

It is ironic that, just as heritage is now an integral brief for designers and engineers, the actual production of cars is more diverse, multi-cultural and inventive than it has ever been. What does all this mean for the consumer? Basically, better cars, better value and reduced list prices. Let the manufacturers solve the formula of world car manufacture and dominance, and enjoy the positive results in the showroom!

WORLD CARS 2002

The 2002 World Car Guide has been totally revised, updated and redesigned to provide you with the best package ever! The Catalogue section that follows contains more cars than ever, yet the information is just as comprehensive as before. What that means for you is a better, more in-depth resource, all laid out in an easy-to-use format - we hope you find it useful.

We pride ourselves in providing accurate, up-to-date information, but as you'll notice when reading, the motor industry is an ever-changing business. New models come out on what seems like a daily basis with pricing and specifications changing too. Use the Guide as a starting point for your research - it's the most invaluable reference tool you'll find.

As in previous years we have driven hundreds of cars, interviewed numerous key industry figures and attended the important international motor shows to ensure we provide you with the most accurate and incisive opinion on every new car available, both in the UK and throughout the rest of the world. With each car we've picked what we consider the 'best all-rounder', not simply the fastest, most expensive or luxuriously appointed model - but the model in the range that offers the best attributes for someone looking for a vehicle in its category. Increasingly you'll see we're picking diesel versions. The best modern diesel cars have all the performance and refinement of petrol models, with the added bonus of increased fuel efficiency. And with ever rising fuel costs economy is a serious consideration when purchasing a new car. Body types, engine choice and prices are also included for each model within the guide, with more detailed technical material contained in data and price sections located within the rear pages. Combine all that with the manufacturer information, our driving impressions and model overviews and the 2002 World Car Guide is the most comprehensive car guide available.

So where should you start? With over 350 cars from over 60 manufacturers in this year's guide you may be bewildered by what's on offer out there. Where you live is a significant factor and may rule out a number of models; many American or Japanese models are unavailable in Europe, conversely many European manufacturers don't sell their vehicles outside of the EC. Don't let that put you off foreign models; there are a number of importers that can get you any car you desire if you're prepared to do a bit of research. It's advisable, however, to stick to cars officially imported into your home market. This ensures if any product recalls are announced - worryingly an increasingly common trend - you'll hear about them and any necessary modifications can be made.

As large manufacturers snap up smaller car makers and undertaking badge engineering, many vehicles that compete against each other share common parts. Here's a taste:

Ford

Ford's portfolio includes Aston Martin, Jaguar, Lincoln, Volvo, Mazda, Land Rover and Mercury - among others. In addition to this it shares models with VW with the Galaxy/Sharan MPV and has recently been involved with the PSA group in the development of small engines.

General Motors

Like Ford its brands are numerous. Cadillac, Chevrolet, Isuzu, Vauxhall, Opel, Holden, Saab, Oldsmobile and Pontiac are just a few of its more recognised outposts. It looks like Daewoo is its next target.

DaimlerChrysler

The German American partnership will resurrect the Maybach marque in a bid to capture the ultra-luxury market while its city car brand MCC smart works at a completely different end of the scale. Mitsubishi is increasingly under DaimlerChrysler control.

Volkswagen Group

VW now owns a number of desirable brands. Audi controls Lamborghini, while ownership of Bugatti and Bentley means the German manufacturer has a foothold in the supercar and luxury markets. Seat and Skoda cover the volume, as does VW itself - but it intends to move upmarket.

Renault and Nissan

The French/Japanese amalgam has just started in its extensive platform and drivetrain sharing scheme. Future models will share technology; the Clio/Micra being the first of many when it's introduced in the next two years.

Fiat

Along with Lancia and Alfa Romeo Fiat owns Ferrari, which in turn controls Maserati. Quite a list. A recent deal means future co-operation with GM too.

PSA

The French group that has Citroen and Peugeot under its control is increasingly becoming involved in partnerships with outside groups to share new model development costs.

Others of note

Honda remains largely independent, while other manufacturers like Toyota has its home grown luxury brand, Lexus, which is now firmly established, to compete in more profitable markets. Hyundai owns Kia and has been linked to DaimlerChrysler. Proton owns Lotus; BMW has Rolls Royce with only a handful of manufacturers being able to claim total independence - Porsche and TVR being two notable examples.

Britain's oldest car manufacturer can boast over 100 years of continuous operation. Set up in 1901, AC has always produced stylish cars – including the first to exceed 100mph – but the company is most famous for a single car. It was all down to one man, ex-racer Carroll Shelby, and his decision to install a big-block ford V8 into the AC Ace; the Cobra was created, and an instant legend was born. Favoured by the rich and famous throughout the 1960s, a Cobra also has the dubious honour of pushing forward speed limits in the UK; one was caught on the M1 in 1964, travelling pretty fast…Things looked shaky for AC in the 1980s, but a recent recovery has seen the Cobra developed, and a new Coupe model launched. The future certainly looks bright.

AC

NEW

AC Mamba

Engine capacity: 3.5V8, 4.0V8, 4.0LPG

Price from: £40,000

Manufactured in: England

Developed from the iconic Cobra, AC's new Mamba coupe is a far more practical proposition, with considerable appeal. As well as luxuries such as a roof and full-sized boot, it can also be equipped with power steering, air conditioning and electric windows, for what AC reckons is a car with great day-to-day usability. It incorporates the advanced carbon-fibre construction seen in the Cobra 212 S/C, for high rigidity and low weight, and is styled very much in the manner of the Cobra. Performance, naturally, will be stunning thanks to the straight-six and V8 engines, and a gas-powered version is also available for those with 'green' concerns. Priced to compete with TVR's Tuscan, the Mamba goes on sale in early 2002.

Best All-Rounder: Too soon to say

AC Superblower/CRS

Price from: £38,950

The loud and lairy Cobra is still as dramatic as ever. Although it is basically nearly four decades old, the Cobra continues to be developed, with 1999's Carbon Road Series models, or CRS, making it far more affordable and accessible. The carbon-fibre bodyshell though more technically advanced, is cheaper to produce than the original aluminium model. All versions feature a 5.0-litre V8 engine, which is super-charged in the Superblower, though there is so much power it hardly needs to be. Incredibly, there is also a Lotus-engined model, the 212SC, using the 3.5-litre twin-turbo V8 from the Esprit. It really is quite staggering. All models still need an experienced hand behind the wheel, but it also remains classically elegant and wonderfully crafted, both inside and out.

Best All-Rounder: 5.0 V8 Superblower

Body styles: Convertible
Engine capacity: 3.5V8, 5.0V8
Manufactured in: England

ALFA ROMEO

If there was any question that the 156 was a desirable but lucky fluke, the 147 has proved otherwise. Stylish in a way that only the Italians seem able to manage, the new 147 combines driver and visual appeal in equal measure. Also new to the range, at least in the British market, is the V6 engine in the drop-top Spider. Now the oldest models in the impressive Alfa range, the GTV and Spider are due to be replaced in 2003 but they are still turning heads despite their advancing years. More powerful 'GTA' versions of both the 156 and 147 are expected soon, challenging the supremacy of the super fast saloons and hatchbacks from BMW and Audi.

Alfa Romeo 147

Body styles: Hatchback
Engine capacity: 1.6, 2.0, 1.9JTD
Price from: £13,175
Manufactured in: Italy

Best All-Rounder: 1.6

Based on a shortened version of the 156 platform, the 147 range is a dramatically styled hatchback that, like the 156, has captured the imagination of the buying public. Available as either a three or five-door, the latter hides its rear door handles so as not to upset the stylish lines. The current rather limited range will gradually be expanded with the addition of a hot GTA version and a turbo-diesel. As a competitor at the higher end of the smaller hatchback market the 147 shouts out sporting appeal, though sadly the driving experience doesn't quite match the drama hinted at by the looks. But the fact that this is the second new Alfa to win European Car of the Year honours just shows how much Alfa has improved of late.

Price from: £14,520

Alfa Romeo 156

Estate

Body styles: Saloon, estate
Engine capacity: 1.6, 1.8, 2.0, 2.5V6, 1.9JTD, 2.4JTD
Manufactured in: Italy

The 156 is the car that marked the turn-around for Alfa. The sporting saloon has won many admirers for both its excellent front-wheel-drive chassis and its characterful range of engines. But initially at least, the most striking thing about the 156 is the fantastic styling, capturing the spirit of Alfas of old while still being utterly contemporary. The later Sportswagon 'lifestyle estate' offers little additional practicality but to some eyes its lengthened roof betters the lines of the saloon. All the engines are willing performers while the Selespeed transmission on the 2.0-litre offers fingertip control over a clutchless manual gearbox. Even the diesel manages to sound sporting, though for outright performance the hot GTA versions coming soon should provide a fantastic driving experience.

Best All-Rounder: 156 2.0 Selespeed

Alfa Romeo GTV

Price from: £19,175

It may be the oldest model in the Alfa range, but the GTV will continue for a few years yet. The reason is simple. despite its advancing years the GTV still has the ability to turn heads, and continues to provide a thrilling drive with either engine choice. There's a 2.0-litre Twin Spark or a 3.0-litre V6 on offer, the four-cylinder 2.0-litre providing an ample 155bhp, the V6 a heady 226bhp. The V6 is a bit of a brute, and while the chassis does a tremendous job transmitting all that power to the road, it can and often does get exciting. Inside it's strictly a two-seater, the tiny rear seats no use for anything except luggage. The quality of the trim has improved with the model's development.

Best All-Rounder: GTV 3.0 V6 24v

Body styles: Coupe
Engine capacity: 1.8, 2.0, 2.0T, 3.0V6
Manufactured in: Italy

Price from: £20,110

Alfa Romeo Spider

Body styles: Convertible
Engine capacity: 1.8, 2.0, 2.0T, 3.0V6
Manufactured in: Italy

Offering the appeal of the GTV, without the roof, the Spider has become a popular choice for those keen on some sharp style. The soft top has been done convincingly, so that the Spider has, arguably, even more appealing lines than its fixed head relative. While the hood may be fiddly and robs the boot of space, the additional thrill of being able to hear the engine working while the sun shines though negates such concerns. Stiff as the chassis is, it still suffers from slight scuttle-shake, which results in the Spider not having quite the composure through the bends as the GTV. But who cares? The 3.0-litre V6 engine is a gem, its aural charm enhanced by drop-top motoring. As a style statement there's little to beat the Spider.

Best All-Rounder: Spider 2.0

Alfa Romeo 166

Price from: £20,410

A commendable alternative to the popular Germanic saloons that so dominate the executive market, the 166 is an individual's choice. Based on the Lancia Kappa chassis, the 166 is powered by a range of four and six-cylinder engines as well as a 2.5-litre common-rail diesel familiar across much of the Alfa range. This means that the 166 has all the sporting appeal of the smaller cars in the Alfa range but with more space inside and more presence on the road. The styling is superb, not as overt as the 156 and 147 models, giving Alfa's executive model a grace more fitting to its class. With front-wheel-drive, slick shifting gearbox and a great driving position the 166 offers a good blend of comfort and sporting appeal.

Best All-Rounder: 166 2.5V6

Body styles: Saloon
Engine capacity: 2.0, 2.0T, 2.5V6, 3.0V6, 2.4JTD
Manufactured in: Italy

AUDI

Following the launch of the latest A4 model, which debuted an all-new platform from the VAG empire, the A6 range has been revised with a host of technical and cosmetic changes. Fans of the luxury A8 will now have to wait longer than expected for its replacement, the arrival of the luxury Volkswagen D1 pushing back its debut. The current model has been fitted with a mighty 6.0-litre W12 engine, for left-hand-drive markets only, to keep interest high for the flagship model. Other new models expected are a replacement A3 and a cabriolet model based on the A4. A mega-performance version of the S6 may also appear with a new S4 also likely.

NEW

Audi A4 Cabriolet

Body styles: Convertible
Engine capacity: 2.4V6, 3.0V6

Price from: £na
Manufactured in: Germany

Based upon the superb new A4 saloon, the new Cabriolet, due in 2002, will be considerably more practical than the old car, with greater room for both passengers and their luggage. The gains are down to an additional 100mm in the wheelbase, but the all-important style aspects have received attention too. The exterior design is strong enough to deal with BMW, while the interior gains the snazzy circular vents from the TT. Initially engines will be either 2.4 or 3.0, both V6, but others will follow. Continuously variable transmission will also be offered. By making the body twice as stiff as before, the Cabriolet should, at last, handle as well as it looks.

Best All-Rounder: To early to say

Audi A2

Price from: £13,095

The A2 is a marvel of packaging, its diminutive proportions clothing a surprisingly spacious interior. Clever aluminium construction means light-weight allowing the A2 to be powered by relatively small engines. The UK market only gets the choice of two 1.4-litre engines, petrol and a TDi, other markets get a 1.2-litre TDi engine that provides super frugal motoring. The snub tail and curving roof certainly make the A2 look distinctive, and help it cleave the air efficiently, though rear visibility is seriously compromised and a rear wiper is impossible. Clever design touches abound in the upmarket interior, removable rear seats, a split-level floor and a partitioned boot all make the best use of the available space. The A2 proves to be an enjoyable car to drive too, if a touch too firm.

Best All-Rounder: A2 1.4TDi

Body styles: Compact MPV
Engine capacity: 1.4, 1.2 TDi, 1.4 TDi
Manufactured in: Germany

NEW

Audi A4

Price from: £18,640

Body styles: Estate
Engine capacity: 1.6, 1.8T, 2.0, 3.0V6, 1.9TDi, 2.5TDi
Manufactured in: Germany

Now the newest car in the Audi range, ignoring the recently re-styled A6, the A4 brings more of what made the old car so popular. This time, allied to the neat styling and very smart interiors, the A4 actually offers some serious driver appeal. It still can't match the outright ability on the road of a BMW 3 Series but the latest A4 is very competent despite its rather firm suspension. The wide range of engines encompasses everything from four and six-cylinder petrol and turbo-diesel units to a powerful 3.0-litre V6 petrol engine, while an impressive CVT automatic transmission is an industry first in this sector. Inside it's typically Audi, simple and stylish, while the Avant (estate) model and Cabriolet are certain to attract many buyers too.

Best All-Rounder: A4 1.9TDi 130 SE

Audi A3

Price from: £14,590

While the A3 shares many components with its VW cousin, the Golf, the benefit of the Audi badge gives it a higher perceived value. Largely responsible for the growth of the premium hatchback sector, the A3 is offered with an extensive range of engines and transmissions. Quattro or front-wheel-drive, with the choice of manual or automatic gearboxes, the range is headed by the stunning S3. The base 1.6 is a fine entry-level model for the range but for those wanting punchy performance and limited visits to the fuel pumps, the new 130bhp turbo-diesel is the one to have. Inside and out the A3 feels like an upmarket machine, deserving the cachet that the four-ring badge from Audi brings.

Best All-Rounder: A3 1.9 TDI SE

5 Door

Body styles: Hatchback
Engine capacity: 1.6, 1.8, 1.8T, 1.9TDi
Manufactured in: Germany, Mexico

Audi A6

Price from: £20,450

Estate

4wd

Engine capacity: 1.8T, 2.0, 2.4V6, 2.7T, 3.0V6, 4.2V8, 1.9TDi, 2.5TDi
Manufactured in: Germany, China

Recently face-lifted, the A6 has always been a handsome alternative to BMW's 5 Series and the Mercedes E-Class. In this area of the market image is everything and the Audi's understatement is its asset. The Avant is the even better looking and more practical of the two models, while those looking for a pseudo off-roader can opt for the Allroad that gets height-adjustable air suspension and more rugged looks. At the top end of the scale there's the S6 that offers supercar rivalling pace, power coming from a 4.2-litre V8 engine and driving through Audi's quattro all-wheel-drive transmission. Spacious inside, the detailing is typically Audi-neat and, while not offering quite the drive of its rear-wheel-drive competition, it's not far off.

Best All-Rounder: A6 2.5 V6 TDi

Audi A8

Price from: £38,250

Since it was originally displayed as a stripped aluminium show car, the Audi A8 has continually impressed. Now one of the oldest models in the Audi range, it's been carrying executives about in style since 1994 with just a mild makeover to freshen it up mid-life. Its popularity has seen 93,000 units sold to date and through it was due to be replaced this year, VW's plans with the big D1 executive have set back the biggest Audi's replacement for a while. That said the A8 still offers class-leading performance and economy, the range of V8 engines mated to the sure-footed quattro transmission, the S8 proving to be a real performance machine. The latest addition is a mighty 6.0-litre W12 engine producing 420bhp, a tempting prospect that's available only in left-hand-drive.

Best All-Rounder: A8 4.2 quattro

Body styles: Saloon
Engine capacity: 2.8V6, 3.7V8, 4.2V8, 2.5V6 TDi, 3.3V8 TDi
Manufactured in: Germany

Audi TT

Price from: £24,050

Convertible

Body styles: Coupe, convertible
Engine capacity: 1.8T
Manufactured in: Hungary

A troubled introduction has done nothing to quell the demand for the TT, Audi recently celebrating the the 100,000th TT off the production line. Power comes from a turbo-charged 1.8-litre engine producing either 180 or 225bhp, though bigger engines are planned. The 180bhp version is available with front-wheel-drive in certain markets but in the UK it's only available with quattro drive. In this form the traction is mind-bogglingly good, so much so that some criticise the TT unfairly as too anodyne. Inside it's a visual and tactile treat in the detailing. The six-speed gearbox can be imprecise and the quattro transmission jerky but otherwise it's a hard package to fault.

Best All-Rounder: TT Coupe 225bhp

ASTON MARTIN

ASTON MARTIN

A busy year ahead at Aston Martin as the eagerly anticipated Vanquish supercar hits the streets. Utilising carbon-fibre in its construction, this Aston couldn't be any more different from the leviathan it replaced, blending British tradition with forward-looking technology. A plaything for the super rich, the Vanquish joins the existing DB7 Vantage, which has assisted the dramatic turn around in fortunes of the Ford-owned company. A third, cheaper, model is expected soon, and though previously planned to be mid-engined, it is now rumoured to feature a front engine, rear drive layout. It should bring Aston Martin to a wider audience, snatching sales from Porsche's 911 and Maserati's 3200GT. Judging by the job done with the Vanquish, the new 'small' car should be a winner.

NEW

Aston Martin Vanquish

Body styles: Coupe
Engine capacity: 6.0V12

Price from: £158,000
Manufactured in: England

It's finally here, and there's no doubting it's been worth the wait. Replacing the V8 series cars, the Vanquish is as futuristic as those cars were backward looking. A technology-fest, the Vanquish gets a carbon-composite tub and a paddle-shift automated six-speed manual gearbox. Power comes from a 6.0-litre V12 which produces 460bhp, giving the Vanquish the potential to dash to 60mph in less than five seconds and onto a 190mph+ maximum. High tech build materials of aluminium and carbon highlight Aston's new role as a technology pioneer for Ford. And though the Vanquish is no stripped-out supercar, the hand-finished interior perhaps lacks that special emotional appeal that enticed buyers in the past. Still, the performance is very hard to ignore.

Best All-Rounder: Vanquish

Aston Martin DB7

Price from: £94,500

As Aston's best-ever selling model, it was a little surprising that the original 3.2-litre car was deleted soon after the significantly more expensive Vantage was introduced. The Vantage is powered by a 6.0-litre V12 producing 420bhp, much more than the the original a super-charged six-cylinder. A serious performance machine, the DB7 Vantage can face up to most of the supercar competition in terms of its on-road ability, yet it remains one of the best looking cars available too. Inside the traditional mix of craftsman fitted wood and leather makes the Aston an appealing driving environment. As the drop-top Volante, it offers all the luxury and performance of the coupe but with a more relaxed appeal.

Best All-Rounder: DB7 Vantage

Coupe

Body styles: Coupe, convertible
Engine capacity: 6.0V12
Manufactured in: England

Quite what is happening at Bentley is a mystery. A return to Le Mans this year raises the sporting value of the marque but quite how this is interpreted by its existing customer base is open to question. Still the Le Mans return gave Bentley the excuse to build a couple of special editions, and charge a handsome premium for them. Perhaps the racing programme is aimed to heighten brand awareness among a potential new, and dare we say it, younger target group. Owner VW is keen to broaden the appeal of the marque, with a smaller, less expensive, model expected later this year. It will, of course, still exhibit the quintessential Britishness that marks Bentley out as a something uniquely special in a growing luxury car market.

Bentley Continental

Body styles: Coupe
Engine capacity: 6.75V8

Price from: £149,000
Manufactured in: England

Best all-rounder: Continental T

The Continental's enormous proportions give it an unparalleled presence to match its incredible performance, its occupants transported in a cabin of leather and wood-trimmed opulence. The engine that propels the Continental is the twin-turbo 6.75-litre V8 that features throughout the Bentley range. In this context it produces between 380 and 420bhp, depending upon your choice of specification. There are two 'standard' models, the Continental T, with a shortened wheelbase aimed at the more sporting driver, and the Continental R which offers similar performance but can be considered more of a grand touring car. If neither of these is enough there's always the ability to specify whatever you desire through Bentley's personal commission scheme - something that most buyers are likely to do with these money-no object machines.

Bentley Arnage

Price from: £149,000

The Arnage shares its shape and the majority of its mechanicals with the Rolls-Royce Silver Seraph – and manages to comprehensively outsell it. Backlash among buyers saw the re-introduction of the classic 6.7-litre twin-turbo engine and it proved so popular that the BMW-sourced 4.4-litre V8 was dropped. That 'old' engine produces more than enough power to propel the hefty Arnage along with alarming vigour, it coping remarkably well when hustled through a series of bends. A sumptuous interior gives the Arnage a 'flying boardroom' feel, though space isn't as generous as you might expect from such a huge vehicle. The Arnage marks the end of a historic period of co-developed Rolls-Royce and Bentley models.

Body styles: Saloon
Engine capacity: 6.75V8
Manufactured in:
England

Best all-rounder: Arnage Green Label

Price from: £230,800

Bentley Azure

Body styles: Convertible
Engine capacity: 6.75V8
Manufactured in:
England

For the ultimate in luxury open-topped motoring there is nothing, except perhaps the closely related Rolls-Royce Corniche, that can come close to the Bentley Azure. A plaything for the extremely wealthy, the Azure is a massive statement of its owner's success, not least because it combines huge overall proportions with somewhat limited interior space. Given its bulk you might expect the Azure to be slow off the mark, but you'd be mistaken. The Azure share its powerplants with the Continental coupes – meaning a twin-turbo 6.75-litre engine with 389bhp, a sub 7 second 0-60mph time and 149mph top speed. Only a handful of these mighty convertibles are produced each year – hardly surprising given you're unlikely to get much change from quarter of a million pounds.

Best all-rounder: Azure

BMW

Flourishing after off-loading Rover, BMW is poised to flood the car market with a host of new models. Up to 10 fresh BMWs are expected over the next 4 years, some totally new, others derivatives or facelifts of existing models. Following the launch of the 3 Series Compact, a more radically styled Z3 is expected within a year. A sub 3 Series Compact model is also predicted, despite BMW producing the MINI, although its arrival is not likely until at least 2004. At the other end of the spectrum the new 7 Series has been revealed, while a new 6 Series coupe/cabriolet extends the range in 2003. The success of the X5 cross-roader means we're certain to see an 3 Series-derived X3, while an X7 is also a possibility. One thing is certain, BMW means business.

NEW

BMW 7 Series

Body styles: Saloon
Engine capacity: 3.5V8, 4.5V8

Price from: £na
Manufactured in: Germany

An all-new car the latest 7 Series has the Mercedes S-Class firmly in its sights. Debuting a number of innovations from BMW, the 7 is a technical tour-de-force, its sharp and neat exterior lines hinting at a more angular look for the marque. Inside the majority of auxiliary controls are operated by what BMW calls iDrive – using a centrally mounted screen and roller-type control between the driver and passenger seats. All the major driving controls are located around the steering column, including the shift control for the six-speed automatic transmission. Two engines are available at present, two V8s, a 272bhp 3.6-litre powering the 735i and a 333bhp 4.4-litre in the 745i. We've yet to drive one but it's certain to be superb.

Best All-Rounder: too soon to say..

BMW Compact

Price from: £16,265

Using the excellent rear-wheel-drive platform from the 3 Series, the Compact proves to be even more enjoyable to drive than the car it's based on. Shortening the rear of the car gives it a distinctive profile, while the nose gets quad headlamps. Inside the 3 Series theme continues, though the trim is available in a wider, more adventurous, range of colours. Power comes from a choice of four engines – a 2.5 six-cylinder, British-built 1.8-litre and 2.0-litre four-cylinder, and a 148bhp 2.0-litre turbo-diesel. Also new is sharper steering which will make its way to 3 Series. As ever, space isn't generous in the Compact, but room isn't bad and inevitably it is a delight to drive, whatever the engine.

Body styles: Hatchback
Engine capacity: 1.8, 2.0, 2.5, 2.0d
Manufactured in: Germany

NEW

Best All-Rounder: 325i

BMW 3 Series

Price from: £17,570

Convertible

Body styles: Saloon, coupe, convertible, estate
Engine capacity: 1.9, 2.2, 2.5, 3.0, 3.2, 2.0d, 3.0d
Manufactured in: Germany, South Africa

Without doubt the BMW 3 Series is the car by which all small executive models are judged. With good reason too, the 3 managing to offer the perfect balance between driver involvement and sophistication. The wide range encompasses a saloon, coupe, convertible and touring (estate) models, with the new Compact hatchback based on its rear-drive chassis. The engine range is just as vast with four and six-cylinder petrol choices and two excellent diesels. It's the new range topper, the M3, that is the model to aspire too – offering Porsche pace in a more practical package. The cabin has near-perfect ergonomics, while a recent facelift on the saloon and touring brings a new headlamp design, an improved steering rack and more standard equipment.

Best All-Rounder: 330d SE

BMW 5 Series

Price from: £23,360

Like the smaller 3 Series the 5 is at the top of its class, still impressing all that drive it despite the advancing years. Those choosing not to wait for the replacement that will be with us in the next year or two won't be disappointed with the current machine, a refined and capable executive car with an underlying sporting character. Even with the smallest engines fitted the 5 is an enjoyable drive, though for the ultimate rapid 5 the M5 has become a legend for its astonishing ability and pace. A touring version adds some practicality; the only real shortcoming of the 5 Series is its limited rear legroom.

Best All-Rounder: 525i SE

Estate

Body styles: Saloon, estate
Engine capacity: 2.2, 2.5, 3.0, 3.5V8, 4.4V8, 5.0V8, 2.0d, 2.5d, 3.0d
Manufactured in: Germany

BMW Z3

Price from: £18,990

Coupe

Body styles: Coupe, convertible
Engine capacity: 1.9, 2.2, 2.5, 3.0, 3.2
Manufactured in: United States

The Z3 has been a resounding success for the Bavarian marque, offering customers all the quality and prestige associated with the brand in a desirable roadster format. The wide range competes with sports cars from virtually all categories, pitting the Z3 against entry-level cars like Mazda's MX-5, with the larger engined 320bhp M versions taking the fight to the Porsche Boxster and beyond. What that means is there's a Z3 for virtually all budgets, all offering an enjoyable open top driving experience. Mainland Europe gets the coupe version with a choice of engines, but only the brawny M coupe is available in Britain. New prototypes have been spotted testing suggesting the Z3 is going to be replaced soon.

Best All-Rounder: Z3 2.0

BMW Z8

Price from: £80,000

Make no mistake, while the Z8 echoes the design of the 1950's BMW 507, it is a thoroughly modern machine. The aluminium alloy spaceframe features aluminium suspension components and is clothed by those retro lines in aluminium too, keeping the weight of the Z8 down. That light-weight means that the 5.0-litre V8 from the M5 gives the roadster mighty performance, covering the 0-62mph dash in 4.7 seconds, all the 400 horses kept reigned in by BMW's impressive Dynamic Stability Control system. Inside the retro theme continues with swathes of chrome and beautiful detailing around the centrally mounted instrumentation. Left-hand-drive (and the price tag) limit its appeal in the UK, though it's only available in limited numbers to maintain exclusivity.

Best all-rounder: Z8

Body styles: Convertible
Engine capacity: 4.9V8
Manufactured in: Germany

BMW X5

Price from: £33,000

Body styles: Estate
Engine capacity: 3.0, 4.4V8, 3.0d
Manufactured in: United States

In previous editions we pondered BMW's decision to produce a luxury 4x4 as it was then the owner of Land Rover. Now LR has been sold to Ford it leaves the X5 to stand on its own, and that it does very well indeed. Not pandering to outright off-road ability has allowed BMW to tune the suspension for road use, making the X5 an accomplished road car - it comprehensively out-drives all comers in the luxury 4x4 market. Power comes from a range of three excellent engines, 3.0-litre six, a 4.4-litre V8 and a 3.0-litre diesel. All give the X5 strong pace. Built in the USA alongside the Z3, BMW's decision now looks like a good one.

Best All-Rounder: 3.0d Sport

The Rendezvous sport utility apart, Buick's range appears tailor-made for the 'more mature' driver. The Century, Regal and Le Sabre all offer a blend of inoffensive styling, reliability and lack of fuss that the golf club set flock to in droves; the Le Sabre is America's best-selling full-size luxury car. But Buick wants to appeal to a younger, more dynamic market, hence the launch of the Rendezvous. With dramatic styling and a less traditional image, it could signal the start of a new direction for the marque. The wild concept cars also continue, proving that General Motors is determined not to let one of its most respected brands meander into extinction, the fate Oldsmobile suffered. The next few years will be crucial, but should be interesting, too.

Buick Le Sabre

Body styles: Saloon
Engine capacity: 3.8 V6

Price from: $24,200
Manufactured in: United States

The 2000 LeSabre may have looked very similar to the aged model it replaced, but it was far better from behind the wheel. Not wishing to alienate its traditional elderly buyers, Buick also wanted to attract younger, keener buyers into America's best selling full-size car. So the suspension was sharpened, which not only benefited the handling but the ride comfort too. Obviously it's no sports car, but the current Le Sabre is a vast improvement over the old model. Today's sedans feature a single engine option, a 3.8-litre V6 engine that produces 205bhp. Although it is an old pushrod design, it is refined and fairly economical. A huge amount of car for the money, it is still possible to see why the appeal is maintained.

Best All-Rounder: LeSabre Limited

BUICK

Price from: $20,400

Buick Century

Body styles: Saloon
Engine capacity: 3.1V6
Manufactured in:
United States

Buick's lowest-priced model certainly doesn't skimp on the luxury. Leather, plenty of electrics and a spacious cabin all suggest excellent value for money. On the road, however, it is a different story. The ride is certainly soft and comfortable, but this comes at the expense of handling ability, which is decidedly vague – the steering is especially light and distant. This is not a car that offers any form of driving excitement. There is plenty of power though, courtesy of a 175bhp 3.1-litre V6 unit driving the front wheels. The slickly-styled Century sells well to older buyers who rate its tremendous value for money and equipment levels; others may find its soggy drive far too plodding and dull.

Best All-Rounder: Century Custom

Buick Regal

The Regal is Buick's car for the younger market – though when this translates to the 'forty-something' market, Buick's status as GM's 'wrinkly' division is reinforced. Closely related to the Century, the Regal is a sporty mid-size saloon, offering plenty of equipment for less than its European rivals. Under the bonnet, there is an impressive 3.8-litre V6 unit, offering 205bhp in standard form, with the supercharged GS version boosting this to 240bhp. The GS also benefits from sportier suspension and wider tyres, making it an entertaining charger – but even the standard model is more agile than the Buick norm. All the ingredients are there, and though rivals offer more sophistication, the Regal's bargain price more than compensates.

Best All-Rounder: Regal GS

Price from: $23,600

Body styles: Saloon
Engine capacity: 3.8V6
Manufactured in:
United States

Price from: $33,900

Buick Park Avenue

Body styles: Saloon
Engine capacity: 3.8V6
Manufactured in:
United States

Buick's large Park Avenue is a favourite of the country club set, but its popularity is waning nowadays as both the car and its buyers age. It can still supply the luxury goods though, with the huge interior coming lavishly equipped with every extra. On the road, soft suspension offers a plush ride at the expense of agility, whilst the V6 engine supplies good performance. The 3.8-litre unit comes in two forms; the base model offers 205bhp, but the maddest model is the supercharged Ultra, with its 240bhp engine. Combined with firmer suspension, it is an odd blend of high performance and old-fashioned refinement. The Park Avenue does the job, but for how much longer?

Best All-Rounder: Park Avenue

Buick Rendezvous

From the manufacturer of the retirement set's preferred modes of transport comes this – Buick's first SUV, and best chance of long-term survival. Like many American-designed rivals, it looks very odd, especially from the rear where the tail appears to have been 'chopped off' and replaced with darkened glass. It's certainly distinctive, and seems to be attracting interest. The seven-seat interior is practical and roomy, and features white instrument dials to add a sporty air; without them, the dash would be dull, as well as cheap-looking. Power comes from a 3.4-litre V6, and both 2WD and 4WD chassis are offered – upper-spec CXL models adding Versatrak 4WD, creating a very capable vehicle. All the ingredients are there, but will the Buick tag hinder its success?

Best All-Rounder: Rendezvous CXL

Price from: $25,500

Body styles: Estate
Engine capacity: 3.4V6
Manufactured in:
United States

NEW

CADILLAC

The stodgy Cadillacs of old are, gradually, being replaced by far more dynamic and hard-edged models, as General Motors continues to overhaul its famous luxury car division. The Seville has been developed into a very fast sports saloon, and even starred as the Le Mans pace car. The Escalade sport utility and Catera saloon also show forward-thinking design, whilst the DeVille luxury model boasts the full range of Cadillac's advanced technology – including Night Vision. The much-previewed Evoq luxury saloon may also appear soon, and will quickly make waves with its dramatic styling. It is younger buyers with plentiful cash that Cadillac desires, and it seems determined to attract them.

Cadillac Seville

Body styles: Saloon
Engine capacity: 4.6V8

Price from: £34,499
Manufactured in: United States

Designed with younger, less traditional buyers in mind, the Seville is noted above all for its huge array of technical features. Multiplex wiring allows the addition of Bose's Infotainment system – for in-car e-mails – as well as StabiliTrak anti-skid control and satellite navigation. The superb Northstar 4.6-litre V8 engine provides the power, offering 275bhp in standard guise and 300bhp in rapid STS form. The engine is effortless, very fast, and generally of the highest calibre. Handling is also more entertaining than expected, though this comes at the expense of an occasionally uncomposed ride. There's a classy interior too, but the popularity of the attractive Seville in the US isn't mirrored in Europe, where the lure of more capable domestic models is just too strong.

Best All-Rounder: Seville

Price from: $31,900

Cadillac Catera

Body styles: Saloon
Engine capacity: 3.0V6
Manufactured in:
Germany

The Catera is based on the Vauxhall/Opel Omega, a car that is considered 'large' in Europe but is pitched in the US for Cadillac owners who want to 'trade down'. It also targets younger buyers who are attracted by European models, but although sales started well, they are slipping now; it is just not seen as a true 'Caddy'. The 3.0-litre V6 engine produces 200bhp – adequate here, but seen as under-powered in the US. The handling, however, is well-rated, especially with the optional Sport package. It also cruises well, and is roomy inside despite its 'small' dimensions. A new model is on the cards, using an all-new platform and much-needed additional power. Until then, the Catera will remain a merely average American saloon.

Best All-Rounder: Catera

Cadillac DeVille

Price from: $41,200

America's best-selling large luxury car, the DeVille, offers even more gadgets than its Seville sister. Items such as the Bose 'Infotainment' system and rain-sensing wipers all feature, and there is also the option of Night Vision – an infra-red 'eye' for driving in the dark. The acclaimed Northstar V8 engine powers it, in 275bhp and 300bhp STS form. The STS model offers electronic suspension control, sensing the road conditions and adjusting accordingly. This makes the DeVille a competent handler with a decent ride quality – some rivals are better, but few are more secure and predictable. The DeVille offers great value and tremendous performance – STS especially – in a discreet, attractively-styled package.

Best All-Rounder: DeVille STS

Body styles: Saloon
Engine capacity: 4.6V8
Manufactured in:
United States

Price from: $40,800

Cadillac Eldorado

Body styles: Coupe
Engine capacity: 4.6V8
Manufactured in:
United States

The European's idea of an American coupe. The Eldorado is big, old and boxy, and is now counting down its final days; buyers have simply dried up. However, although the styling is dated, underneath it far more up-to-date. The 4.6-litre V8 engine is typically superb, and is offered in both 275bhp and 300bhp forms. There is also plenty of chassis technology, including StabiliTrak anti-skid system and road-sensing suspension that 'reads' the tarmac for bumps. This all means the Eldorado drives surprisingly well, far better than it looks like it should. It is also spacious, with plenty of room inside for four. However, its looks place it in a bygone era; expect the Eldorado, like its buyers, to retire soon.

Best All-Rounder: Eldorado

Cadillac Escalade

Price from: $48,000

The Escalade was revised last year, with a far more modern look bringing it bang up-to-date. There were also improvements under the skin, with the introduction of a new 6.0-litre V8 engine offering 345bhp running alongside the 5.3-litre 285bhp V8. However, although the sports-utility Escalade looks like a butch off-roader, it's not designed for off-road use; only the 6.0-litre model sports four-wheel-drive, for example. This means it offers a fine road-biased ride and handling mix, along with very rapid performance – at the expense of horrific fuel economy. The Escalade is well equipped too, with plenty of features that include Night Vision – Cadillac's innovative night-time image-sensing infra-red system. A large, luxurious, expensive battleship, ideally suited to American tastes.

Best All-Rounder: Escalade

Body styles: Estate
Engine capacity: 5.8V8
Manufactured in:
United States

CHRYSLER

In recent years Chrysler has been one of America's most forward-thinking manufacturers. Exciting show-car concepts have often been translated into real products that people can buy. The latest Neon maintains the distinctive 'cab forward' design which the LH series of cars also features. The new Voyager continues to be a hugely popular minivan – especially now safety criticisms of the previous model have been addressed. But it is the radical hot-rod inspired PT Cruiser that is breaking all the records, Americans simply cannot get enough, and the lengthy waiting lists mean premiums of over $10,000 have been commanded and production has been replicated in Austria. Throw in a new Viper supercar, with 500bhp and traffic-stopping looks, and Chrysler's current financial problems could soon be eased; parent company DaimlerChrysler will certainly hope so.

Chrysler Prowler

Body styles: Convertible
Engine capacity: 3.5V6
Price from: $44,600
Manufactured in: United States

The PT Cruiser isn't the first recent Chrysler to be inspired by a hot rod – the Prowler was. Formerly called Plymouth, the Chrysler Prowler really is a show car for the road, complete with 20-inch rear wheels and looks like those of no other car. The interior is just as outlandish, yet packs a decent amount of equipment, too. Under the hood lies a 3.5-litre V6 – sadly not a V8 – but it still does the job very well. 0-60mph takes 6.5 seconds, thanks to an impressive 253bhp. Handling is also sharp, especially since retuning last year, and the ride quality is reasonable – despite the liqourice-profile tyres. Most prefer to drive slowly though, making sure people see them and their Prowler!

Best All-Rounder: Prowler

Chrysler PT Cruiser

Price from: £14,995

One of America's most sought-after cars, the PT Cruiser commands huge demand. Retro is the word, hot rod the inspiration, the result unlike anything else. It is also surprisingly practical, with mini-MPV space and great flexibility within the equally outrageous interior. Standard equipment is also generous, and passenger comfort is great. However, the drive-train is more down-to-earth, with a vocal 2.0-litre engine providing noisy performance. The gearchange is smooth though, with racecar-like snick shifts. Handling is also sporty, with sharp steering and a firm but composed ride. To many though, the way the PT Cruiser drives is almost immaterial; they buy it for the way it looks, and in huge numbers.

Body styles: Compact MPV
Engine capacity: 2.0, 2.4
Manufactured in: Austria, United States

Best All-Rounder: PT Cruiser Touring

Chrysler Neon

Price from: £10,995

Body styles: Saloon
Engine capacity: 2.0
Manufactured in: United States

Chrysler's cheapest model continues to offer great value for money, especially for UK buyers. A redesign last year added more mature styling and an attractive interior, though underneath things remained pretty much the same. That means a vocal 2.0-litre engine is the only option, requiring hard work to extract admittedly reasonable performance. The Neon can be fun to drive, though not up to the standards of composure of newer competitors. Noise levels can also be high, from wind rustle and suspension as well as the engine. The equipment is generous though, especially considering the competitive price tag. It may have the all-round competence of more expensive rivals but for the bargain-hunter, Chrysler's Neon still appeals.

Best All-Rounder: Neon 2.0 LX

Price from: £22,995

Chrysler Sebring

Body styles: Saloon, coupe, convertible
Engine capacity: 2.0, 2.4, 2.7V6
Manufactured in: United States

Last year's all-new Sebring range replaced Chrysler's previously confusing mid-size model range, bringing saloon, coupe and convertible under the same umbrella. All models are stylish and attractive, and well-built too. The saloon, previously called the Cirrus, offers a choice of 2.4 four-cylinder or 2.7 V6 engines, and is very refined and spacious. Similarly, the coupe – built by Mitsubishi – offers 2.4 four-cylinder or 3.0-litre V6 engines, and an extremely attractive design both inside and out. The equally pretty convertible uses the 2.7-litre engine, and is just as spacious and solid as its hard-top sisters. All Sebrings are fun to drive, and offer a strong package in a competitive class. Pity they're sold in Europe, but not in the UK.

Best All-Rounder: Sebring LXi Sedan

Chrysler LHS

Price from: $28,700

The LHS name is one steeped in history, dating back to Chrysler's prestigious era of the '30s. However, although it is just as luxurious as those older models were, today's Concorde-derived LHS is not viewed as such, which explains the bargain price. For under $30,000, buyers get an excellent 3.5-litre V6 engine, sleek and distinctive styling and a huge amount of interior room. They also benefit from a cabin of high luxury, one that contains almost every refinement and addition. On the road, the silky V6 complements a very smooth ride to create a great air of refinement. It handles competently too, but this will be of little consequence to many. It is a car to waft around in.

Body styles: Saloon
Engine capacity: 3.5V6
Manufactured in: United States

Best All-Rounder: LHS

Price from: $22,500

Chrysler Concorde

Body styles: Saloon
Engine capacity: 2.7V6, 3.2V6
Manufactured in: Canada

Chrysler's Concorde is a remarkably spacious car that, unlike some of its US rivals, is also attractive and innovative. It was the world's first 'paperless' car, designed entirely on a computer screen, and sports an attractive 'cab forward' style. This pushes the base of the windscreen towards the front wheelarches which, along with the long wheelbase, creates the interior room. Engines are all-alloy V6s, of 2.7-litre and 3.2-litre displacements, and both are efficient and powerful. The Concorde drives well too, in a sporty manner that's lacking in many American cars – though not at the expense of ride quality. It's a dramatically-styled car, that is as good on the road as it looks on a computer screen.

Best All-Rounder: Concorde LXi

Chrysler 300M

Price from: $29,600

Derived from the Chrysler LHS, the 300M is a well-equipped large saloon with a very sophisticated style. It was designed to take on luxurious European models, so is not brash but elegant, modern and attractive. It offers similar interior room to the LHS, but is shorter to meet the requirements of European markets. It is also styled in a sportier manner, and features a more upmarket interior. It uses the same 3.5-litre V6 engine though, for rapid and smooth performance. The handling is also sharp, especially with the optional handling pack, though even the standard model is tuned for a sportier feel than the LHS. Add in a huge amount of standard equipment and a low list price, and the 300M seems a bargain.

Body styles: Saloon
Engine capacity: 2.7V6, 3.5V6
Manufactured in: Canada

Best All-Rounder: 300M

NEW

Price from: £18,495

Chrysler Voyager

Body styles: MPV
Engine capacity: 2.4, 3.3V6, 3.8V6, 2.5CRD
Manufactured in: Austria, United States

The original 'minivan', Chrysler's second generation Voyager was comprehensively revised last year to produce this new model. Generation three was vital, for the previous model fared appallingly in Euro NCAP crash safety tests. It is also more refined, sleeker and boasts innovative features – such as a power-operated tailgate and doors, and a three-zone climate control system. The interior is also more attractively-designed, with improved seats and better noise suppression at speed. The engine range is extensive, with revised V6 units, as well as an excellent 2.5-litre turbo-diesel for Europe. It offers a superior drive too, with a smoother ride and more composed handling. For many, only the original will do, yet Chrysler has not rested on its laurels with the improved new Voyager.

Best All-Rounder: Voyager LX

CHEVROLET

The high-volume division of General Motors, Chevrolet has one of America's most extensive model ranges. From the budget Malibu to the rumbling, testosterone-charged Corvette, Chevrolet has all bases covered. However, apart from the squat sports cars and huge off-roaders, Chevrolet's model range appears dull nowadays, with unadventurous design and a lack of engineering innovation. The Corvette may well use an advanced electronic handling system, and the Silverado may be one of the most competent luxury off-roaders, but when the basic mechanicals are, like the rest of the range, rooted in the 1970s, Chevrolet's problems become clear. What's more, the looks and interiors of many models are ageing; action will have to be taken over the next few years to ensure Chevrolet remains the 'Heartbeat of America'.

Chevrolet Corvette

Body styles: Coupe, targa, convertible
Engine capacity: 5.7V8

Price from: £33,999
Manufactured in: United States

America's favourite sports car approaches its half-century in better shape than ever. Available in coupe and convertible form, the Corvette is dramatic, distinctive, and unashamedly American. The 5.7-litre V8 makes all the right noises, whilst the suspension is basic in architecture but fine on long, straight roads. The Active Handling system should ensure there's no tail-out action through corners, but it's too slow to respond. Most headlines are saved for the sensational Z06 model, though; the V8 is tuned to produce 386bhp, offering 170mph potential and 0-60mph in 4 seconds; ferocious performance in anyone's book, and incredible given the car's list price. It has re-created an instant classic that has renewed interest in Chevrolet's classic sports car.

Best All-Rounder: Corvette Z06

Chevrolet Tahoe

Price from: $25,700

One of the original 'full-size' 4x4s, Chevrolet's Tahoe was completely redesigned last year, and now sports a far more modern chassis and exterior style. The ladder-type layout offers independent front and multi-link coil rear suspension, in both 2WD and 4WD formats. The V8 engine is available in either 4.8-litre or 5.3-litre guise, for rapid performance and great pulling power, which can be utilised fully thanks to the improved suspension. Handling is controlled and body roll is not an issue, whilst the ride is smooth – very good for a 4x4-type vehicle. The Tahoe is typically well equipped too, and offers a great deal of vehicle for the money. Few such machines are more competent or better value, explaining its strong following in the US.

Body styles: Estate
Engine capacity: 4.8V8, 5.3V8, 6.0V8
Manufactured in: United States

Best All-Rounder: Tahoe 4WD

Chevrolet Malibu

Price from: $17,700

Body styles: Saloon
Engine capacity: 3.1V6
Manufactured in: United States

Chevrolet's mid-size family saloon offers exceptional value for money. It may not be as advanced as the European rivals it competes with, but it counters with plenty of standard equipment and a 170bhp 3.1-litre V6 engine. There is ample passenger and luggage space, and the interior is a very comfortable place to spend time in. The ride and handling may not be up to the standards of the best class rivals, but both are competent enough. The Malibu's real strengths lie in the overall package; how many other models offer as much space, along with air conditioning, ABS and four airbags, for the equivalent of around £12,000?

Best All-Rounder: Malibu LS

Price from: $13,800

Coupe

Body styles: Saloon, coupe
Engine capacity: 2.2, 2.4
Manufactured in: United States

Chevrolet Cavalier

General Motor's top-selling car, the Cavalier, has been around since the mid '90s, yet its popularity shows no signs of slowing. It is starting to feel its age though, in both the way it looks and the way it drives. The engines, either 2.2-litre or 2.4-litre four-cylinder units, are vocal, though they produce the goods well enough. It also shows its age through its ride and handling, both of which are some way off the class leaders. Still, it is cheap and comes loaded with a huge amount of equipment. Sales have been declining recently, and whether the Cavalier can continue to sell on value for money alone remains to be seen; revisions are long overdue.

Best All-Rounder: Cavalier LS Sedan

Chevrolet Monte Carlo

Price from: $20,300

Chevrolet's Monte Carlo coupe, like today's Corvette, has a long history and strong image. Today's model is quite different from the V8 chargers of the past though; it is front-wheel-drive and based on the chassis of the Chevrolet Impala. It also now uses V6 engines of 3.4-litre and 3.8-litre capacity. Equipment is generous, with both standard and SS models featuring air conditioning and alloy wheels. The SS also sports firmer suspension, to handle its 200bhp. Neither model is hugely inspiring though. The simple fact that the Monte Carlo is fast, looks good and is great value explains the loyal following.

Best All-Rounder: Monte Carlo

Body styles: Coupe
Engine capacity: 3.4V6, 3.8V6
Manufactured in: United States

Price from: $15,900

5-Dr

Body styles: Estate, convertible
Engine capacity: 2.0, 2.5V6
Manufactured in: United States

Chevrolet Tracker

Chevrolet's smallest sports-utility vehicle, the Tracker offers plenty of ability for not much cash. Basically a rebadged Suzuki Grand Vitara, the Tracker is naturally well-equipped with a choice of 2.0-litre four-cylinder and 2.5-litre V6 engines. The latter is especially strong, with excellent refinement and a broad spread of power. The chassis is also well-developed, with the tracker as good off-road as well as it is on it; a rare combination. Off-roaders will prefer the soft-top version, whilst city dwellers may stick to the hard-top. However, either Tracker takes all the ability of the Grand Vitara, adds a high specification and sells under the strong Chevrolet brand for a low price. No wonder sales are strong.

Best All-Rounder: Tracker LT 4WD

Chevrolet Suburban

Price from: $26,700

Another long-running, well-known name, the Suburban is a large, bulky, full-size 4x4, complete with the huge engines that Americans love. A choice of large 285bhp 5.3-litre, larger 300bhp 6.0-litre or simply huge 340bhp 8.1-litre V8s means fuel economy will be poor, but buyers of the Suburban don't seem to mind. They love its engines, along with its huge interior space that can seat up to nine people, and if the pay-off is soft and vague handling, then so be it; at least the ride is smooth. Available with both 2WD and 4WD, the latter is the preferred option, especially if all the pulling power of the V8s is to be fully used. An American icon – but in a greener world, for how long?

Best All-Rounder: Suburban K2500 4WD LS

Body styles: Estate
Engine capacity: 5.3V8, 6.0V8, 8.1V8
Manufactured in: United States

Price from: $19,800

Body styles: Estate
Engine capacity: 4.3V6
Manufactured in: United States

Chevrolet Blazer

It may be Chevrolet's mid-size 4x4 contender, but the Blazer still packs a 190bhp 4.3-litre V6 engine. Available in 2WD and 4WD forms, the Blazer offers reliable transport for a very reasonable price. Just don't expect sharp handling; it is soft, providing interesting moments when the full power of the engine is used. The ride is cossetting though, making it a fine car for loping along in. It is also competent off-road, thanks to its rugged construction and advanced 4WD system. Inside, there is plenty of equipment and a lot of space for five people – and the luggage area is vast, too. For many Americans, it is an ideal compromise – especially considering the competitive price.

Best All-Rounder: Blazer

CHEVROLET

Chevrolet Venture

Price from: $21,800

Body styles: MPV
Engine capacity: 3.4V6
Manufactured in:
United States

Chevrolet's 'minivan' people carrier is available in two sizes – standard and long-wheelbase. Both versions seat seven people, though space is tighter than in some rivals. Equipment levels are very high though, and the standard 185bhp 3.4-litre V6 is reasonably smooth and offers decent performance. New last year was a redesigned fascia and a power sliding door. Chevrolet has gone to some lengths to make the Venture car-like to drive, with predictable handling and a smooth ride. It is only the size of the long-wheelbase version that can cause problems, especially in tight parking spaces. Trim levels and the options catalogue are both vast, offering the potential to create a unique and practical family car that is also fine value.

Best All-Rounder: Venture Ext LT

Chevrolet Impala

Price from: $19,900

Launched two years ago, the good-looking Impala revives another of Chevrolet's long-running names, though again it doesn't boast the huge V8 engines of its predecessors. Instead, it uses 3.3-litre and 3.8-litre V6 units that supply reasonable power and acceleration, but are noisy when fully stretched. The handling is competent but with a similar dislike to being pushed, when feedback becomes limited. The ride is typically soft and cosseting, providing good comfort for the five occupants, who also have plenty of room and equipment to play with. It lacks ability or sophistication against the best-selling Honda Accord, but as a great-value large saloon, the Impala holds considerable appeal to patriotic American buyers.

Best All-Rounder: Impala LS

Body styles: Saloon
Engine capacity: 3.4V6, 3.8V6
Manufactured in:
United States

Chevrolet Camaro

Price from: $17,900

Coupe

Body styles: Coupe, convertible
Engine capacity: 3.8V6, 5.7V8
Manufactured in:
United States

Representing exceptional value, the Camaro may be getting on a bit, but there's no denying its credentials as an accessible sports car. Offered with a 3.8-litre V6 or a superb 5.7-litre V8 – the latter in either 310bhp Z28 or 325bhp Z28 SS form – no Camaro lacks in power. However, although straight-line pace is superb, the Camaro's handling ability is less impressive. The live rear axle means composure is lacking, and it quickly runs out of ideas when pressing on; the ride is also fidgety. It is also remarkably tacky inside - no European manufacturer could get away with such a poorly-designed. low-rent interior. This seems of little consequence to its buyers though, who get huge power and head-turning looks all for the price of an average family saloon.

Best All-Rounder: Camaro Z28

Chevrolet TrailBlazer

Price from: $25,800

Replacing the long-running Blazer, Chevrolet's Trailblazer is pretty much the same vehicle with a few styling modifications, chassis revisions and a brand-new engine. The 4.2-litre straight-six unit produces 250bhp, and is smoother and more balanced than the old 4.3-litre V6. To drive, the Trailblazer is far more composed, thanks to the new coil-link rear suspension which aids both ride and handling accuracy. Off-road, it remains competent, and is limited more by its vast size rather than by any lack of ability. Inside, there is huge passenger and luggage space for five people, plus a full complement of standard equipment. A strong seller that has been greatly improved, the Trailblazer is also now available in the UK.

Best All-Rounder: Trailblazer LS

Body styles: Estate
Engine capacity: 4.2
Manufactured in:
United States

Chevrolet Prizm

Price from: $14,600

Body styles: Saloon
Engine capacity: 1.8
Manufactured in:
United States

Chevrolet's popular Prizm family saloon offers just a single engine option, a 125bhp 1.8-litre four-cylinder unit. This may seem unusual in a land so keen on V6s and V8s, but even the Yanks have to accept small engines in their budget cars. There are benefits in good fuel economy, and performance is also reasonably strong. However, equipment levels are lower than some competitors, especially considering the list price. Ride and handling is well up to class standards, with the sharper LSi offering a fairly sporty drive. Comfort is of far more importance to families though, and the Prizm scores here, with low noise levels and a well-furnished interior. An honest car, that fills the role of family car well.

Best All-Rounder: Prizm LSi

As valiant an effort as the 21 was, Caterham customers know what they like and they like their Caterhams raw. Now preferring to leave more civilised sports cars to people like Lotus, the 21 is no more. Of course, the legendary Super Seven soldiers on, continually updated to provide even greater motoring thrills. People are bigger than way back in the 1950s when the Seven was first conceived and to make sure even the tallest or fuller-figured driver can get behind the wheel, Caterham now produces larger SV versions of the majority of its models. Concurrently more and more wild versions of the Seven keep coming from the factory, a nod to the growth of track days as a leisure activity. Most recent are the manic high-revving super-bike engined versions that blur the divide between bikers and sports car enthusiasts.

Super Seven

Body styles: Convertible
Engine capacity: 1.1, 1.6, 1.8

Price from: £13,245
Manufactured in: England

Best All-Rounder: Seven VVC

No matter which Seven you go for you can be certain that there will be little to match the sheer thrill of driving it. Various engine choices are available, ranging from fast to faster and onto manic. Superbike-engined models are featherweight-light with real punch from their stratospherically high revving units - though are more suited to track driving than everyday use. That said, any Seven is a compromise as an only car, though those looking for a bit more space can now opt for SV versions which fit fuller and taller frames. Race car responses and supercar performance at prices that are impossible to match on a pound-to-thrill ratio, Caterham must be rubbing its hands in delight at the increased interest in track days. A 'must drive' for any motoring enthusiast.

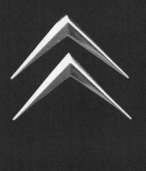

CITROËN

The new C5 has received mixed reviews, praised for its massive interior space, cosseting ride and refinement but criticised for its rather odd looks. It seems Citroen cannot win in the styling department, unable to strike a balance between its historically quirky design and mainstream acceptability. The Xsara is long overdue for replacement, as is the Saxo, with both likely within the next year, following the 'C' badge designation started by the C5. The Synergie MPV is also due to be replaced, the development costs shared between Peugeot and Fiat, like the current model. A sub-supermini C2 looks likely given the small car tie up with Toyota, but perhaps more importantly Citroen needs a sport-utility 4x4 vehicle to expand its overall market share.

NEW

Citroën C5

Estate

Body styles: Hatchback, estate
Engine capacity: 1.8, 2.0, 3.0, 2.0HDi, 2.2HDi

Price from: £14,580
Manufactured in: France

Replacing the respected Xantia, the C5 couldn't look more different - the Xantia's sharp, neat lines being substituted by the rather ungainly look of the C5. Once inside though things get better, this is a very spacious car for its class. Currently the C5 has the job of two cars, looking after the executive market too until the C6, XM replacement, arrives. Much has been made of the technology included in the C5 but in fact it offers little more than trickle-down technology from other executive models. Ride and handling is erred toward comfort rather than sporting prowess but when pushed hard the C5 copes admirably. Diesels offer the best all-round performance and the estate is a seriously capacious machine.

Best All-Rounder: C5 2.2HDi SX Estate

Citroën Saxo

Price from: £5,940

The Saxo, like the AX before it, has had its life stretched to the limits and is now long overdue for replacement. We should see a new car soon, though to be fair the current car still has something to offer. It's the entry-level and range-topping models that hold the most appeal. The base First model offers cheap, fuss-free motoring while the rapid VTR and VTS models are hot hatchbacks of acclaim. Enjoyable and comfortable to drive, the only niggle is the cramped driver's footwell. Others may offer more rear space but the Saxo is still a worthwhile contender. Buy it for the driving experience alone, for when the roads get windy the Saxo just gets better and better.

Best All-Rounder: Saxo 1.4 Furio

5 - Dr

Body styles: Hatchback
Engine capacity: 1.1, 1.4, 1.6, 1.5D
Manufactured in: France, Portugal

CITROËN

Price from: £9,660

Citroën Xsara

Body styles: Hatchback, estate, coupe
Engine capacity: 1.4, 1.6, 2.0, 1.9D, 2.0HDi
Manufactured in: France, Spain

Like the Saxo the Xsara is ready to be replaced. The market has moved on with its newer competitors all offering much more interior space than the Xsara can muster. It's established a good reputation however, offering value with the added bonus of being an accomplished driving machine with any engine choice. The five-door hatchback is the volume seller though three-door 'coupe' and estate models are also offered. The range topping VTS offers a tremendous package, 167bhp and that responsive chassis making it the one to have for enthusiasts - quite a 'Q-car'. Inside the fixtures and fittings betray its age, though the exterior lines still look good after what seems like continual facelifts. The replacement will have a tough act to follow.

Best All-Rounder: Xsara 2.0 HDi LX 110

Citroën Picasso

Price from: £12,780

The Picasso, like its namesake, is a slightly off the wall alternative to its contemporaries. Oddball styling falls into the love it or loathe it category and the steeply raked rear screen compromises space inside. There are some neat touches inside that hint at the Citroën's aim to offer a versatile vehicle, things like cubby storage and a dashboard-mounted gearlever; like many in its class, however, the Picasso is only a five-seater. Three engines are on offer: 1.6, 1.8 and the lower-powered version of Citroen's 2.0HDi diesel, which proves rather sluggish, if frugal. If you're after practicality then Citroen's own Berlingo Multispace offers much more, for much less money, but the Picasso is far more plush than its utilitarian relative.

Best all-rounder: 1.8iSX

Body styles: Compact MPV
Engine capacity: 1.6, 1.8, 2.0HDi
Manufactured in: Spain, Brazil

Price from: £8,980

Citroën Berlingo Multispace

Body styles: Estate
Engine capacity: 1.4, 1.6, 1.9D, 2.0HDi
Manufactured in: Spain, Portugal, Argentina

The Berlingo makes a great deal of sense as a practical and spacious alternative to the current crop of compact MPVs and estate cars. Based on a van, the Berlingo is unashamedly pushed at those more concerned with utility than anything else. As a package it makes a great deal of sense. Loads of space, two sliding rear doors and a massive rear hatch gives great access, the rear easily transformed back to its van origins. Room inside is good, with plenty of door bins for all your oddments while the high driving position and large glass area gives excellent visibility. Engine choice is wide, all offering adequate performance, the ride and handling being acceptable too. If we all were to buy cars with our heads we'd all have one of these.

Best All-Rounder: Berlingo 1.8

Citroën Synergie

Price from: £17,670

In the highly competitive MPV market the Synergie is simply beaten by the majority of its competitors in the desirability stakes. Large proportions don't necessarily translate to massive amounts of interior space, and Citroen's full-sized MPV is not as practical as its van-like looks may suggest. It's a shame, because underneath the bland exterior lies a competent chassis, once you get used to the peculiar gearchange. Sliding rear side doors are a boon in supermarket car parks, though with all seven seats in place you won't get much shopping in the boot. Engine choice is limited to two 2.0-litre choices in the UK, one petrol, the other a frugal turbo-diesel. Soon to be replaced the Synergie will, like the current model, be developed with Fiat, Peugeot and Lancia.

Best All-Rounder: Synergie 2.0HDi

Body styles: MPV
Engine capacity: 2.0, 2.0HDi
Manufactured in: France

DAIHATSU

Pre-empting the rise in demand for small cars, Daihatsu is a small car expert. Toyota holds a controlling interest in the company, giving it access to its technical expertise. The model line-up remains largely unchanged over last year, though the Sirion and Terios have benefited from engines from its Toyota partner and a host of other technical revisions. The Fourtrak off-roader is the oddity in the range, a genuinely competent, tough off-roader in the vein of Land Rover's Defender which continues to sell well among those needing a 'proper 4x4'. Given the amount of interest (and business) its small car rival Suzuki is generating at present, it's only a matter of time before more manufacturers come knocking for assistance in developing, or re-badging Daihatsu models to get a foothold in this growing market.

Daihatsu YRV

Body styles: Hatchback
Engine capacity: 1.0, 1.3, 1.3T

Price from: £7,995
Manufactured in: Japan

The YRV is the newest and most characterful car of the Daihatsu range. The relatively small exterior dimensions hide a capacious cabin, offering almost family hatchback sized accommodation in a supermini-sized package. Powered by the same engine as 1.3 Toyota's top Yaris, the YRV offers good performance. The snappy gearshift and light, though direct, steering make the YRV an enjoyable drive, the overall experience only dulled by the ride which becomes choppy when pushed hard. An automatic - dubbed F-speed - with steering mounted button shift, is also available. Bold styling marks the YRV out from the competition, and the interior has some clever MPV-like touches adding to practicality, while a phenomenal warranty package - five years on some versions - is a serious draw.

Best All-Rounder: 1.3 Premium

Daihatsu Sirion

Price from: £7,495

Body styles: Hatchback
Engine capacity: 1.0, 1.3
Manufactured in: Japan

Easily overlooked, the Sirion is a credible supermini, with a high specification in the UK and distinctive looks to boot. Improved in 2001 it, like many models in the Daihatsu range, has been transformed by the use of the 1.3-litre VVTi engine from Toyota. The cabin has a quality about it that is unexpected for a car in this price category, it's pretty spacious and the boot too is one of the largest in its class. There is a fair degree of refinement for such a small car - the ride and noise levels are both good. Distinctive without being weird, it offers an impressive combination of virtues and its heavily revised 1.0-litre three-cylinder engine is remarkably economical, though is hardly the quickest means of getting about.

Best All-Rounder: Sirion 1.3

Price from: £6,445

Daihatsu Cuore

Body styles: Hatchback
Engine capacity: 0.7, 1.0
Manufactured in: Japan

Blink and you'll miss it. The Cuore is the smallest car in Daihatsu's small car range. That smallness isn't just constrained to its proportions - the Cuore offers motoring to those on even the smallest of budgets. Fuel consumption is remarkably meagre no matter how the Cuore is driven. Yet while its small on the outside there's surprising space inside. The narrow width means you're closer to the door than you would be in other cars but there's enough head and legroom for both front and rear seat passengers. Coming with a 1.0-litre engine in most markets, a 700cc three cylinder is still offered in its native Japan. The 5-door body gives a healthy dose of practicality, as do split/fold rear seats.

Best all-rounder: Cuore

Daihatsu Move

No longer sold in the UK, the Move is Daihatsu's city car that places practicality above style. The design means that there is room for four tall adults to sit in relative comfort yet the car is short enough to fit in the tightest parking spaces. It is achieved by making the Move TALL rather than long. There is flexibility too, with rear seats that fold down or slide back and forth so that if kids are carried, luggage space can be increased. Not that in any condition there is a surplus of room for luggage, and even if there were, there is an inevitable conflict with the 1.0-litre engine that sounds gutsy but lacks the punch to give decent performance.

Best All-Rounder: Move 1.0

Price from: £na

Body styles: Hatchback
Engine capacity: 1.0
Manufactured in: Japan

Price from: £9,980

Daihatsu Terios

Body styles: Estate
Engine capacity: 1.3
Manufactured in: Japan

While the Terios may have the looks of an off roader its rather ungainly tall and narrow stance mark it out as a twist on the city car theme. With a locking differential and permanent four-wheel-drive the Terios will get you across a muddy field but is more suited to supermarket car parks than serious off-roading. Inside its narrow width means you need to be on good terms with your passengers, though the driving experience is better than you might expect. The 1.3-litre engine, sourced from the Toyota Yaris, is keen, the steering direct; the Terios is available with either a manual or automatic gearchange. As an alternative to regular city cars the Terios is an interesting choice.

Best All-Rounder: Terios 1.3

Daihatsu Fourtrak

A proper off-roader from the old school, the Fourtrak's appeal lies in its honest non-nonsense attitude. Basic and unrefined by modern standards, the Fourtrak is a four-wheel-drive of serious capability, and thus is still popular among rural communities. The Fourtrak is only available with one engine option in the UK - a fine performing 2.8-litre turbo-diesel. It has great pulling power for sticky situations or towing, and is also a relaxed motorway cruiser, though the suspension provides a bouncy ride that becomes tiresome over long journeys. Despite newer and more attractive looking competition, the Fourtrak will remain popular with farmers with its ability in the mud, huge towing capacity, and faultless reliability in all weathers.

Best All-Rounder: Fourtrak TDX

Price from: £19,000

Body styles: Estate
Engine capacity: 2.2, 2.8D, 2.8TD
Manufactured in: Japan

DAEWOO

Daewoo Motor in Korea is bankrupt. That is the harsh, unpalatable truth. There are hopes that it will be purchased by another major manufacturer – Ford looked likely for a long time, now General Motors is in the frame. The situation should, hopefully, be resolved before the end of 2001. Otherwise it has been business as usual. The company is still producing cars, and the separate distributors around the world are still selling them and providing the backup buyers expect. The two strongest models in the range are the Matiz and Tacuma. Everything else sells on price, a comprehensive new-car package and great back-up. The radical direct-to-the-customer sales operation in the UK, however, has just been replaced by a traditional dealer network.

Daewoo Matiz

Body styles: Hatchback
Engine capacity: 0.8

Price from: £5,995
Manufactured in: Korea

Without doubt the most convincing car in the Daewoo range, the Matiz stacks up remarkably well against its city car competition. That it is can be seen by the remarkable fact that the Matiz is one of Italy's most popular small cars. Compact proportions mean it's a cinch to slot through gaps in busy traffic and there's a willing engine, though it's 800cc can't quite cut it on the open road. The diminutive Daewoo is a fun car to drive, all-the-same. Give-away prices are combined with excellent interior space, the Matiz easily accommodates four six-footers. The Matiz is a car that holds its head up proudly against any competition, something it is difficult to say of any other car in the Daewoo range.

Best All-Rounder: Matiz SE

Daewoo Lanos

Price from: £7,495

Daewoo is recognised as a budget brand in the majority of its markets, making comparisons with more mainstream rivals seem a little unfair. However, the rise of the budget market has seen Daewoo pitted against ever improving competition. The Lanos sits somewhere between the supermini and family hatchback classes and, despite the rather cheap plastics, feels well put together. Two engines are available, a 1.4-litre and a 1.6-litre; neither offers much in the way of refinement or, indeed, performance. Impressive standard specifications allied to good warranties and fuss free sales keep up enough interest, as does the pricing which remains class competitive. It's just the class keeps on getting bigger.

Body styles: Hatchback, saloon
Engine capacity: 1.4, 1.5, 1.6
Manufactured in: Korea

Best All-Rounder: Lanos 1.4 SE

Price from: £10,995

Body styles: Compact MPV
Engine capacity: 1.8, 2.0
Manufactured in: Korea

Daewoo Tacuma

A touch late joining the burgeoning compact MPV market, the Tacuma has its sights firmly set on stealing sales from established competition like the Renault Scenic and Citroen Picasso. As with the majority of Daewoo's models the Tacuma brings little new to the party except the usual combination of good price and high specification levels. The distinctively styled tall body, with a commanding seating position, five individual seats (all of which slide) and removable rear seats are nothing new in this class but worthwhile nonetheless. Engines are familiar 1.8 or 2.0-litre units with the option of automatic transmission on the larger capacity model. A diesel version has been rumoured for sometime now but the UK market has yet to see it.

Best All-Rounder: 1.8 SE

Daewoo Nubira

Price from: £9,995

Daewoo's family car is, like the smaller Lanos, largely forgettable until you consider its pricing and specification. Revised early on in its life, the car was transformed visually, the interior benefited from a makeover the seats upgraded. Two body styles are offered - saloon and estate - with two petrol engines, a 1.6 or a 2.0-litre available. Specification is where the Nubira makes a case for itself, with even the cheapest models coming with dual airbags, ABS and air conditioning as standard. Allied to the low purchase costs and impressive after-sales package, the Nubira makes sense to the motorist who wants nothing more than a comfortable means of getting from A to B.

Best All-Rounder: Nubira 1.6 SE

Estate

Body styles: Saloon, estate
Engine capacity: 1.5, 1.6, 1.8, 2.0
Manufactured in: Korea

Price from: £12,495

Body styles: Saloon
Engine capacity: 1.8, 2.0, 2.2
Manufactured in: Korea

Daewoo Leganza

The large car market is a particularly unforgiving one, with the majority of customers already entrenched in long-held brand loyalty. So it's easy to see why Daewoo has a tough job convincing buyers that the Leganza is a credible alternative to the established competition. Coming as ever with loads of standard equipment as well as a wide-reaching after-sales package, the Leganza is at least cheap. For keen drivers the Leganza falls a bit flat, with an engine that's too coarse when revved and soft handling. But others will appreciate the amount of space front and back, the comfort and the lack of noise when cruising. It is well finished as well, making it a Daewoo you don't need to justify to your friends.

Best All-Rounder: Leganza 2.0 SX

Daewoo Korando

Price from: £15,995

Quirky Jeep-esque styling doesn't translate to large sales for Daewoo's entry-level off-roader. That guarantees exclusivity, but would you want to join the club? Two engines are available, a 2.3-litre petrol unit and a turbo-charged 2.9-litre diesel. Neither is particularly quick, both struggling to keep up with the more sprightly competition. Competitive due to low pricing, the Korando is outclassed by Japanese competition, which while admittedly smaller, offer so much more - particularly desirability. Reasonably spacious, the interior has a solidity that's impressive given the price, though the front seat adjustment is limited. If you're after a work horse that drives reasonably well the Korando may well be the answer; but just look around first.

Best All-Rounder: Korando 2.3

Body styles: Estate
Engine capacity: 2.0, 2.3, 3.2, 2.3D, 2.9D, 2.9TD
Manufactured in: Korea

Price from: £17,995

Body styles: Estate
Engine capacity: 2.0, 2.3, 3.2, 2.3D, 2.9D, 2.9TD
Manufactured in: Korea

Daewoo Musso

For about the same money that you might pay for a family estate you could have a fully loaded four-wheel-drive Musso on your drive. It gets even better when you consider that the engines are Mercedes-Benz designed, though sadly these don't offer quite the performance of their current units. Despite having all these forces working for it the Musso is still seen as a bit of an oddity. Perhaps it's the styling, which tries to blend 4x4 and estate car, rather unsuccessfully. The turbo-diesel is refined, though slow and the 2.3-litre petrol isn't much better. On road it performs well, to the detriment of its off-road ability, but it seems to have won favour among those looking for a capacious towcar.

Best All-Rounder: Musso 2.3

FERRARI

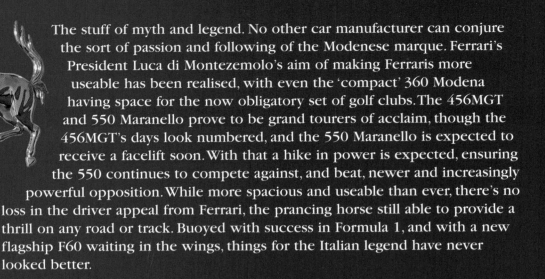

The stuff of myth and legend. No other car manufacturer can conjure the sort of passion and following of the Modenese marque. Ferrari's President Luca di Montezemolo's aim of making Ferraris more useable has been realised, with even the 'compact' 360 Modena having space for the now obligatory set of golf clubs. The 456MGT and 550 Maranello prove to be grand tourers of acclaim, though the 456MGT's days look numbered, and the 550 Maranello is expected to receive a facelift soon. With that a hike in power is expected, ensuring the 550 continues to compete against, and beat, newer and increasingly powerful opposition. While more spacious and useable than ever, there's no loss in the driver appeal from Ferrari, the prancing horse still able to provide a thrill on any road or track. Buoyed with success in Formula 1, and with a new flagship F60 waiting in the wings, things for the Italian legend have never looked better.

Ferrari 360 Spider

Body styles: Convertible
Engine capacity: 3.6 V8

Price from: £109,101
Manufactured in: Italy

Best All-Rounder: F360 Spider

Open-topped Ferraris are often criticised for being the poorer relative of their fixed-head counterparts, compromising the stiffness and hence steering response for posing appeal. Not so the 360 Spider. More than a simple cropping job, the Spider was thoroughly re-engineered to ensure that its credibility as a driving machine stayed intact. The penalty is a slight increase in weight, though not so you'd notice when that characterful 4.0-litre engine produces its goods. Indeed it's that engine that encourages you to lower the hood, allowing you to revel in its tuneful bark more than is possible with the 'standard' car. Like the coupe it's a phenomenal driving machine, Ferrari having done an amazing job to maintain structural rigidity despite the removal of the roof. Hood up, the 360's no beauty - but with the top down the Spiders lines better that of the coupe. More expensive, the extra outlay's worth it to hear that engine more clearly. Oh, and everyone looks at you too.

Ferrari 360

Price from: £103,068

Body styles: Coupe
Engine capacity: 3.6V8
Manufactured in: Italy

When it was first introduced the 360 was criticised for not having the purity of line of its predecessor, the 355. As with the rest of the current Ferrari range, though, its looks seem to get better every time you are lucky enough to see one. While no longer pretty its lines are purposeful in so much as they allow the 360 to cut through the air with incredible efficiency, increasing down force without the need for unsightly spoilers. Inside too is a triumph of packaging, the 360 having a genuinely roomy interior, with space for the all-important golf clubs behind the front seats. The aluminium V8 pumps out 400bhp at 8,500rpm, Ferrari using a trick exhaust system that allows it to pass drive by noise legislation, but unleashes its full triumphant wail in the upper rev ranges. The gearshift action retains a mechanical feel, though if you want the car to work the clutch for you there's the popular F1 paddle-operated transmission. Dynamically the 360 eclipses the highly regarded 355, meaning it's one of the most accomplished sports cars ever.

Best All-Rounder: F360 Modena

Ferrari 550 Maranello

Price from: £152,345

Body styles: Coupe
Engine capacity: 5.5V12
Manufactured in: Italy

Less brash than the mid-engined monsters that preceded it, the 550 is a consummate performer - while being a useable day-to-day proposition. How many other cars can claim that and have 200mph capability and a 0-60 time in the low fours? While not the most exciting Ferrari in the styling department, the 550 Maranello is still a sight to behold. It doesn't shout about its power like supercars of old, but there's still plenty on offer from the magnificent 5.5-litre V12 - a 'mere' 485bhp. Given the competition's been catching up ever since its introduction, with new challengers including the Aston Martin Vanquish, the Maranello is due a mild make-over to enhance its performance, the styling likely to be tweaked slightly to signify the engineering changes. Even though it's currently the most powerful Ferrari in the range it's a surprisingly easy machine to drive. Clever electronics keep the power in check when you overstep its, or your, limits - the 550 is an incredibly rapid and thoroughly sorted driving machine.

Best All-Rounder: 550M

NEW

Price from: £172,358

Ferrari 550
Barchetta Pininfarina

Body styles: Convertible
Engine capacity: 5.5V12
Manufactured in: Italy

To celebrate the 70th anniversary of Pininfarina Ferrari asked the legendary coachbuilder to produce a design for a roadster based on the 550 Maranello. The result is this strictly limited run model which has been pre-sold to Ferrari aficionados across the world. Designed to recapture the spirit of classics like the Daytona Spider and the California series 250 GTs, the lengthily titled Ferrari 550 Barchetta Pininfarina is a dry weather toy for the seriously wealthy. There is a hood, but it's for emergency weather protection only; instead customers will be able to shield their heads with the exclusive Barchetta open faced helmets that come with the car. No conventional beauty, the 550 Barchetta Pininfarina does have a menacing stance, with the lowered and strengthened windscreen and rather clumsy looking bars behind the driver and passenger providing rollover protection. The powertrain remains unchanged, though without a roof the full aural effect of the 12-cylinder is more accessible - which to many is worth the extra money alone.

Best All-Rounder: 550 Barchetta Pininfarina

Ferrari 456M GT

Price from: £170,358

Body styles: Coupe
Engine capacity: 5.5V12
Manufactured in: Italy

Arguably the ultimate GT car, the 456M GT is nearing the end of its life cycle. It remains an ultra-desirable model, for while following the formula of the Ferrari greats like the Daytona, the 456M GT boasts sufficient performance to take the breath away from all four occupants. Under that long bonnet nestles a V12 that produces a not inconsiderable 442bhp – giving this, the most practical of Ferraris, 186mph capability. Inside the classically styled interior is sumptuously appointed in the finest leather, with tailored luggage available - underlining its grand touring credentials. Not that the 456M GT falls short in other areas, for it proves a surprisingly agile steed given its size and weight. Near perfect weight distribution aids this, the rear mounted transaxle going some way to countering the weight of the 5.5-litre V12 up front. The most expensive car in the current range, this is the 'gentleman's Ferrari', and can even be specified with an automatic transmission.

Best All-Rounder: 456M GT

FIAT

The replacement for the Brava/Bravo range is finally upon us and brings new levels of versatility to the hatchback class with its MPV inspired interior. It's the first of a whole new range of Fiats; it looks good too, spearheading a new range of models that will be introduced over the next four years. The quirky, though thoroughly practical, Multipla hasn't been the success the Italian firm had hoped, suggesting that the public were not yet ready for such a radical looking vehicle. This is likely to influence the design of future models, the emphasis more on good design than radical change. Aiming to compete with the Germans in the build quality stakes Fiat is involved in technology sharing with GM - reducing development times, costs and increasing flexibility.

NEW

Stilo

Fiat Stilo

5 - Dr

Body styles: Hatchback
Engine capacity: 1.2, 1.6, 1.8, 2.4, 1.9JTD

Price from: £na
Manufactured in: Italy

Like the Bravo and Brava range before it, the Stilo will be offered in two distinct versions for its three and five-door models. The three-door will, unsurprisingly, be aimed at the sportier area of the market, getting a lower driving position and sharper looks. The five-door is the more sensible proposition with interior detailing offering MPV-like practicality and a raised driving position. The engine range will be largely carried over from the Brava/o range, albeit with significant revisions. Based on a new platform, which will underpin a number of new Fiat products, the Stilo features build techniques that were introduced with the Multipla that maximise the useable interior space. On sale from late in 2001, the Stilo will have a tough job against the established Ford Focus and VW Golf.

Best All-Rounder: Too soon to say

NEW

Price from: £8,695

Fiat Doblo

Body styles: Estate
Engine capacity: 1.2, 1.6, 1.9D, 1.9JTD
Manufactured in: Italy

The Doblo is the latest entrant in the budget multi-purpose vehicle sector. It has, Fiat reckons, a sense of fun. To others it will look just plain funny, without the Postman Pat appeal of the Renault Kangoo or Citroen Berlingo. Like the French vehicles, this is a van with seats and rear windows, and so has the same benefits – enormous amounts of interior space for a bargain price. That means in reality it is no joke, but sensible transport for the new millennium, cheap and practical. The Doblo's weak points are its enormous tailgate and engines which seem too small to provide the necessary get-up-and-go when loaded.

Best All-Rounder: Doblo 1.9D

Fiat Seicento

Price from: £5,940

Fiat is the European master of the small car, with Italian buyers traditionally snapping up its diminutive models like the Seicento. Up front there's enough room, though the rear seats are best used for short journeys only - or small children. Inside a feature is made of the body-coloured exposed metal, which is better than covering it up with cheap plastics, though the upright facia betrays the Seicentos advancing years. Competition from the East has seen the city car segment become highly competitive, newer cars showing the diminutive Fiat how it should go about its interior packaging. Still managing to sell well with its combination of character and good looks, the Fiat is comprehensively beaten by its newer rivals. Expect a new model soon.

Body styles: Hatchback
Engine capacity: 0.9, 1.1
Manufactured in: Poland

Best All-Rounder: Seicento Sporting

Price from: £6,940

Fiat Punto

5 - Dr

Body styles: Hatchback
Engine capacity: 1.2, 1.8, 1.9D, 1.9JTD
Manufactured in: Italy

The Punto brings a dash of style to the supermini range as Fiat's best ever competitor in this hotly contested market segment. Even the most basic models look great, the neat detailing carried through to one of Fiat's neatest interiors. The range of engines runs from 1.2-litre to the 1.8 from the barchetta roadster in the HGT models, as well as a couple of diesels. Manual gearboxes have five or six speeds, but there is a clever CVT automatic that offers a seven-speed sequential shift. The key weakness is the rear vision in the five-door, obscured by the thick pillars. Sporting models offer little of what their name promises but they come with an excellent specification. Lacking in outright driver appeal, the Punto is a stylish, refined and characterful choice.

Best All-Rounder: Punto 1.2-16v

Fiat Palio

Price from: £na

Available in Europe only as an estate model, the Palio is Fiat's world car. Built in a number of factories world-wide, it is a simple, though labour-intensive, vehicle to build. Suited to the rougher conditions of developing economies, the Palio rides on higher suspension than you'd expect on European cars. Available in a number of body styles including three and five-door hatchbacks, a saloon, an estate, a van and also as a pick-up, there's a Palio to suit every conceivable market. All those derivatives means that the Palio is a big seller, reaching a staggering one million units a year. A wide range of engines is available, with the petrol line including 1.0, 1.2, 1.4, 1.5 and 1.6-litre capacities, while a 1.7-litre diesel is also available.

Body styles: Hatchback, saloon, estate
Engine capacity: 1.0, 1.2, 1.6, 1.7TD
Manufactured in: Worldwide

Best All-Rounder: Palio 1.4

FIAT

Price from: £11,995

Fiat Marea

Estate

Body styles: Saloon, estate
Engine capacity: 1.6, 1.8, 2.0, 2.0T, 2.4, 1.9JTD, 2.4JTD
Manufactured in: Italy

Based on the now obsolete Brava/Bravo range the Marea saloon and estate (Weekend) falls between the Focus and Mondeo-sized car categories. Of the two models it's the estate that is the most convincing package, both for its practicality and its styling. Despite selling in small numbers in the UK, if you want one there's an broad range of engines available - including the impressive 2.0-litre five-cylinder unit that powered the old Fiat Coupe. The top of the range diesel is the 2.4-litre five-cylinder - which performs like no other car in its class. Well made and comfortable the Marea deserves to sell in bigger numbers, something we're sure Fiat would like when it's replacement is finally unveiled.

Best All-Rounder: Marea Weekend JTD ELX

Fiat Multipla

Price from: £12,995

The trouble with the Fiat Multipla is that most people can't see past the rather wacky styling to appreciate what a fantastically space-efficient piece of design it is. Two rows of individual chairs give six-seater capacity, without encroaching on boot space, while the upright sides make for an airy and light cabin. Clever build processes also help make the most of the available space, the wheels being pushed out wide into each corner to help. As a bonus this endows the Multipla with surefooted, even entertaining, handling. If there are any faults it's the engines, a 1.6-litre petrol and 1.9-litre turbo-diesel, which struggle when the Multipla is used as intended - fully loaded. Sadly the styling has proved too odd for the majority, the Multipla selling fewer than Fiat would like .

Best All-Rounder: Multipla 1.9TD.

Body styles: Compact MPV
Engine capacity: 1.6, 1.9JTD
Manufactured in: Italy

Price from: £16,995

Fiat Ulysse

Body styles: MPV
Engine capacity: 2.0, 2.0 JTD
Manufactured in: France

This collaborative project between Fiat, Citroen and Peugeot shall be repeated soon with a new model. The Ulysse, unlike the majority of the newer competition, harks back to a time when the MPV was little more than a van with windows and seats, so a commercial version of the Ulysse is also available. Its sliding rear doors are useful in tight spaces, but the downside is that rear seat passengers can't open their windows. The engine choices are limited in the UK to a 2.0-litre petrol or a 2.0-litre turbo-diesel and both have a hard time of it when the Ulysse is fully laden. As a seven seater it's comfortable and reasonably spacious, but not as easy to drive or car-like on the road as its rivals.

Best All-Rounder: Ulysse 2.0 JTD

Fiat Barchetta

Price from: £13,815

The barchetta is a relatively rare sight on UK roads by virtue of the fact that it's only available with left-hand-drive. Unique in the roadster market, it has front-wheel-drive rather than the more traditional rear-wheel-drive, though the barchetta is still an enjoyable drive in spite of this. The eager twin-cam 130bhp 16-valve 1.8-litre engine gives a suitably sporting rasp, while offering respectable performance too. Scoring most strongly on its stylish detail touches - the retro-style chrome door handles which pop out at the press of a button and the cute dashboard, for example - the barchetta also offers a degree of practicality with a good-sized boot. Style, a characterful engine and a hood that's easy to operate, lie at the heart of the car's appeal.

Best All-Rounder: barchetta 1.8

Body styles: Convertible
Engine capacity: 1.8
Manufactured in: Italy

While the Firestone debacle is still roaring in the USA, the European division of the automotive giant has had a busy year. The launch of the Mondeo saw Ford upset the balance in the highly competitive medium sector. It received all-round acclaim, so now the Mondeo is firmly positioned as a benchmark car in its class. This year sees the introduction of the long overdue Fiesta - expect it to take class honours in the near future. Performance versions of the Focus will revive the legendary RS badge, while the European Maverick is finally available. The superb product range is let down by the badging, and with consumers switching to more aspirational marques, Ford is losing sales. This makes the purchase of Volvo and Jaguar look like excellent foresight.

FORD EUROPE

NEW

Ford Fiesta

Body styles: Hatchback
Engine capacity: 1.3, 1.4, 1.6, 1.4TDCi

Price from: £7,000 est
Manufactured in: England

The long-awaited replacement for the Fiesta looks set to cause headaches for its competition. After all, the old model remained a best-seller throughout its life, so the vastly improved all-new model can only add to this success. Ford promises class-leading interior space – always a weakness of the old model – whilst attention has also been paid to ergonomics, too. Advanced engines offer improved economy and emissions performance, without sacrificing performance, and the handling should be even better than the highly-acclaimed late-'90's Fiesta. Like all modern cars, safety equipment is extensive and crash performance should be strong; Ford's Intelligent Protection System boosts both passive and active safety. Addressing its predecessor's weaknesses whilst retaining its dynamic strengths should ensure success for Ford's supermini; expect it to quickly become familiar.

Best All-Rounder: Too soon to say

Price from: £6,960

Ford Ka

Body styles: Hatchback
Engine capacity: 1.3
Manufactured in: Spain, Brazil

The Ka continues to be the city car class's most radical entrant, and also one of the best to drive. It is as agile as a roller-skate around town, yet is also the equal of many larger cars on the open road. Bumps are absorbed without fuss, whilst high grip levels mean enthusiastic drivers won't be caught out. It really begs for more power, which the economical but aged 1.3-litre engine can't really supply. Rear seat passengers may also complain about the lack of space, especially if luggage from the tiny boot spills over, but front-seat passengers will be able to ignore them in comfort. They'll enjoy a radical dash design that is great to use too; the dramatic Ka is a deserved success.

Best All-Rounder: Ka Collection

Ford Focus

Price from: £10,460

The Focus single-handedly revolutionised the family car sector. Never before had a mass-market hatchback turned so many heads, with curves intersected by sharp creases, bold headlights and arrow-like high-mounted tail lights. It looks like no other car and is still attractive today, as is the equally dynamic interior. The large body means it is roomy, and ergonomically perfect, too. But it is on the road where the Focus really scores, thanks to a remarkable blend of handling precision and ride comfort; it feels like a sports car and luxury cruiser rolled into one, which a crisp gearchange, eager engine range and high levels of refinement all reinforce. Throw in competitive pricing and high levels of safety, and it could be the only car you ever need.

Best All-Rounder: Focus 1.6 Zetec

5-DR

Body styles: Hatchback, saloon, estate
Engine capacity: 1.4, 1.6, 1.8, 2.0, 1.8TDdi
Manufactured in: Germany, Spain, Argentina, United States

FORD EUROPE

Price from: £14,580

Ford Mondeo

Estate

Body styles: Hatchback, saloon, estate
Engine capacity: 1.8, 2.0, 2.5V6, 2.0D
Manufactured in: Belgium, South Africa

The discrete and classy Mondeo may not be as radically-styled as some rivals, but is up among the very best from behind the wheel. Handling is superb, with few roads upsetting the car's considerable composure. It provides great feedback for the driver too, thanks to the well-weighted and accurate steering. All this comes with firm but relaxing ride comfort and fuss-free refinement. Engines are all familiar, and provide adequate performance – though the noisy diesel and thirsty V6 make the four-cylinder petrol units the best choice. Inside, the Volkswagen-influenced dashboard is attractive and logical, and equipped to a high standard. Safety kit is comprehensive, and passengers also benefit from one of the roomiest interiors in the class. In hatchback, saloon or estate form, it's a winner.

Best All-Rounder: Mondeo 2.0 Zetec

Ford Puma

Price from: £12,280

The kitten-cute Puma fools the world with its delightful lines, for underneath sits the chassis of the previous Fiesta. This is no bad thing though, for the Puma drives even better than the acclaimed hatch, making it an enthusiast's delight. Handling is superb, and the constant flow of feedback makes it an entertaining back-road rocket, especially in free-revving 1.7-litre form. Refinement is admirably good too, and the Fiesta-based dashboard is easy to use and quite well-equipped. However, although front passengers will be comfortable, those in the rear won't rate the lack of space – if they can get in at all. The boot is a bit better, but still not huge. Find the right road though, and none of this will matter.

Body styles: Coupe
Engine capacity: 1.6, 1.7
Manufactured in: Germany

Best All-Rounder: Puma 1.7

Price from: £18,245

Ford Galaxy

Body styles: MPV
Engine capacity: 2.0, 2.3, 2.8, 1.9TD, 1.9TDi
Manufactured in: Portugal

Always one of the best MPVs to drive, the latest Galaxy is also one of the best-looking thanks to recent revisions. It took on a far more luxurious air, with huge aircraft-style seats, darkened rear windows, and even head restraint-mounted DVD screens. The engines are well-mannered, with the V6 unit producing remarkable amounts of power considering the Galaxy's main duties. Most private buyers prefer the economical TDI turbo-diesel though. Good handling characterises the driving experience, and passengers won't find cause for complaint about either body roll or ride comfort. And although the bulky body makes car parks a challenge, the benefits in interior space are clear. Altogether a very strong package, with some keenly-priced entry models, too.

Best All-Rounder: Galaxy Zetec 1.9 TDI`

Ford Maverick

Price from: £17,995

The US-built Maverick is an all-new model, built to compete with the hugely successful Land Rover Freelander. However, since Ford acquired Land Rover, the Maverick's success in the European market is not as important, so it may well remain a niche player. This would be a shame, as it is a very talented vehicle with many strengths, not least the controlled, car-like driving experience. It is not as cumbersome as more traditional 4x4s, yet is just as impressive off-road as many, thanks to the clever electronic four-wheel-drive hardware. The engines are powerful and smooth, though the steering column-mounted automatic gearshift can be a little tricky to use. The tough, chunky looks should win it fans.

Body styles: Estate
Engine capacity: 2.0, 3.0V6
Manufactured in: United States

Best All-Rounder: Maverick 2.0

NEW

Price from: £25,895

Ford Explorer

Body styles: Estate
Engine capacity: 4.0V6, 4.6V8
Manufactured in: United States

In the US, the previous Explorer's reputation was rocked by a massive high-profile safety scare. The new model couldn't come soon enough, so it was with relief at Ford that it was launched to a receptive public. It is now available in Europe too, and is a vast improvement over the cumbersome old model. Wider and longer to offer even more space inside, there's extra safety kit too. Driver comfort is boosted by a moveable pedal box, and a driving experience that is far less anxious when pressing on. Ride quality is also far better, and is now a match for the class best. Europeans seeking a huge 4x4 to conquer all could do far worse than visit their Ford dealership.

Best All-Rounder: Explorer 4.6 V6

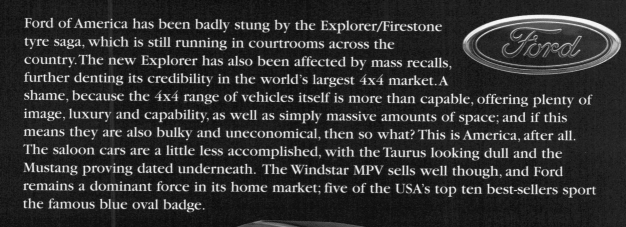

Ford of America has been badly stung by the Explorer/Firestone tyre saga, which is still running in courtrooms across the country. The new Explorer has also been affected by mass recalls, further denting its credibility in the world's largest 4x4 market. A shame, because the 4x4 range of vehicles itself is more than capable, offering plenty of image, luxury and capability, as well as simply massive amounts of space; and if this means they are also bulky and uneconomical, then so what? This is America, after all. The saloon cars are a little less accomplished, with the Taurus looking dull and the Mustang proving dated underneath. The Windstar MPV sells well though, and Ford remains a dominant force in its home market; five of the USA's top ten best-sellers sport the famous blue oval badge.

NEW

Ford Thunderbird

Body styles: Convertible
Engine capacity: 4.0V8

Price from: $35,500
Manufactured in: United States

The fantastic-looking new Ford Thunderbird proves that, given a clean sheet of paper, American designers really come up with the goods. Initially previewed as a concept car, the Thunderbird is the latest in a line of models that stretches back to the '50s. The interior is just as outlandish, and features plenty of equipment; climate control, power leather seats and a 6-CD stereo are all standard. A 3.9-litre V8 engine provides 252bhp and a great soundtrack, whilst the modern rear-wheel-drive chassis ensures the driving experience is enjoyable, too. Most will be used for cruising though, where the retro design cues and wonderful lines ensure the Thunderbird is a great head-turner. It may cost more than some other 'muscle cars', but the 'T-Bird' is worth it.

Best All-Rounder: Thunderbird Premium

Ford Mustang

Price from: $17,700

Convertible

Body styles: Coupe, convertible
Engine capacity: 3.8V6, 4.6V8, 5.4V8
Manufactured in: United States

Probably Ford's most famous model, the Mustang offers tremendous value for money. The base model sells for an incredible $17,000 and features a 3.8-litre V6 engine. There is also a 4.6-litre V8, offering outputs from 260bhp to 320bhp. Equipment levels are also high, and there is a convertible option, too. The chassis lacks polish though, for it is not only aged but unsophisticated too; only the Cobra model gets independent rear suspension. The ride is also skittish, another deterrent to using all the Mustang's substantial power. Still, most accept these major compromises for the benefits they bring in costs; the Mustang remains America's best-selling muscle car.

Best All-Rounder: Mustang GT

Ford Taurus

Price from: $19,200

Revisions two years ago gave the Taurus a more attractive look as well as a better chassis, making it a much improved car overall. With seating for up to six people, the Taurus is very practical, and safe too, with a number of unique crash protection systems appealing especially to families. Power is provided by a 3.0-litre V6 unit; the base unit offers 155bhp, with the 24-valve version boosting this to 200bhp. It is perfectly adequate, which can be used to describe the ride and handling; both are crisp and well up to class standards. The previous version may well have been controversially-styled, but the new Taurus is far more conventional, which has helped its success in a competitive market.

Estate

Body styles: Saloon, estate
Engine capacity: 3.0V6
Manufactured in: United States

Best All-Rounder: Taurus SE

FORD USA

Price from: $22,900

Ford Crown Victoria

Body styles: Saloon
Engine capacity: 4.6V8
Manufactured in: United States

Built on a platform introduced in the '70s, the Crown Victoria is one of the last top-level large rear-wheel-drive saloon cars sold in America. Powered by a 4.6-litre V8 engine, it offers seating for up to six people along with a mass of equipment, especially on the high-spec LX model. That aged platform soon reveals itself on the road though, for although the ride is very soft, the handling is unsophisticated. The optional Performance Pack improves things, but there is no escaping this car's 1970s roots. American buyers don't seem to mind though, for the Crown Victoria still sells strongly. Considering the space, value and equipment it offers, this is perhaps not surprising; more sophistication can be bought, but only for more cash.

Best All-Rounder: Crown Victoria LX

Ford Excursion

Price from: $35,400

Fuel economy that struggles to make double figures, a weight greater than some trucks and an inability to fit into domestic garages mark out the Excursion as a pointlessly large sport-utility vehicle. Engines can be chosen from a 5.4-litre V8, a 6.8-litre V10 or a 7.3-litre V8 turbo diesel; Ford says they meet tough emissions regulations, but they are still woefully uneconomical. The ride is good, thanks to the sheer weight, and the handling does a reasonable job of disguising that mass. Equipment levels are also good, and there is plenty of space inside for up to nine people. However, this is because the Excursion is the world's largest and heaviest SUV; how long will this dinosaur last in the greener new millennium?

Best All-Rounder: Excursion XLT 6.8 4WD

Body styles: Estate
Engine capacity: 5.4V8, 6.8V10
Manufactured in: United States

Price from: $30,900

Ford Expedition

Body styles: Estate
Engine capacity: 4.6V8, 5.4V8
Manufactured in: United States

Ford's full-size 4x4, the Expedition, was first introduced in 1997, and remains a vast-selling favourite with American buyers. Like many sports-utility vehicles, it is available in both 2WD and 4WD format, with either a 4.6-litre or 5.4-litre V8 engine; power is certainly not lacking, with refinement and crushing ability also proving first-rate. Like the larger Excursion, the Expedition can also seat nine people, and is just as luxurious and, sadly, as inefficient. It handles in a similar fashion too, using its sheer mass rather than any finesse to aid comfort levels. Large, heavy and bulky, the Expedition is another vehicle it is all too easy to mock – but it still sells in huge numbers. The low list price probably explains why.

Best All-Rounder: Excursion Eddie Bauer 4WD 5.4

Ford Windstar

Price from: $22,700

A strong seller, Ford's Windstar has become an increasingly popular 'minivan', thanks to its impressive safety, good value and high specification level. Power sliding doors make harassed mums' live's easier, whilst the electrically-adjustable accelerator and brake pedals help them find the safest and most comfortable driving position, too. It performs well in American crash tests, making a natural choice for families. The 3.8-litre V6 engine provides good performance, whilst the ride and handling are comfortable and predictable. Choosing a Windstar could prove a weekend-long family debate, thanks to the sheer number of trim levels and options, but this ensures there is a vehicle out there to suit most needs.

Best All-Rounder: Windstar LX

Body styles: MPV
Engine capacity: 3.8V6
Manufactured in: Canada

Price from: $12,800

Ford ZX2

Body styles: Coupe
Engine capacity: 2.0
Manufactured in: United States

Based on the Escort chassis, which was discontinued in 2000 with the introduction of the Focus, the ZR2 remains on sale thanks to continuing demand; it is Ford's second-best-selling car. It sells above all because of its very low price – just $12,000 buys you a 130bhp 2.0-litre ZX2, with a decent standard equipment level and fairly sleek looks. To drive, it is some way off the standards set by the new Focus, but is fine for the undemanding driver who rates comfort far higher than handling precision. It offers decent passenger room for a coupe too, though in many respects there is no hiding its age. Modern rivals offer far more ability – but the ZX2 is cheaper than most, explaining its continuing popularity.

Best All-Rounder: ZX2

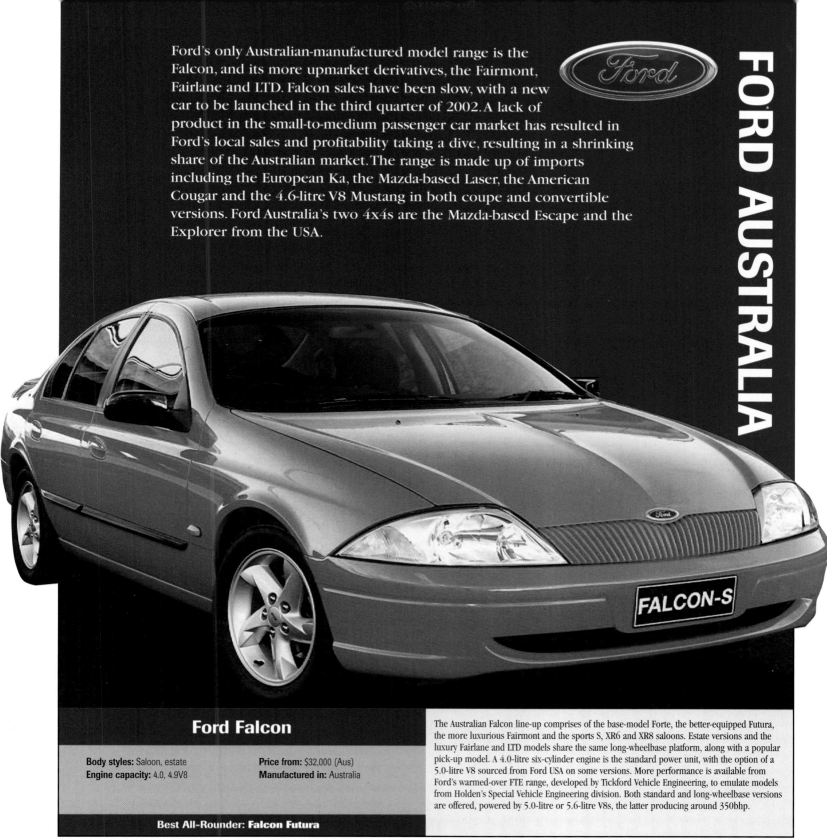

Ford's only Australian-manufactured model range is the Falcon, and its more upmarket derivatives, the Fairmont, Fairlane and LTD. Falcon sales have been slow, with a new car to be launched in the third quarter of 2002. A lack of product in the small-to-medium passenger car market has resulted in Ford's local sales and profitability taking a dive, resulting in a shrinking share of the Australian market. The range is made up of imports including the European Ka, the Mazda-based Laser, the American Cougar and the 4.6-litre V8 Mustang in both coupe and convertible versions. Ford Australia's two 4x4s are the Mazda-based Escape and the Explorer from the USA.

FORD AUSTRALIA

Ford Falcon

Body styles: Saloon, estate
Engine capacity: 4.0, 4.9V8

Price from: $32,000 (Aus)
Manufactured in: Australia

The Australian Falcon line-up comprises of the base-model Forte, the better-equipped Futura, the more luxurious Fairmont and the sports S, XR6 and XR8 saloons. Estate versions and the luxury Fairlane and LTD models share the same long-wheelbase platform, along with a popular pick-up model. A 4.0-litre six-cylinder engine is the standard power unit, with the option of a 5.0-litre V8 sourced from Ford USA on some versions. More performance is available from Ford's warmed-over FTE range, developed by Tickford Vehicle Engineering, to emulate models from Holden's Special Vehicle Engineering division. Both standard and long-wheelbase versions are offered, powered by 5.0-litre or 5.6-litre V8s, the latter producing around 350bhp.

Best All-Rounder: Falcon Futura

Price from: $21,000 (Aus)

Ford Laser

Body styles: Hatchback
Engine capacity: 1.6, 1.8, 2.0
Manufactured in: Australia

While Ford buyers wait for the acclaimed Focus to arrive, they have to make do with the Laser, a Mazda 323 clone imported from Japan. Not that there is a lot wrong with the Laser. It's a solid and well-made, available in hatchback or saloon form with a range of engine from cooking 1.6 LXi to the sporty 2.0-litre SR2. The new Laser R combines the economy of the 1.6 with the sporty style of the SR2. Inside the Laser is entirely average in terms of accommodation, and even with the sports bits it doesn't drive as well as the Focus. But for a budget model it has all a lot of buyers require.
Best All-Rounder: Laser 1.8 GLXi

HONDA

Honda has grand plans for the new Civic, which while a trifle dull in the looks department is a spacious and practical alternative to its competition. The basic platform is being used to sire a host of new models including the Coupe and the Stream compact MPV. Of the two models it's the Stream that is most interesting, the first vehicle of its type to be aimed at the more enthusiastic driver, it offers the unusual combination of space and pace. The Type-R version of the Civic is finally here as is the Jazz supermini – while Honda has also conceded to the production of diesel versions of its cars with a new range of engines developed with Isuzu.

NEW

Honda Integra

Coupe

Engine capacity: 2.0

Price from: £na

Manufactured in: Japan

The old Integra Type-R was the only Integra model that was imported officially into the UK. It gained quite a following too - among those that really enjoy their driving. As fun on the roads as on the track the Type-R had performance unlike no other front-wheel-drive machine. The new Integra, called RSX in the USA, is slightly larger than the old car and should also cover the hole in the range left by the Prelude coupe. Good news for Type-R fans is that this car will receive the racing treatment, with the same 2.0-litre iVTEC engine that powers its Civic Type-R sibling. Sadly for British buyers, Honda reckons it is too close to its hatchback relative, and will not be importing the new car to the UK.

Best All-Rounder: Integra Type-R

Honda Jazz

Price from: £8,000 est

For too long Honda has not had a serious contender in the supermini market, the Logo being brought in late in its life cycle and making little impact on the UK buying public's imagination. With the new Jazz Honda will at last have a competitive supermini when it arrives early in 2002. Styled in the 'mini-MPV' fashion adopted by the Civic, it features advanced petrol engines, with twin spark plugs in each cylinder to boost efficiency. Continuing the 'mini-MPV' theme the interior is also flexible, and said to offer class-leading space. Expected to be a good drive, the Jazz features an all-new platform. If it drives as well as promised don't rule out a Type-R version.

Body styles: Hatchback
Engine capacity: 1.2, 1.4
Manufactured in: Japan

NEW

Best All-Rounder: Too soon to say

NEW

Price from: £10,795

Honda Civic

Coupe

Body styles: Hatchback, saloon, coupe
Engine capacity: 1.4, 1.6, 1.7
Manufactured in: England, Worldwide

The all-new Civic follows the current trend in the family hatchback class by offering space and innovation to rival a compact MPV. The new Civic offers a vast amount of room compared to its predecessor, it's flat floor and dashboard-mounted gearshift increasing useable space. Well equipped, the engine range is limited to two petrol units at present, of 1.4 and 1.6-litre capacity but a new turbo-diesel is expected soon. It's platform forms the basis for a number of spin-off models including the Coupe and Stream MPV, the core range just extended with the introduction of the three-door version. With it the eagerly anticipated Type-R model is now available, featuring a 2.0-litre 200PS VTEC engine and significantly revised suspension making it a thrilling proposition

Best All-Rounder: Civic 1.4 SE

Honda Stream

Price from: £16,395

NEW

This is Honda's idea of a new market niche, a cross between a GTi and a compact MPV. So the Stream gets a couple of powerful VTEC engines, sports chassis tuning and sports seats – MPV owners will be amazed at how well it drives. The new 2.0-litre engine is arguably Honda's best yet in its family cars, and the chassis tuning is exemplary – this car handles superbly. It's comfortable inside too, though not very "GTi". It's as a seven-seater that the Stream works least well. The packaging hasn't been thought out well enough – it works best as a six-seater with a couple of kids in the back. But it's an interesting idea.

Best All-Rounder: Stream 2.0

Body styles: MPV
Engine capacity: 1.7, 2.0
Manufactured in: Japan

Price from: 14,645

Honda Accord

Coupe

Body styles: Hatchback, saloon, coupe
Engine capacity: 1.6, 1.8, 2.0, 2.2, 3.0V6, 2.0TD
Manufactured in: England, Worldwide

The Accord is built to a number of different specifications world-wide that are barely related. The Americans get a slightly larger model while the European market gets this more sporting model, with the option of either saloon or hatchback body styles. It faces tough competition from newer rivals so has recently been revised to keep it class competitive. The American built coupe is available with a 3.0-litre V6, but overall the saloons and hatchback are a better proposition. Engine choice for these models include a 1.8, 2.0 and a 2.3 with a manic high revving 2.2-litre also available in the superb Type-R version. Space inside could be better, though the interior feels like it will last forever.

Best All-Rounder: Accord 1.8 SE

Honda Legend

Price from: £31,995

Against the German competition the Legend has a great deal of on-paper promise. A fully loaded specification with a suitably powerful and refined 3.5-litre V6 engine has failed, however, to tempt buyers away from more prestigious brands. Big and comfortable, the Legend offers little in the way of driver involvement, the suspension struggling when the roads get challenging. There are few extras available, as almost everything is standard, from leather upholstery to CD player. Honda's reliability is good too, but you are offered more choice, and a better drive, in other manufacturer's ranges. The Japanese have proved that they can compete in this class, Lexus being a prime example; sadly the Legend is a long way off the mark.

Best All-Rounder: Legend 3.5 V6

Body styles: Saloon
Engine capacity: 3.5V6
Manufactured in: Japan

Price from: £17,000

Honda Insight

Body styles: Coupe
Engine capacity: 1.0
Manufactured in: Japan

Showcasing clever technology to provide a partial solution to the environmental problems associated with the internal combustion engine the Insight utilises Integrated Motor Assist (IMA). Both an electric motor and conventional engine work in tandem when accelerating, the electric motor becoming a generator when the Insight is decelerating, producing both excellent drivability and outstanding fuel consumption. Removing the need to re-charge is one of the Insights many tricks. Honda has around 300 patents covering the innovative technology used not only in the drivetrain but also the oddly styled coupes aluminium construction. Being a coupe it's not too practical but limited numbers and potentially enormous fuel bill savings ensure interest is high.

Best all rounder: Insight

HONDA

Honda S2000

Price from: £25,995

Body styles: Convertible
Engine capacity: 2.0
Manufactured in: Japan

While the S2000 may not look particularly exciting it's the engineering that goes into Honda's roadster that's extraordinary. The driving experience is the attraction, enough to forgive the rather unimaginative and plain interior. The 2.0-litre VTEC engine that powers the S2000 develops an incredible 240bhp - without the assistance of forced induction. Revving to a heady 9,000rpm, the means by which the engine delivers its power above 6,000rpm is intoxicating, pushing you deep in to the hugging sports seats as you press the throttle. Not that it's not quick below the 6,000rpm threshold, it's just exceptionally so above it. Steering, handling and a near perfect gearchange add to its appeal, all at a price that trounces the competition.

Best All-Rounder: S2000

Honda NSX

Price from: £69,590

Honda's interpretation of the supercar rocked the establishment when it was launched with its sublime combination of fantastic performance and all-round user friendliness. Logic says it should sell in greater numbers but the Honda badge seems to work against it. People with £70,000+ look for their thrills from German or Italian manufacturers. Despite this, the package remains impressive; aluminium bodywork, a powerful 3.2-litre V6 and lightweight wishbone suspension provides a memorable drive - especially when that engine is on full chat. Inside the NSX lacks any drama, the facia being too ordinary for a car of this type. It seems Honda may have been a bit early with the NSX. As rivals supercars become easier to drive the NSX is nearing the end of its life.

Best All-Rounder: NSX 3.2 Coupe

Body styles:
Coupe, targa
Engine capacity:
3.0V6, 3.2V6
Manufactured in: Japan

Honda HR-V

Price from: £13,695

Body styles: Estate
Engine capacity: 1.6
Manufactured in: Japan

The HR-V doesn't fit comfortably in any specific car category but that's where a great deal of its appeal lies. While it's based on the ancient mechanicals of the now defunct Logo supermini, the HR-V comes with either two or four-wheel drive, with three or five-doors. Wacky styling turns heads and the high seating position is an advantage around town, the HR-V driving more like a jacked up hatchback rather than an off-roader. Inside there is lots of blue - dials, switch gear and seats. It looks good, and front seat comfort is fine, but legroom is mediocre in the rear. Fun to drive and surprisingly practical, the HR-V is a great car for those that don't like to be categorised.

Best All-Rounder: HR-V 1.6i VTEC

Honda CR-V

Price from: £16,495

The CR-V offers little of the off-road capability suggested by it looks, though as the majority of buyers are unlikely to ever encounter anything other than a deep puddle, it's of little consequence. In fact it gives it a useful edge, offering more car like performance in a practical package. The floor is completely flat, allowing the seating positions to be changed, and there's a concealed luggage area under the floor. The 2.0-litre engine gives performance which is usefully brisk, though it's hardly the GTi in 4x4 clothing that makes the Toyota RAV4 such a hit. Well built, roomy and quite entertaining to drive, the CR-V is due to be replaced by an all-new, British-built car for the 2002 model year.

Best All-Rounder: CR-V 2.0 ES

Body styles: Estate
Engine capacity: 2.0
Manufactured in:
England

Holden, General Motors' Australian satellite, manufactures the locally-designed Commodore, in saloon, estate and utility (pick-up) derivatives, together with its long-wheelbase Statesman and Caprice cousins. Holden's Special Vehicles division (HSV) produces enhanced versions of the local fare, all but one featuring V8 power, with the range-topping 5.7 GTS versions producing around 400bhp. Holden's other passenger cars are sourced form the Opel range; the Barina (Corsa), the Astra in three and five-door hatchback and saloon versions, and the Vectra four and five-door, too. The Coupe and convertible version of the Astra are expected in early 2002, while the just-released Zafira gives Holden a player in the rapidly-expanding people-carrier sector. It also offers two 4x4s, sourced from GM's Isuzu division - the Frontera and the Jackaroo (Isuzu Trooper).

Holden Commodore

Estate

Body styles: Saloon, estate
Engine capacity: 3.8V6, 5.7V8
Price from: $29,500(Aus)
Manufactured in: Australia

The Commodore range is largely unchanged for the 2002 model year, and continues to outsell rivals with a market share close to 50% of all large passenger cars. The base Executive model is aimed at the fleet market, and anchors a range that also consists of the well-equipped Acclaim, luxurious Berlina and Calais, and the sporty S and SS derivatives. The cavernous estate and luxury Statesman and Caprice models all share the same long wheelbase platform. Power options are shared between either a 3.8-litre V6 in standard or super-charged form, or a Chevrolet-sourced all-alloy 5.7-litre V8. Anticipation is currently building for the launch of the Commodore coupe, to be badged Monaro, in late 2001. It will wear a unique nose and tail to differentiate it from the saloons.

Best All-Rounder: Commodore 3.8 V6 Acclaim

Holden Jackaro

Price from: $38,800(Aus)

Holden brings in the Isuzu Trooper from Japan to fill its large 4x4 niche, as Opel does in Europe. It may have been around for a good few years now, but regular updates keep the Jackaroo a viable contender as a rugged, no-nonsense offering. The range was upgraded recently by widening the track in all but the base model to improve the stability and ride quality. There is also longer rear suspension travel which makes the Jackaroo work better off-road. Engine choice is between a refined 3.5V6 and a solid 3.0-litre turbo-diesel which claims to be the most powerful in its class. Top-of-the-range Monterey models, with full leather and power seats, get the option of the diesel for the first time.

Body styles: Estate
Engine capacity: 3.5V6, 3.0TD
Manufactured in: Australia

Best All-Rounder: Jackaroo V6

HYUNDAI

Currently riding on the crest of a wave, with the impressive Santa Fe 4x4 selling strongly in the US market and performing well in crash tests, Hyundai has recently launched the new Elantra in Europe. Larger than the car it replaced, it is now positioned to take sales from competition like the Vauxhall Vectra and Peugeot 406. As a brand for the more budget conscious buyer, Hyundai remains refreshingly free from the stigma associated with some of its competition. A new coupe is expected soon, with rumours persisting that it will feature Mercedes power, the tie-up giving the German giant access to Hyundai's extensive small car knowledge.

NEW

Hyundia Elantra

Hatchback

Body styles: Hatchback, saloon
Engine capacity: 1.6, 1.8, 2.0, 2.0TD

Price from: £10,999
Manufactured in: Korea

Hyundai's Mondeo and Vectra competitor offers impressive on-paper value. Along with prices much lower than its rivals, it is very well-equipped, cheap to run, and quite lively in 2.0-litre guise. It also looks reasonable in the metal; not all that exciting, but inoffensive and quite mature in places. The interior is spacious and comfortable, and a fairly relaxing place to spend time in. Of course, the Elantra can't match the dynamic excellence of the Mondeo, majoring instead on refinement and fair ride comfort; it handles securely, but with little real enthusiasm – though its drivers probably won't be looking for such qualities, anyway. Available in saloon or hatchback form, the Elantra is a reasonable alternative to more expensive European models.

Best All-Rounder: Elantra 1.6 GSi

Price from: £6,599

Hyundia Amica

Body styles: Hatchback
Engine capacity: 1.0
Manufactured in: Korea

Hugely popular in the Far East, Hyundai's small city cars are gaining acceptance in Europe, too. The Atoz was the ugly one, with the Amica offering similar mechanicals with a more acceptable style. It's fine to drive too, especially around town where tiny dimensions pay dividends. An upright driving position means visibility is fine, and the lively 1.0-litre engine ensures gaps are rarely missed. A good ride and surprising amount of space means passengers shouldn't be uncomfortable, either. Surprisingly , the Atoz is capable outside town too, so long as you accept the lack of ultimate performance. Refinement is impressive, and generous equipment levels provide plenty of comfort; throw in low prices, and the Amica looks appealing.

Best All-Rounder: Amica 1.0 GSi

Hyundia Accent

Despite a successful World Rally Championship campaign with the Accent WRC, Hyundai's small hatch still lacks recognition with new buyers. There's no denying the space and equipment it offers for the money – it is larger than many superminis, yet costs less than most – but the dull styling and 'basic' air mean it holds only limited appeal. It provides an easy-going drive, though with no real enthusiasm. Noise levels are low, ride quality is good, and as long as you don't drive it hard, the Accent remains well-composed. Watching the rally cars may well be more exciting than driving the road car, but there is no denying the Accent's appeal to value-seeking drivers.

Best All-Rounder: Accent 1.3 GSi

Price from: £6,995

Saloon

Body styles: Hatchback, saloon
Engine capacity: 1.3, 1.5
Manufactured in: Korea

HYUNDAI

Price from: £15,499

Hyundia Trajet

Body styles: MPV
Engine capacity: 2.0,
2.7V6, 2.0TD
Manufactured in: Korea

Although not as widely recognised as other full-sized MPVs, the Trajet is a surprisingly good entrant into a competitive market. Like many rivals, it has seven seats with plenty of folding and removing options, and a roomy cabin with fair luggage space and high levels of comfort. There are plenty of gadgets too, including standard air conditioning on all models. It is even good to drive, with precise handling and high levels of ride quality ensuring passengers won't complain. The most desirable engine option is the 2.7-litre V6, though owners watching the pennies will prefer the turbo-diesel; the 2.0-litre petrol unit demands hard work to maintain pace. Overall, the Trajet is an impressively able, well-priced MPV, that needs no excuses from those who buy it.

Best All-Rounder: Trajet 2.0 TD GSi

Hyundia Santa-Fe

Price from: £15,999

Despite the American soap opera name, the attractive Santa Fe is actually a high-quality machine, and is currently taking the US by storm. 'Mercedes M-Class space for Toyota RAV4 money' means the cabin is comfortable for passengers, and also very well-designed from high-quality materials. It is mature to drive too, with far more composure, ride comfort and handling agility than more traditional off-road vehicles can offer. This means it cannot conquer the harshest of terrains, but in most off-road conditions, the Santa Fe will not disappoint. Engines are all competitive, though only the V6 offers the manners equal to the rest of the car. More distinctive than other more expensive rivals, the Santa Fe's success is down to far more than good value.

Best All-Rounder: Santa Fe 2.7 V6

Body styles: Estate
Engine capacity: 2.0,
2.4, 2.7V6, 2.0TD
Manufactured in: Korea

Price from: £20,999

Hyundia XG

Body styles: Saloon
Engine capacity: 2.5V6,
3.0V6
Manufactured in: Korea

The Hyundai that looks like a Rolls-Royce is the cheapest luxury car you can buy, though whether buyers are convinced by the 'luxury' status is debatable. However, if they drive one without looking at the badge, they might well be. As well as the usual mass of standard equipment and space, and high levels of build quality, the XG is also very smooth to drive. The V6 engine is quiet and powerful, and the Tiptronic-style five-speed automatic transmission shifts imperceptibly. The expected ride quality is present, as are impressive levels of refinement, and it's really only the XG's vague handling and silly foot-operated handbrake that fail to attract. For the money, few cars are as spacious or well-equipped – or as expensively-looking and eye-catching.

Best All-Rounder: XG 3.0 V6

Hyundia Coupe

Price from: £12,879

After the smooth and attractive style of the original Coupe, 2000's revised model lead many to believe Hyundai had gone mad. Elegance made way for impact, dividing opinion like no other Korean car. Things were a little better inside, with modern aluminium-look trim, but the Coupe lacks the quality feel of more recent Hyundais. It drives well though, and still provides entertaining handling that is surprisingly engaging when you really begin to push it. It is a shame the engines are not more powerful, as the chassis encourages you to drive faster than the engines deliver. Rarely for a coupe, the 1.6-litre is available with automatic transmission, adding further all-round appeal.

Best All-Rounder: Coupe 2.0 SE

Body styles: Coupe
Engine capacity: 1.6,
1.8, 2.0
Manufactured in: Korea

NEW

Price from: £na

Hyundia Sonata

Body styles: Saloon
Engine capacity: 2.0,
2.7V6
Manufactured in: Korea

The Sonata is the forgotten model in Hyundai's range, lacking the stylish appeal of more expensive models, and the great-value pricing of the cheaper cars. However it has numerous strengths, not least an impressive amount of space and equipment, and the option of smooth 2.0-litre or 2.5-litre V6 engines. Competent in most respects too; ride, handling and refinement are all perfectly adequate, as is performance from the evenly-matched engines. The V6 is the nicer unit to use, but this is at the expense of fuel economy. The Sonata is a car for passengers, offering great comfort levels and a huge boot. With such generous equipment levels, the overall sales package looks appealing. But will buyers notice?

Best All-Rounder: Sonata 2.5 V6

ISUZU

ISUZU

As an off-road specialist Isuzu is a useful ally for General Motors - the US giant has a stake in the company. The General taps into its extensive expertise in the field of 4x4 vehicles to sell a variety of GM-badged Isuzu models around the world. Respected as more than just a manufacturer of fashionable 'Sports Utility Vehicles', Isuzu products have a level of competence off-road that makes them popular among those who actually require their 4x4 to cope with off-road exploits. Until now Isuzu's reliance on 4x4 models has been beneficial, allowing it to tap into a highly popular market segment. But the current reversals of opinion regarding such vehicles in the US may signify interesting times ahead for the marque.

NEW

Isuzu Axiom

Body styles: Estate
Engine capacity: 3.5V6

Price from: $26,500
Manufactured in: Japan

The modern, good-looking Axiom is causing much debate in the US over its futuristic style. Odd, considering the Pontiac Aztec was born there. Still, the Axiom has plenty to commend it, not least an advanced chassis with computer-controlled suspension – dubbed 'Torque On Demand' by Isuzu. This gives it good on-road manners, along with supreme off-road ability thanks to the rugged off-road chassis. There's also plenty of power from the 3.5-litre V6 engine, though this comes at the expense of fuel economy. Two trim levels, base and XS, feature plenty of standard kit, and the interior is also very practical, a necessary requirement of any new vehicle in the booming SUV market. Two-wheel-drive versions are also available, but the four-wheel-drive models are preferable.

Best All-Rounder: Axiom 4WD

Price from: £17,950

Isuzu Trooper

Body styles: Estate
Engine capacity: 3.5V6, 3.0TD
Manufactured in: Japan

A long-running off-roader with a huge but understated reputation, the Trooper maintains healthy sales despite seemingly flashier and more desirable rivals. However, for those who really use their vehicles as they were intended, the Trooper ranks among the best. Off-road, it is superb, and is rugged enough to soak up harsh conditions for years. The lusty engines provide plenty of pulling power, but the V6 petrol unit is thirsty. On-road, the Trooper may lack the refinement of newer models, but it is still perfectly acceptable, and very practical and comfortable too – especially in long-wheelbase format. Only a dull dash design finds criticism, compensated for by decent equipment levels. It may not be the obvious choice, but the Trooper has a discreet class that many others lack.

Best All-Rounder: Trooper 3.0 TD Duty

Isuzu Vehi-cross

If the Trooper is too restrained for Isuzu fans, there's always the VehiCross to redress the balance. It is based upon the running gear of the short-wheelbase Trooper, but features a body that comes straight off a Motor Show concept car stand. Rugged plastic lower mouldings, bizarre headlights and extreme curves ensure it looks like no other 4x4 – and extensive work to the chassis means it doesn't drive like traditional 4x4s, either. Sportier settings and a 212bhp V6 engine provide great fun, making it an unlikely hot hatch-chaser. Of course, this means it is unlikely to excel off-road, but who will ever drive this outlandish vehicle through the rough stuff? It is a street cruiser that continues to turn heads.

Best All-Rounder: VehiCross V6

Price from: £na

Body styles: Estate
Engine capacity: 3.2V6
Manufactured in: Japan

The great granddaddy of off roaders, Jeep's range is updated with the addition of the Liberty model that replaces the ancient Cherokee. Even though its vehicles are growing more and more luxurious to cater for a wider audience, they remain competent off-road machines. Despite assertions to the contrary, the financial burden Chrysler has landed on owner Daimler may yet result in future Jeep and Mercedes SUV models sharing platform and powertrains to keep production and development costs to a minimum.

Jeep

JEEP

NEW

Jeep Cherokee/Liberty

Body styles: Estate
Engine capacity: 2.4, 3.7V6, 2.5CRD

Price from: £na
Manufactured in: United States

Out goes the elderly previous model's flat, angular style, to be replaced by a far more modern and attractive design – with plenty of swoops and curves. The latest Cherokee is the first all-new model since the early 1980s, and Jeep hopes it will further improve on the old model's surprisingly strong sales. And if the exterior is a shock to fans of the previous car, they'd better hold on when they step inside – once again, curves abound instead of blocks. The Cherokee is likely to be impressive off-road, but should also be far more refined than the old model on the highway. Engines are improved, and include a great new 2.5-litre turbo-diesel that will be popular thanks to its refinement, economy and huge reserves of torque.

Best All-Rounder: Too soon to say

Price from: £27,995

Jeep Grand Cherokee

Body styles: Estate
Engine capacity: 4.0, 4.7V8, 3.1TD
Manufactured in: Austria, United States

The Grand Cherokee is one of the most powerful large off-roaders you can buy – qualities that command huge respect across the globe. This model, launched a few years ago, may not look too different to older versions, but thorough engineering mean it is great to drive. The multi-cylinder petrol and turbo-charged diesel engines provide plenty of pulling power, whilst the advanced chassis provides reassuring grip, balance and steering precision. Even the ride quality is good, which is commendable in an off-roader. However, interior space levels find criticism, which is surprising considering the Jeep's bulk. It is extremely comfortable inside though, with huge seats, an attractive dash and all the toys usually associated with the luxury cars that the Grand Cherokee competes with.

Best All-Rounder: Grand Cherokee V8

Jeep Wrangler

Price from: £15,795

The World War II icon remains on sale, continuing the familiar styling that has been in production for over half a century. Of course, today's models benefit from a smart interior, modern independent suspension and a heater – but comfort and refinement levels remain 'rugged' compared to newer rivals. The Wrangler has an ace though, in the form of powerful turbo-diesel and straight-six petrol engines; the latter sounds like a NASCAR racer, with the former providing high levels of low-down torque. In terms of driving, the Wrangler is best off-road, which is where it was designed to excel; on-road, the jiggly ride, and handling that is at times demanding, both tax the driver. It requires compromises, but many willingly accept them, so unique is the Wrangler.

Best All-Rounder: Wrangler 4.0 Sport

Body styles: Estate, convertible
Engine capacity: 2.5, 4.0
Manufactured in: United States

JAGUAR

The big cat leaps into a whole new market with the X-Type range, which should see production volumes eventually double for the Coventry marque. Competing against established rivals like the BMW 3 Series and Mercedes C-Class, the X-Type has been warmly received by the press and public alike. While the X-Type may be based on Ford underpinnings, the blue oval's involvement with Jaguar has been its saviour - clearly exhibiting how brands can remain distinct under control of a larger manufacturer. New models expected in the near future include a replacement XJ series model, thought to utilise aluminium construction, hotter XK8 variants and the F-Type sports car which is now looking likely to be mid rather than front engined as first expected.

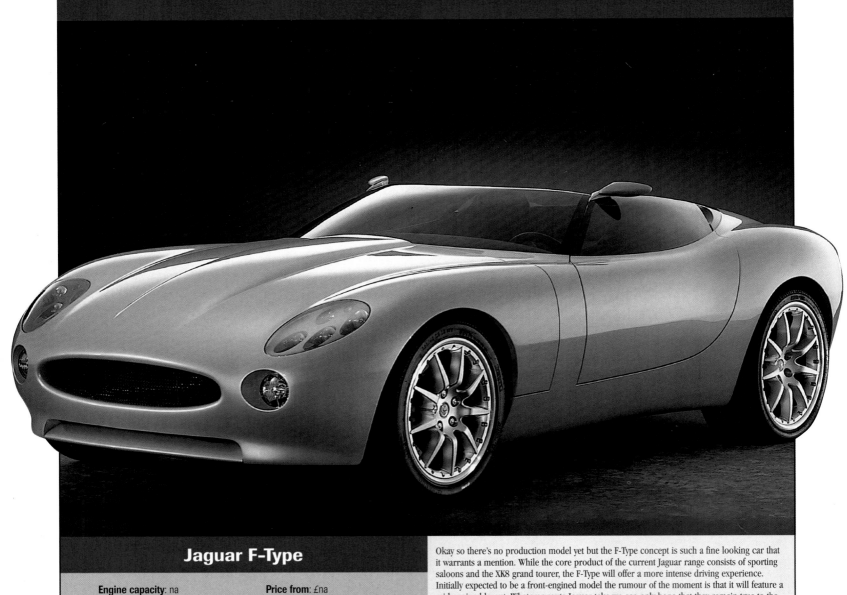

Jaguar F-Type

Engine capacity: na   **Price from**: £na

Manufactured in: na

Okay so there's no production model yet but the F-Type concept is such a fine looking car that it warrants a mention. While the core product of the current Jaguar range consists of sporting saloons and the XK8 grand tourer, the F-Type will offer a more intense driving experience. Initially expected to be a front-engined model the rumour of the moment is that it will feature a mid-engined layout. Whatever route Jaguar take we can only hope that they remain true to the concept cars purposeful flowing lines; that while unmistakably Jaguar are bang right up to date. Expect it to be hugely powerful, massively entertaining and ultra desirable – if you want to be one of the first to own one you'd be advised to get a deposit in at your local dealership – as it's certain to be a sell out.

Best all-rounder: Too soon to say

NEW

Price from: £22,000

Jaguar X-Type

Body styles: Saloon
Engine capacity: 2.5V6, 3.0V6
Manufactured in: England

The X-Type is the most important new Jaguar for years; the company's future growth depending on its success. Entering the cut-throat 'junior executive' class for the first time, the X-Type goes head-to-head with the dominant BMW 3-Series, and offers a number of unique features to sway buyers. The four-wheel-drive chassis supplies plenty of grip, stability and composure, whilst the V6 engines are smooth and refined. Inside, the optional high-tech 'touch-screen' centre console display controls heating, stereo and satellite navigation, but doesn't detract from the luxurious wood and leather. There is also plenty of space which, along with the traditional large-car styling, should ensure Jaguar continues its remarkable rate of growth for some years.

Best All-Rounder: X-Type 2.5 V6 Sport

Jaguar S-Type

Before the X-Type, this was Jaguar's 'smallest' model – yet it is still a BMW 5-Series and Mercedes E-Class rival. The styling, like the name, harks back to the classic saloons of the 1960s, but is full of modern details too, like the LED rear tail lights and the complicated curvaceous bonnet. Effortless performance is provided by refined 3.0-litre V6 and 4.0-litre V8 engines, while the S-Type is a responsive machine through the bends; optional semi-active suspension adds a further degree of control and agility. Inside, there is plenty of wood and leather, and fine comfort too; the only criticism is limited space compared to some rivals. Otherwise though, the S-Type is a great car that is proving to be a huge success for Jaguar.

Best All-Rounder: S-Type 3.0 Sport

Price from: £26,700

Body styles: Saloon
Engine capacity: 3.0V6, 4.0V8
Manufactured in: England

Price from: £35,950

Jaguar XJ8

Body styles: Saloon
Engine capacity: 3.2V8, 4.0V8
Manufactured in: England

Offering a unique blend of British style and German-like quality and build, the XJ8 is now one of the executive class's more 'mature' players. This does not mean it is off the pace - for dynamically it remains strong. The 3.2-litre and 4.0-litre V8 engines are refined and, in supercharged XJR form especially, tremendously powerful. However the chassis can cope, and is both eager and smooth-riding, just as a Jaguar should be. Of course, many are attracted by the beautifully elegant lines and cosseting interior; space may be tight, but no other rival has such a charismatic and stylish interior. A replacement may well be on the horizon, but the current XJ8 remains a highly desirable executive sports saloon.

Best All-Rounder: XJ8 4.0 Sovereign

Jaguar XK8

Price from: £48,700

A sensation at its launch, the XK8's huge appeal shows no signs of diminishing The sleek lines already approach classic status, boasting a muscular look that is also beautiful, whether in coupe or cabriolet form. The interior is also traditional and very comfortable for a 2+2, but features plenty of gadgets, too. Under the long nose is a 4.0-litre V8 that is effortlessly fast, and sensationally rapid in supercharged form. It is smooth to drive too, especially over long distances across challenging roads. Other rivals may offer more space, but the Jaguar is a formidable competitor in almost every other area. Add in value that makes others look over-priced, and the reasons for its continued success are clear.

Best All-Rounder: XK8 Coupe

Convertible

Body styles: Coupe, convertible
Engine capacity: 4.0V8
Manufactured in: England

KIA

With a range expanding faster than the waistline of a middle-aged man, Kia is nothing if ambitious with its new models. The Mentor has been replaced with the imaginatively-badged Mentor II while the Rio reached Europe late in 2001. The Magentis flagship model offers all the luxury of more costly competition, without the expense - an impressive alternative to other budget luxury models. Sadly European markets don't get the benefit of the aggressive after-sales warranty and servicing package offered to American consumers. Owned by Hyundai, the Kia range has benefited from shared technology but doesn't offer the same badge appeal of its parent, despite competing in similar budget markets.

NEW

Kia Magentis

Body styles: Saloon
Engine capacity: 2.0, 2.5V6

Price from: £12,995
Manufactured in: Korea

Using the Hyundai Sonata as its base, Kia's new Magentis offers remarkable space and equipment for the money. It is half a class bigger than Mondeo-sized cars, yet costs less than the vast majority of them. Surprisingly, it is also fairly attractive, in a discrete, understated way. Under the bonnet sits a 2.5-litre V6 engine, again a rare luxury for this budget; it is powerful, but not the most efficient. To drive, the Magentis is competitive too. Those Sonata underpinnings mean the ride and handling are reasonable, and while it is never likely to set any new standards, it is more than acceptable. The equipment levels are the key to this car's attraction - making it a specification-sheet winner.

Best All-Rounder: Magentis 2.5 V6 LX

Kia Rio

Price from: £5,995

Glance at the Rio and you could be forgiven for thinking it is an estate model. You'd be mistaken though, as the Rio is only available as a hatchback. And there is where the appeal lies in the Rio range – you get a lot of car for your money. Recognised as a budget brand the Rio is Kia's latest model to enter the British market. Inside there's Focus-sized space, and while the dashboard and trim design may hardly be cutting edge they are suitably sturdy without the cheap feel of much of the competition. Two engine choices are available, a 1.3 and a 1.5 – the difference between the two so imperceptible to make the 1.3 the better choice. A budget buy that's hard to beat.

Body styles: Hatchback,
Engine capacity: 1.3,
1.5
Manufactured in: Korea

NEW

Best all-rounder: Rio 1.3

Price from: £8,995

Kia Mentor II

Body stlyes: Saloon
Engine capacity: 1.6
Manufactured in: Korea

Kia hopes its new Mentor saloon will make more of an impact than its unadventurous predecessor which was usually ignored by UK buyers. It offered lots of car for the money though, and if anything, the new model offers even better value. Comparisons of equipment levels and list prices reveal the Mentor to be a very good deal indeed. Its 100bhp 1.6-litre engine is also powerful, offering more performance than many rivals. And although the chassis is not class-leading, with a car like this it's not that important; Mentor buyers will be more interested in the spacious interior that supplies medium-class space for family-class money. More of an appliance than a car, there is no denying the Mentor's bargain status.

Best All-Rounder: Mentor 1.6 LX

Kia Shuma

Price from: £8,495

Criticism of the dull Mentor saloon inspired Kia to produce a more stylish hatchback variant of the car. The Shuma uses a twin-headlight Mercedes-style nose, that is distinctive, if not exactly pretty. Underneath lies the standard Mentor chassis, which means the ride and handling are fail-safe but uninspiring, and the engines are surprisingly powerful but not exactly refined when used hard; most won't be pushed hard enough to reveal such faults, though. Inside, it is extremely dull, though reasonably well-equipped and quite spacious front and rear. But it is not a car that drivers will relish for long-distance trips, unless their expectations are low; it is an acceptable choice only for those who prefer lots of kit for not much cash.

Best All-Rounder: Shuma 1.5 SX

Body styles: Hatchback, saloon
Engine capacity: 1.6
Manufactured in: Korea

Price from: £9,995

Kia Carens

Body styles: Compact MPV
Engine capacity: 1.8
Manufactured in: Korea

Offering mini-MPV practicality yet costing significantly less than more established rivals, the Carens is a typical Kia bargain. Seating five in standard form, a six-seat version is also offered, though the rear two in that model are only really suitable for children. Otherwise, the interior is practical, if dull, and very well-equipped. However, engine choice is limited to a single 108bhp 1.8-litre unit; a turbo-diesel option would be welcome. The chassis is also not particularly inspiring – it does the job, but no more. However for the money, few will complain, as on a practical, value-for-money front, the Carens is strong. Others are more flexible and better to drive, but how many offer brand-new car enjoyment for so little?

Best All-Rounder: Carens 1.8 SX

Kia Sedona

Price from: £13,995

A full-size MPV for mini-MPV money; that's the key to the Sedona's attraction. It is similar in size to Renault's Grand Espace, and seats seven people with plenty of space for their luggage, too. There are also sliding doors to ease entry in tight parking spaces. However, as a load-carrier, the Sedona is poor – because until 2002 the seats could be removed, unlike in most other MPVs. It does not provide the greatest driving experience in the world, either: ride and handling are OK, no more, whilst the surprisingly powerful engines are noisy when revved hard. Still the diesel is economical, and features a bizarre air scoop on the bonnet for added visual interest. A bargain, despite its obvious weaknesses.

Best All-Rounder: Sedona 2.9 TDi SX

Body styles: MPV
Engine capacity: 2.5V6, 2.9TD
Manufactured in: Korea

Price from: £12,995

Kia Sportage

Body styles: Estate
Engine capacity: 2.0, 2.0TD
Manufactured in: Korea

The Sportage may well be Kia's oldest vehicle, but it remains surprisingly competitive. The rugged looks hide an effective four-wheel-drive chassis, that makes a fair fist of off-road mud plugging. Revisions in 2000 also helped on-road comfort and agility too, though it is still some way off the class best. A 2.0-litre engine helps the Sportage perform reasonably well, but the 2.0-litre turbo-diesel is a better all-rounder, though its availability is limited. The five-door Sportage is well-equipped and offers a competent budget alternative to the Land Rover Freelander. Just don't expect to turn many heads, or experience the cutting edge of off-road technology and refinement.

Best All-Rounder: Sportage 2.0 SX

LAMBORGHINI

The definitive supercar manufacturer to some, Lamborghini continues to offer outrageous machines without the concessions to practicality that competitors now consider essential. Under Audi's stewardship the Diablo replacement has been pushed back to ensure that it meets the high expectations of both Lamborghini's customers and the bosses back in Germany. In the meantime the Diablo has been given a thorough rework, taming the outrageous beast into a consummate performance machine, allowing drivers to actually drive it rather than be scared by it. The one-model range won't do these days so it's likely that following the Diablo's imminent replacement, a new smaller car will join the stable to compete against rivals like the Ferrari 360 Modena and a proposed new Aston Martin. We, like many, can't wait.

Lamborghini Diablo

Body styles: Coupe, convertible
Engine capacity: 5.7V12, 6.0V12

Price from: £152,500
Manufactured in: Italy

They still build cars like this? Unashamedly huge in every respect, the Diablo is a true old-school supercar, where size matters above all else. Installed in the tight interior, you may wonder why the thing is so large; firing up the 6.0-litre V12 engine may provide an answer. It really is an all-time great, with immense power and a quite brilliant soundtrack. A four-wheel-drive chassis keeps it all under control, and allows the driver to travel as fast as he dare – though few roads are big enough to fully unleash the Diablo. Far more of a complete car since Audi's input, the big Diablo's days are nevertheless numbered. Don't worry though, for its successor will be just as dramatic. The dinosaur will be reborn.-

Best All-Rounder: Diablo VT

Now a distant memory to the majority of British consumers, the Lancia name lives on in the rest of Europe. The marque, once famed for its rally success with the Delta Integrale, has changed its direction leaving the sporting models to Fiat stable-mate Alfa Romeo to concentrate on the luxury end of the market. The current range barely reflects this, however, with the quirky Y supermini still on the price lists. Perhaps a better indicator of the future for the marque is in its concept models, which are being paraded around the European motorshow circuit to gauge public reaction. They look good too, stylish and discrete - but offering all the luxury associated with premium German brands. Given the resurgence of Alfa Romeo in Britain it might be right time to reintroduce Lancia to a more receptive audience.

Lancia Lybra

Body styles: Saloon, estate
Engine capacity:
1.6, 1.8, 2.0, 1.9JTD, 2.4JTD

Price from: £na
Manufactured in: Italy

Best All-Rounder: Lybra 2.0

In a marketplace full of 'sporting' models, Lancia's Lybra stands almost distinct in offering a luxury-biased style. Like the Rover 75, emphasis is placed on refinement and elegance, to distance it from the more focused and dynamic Alfa Romeo 156. As such, noise levels are low, and there is an advanced air conditioning system and sophisticated Bose stereo, set into a centre console designed to reflect the Lancia grille. It is all executed very well indeed, making the Lybra a desirable medium-sized luxury car. The engines, ranging from 1.6-litres to a 2.0-litre 155bhp five-cylinder unit, are all powerful and eager, and the ride is suitably soft and comfortable, without sacrificing handling agility. An interesting and attractive medium-sized alternative to the usual sporty fare.

Lancia Y

Price from: £na

Body styles: Hatchback
Engine capacity: 1.1, 1.2
Manufactured in: Italy

Using the chassis of the previous Fiat Punto, it is to Lancia's credit that the Y still handles and – especially – rides commendably well. It is the styling that will attract most though, for few superminis are as distinctive and unique as the smallest Lancia; the option of 112 colours makes it even more individual, too. The luxurious interior is equally stylish, with central-mounted instruments and the use of sensuous Alcantara trim for the seats and dashboard. Beneath the faired-in bonnet sit Punto engines of 1.1-litre or 1.2-litre capacity; both units are smooth and eager, especially the higher-output 86bhp 1.2-litre variant. Sadly, it will never be engineered for right-hand-drive, so sales in the UK will never happen. Pity.

Best All-Rounder: Y 1.2 86bhp

Lancia Z

Price from: £na

Body styles: MPV
Engine capacity: 2.0, 2.0JTD
Manufactured in: Italy

If ever there was an example of the confused direction Fiat has chosen for Lancia, it is the Z. Quite what a company with Lancia's heritage is doing producing a people carrier is a difficult question to answer. But you can guess the way the thinking went - Lancia has the right image, and Fiat has an MPV, so why not combine them to produce a really upmarket luxury six-seater? The trouble is, it looks like a van and is the car that, in Fiat form, is seen bashing around Italy's streets as a taxi. It is, of course, the same as the Peugeot 806 and Citroen Synergy too, and to top it all, built in France. Expect a new model soon.

Best All-Rounder: Z 2.0 Turbo

LAND ROVER

Now under Ford's control Land Rover can look forward to the success that Jaguar has demonstrated under the wing of the automotive giant. Like the Coventry cat the legendary off-road manufacturer now benefits from more efficient production techniques and a much needed increase in quality control. Strong sales should continue, though expect volume to increase significantly with Freelander going on sale in the USA this year. An important market, the USA love the Range Rover, a new super-luxury replacement model is expected within the next year. That may have been enough in the past but Land Rover looks likely to introduce a further four models in the next four years, covering every conceivable market segment. The plans may sound ambitious but Ford has proved what it can do with a premium brand in the past - Land Rover almost certain to replicate that success.

Land Rover Defender Tomb Raider

Engine capacity: 2.5TD5

Price from: £22,995

Manufactured in: England

Best all-rounder: it's a film prop!

So the car from the film may not available in your local Land Rover dealership but it's probably the most famous Solihull product at the moment. Featuring in the Hollywood smash Tomb Raider, Lara Croft's vehicle is certain to do the famous off-road brand no harm at all. Rugged and purposeful, the Defender that features on screen is powered by a rumbling V8 and while not a production model there's a number of Tomb Raider special editions (pictured) available with some of the additions that feature on Lara's steed. As a marketing exercise Land Rover couldn't ask for better exposure, for while their 4x4 range may now include luxury models the brand is keen to continue its association with real off-road vehicles. As such don't rule out a sub Defender model with emphasis on off-road ability over everything else.

Price from: £15,995

Land Rover Freelander

Body styles: Estate, convertible
Engine capacity: 1.8, 2.5V6, 2.0Td4
Manufactured in: England

Only the Land Rover faithful didn't take to the Freelander 'soft roader'; everyone else across Europe took to it in droves, creating great demand and even waiting lists in some parts. Buyers were attracted to the rugged looks, car-like driving style and commanding driving position, and reassured by the clever Hill Descent Control and all-wheel-drive composure. The interior is just as tough as the exterior, and impressively flexible too, whilst the engines are smooth and fairly powerful. Last year's revisions brought many under-skin improvements and a superb BMW-supplied 2.0-litre Td4 diesel engine, of which they can't build enough to meet demand. The Freelander, available in three-door soft-top or five-door estate style, remains a desirable and impressive trend-setting vehicle.

Best All-Rounder: Freelander 2.0 Td4 Softback

Land Rover Defender

Price from: £19,925

As much as an icon as the Mini and Volkswagen Beetle, the Defender is one of a select few 'immortal' vehicles. It has survived pretty much unchanged for over half a century, yet it still continues to sell to loyal followers and fashion-conscious buyers. Built from aluminium, it is the 'no-nonsense' design that is the key to its appeal. Function instead of form, practicality instead of panache. It was designed to drive off-road, which it still does better than anything else, so, not surprisingly it is not as refined as modern vehicles on it. However, the excellent Td5 turbo-diesel engine helps, as does slightly more refined seats and trims in latest versions. It will always remain a 'physical' vehicle though, and is all the better for it.

Best All-Rounder: Defender Td5

Body styles: Estate
Engine capacity: 4.0V8, 2.5Td5
Manufactured in: England

Price from: £21,995

Land Rover Discovery

Body styles: Estate
Engine capacity: 4.0V8, 2.5Td5
Manufactured in: England

It may look like the 1989 original, but Land Rover's Discovery was thoroughly redesigned in 1998, bringing it bang into the 20th Century. A larger, better-quality interior, refined new turbo-diesel engine and advanced suspension system all featured; the latter is available with Active Cornering Enhancement, which optimises the ride and handling for both on and off-road use – impressive. The dramatic roll of older models is no more, for today's Discovery feels more stable than any other serious off-roader. Although there is a V8 engine offered, the smooth, powerful and economical five-cylinder turbo-diesel is good enough to question it. In all, a fine 4x4, which remains incredibly popular even after a decade. It sets the standards that other manufacturers aspire to.

Best All-Rounder: Discovery Td5

Range Rover

Price from: £36,995

The King of off-roaders may well be approaching the end of its lifespan, but its appeal shows no signs of fading. It is a cult vehicle across the world, especially in America, where its presence and refined but rugged class hold particular appeal. The interior ambience is even more desirable, with tremendous comfort and stately furnishings. The fact that the Range Rover no longer drives as well as the best is almost irrelevant. It rides well but handling is soft, whilst the V8 engines are powerful but frighteningly thirsty. The BMW-sourced six-cylinder turbo-diesel is a popular choice though coupled to the auto gearbox it can feel desperately sluggish. The Range Rover's 'niggles' don't really matter though; its tremendous allure easily overrules them.

Best All-Rounder: Range Rover 2.5 TD

Body styles: Estate
Engine capacity: 4.0V8, 4.6V8, 2.5Td5
Manufactured in: England

LEXUS

Few could have predicted the tremendous success of the luxury division of Toyota, not just in the US but on a world-wide scale. The American market can't get enough of them, Europeans too are attracted to the superb blend of luxury and, key in this marketplace, exceptional reliability. New models join the range, the SC430 luxury sports car selling out before official prices were even announced. A wagon version of the IS200/300 models also joins the model line up while the RX300 crossover SUV can't be built quick enough to satisfy demand. All in the Lexus brand continues to grow in strength by offering all that of the competition, at lower prices, without some of the associated badge snobbery of some of its European rivals.

NEW

Lexus SC430

Body styles: Convertible **Engine capacity:** 4.3V8

Price from: £50,850
Manufactured in: Japan

The new Lexus coupe is a stunning-looking car. But press a button, and you've got an equally-stunning Lexus convertible – it may be a copy of the Mercedes system, but it is still great. Underneath the yacht-like curves sits a wealth of advanced technology that makes driving the SC430 an effortless, but hugely rewarding experience. It is extremely quiet and smooth, but is softer than the competition and and as a result cannot compete through the bends - however advanced electronics keep everything on an even keel. Inside, as it is a Lexus for the American market, there is both plenty of space and loads of equipment. Best of all though, the SC430 is at last offered in Europe, which should offer strong competition to the similarly-priced class-favourite, the Jaguar XK8.

Best All-Rounder: SC430

Lexus IS200/300

Price from: £18,380

Designed to compete head-on with the legendary BMW 3-Series, the IS200 is a Japanese copy of the German icon; rear-wheel-drive, straight-six engine and a driver-focused feel. The exterior is attractive and distinctive, though the interior is more fussy and over-stylised in places. However, on the road, the IS200 excels, with a responsive, well-balanced chassis, sharp steering and a ride quality that is relaxing over long distances. The engine is also accomplished, with a wonderful soundtrack combined with uncanny smoothness that makes up for a lack of ultimate power; the upcoming 3.0-litre IS300 will solve this. Overall, the smallest Lexus is very impressive indeed, its appeal broadened with the addition of 'lifestyle estate' version - the Sportcross.

Best All-Rounder: IS200 2.0 Sport

Estate

Body styles: Saloon, estate
Engine capacity: 2.0, 3.0
Price from: £18,380
Manufactured in: Japan

Price from: £28,450

Lexus GS300/430

Body styles: Saloon
Engine capacity: 3.0, 4.3V8
Manufactured in: Japan

Lexus's stylish and distinctive BMW 5-Series and Mercedes E-Class rival is far more striking than its anonymous predecessor, launched in the mid 1990s. However, its appeal remains limited in Europe, a shame for its talents are wide-ranging. The interior, for example, is smart and flawlessly built, and equipped to a very high standard. It is also extremely refined. The GS300's 3.0-litre straight-six engine is smooth, while the GS430's 4.3-litre V8 engine is just as quiet, but impressively rapid, too. Handling is safe and precise, if not as sharp as the BMW, with the ride proving comfortable. Only very strong competition limits the success of the Lexus GS saloons. However, as a capable and individual alternative, it makes a fine buy.

Best All-Rounder: GS430

Lexus LS430

Price from: £49,950

All-new and even more crushingly capable than its predecessor, the Lexus LS430 is the largest and most advanced model in today's Lexus range. Equipped with the latest technology; air-conditioned seats, water-repellent glass and air suspension are highlights of a very long list. As ever, it is whisper-quiet inside at all speeds, riding and handling better than ever, too. It dismisses both bumps and corners as if they simply weren't there. The V8 engine supplies plenty of power – 373bhp means performance is effortless, while economy is reasonable too. Ten years ago, the original LS400 frightened European manufacturers into action, and the current LS430 remains a fine example of Japanese luxury saloon car engineering.

Best All-Rounder: LS430

Body styles: Saloon
Engine capacity: 4.3V8
Manufactured in: Japan

Price from: $32,000

Lexus ES300

Body styles: Saloon
Engine capacity: 3.0V6
Manufactured in: Japan

Enlightened buyers reckon the Toyota Camry is a more affordable Lexus, and this is confirmed in the US. The entry-level Lexus over there is no other than a rebadged Camry, complete with 3.0-litre V6 engine and distinctly 'Toyota' style. Thanks to a price almost $10,000 less than the GS saloon, it is Lexus of America's best-selling model – and it has enough ability to make it seem great value, especially when compared to US rivals. Refinement is the key, with a whisper-quiet engine, low road and wind noise, and a general feeling of serenity at all speeds. Handling isn't bad, the ride is commendable, but this is a car that excels at low-effort cruising. And, being a Lexus, build quality is faultless, too.

Best All-Rounder: ES300 V6

Lexus RX300

Price from: £28,950

A hit in America, the RX300 is rapidly gaining fans in the UK too. It is a stylish, modern-looking off-roader, with the all-important high seating position of 4x4s, but none of the on-road compromises. The car-like ride is smooth, and the handling is very safe and secure, with little of the typical 4x4 'lean' around bends. Interestingly, it is based on a car platform – that of the old Celica 4x4. The interior is extremely luxurious, and features plenty of high-tech gadgets and electronic aids. Quality is high, and refinement is well up to Lexus standards. A 3.0-litre V6 provides the power, and though it doesn't offer traditional 4x4 'crawler' ratios, few seem to mind; this is a 4x4 for the highway.

Best All-Rounder: RX300

Body styles: Estate
Engine capacity: 3.0V6
Manufactured in: Japan

Price from: $62,000

Lexus LX470

Body styles: Estate
Engine capacity: 4.7V8
Price from: £na
Manufactured in: Japan

Based on the enormous Toyota Landcruiser Amazon, few luxury off-roaders are as big as the Lexus LX470. But, as long as you don't have to park it or use it in town, the biggest Lexus is actually easy to drive, one of the benefits of such a commanding driving position. The huge 4.7-litre V8 engine provides plenty of power – just don't look at the fuel economy – and both ride and handling are impressive, considering the LX470's size. Noise levels are low, which, combined with a plush interior, make this huge 4x4 an effective luxury car, too. It may look little different to the Landcruiser from the outside, but the LX470 is an effective, expensive vehicle, that is very popular in the 4x4-obsessed US.

Best All-Rounder: LX470

LINCOLN

What used to be Ford's 'pensioner' division is now one of the USA's most modern and dynamic brands, with sleek designs and desirable all-new models constantly joining the fray. The Lincoln LS is the brand's newest entrant, taking its base from the Jaguar S-Type but adding its own blend of style and value; competitors are still reeling over the superb dynamics, good looks and remarkably low prices. Meanwhile, the huge Navigator appeals to upmarket SUV-seekers, whilst the traditional Continental and Town Car remain fine luxury limousine contenders. Ford seems set to keep Lincoln on its current sharp-edged course, meaning we can look forward to further attractive models in the future – and on today's evidence, subsequent increases in sales, too.

Lincoln Navigator

Body styles: Estate
Engine capacity: 5.4V8

Price from: $44,700
Manufactured in: United States

As huge as the Ford Expedition upon which it is based, the Navigator can rightly be called Lincoln's saviour. Since its introduction, it has sold in huge numbers and shows no signs of losing any popularity yet. Powered by a 5.4-litre V8 engine, the Navigator is available in 2WD and 4WD form, and uses the Expedition's fairly crude underpinnings. This means it does not drive with anything like the sophistication of more modern rivals, but it remains comfortable and smooth if you don't push it too much. The engine may offer plenty of encouragement, but this is best as a cruiser, a job helped by the chunky looks and glitzy details. Huge space and equipment levels add further desirability to this gargantuan vehicle.

Best All-Rounder: Navigator 4WD

Price from: $34,200

Lincoln LS

Body styles: Saloon
Engine capacity: 3.0V6, 4.0V8
Manufactured in: United States

All you need to know is that, under the Lincoln LS's attractive styling, lies the chassis of a Jaguar S-Type. An instant fine pedigree, that has ensured the LS is well-known in Europe as well as the US. Engines are either 3.0-litre V6 or 3.9-litre V8, but it is the way the LS drives that is of more interest; it is said to handle even better than the Jaguar, yet still retains a fine ride. Such an inspired drive is helping to attract younger drivers into the Lincoln brand, essential if it is to expand further. If future models are as good as the LS – and remain as incredibly well-priced – Lincoln's future looks bright. The LS is certainly a very desirable car.

Best All-Rounder: LS V8

Lincoln Continental

The luxurious Continental features an extravagant level of standard equipment, which helps add appeal to an otherwise fairly dull car. The Driver Select System, for example, allows customisation of areas such as steering weight and seat firmness; even the tone of the horn can be chosen. A voice-activated telecommunication system is also on the way. All this diverts attention from the Continental's looks, which are not as sharp as some rivals, and handling agility that only moderately succeeds in hiding its bulk. The ride is cosseting though, which in truth is what most drivers and passengers demand. The 4.6-litre V8 engine also provides plenty of silent power. Few limousines are more comfortable – if only it was a little more distinctive.

Best All-Rounder: Continental

Price from: $40,400

Body styles: Saloon
Engine capacity: 4.6V8
Manufactured in: United States

LOTUS

Surprising everybody with its new Elise, it is clear that Lotus can't afford to lose sales to recently introduced rivals - specifically the Vauxhall VX220/Opel Speedster that it produces for GM at its UK production facility at Hethel. Despite the factory being busier than it ever has there have been job loses, and production of the M250 Porsche Boxster-rivalling model has been shelved on the instructions of Malaysian owners Proton. Lotus expertise is still used by numerous car manufacturers, particularly to hone the ride and handling, activities that bring in more money than the car production division.

NEW

Lotus Elise

Body styles: Convertible
Engine capacity: 1.8

Price from: £22,995
Manufactured in: England

Recently fully revised, the best-selling Lotus ever is also one of the greatest. Staying true to the company's lightweight ethos, the Elise is a simple, elegant and devastatingly effective sports car that can outhandle almost anything else on the road. The key to its supremacy is the bonded aluminium chassis - exceptionally light, it is also extremely strong and rigid. When allied to the MGF's 1.8-litre engine, performance is incredibly rapid, and better than many more powerful rivals. Handling is delicate and intimate, with superb steering and wonderful feedback through all controls. It feels just like a single-seater race car. The new styling adds harder-edged looks, while it is a little more refined in the modified cabin, too. The Elise remains a landmark car.

Best All-Rounder: Elise 1.8

Price from: £na

Lotus Exige

Body styles: coupe
Engine capacity: 1.8
Manufactured in:
England

The race-track refugee Exige is basically an Elise coupe, and all the more outrageous for it. It is also directly derived from the Elise Championship race car, so is hot, noisy and difficult to get in and out of. Even Lotus admits it is not really a road car - but find the right road, or better still, the right race track, and few other cars can match the Exige for sheer thrills. Handling is superb, feedback is extraordinary, and if you want to know how a Le Mans car feels, this is a great place to start. Even the 1.8-litre Rover engine is authentically grumbly at low revs, but as you approach 8000rpm, the power and soundtrack thrill just like a racer. Sensational, affordable fun.

Best All-Rounder: Exige 1.8

Lotus Esprit

Price from: £49,950

Officially the world's most elderly supercar, the Esprit can still teach the younger generation a few tricks. Despite its age, for example, it always turns heads, with its rakish lines and ground-hugging stance. It also stays true to the supercar rulebook inside too, with limited visibility and a heavy gearchange and clutch. Find an open road, however, and all such niggles are forgotten - the Esprit handles astonishingly well. The steering is magic, grip is abundant and feedback is remarkable. It is a huge car, but it shrinks around you to feel almost like a race car - but with good ride quality and fair refinement, too. Add the very fast twin-turbo V8 engine, and the Esprit's survival is understandable. Compromised, aged, but great nonetheless.

Best All-Rounder: Esprit V8 GT

Body styles: coupe
Engine capacity: 3.5V8
Manufactured in:
England

MAZDA

Mazda has shown that it can successfully compete, indeed introducing, niche markets with the MX-5. Now looking to replicate that experience with a new range of more adventurous vehicles - including the dramatic RX-8 - the Japanese company is undergoing a transformation. The RX-8 features a new rotary engine - Mazda being the world leaders in the production of this radical technology. Meanwhile the existing model range has been revised to improve performance, while styling tweaks give them a more corporate look. Part owned by Ford Mazda is looking to become a larger global player, something it looks increasingly likely to achieve.

NEW

Mazda MX-5

Body styles: Convertible
Engine capacity: 1.6, 1.8
Price from: £14,995
Manufactured in: Japan

The world's best-selling sports car just gets better as the years go by. 2002 models feature a revised interior and engine line-up, though the classic looks have essentially been left well alone; the MX-5 still pays homage to the original Lotus Elan. The way it drives is also fabulous, with an immensely exploitable rear-wheel-drive chassis that is one of the friendliest and least intimidating around, tremendous steering feel and surely the world's best flick-switch gearbox. The latest engines are strong too, making the MX-5 a surprisingly rapid cross-country car. Best of all, the MX-5 is a supreme 'feel-good' car; throw in some sunshine to bask in, and few cars are as enjoyable as Mazda's popular roadster. Familiar, but still great.

Best All-Rounder: MX-5 1.8i

Mazda Demio

Price from: £8,735

Body styles: Hatchback
Engine capacity: 1.3, 1.5
Manufactured in: Japan

The concept is sound; a supermini-sized car with the space of a family model and styling that hints at MPVs and off-roaders. The high-set driving position gives good visibility, and the rear seats can slide to boost either luggage or passenger space. However, in practice, things are a little less clear-cut. The 1.3 and 1.5-litre engines are fine around town but struggle on the open road. The chassis runs out of ideas when pushed too, and ride comfort is always firm becoming quite bumpy over poor surfaces. Really, the Demio is a car best restricted to town use, where its ease of use make it a good choice for the practical but undemanding driver.

Best All-Rounder: Demio 1.3

Mazda 323

Price from: £10,780

NEW

The cleanly-styled 323 is Mazda's very attractive and solid-looking VW Golf-class competitor. A recent facelift adds a revised front end and new engines, making the five-door hatchback look even more attractive. Build quality is naturally excellent, and though the interior is a little dull, it is comfortable and well-equipped. On the road, the 323 is very eager, with smooth, powerful and refined engines, and sharp handling that is very responsive and composed. The ride quality is also reasonable, taking the rough edges off poor surfaces. High-mileage reliability is assured, and the 323 will also be economical and cheap to run, too. Not the most outlandish car in its class, it is nevertheless a fine and capable all-rounder.

Best All-Rounder: 323 1.5 GXi

Hatchback

Body styles: Hatchback, saloon
Engine capacity: 1.3, 1.6, 2.0, 2.0TD
Manufactured in: Japan

Price from: £13,980

Mazda 626

Estate

Body styles: Hatchback, saloon, estate
Engine capacity: 1.8, 2.0, 2.5V6, 2.0TD
Manufactured in: United States

The forgotten family car. Mazda's 626 may well offer superb refinement, good comfort and top-notch build quality, but it fades into the background against the likes of the Ford Mondeo and Volkswagen Passat. This is a pity, for it has many attributes, including a range of effortless and subdued engines, an easy-going nature and generous equipment levels. Unfortunately, the smooth but bland styling and interior also sum up the driving experience; it is competent, but unexciting. Ride quality is fair, as is the handling, but it is never a car you'll drive just for the sake of it. This is the 626's biggest problem, especially as many rivals are so exciting in comparison. Great for the undemanding, value-seeking driver.

Best All-Rounder: 626 2.0 Sport

Mazda Premacy

Price from: £13,995

Based on the good-to-drive 323, the Premacy is Mazda's answer to the hugely successful Renault Scenic mini-MPV. It is a very well-developed car, with plenty of space for passengers and a huge boot. The seats are also multi-adjustable, though a little firm for some tastes. There are not as many of the nice touches that makes the Scenic so desirable though - but high equipment levels compensate. The engines - 100 or 115bhp 1.8-litre petrol, or 2.0-litre direct injection turbo-diesel - are all strong, and the driving experience is just as good as the 323 hatchback's. Add in the fine build quality and promise of strong reliability, and the Premacy appears to offer a strong package in what is now a very crowded marketplace.

Best All-Rounder: Premacy 1.8 GSi

Body styles: Compact MPV
Engine capacity: 1.8, 2.0TD
Manufactured in: Japan

Mazda Xedos 9

Price from: £na

Body styles: Saloon
Engine capacity: 2.0V6, 2.3V6, 2.5V6
Manufactured in: Japan

The executive marketplace is one of the most cut-throat of all; prestige badges rule, with few others getting a look-in. So with the benefit of neither a 'badge' nor real presence, Mazda's Xedos 9 struggles in the UK. It does have its merits though. The styling, although discrete, is actually quite sleek and good-looking, and all engines are quiet and powerful - especially the unique Miller Cycle unit. Inside, it is a little dated, but very well-equipped and comfortable, though room in the rear is a little tight. It provides a sporty drive, with a firmish ride that benefits cornering agility and composure. However, it takes a brave buyer to choose the Xedos 9 over the more obvious choices. Not many dare to be different.

Best All-Rounder: Xedos 9 2.5

Mazda Tribute

Price from: £na

It certainly is a tribute to the Ford Maverick upon which it is based. The Mazda is arguably the better-looking of the two models, and should offer better resale value thanks to greater exclusivity. It is a proper 'sports utility', for American consumption above all, so offers fine handling and on-road comfort at the expense of ultimate off-road ability. The cabin is also spacious, and practical enough for five people and all their luggage. Mazda offers the same 2.0-litre four-cylinder and 3.0-litre V6 engines as the Maverick, with both proving fairly lively and not too uneconomical. It promises to be a fine, if understated vehicle, that may well be a rare sight in the UK.

Best All-Rounder: Tribute V6

Body styles: Estate
Engine capacity: 2.0, 3.0V6
Manufactured in: United States

Price from: £16,995

Mazda MPV

Body styles: MPV
Engine capacity: 2.0, 2.5V6
Manufactured in: Japan

A late entrant into the full-size MPV market, Mazda's cunningly-titled MPV should be one of the best. In areas such as seat comfort and interior room, it is. Entry is easy thanks to the sliding rear doors, and there is plenty of luggage space - not always the case for MPVs. However, the sheer size of the Mazda means the 2.0-litre and 2.5-litre V6 engines struggle to haul it along - they're also fairly intrusive when worked hard, too. Add in a slightly awkward driving position, occasionally jittery ride quality and handling that is not all that responsive, and it becomes clear the Mazda is not an MPV for those who enjoy driving. Impressively practical, but its rivals make better overall packages.

Best All-Rounder: MPV 2.0

MASERATI

There was a time when the Maserati was a serious rival for its Italian compatriot Ferrari - but then its fortunes became bleak. Now under Ferrari's control the Trident badged cars have had a remarkable turn around, the 3200GT coupe being the model that has led the revival. Now a Spyder (convertible) version joins the coupe; more than a simple roof removal conversion, it gets a shortened wheelbase and an all-new V8 fitted .The Spyder spearheads a return to the lucrative North American market, while a new Quattroporte (four-door) model is also planned, though quite when it will appear is still unknown. Despite improved sales, the 3200GT still remains a relative rarity, if anything increasing its desirability to a market largely dominated by the Porsche 911 and Jaguar XK8.

NEW

Maserati Spyder

Engine capacity: 4.2V8

Price from: £na

Manufactured in: Italy

Just to confirm its renaissance, Maserati reveals the Spyder, which is, in every respect, a stunner. It not only embodies a new and even-more desirable style, but features an engine whose pedigree and breeding is among the finest on earth. Developed by Ferrari, the 4.2-litre V8 produces an astounding 390bhp, offering a maximum speed of over 175mph - said to be almost unbeatable for a sports car. Furthermore, the fantastic noise it makes will be offered in surround-sound thanks to the convertible roof; plan your journeys around tunnels. An optional F1-style paddle-shift gearbox and computer-controlled automatic suspension complete the finely-honed driving picture, while inside, improved details and even more luxury further add to the Spyder's desirability. An instant classic.

Best All-Rounder: Spyder V8

Maserati 3200GT

Price from: £60,950

The 3200GT marks the stunning return to form for the mystical sports car manufacturer. Maserati's rediscovery of the magic it had in the 1960s is evident both in the stylish exterior and lavish, leather-lined interior; it is a classically elegant car, and now built to a high standard too, thanks to input from owner Ferrari. The twin-turbo 3.2-litre V8 engine produces massive power - 370bhp - but is rather languid at low revs, until the turbos spool up to provide slingshot pace. It sounds great too. The handling is also impressive, and can be varied via the adjustable suspension settings, but on any mode the ride is sportingly firm. It may not appeal to everyone, but the 3200GT is a stylish car that offers a charismatic driving experience.

Body styles: Coupe
Engine capacity: 3.2V8, 4.2V8
Manufactured in: Italy

Best All-Rounder: 3200GT

A couple of years back things weren't looking good for the funky city car, though there is now a revival of interest in the diminutive two-seater. The wacky styling certainly turns heads but for those wanting more attention there's a new convertible offering. A sports version has been shown as a concept for years, but recent shots of it out testing on European racetracks means that it is finally looking close to production. Still only available in left-hand-drive (which seems to do little to curb sales in the UK) the smart is a fun, if expensive, alternative to a scooter, or even public transport around city centres. As much a fashion statement as a personal transport solution, the brand's reliance on fickle young buyers may prove costly in the long run.

smart

NEW

smart Convertible

Body styles: Convertible
Engine capacity: 0.6, 0.8CDi

Price from: £9,600
Manufactured in: France

The cheekiest soft-top on sale is also the UK's cheapest sun-seeker. Apart from the folding roof, it is basically identical to the smart city car, which means performance from the three-cylinder turbo-charged engine is nippy, and handling is perfect for car-jammed city centres. Generous equipment and extensive options lists mean personalisation is easy, and the plastic body panels make colour changes simple to achieve, too. The convertible roof is a further boost to the smart's appeal, proving both easy to use and well-insulated when raised. It is not a full 'drop-top', but is the next-best thing - and just as safe as the hard-top. A very appealing car for all weathers, it will further broaden the smart's already-considerable success.

Best All-Rounder: smart Passion convertible

smart Coupe

Price from: £5,700

In the most stylish cities across Europe, it is one of THE cars to be seen in. Conceived by watch maker Swatch but developed and produced by Mercedes, the two-seat city-car really is a car for the millennium; it is unlike anything else on the road. Only in real life can its minuscule size be fully appreciated, though incredible packaging yields more than enough room for two passengers, and a fair amount of luggage. The tiny three-cylinder turbo-charged engines feature a six-speed semi-automatic 'Tiptronic' style gearchange, and offers more than enough performance for town and motorway use. Handling is extremely safe and the ride is better than it was.

Body styles: Hatchback
Engine capacity: 0.6, 0.8CDi
Manufactured in: France

Best All-Rounder: smart Pulse

MERCEDES-BENZ

Celebrating 100 years of building cars, Mercedes-Benz has never offered so much to so many. The marque has introduced and renewed a number of key models in the past year, though there's more to come, including a new E-Class, M-Class and an A-Class based mini-sports utility vehicle. The SL has been replaced with a striking new model featuring an innovative roof folding mechanism like that on the SLK, while a significantly revised E-Class also joins the model line up. A new compact MPV dubbed Vaneo is due soon while the SLR McLaren supercar promises to be something special for the super wealthy. Add in the ultra luxury Maybach and Mercedes looks like it's in fine fettle. Under the façade, though, there's financial woe as the Chrysler partnership draws heavily on the German giant's coffers.

NEW

Mercedes-Benz SL

Body styles: Convertible
Engine capacity: 5.0V8
Price from: £na
Manufactured in: Germany

Best All-Rounder: SL500

Like so many classic models there's always a fear that their replacement will mean a dilution of the characteristics that made the original so special. The old SL ran for 12 years, still being a deeply impressive car prior to its replacement. The new model picks up where the old car left off. Now featuring a folding hard top among its extensive technical specification, the SL is a fantastic looking car that combines hints of SL models throughout the ages while looking thoroughly contemporary. Available initially with a 5.0-litre V8 engine, the range will be extended through time with the addition of six–cylinder units and, naturally, more powerful versions. The first car to feature electronic brake-by-wire, the SL is a technological tour-de-force, and as such is a fitting figurehead to the Mercedes range.

Mercedes Sports Coupe

Price from: £21,140

Based on the C-Class platform, Mercedes is targeting a more youthful market with this 'Sports Coupe'. Little more than a hatchback C-Class, and, despite protestations to the contrary, a rival for the BMW Compact, the C-Class Sports Coupe goes some way to fulfiling its grandiose title. Fun to drive, the chassis is never really troubled by the power from the wide range of engines, which includes two super-charged models of 2.0 and 2.3-litre capacity, a 1.8-litre petrol and a 2.2-litre diesel. Indeed of all the engines it's the diesel that offers the best all-round package, with enough punch to make it an able cross country performer and economy to keep trips to the pumps to a minimum.

Best all-rounder: C220 CDi

Body styles: Coupe,
Engine capacity: 1.8, 2.0K, 2.3K, 2.2CDi
Manufactured in: Germany, South Africa

Price from: £13,025

Mercedes-Benz A-Class

Body styles: Hatchback
Engine capacity: 1.4, 1.6, 1.9, 1.7CDi
Manufactured in: Germany

Astonishingly the standard A-Class is shorter than a Ford Ka in standard form, though the new long-wheelbase version offers more rear legroom than the S-Class luxury car. A very clever car indeed, it has now fully recovered from its troubled birth. Its height allows occupants to sit more upright, benefiting legroom as well as giving a commanding feel on the road. It is extremely safe, with lots of electronic aids deigned to help accident avoidance in the first place. Engines are economical and perform well, and it is only really the A-Class's chassis that lets the side down; the ride can get jittery, and the handling is dull because of inert steering. Better in town than on the open road, its popularity is understandable.

Best All-Rounder: A160 Elegance

Mercedes-Benz C-Class

Price from: £21,140

Mercedes has ditched its mature image over the past few years, as it chases a younger, more dynamic group of buyers. The C-Class is the latest model to benefit from this shift in outlook, sporting a look not unlike that of the S-Class. Rewarding to drive, the new Mercedes is aiming directly at BMW's 3-Series, so it is far sportier than the model it replaces. It is also better equipped, with plenty of gadgets and unique features, and the option of five-speed automatic or six-speed manual gearboxes. The engine range is extensive, and although the four-cylinder units are harsh when extended, the V6s are fine, and the CDI diesels are economical. A very strong entrant in the competitive junior executive market.

Best All-Rounder: C200 Kompressor

Estate

Body styles: Saloon, coupe, estate
Engine capacity: 2.0, 2.6V6, 3.2V6, 2.2CDi, 2.7CDi
Manufactured in: Germany, South Africa

Price from: £24,040

Mercedes-Benz E-Class

Estate

Body styles: Saloon, estate
Engine capacity: 2.0, 2.6V6, 2.8V6, 3.2V6, 4.3V8, 5.5V8, 2.2CDi, 2.7CDi, 3.2CDi
Manufactured in: Germany

This is an 'old style' Mercedes, before the current sportier edge took hold. As such, it is large, bulky, imposing but thoroughly competent. There is also an estate version, which is simply enormous, but again aesthetics take second place to practicality. The E-Class is very safe, with side and window airbags being added a few years ago to further enhance its record. Otherwise, standard equipment levels can be a little mean, though all the essentials are usually found as standard. The engine range is simply huge, and all variants are smooth and refined; the V6 and V8 versions proving rapid. Although the E-Class can be dull to drive, it is supremely comfortable and refined. The imminent next version will be far sportier, too.

Best All-Rounder: E280 Elegance

Mercedes-Benz S-Class

Price from: £41,540

The S-Class is surely one of the most attractive Mercedes road cars ever - elegant and sleek, it disguises its substantial size incredibly well. The interior is just as elegant, and has been designed to create a wonderfully cohesive and inviting ambience. So it should come as no surprise to discover the S-Class drives superbly too. Air suspension means it both rides brilliantly and handles with small car-like agility, while all engines are refined and powerful. Interior comfort is supreme, with some of the best seats in the business - long-distance comfort is second to none. Its vast range of ability is quite remarkable, especially considering its very talented rivals. The best car in the world? By most standards, it is unquestionably so.

Best All-Rounder: S320

Body styles: Saloon
Engine capacity: 2.8V6, 3.2V6, 4.3V8, 5.0V8, 6.0V12, 3.2CDi, 4.0CDi
Manufactured in: Germany

Price from: £23,230

Mercedes-Benz V-Class

Body styles: MPV
Engine capacity: 2.3, 2.8, 2.2CDi
Manufactured in: Spain

Without doubt this is the weakest model in the current Mercedes range. Take note of the usual MPV criticism about vans with windows – for this is a van with windows, and it makes little effort to hide the fact. The benefit of this is tremendous interior room, with plenty of space for six comfortable 'captain's chairs', and the added benefit of sliding rear doors. There is a large luggage area too. However, on the road, the V-Class is much less convincing. Ride quality can be awful when compared to other Mercedes cars, while the handling is ponderous. The smaller engines struggle against the sheer mass of the V-Class, though the 2.8-litre V6 is better, if much thirstier. In all, unconvincing.

Best All-Rounder: V220 CDI

MERCEDES-BENZ

Mercedes-Benz SLK

Price from: £24,790

Body styles: Convertible
Engine capacity: 2.0, 2.3, 3.2V6
Manufactured in: Germany

'Sensible' sports cars rarely come more stylish than this. Famous for its clever folding hard top roof and trendy good looks, the SLK remains a car very much in demand. Inside, the retro-Mercedes dash has deeply-cowled instruments and brushed aluminium trim, as well as a comfortable driving position that calls for few compromises. On the road, however, it is not quite as sharp as the looks suggest being tuned more for comfort than ultimate cornering agility. This pays dividends on motorways but is not so good on back roads, where the dull steering and lack of feedback take the edge off things. Unusually it's the automatics that offer the better choice, Mercedes never quite mastering manual transmissions. Refined, all engines are powerful – the best being the 3.2-litre V6.

Best All-Rounder: SLK 320

Mercedes-Benz CLK

Price from: £26,340

Based on the old C-Class chassis but looking like an E-class coupe, the CLK is a Mercedes that still creates huge demand; both coupe and cabriolet models command waiting lists, and depreciation is negligible – thanks, no doubt, to the expensive image the car creates. The interior is just as tasteful, with classy trims and materials, comfortable seats and plenty of room for rear passengers, too. The fact that the CLK is not the most inspiring car to drive is therefore unimportant; it is very refined, smooth-riding and relaxing, but simply not the most dynamically-sharp coupe on sale. Better to use the power of the large engine range to cruise, and enjoy the attention.

Best All-Rounder: CLK 320

Coupe

Body styles: Coupe, convertible
Engine capacity: 2.0, 2.3, 3.2V6, 4.3V8, 5.5V8
Manufactured in: Germany

Mercedes-Benz CL

Price from: £66,440

Body styles: Coupe
Engine capacity: 5.0V8, 5.5V8, 6.0V12
Manufactured in: Germany

Even more beautiful than the S-Class upon which it is based, the CL coupe is a tremendous improvement over its ungainly predecessor. Sleek and svelte, it does not look like a two-tonne car – a remarkable achievement. Inside, it is just as inviting as the S-Class, with supremely comfortable seats, a great dash layout and almost every convenience imaginable. Semi-active suspension means it drives with unequalled composure too, using hydraulic pumps to maintain ride comfort without becoming wallowy over taxing surfaces. Ample power is provides by the large V8 and V12 engines, easily helping the CL reach high speeds on the autobahn, with no fuss. It is expensive, but it is a technological wonder that is currently all-but unrivalled.

Best All-Rounder: CL500

Mercedes-Benz M-Class

Price from: £31,140

This is the car that Mercedes-Benz hoped would knock the Range Rover off its perch. Built in the US, where the majority of the buyers are to be found, it never quite managed to gain the cachet of the British rival, even though it offered the space and the performance to compete on equal terms. One issue was the style, just too plain for a car of this price. Now it has been face-lifted for 2002, with improvements inside and out, as well as to the mechanicals. Now it is a much more viable contender, with two great diesels and a 5.0-litre V8 replacing the previous 4.3. The ML320 is a little under powered for the task; the ML55 fills the final piece of the jigsaw, though it is not as fast as you might expect.

Best All-Rounder: ML400CDI

Body styles: Estate
Engine capacity: 3.2V6, 5.0V8, 5.5V8, 2.7CDi, 4.0V8CDi
Manufactured in: Austria, United States

NEW

Mercedes-Benz G-Class

Price from: £na

Body styles: Estate
Engine capacity: 3.2V6, 5.0V8, 2.9TD, 4.0CDi
Manufactured in: Germany

Think again, if you thought all of today's Mercedes were sleek and sporty-looking. The G-Wagon dates back to 1980, and even then it looked square-set and angular. Nowadays, it is a tough, indestructible go-anywhere 4x4 with plenty of luxury and power. The interior is particularly plush, with plenty of walnut and leather trimmings. Impressively, it is available with a 5.0-litre V8 engine, producing nearly 300bhp, for eye-opening performance that is controlled admirably well by the rugged chassis. Although it used to be available officially in the UK, the G-Class is currently only offered in Europe. This may well change in the future – but with prices greater than the Range Rover, appeal may be limited. Desirable if you can afford it, though.

Best All-Rounder: G500

Fears that the MINI's appeal may be sullied by BMW ownership seem unfounded. The public's reaction to the cars is rapturous enthusiasm. Ever-lengthening waiting lists are testament to this, with the two model, One and Cooper, range being joined by the fire-cracking Cooper S in the spring of 2002. Other derivatives may follow, including cabriolet and Clubman (estate) versions - with a pick-up even rumoured. Aggressive pricing and a comprehensive after-sales package make the fashionable MINI a seriously tempting ownership proposition. While cynics may lament its lack of innovation, buyers are ignoring this and snapping them up quicker than BMW can make them. Production had better step up too, with entry to the US market on the cards, where, if it's marketed right, it should be a huge hit.

MINI

NEW

Mini Cooper

Engine capacity: 1.6

Price from: £11,600
Manufactured in: England

Instantly recognisable, the Cooper heads the MINI range until the arrival of the 160+bhp Cooper S version. Cynics still criticise the new MINI but the majority of people seem to be bowled over by its combination of the retro Mini lines in a modern, and incredibly well built, package. Inside there's still little space in the rear, but the rest of the Cooper feels right and suitably 'MINI'. As a sporting model the Cooper is certainly fun, with faithful and direct steering combined with a punchy 1.6-litre engine, giving it sufficient pace to beat the traffic around town and be an entertaining back road companion. Sure to be a sales success, the MINI may offer little of the innovation of the original but everything else is there, from its lively driving experience to its unmistakable character.

Best all-rounder: Cooper

Mini One

Price from: £10,300

While the One may be the 'entry-level' model in the current MINI line-up it's certainly no poor alternative to the more powerful and showy Cooper. With the same pert looks that make the Cooper so appealing, without some of the more obvious sporting accoutrements, the One is stylish and fun way to get about. Power from the 1.6-litre engine may be only 90bhp against the Cooper's 115bhp but it's only when you're pressing hard that you'd notice – the One being a perfectly capable all-round performer. The cabin is brimming with period details that hint to the old Mini, though the driving experience is thoroughly modern – and far safer with modern safety equipment. Of course it lacks space in the rear – but you'll be having too much fun to notice such trivialities.

Best all-rounder: One

Body styles: Hatchback
Engine capacity: 1.6
Manufactured in: England

NEW

The Mountaineer signals Ford's intended direction for its Mercury brand – dramatic styling with a sportier air than many of its rivals. However, the need to establish Lincoln as a global brand means Mercury has been left to meander a little – the Taurus-based Sable and large, outdated Grand Marquis show little of the Mountaineer's cutting-edge design, and appeal mainly to value-orientated retirees, who are seeking as much car as possible for their cash. The Explorer-based Mountaineer appears to signal the direction Mercury is going to take in the future though, so hopefully buyers will be able to look forward to more dramatic new designs in the next few years, especially as Lincoln is now well on the way to success.

Mercury Cougar

Body styles: Coupe
Engine capacity: 2.0, 2.5V6

Price from: $17,200
Manufactured in: United States

The Mercury Cougar may well look familiar – until recently it was also sold in the UK as the Ford Cougar. The American version is just as striking, and could be just the car Mercury needs to appeal to younger, sportier drivers. Engines are the familiar 2.0-litre four-cylinder and 2.5-litre V6 units, both providing decent power, and the V6 an eager soundtrack too. The UK Cougar always rode and handled well, something the US car replicates. The front-wheel-drive chassis is informative, whilst the ride deals with imperfections well. The Cougar also offers more room than most coupes for four passengers and the low list price makes it a strong competitor to less sporty rivals.

Best All-Rounder: Cougar V6

Price from: $23,800

Mercury Grand Marquis

Body styles: Saloon
Engine capacity: 4.6V8
Manufactured in: Canada

Incredibly, the Grand Marquis is basically more than two decades old, yet still shows no signs of going out of production. The separate-frame chassis, bench seats for six and lazy 4.6-litre V8 engine all show where its roots lie, yet it still appeals to a certain class of buyer; few cars are as supple, making it a superb cruiser. That V8 offers strong performance, and the armchair-like seating, especially with optional leather trim, create more of a sitting-room atmosphere – it feels far more than 'just a car'. Of course, the dynamics belong to a past era too, and pressing the Grand Marquis hard is inadvisable. Just look at the price, the equipment, the big V8 and the comfort offered for reasons why the big Mercury still sells.

Best All-Rounder: Grand Marquis GS

Mercury Villager

Price from: $23,300

The Mercury Villager is also sold as a Nissan, but the American version is much glitzier than its Japanese sister. The Nissan 3.3-litre V6 also helps further the classy image; it is extremely sweet and quiet, and fairly powerful, too. Equipment is generous, with all models featuring air conditioning and power operation of the usuals. Those Japanese roots also show in the way the Villager drives, for it is very competent in both ride and handling, with no nasty surprises or lack of composure. Mercury's minivan is a very competent and classy vehicle; with just a little more space inside, it would provide stiff competition to rivals. As it is, others offer that crucial extra edge in practicality.

Best All-Rounder: Villager Estate

Body styles: MPV
Engine capacity: 3.3V6
Manufactured in: United States

Price from: $29,300

Mercury Mountaineer

Body styles: Estate
Engine capacity: 4.0V6, 4.6V8
Manufactured in: United States

Great styling, especially at the front-end, marks the Mountaineer out as an extremely desirably sports utility vehicle. Based on the new Ford Explorer, its roots become clear as you move back, but it is still far more distinctive than Ford's offering. Engines are the same, offering a choice between 4.0-litre V6 and a 4.6-litre V8. Both are impressive, but it is the improvements to the chassis that really mark out the Mountaineer as something special. Just as Ford's new Explorer is a huge advance over the old model, so too is the Mercury a vast improvement – both ride and handling are now up with the class best. Comfort is good and, with seating for up to eight people, the Mountaineer is one of the most practical vehicles of its size.

Best All-Rounder: Mountaineer 4WD

Mercury Sable

Price from: $20,100

Based on the chassis of the Ford Taurus, Mercury's Sable is far more subtly-styled. However, as the Taurus itself had to be redesigned because its looks were a turn-off, this is probably not a bad thing. Power is provided by to 3.0-litre V6 engines, providing power outputs of 153bhp and 215bhp. Like the Taurus, the Sable provides an adequate drive; it is not exciting, but competent in all conditions, with a well-controlled ride. Equipment is also generous, and a front bench seat is offered, which means up to six people can be seated. It is more expensive than the Taurus but has a classier image, making it a more exclusive choice while keeping all the Ford's many strengths.

Best All-Rounder: Sable LS

Body styles: Saloon, estate
Engine capacity: 3.0V6
Manufactured in: United States

MG ROVER

Last year it looked like the writing was on the wall for the troubled Rover marque. The acrimonious divorce from BMW had business commentators forecasting doom, though the reality has been more promising. Despite announcing huge losses the ambitious revival plan is starting to take shape. New MG models underline the engineering talent in the company, transforming the middle of the road Rover range into more focussed driver-orientated machines. The take over of Qvale, the Italian company which produced the Mangusta, gives MG the base for a new flagship sports car, and more importantly a useful entry into North America – the Mangusta already having type-approval for the US market. Working with motorsport suppliers MG Rover hopes to turn around new models quickly, a 45 / ZS replacement expected sometime in 2004.

NEW

MG ZT/Rover 75

Estate

Body styles: Saloon, estate
Engine capacity: 1.8, 2.0V6, 2.5V6, 2.0CDT

Price from: £16,495
Manufactured in: England

The Rover 75 is the youngest model in the MG Rover range and by a significant margin. Developed during the BMW years, the 75 is a junior executive model of acclaim, blending a modern front-drive chassis, smooth and powerful power trains with a traditional look and feel that is unmistakably Rover. The hot MG version, the ZT, takes this relaxed cruiser and turns it into a more focussed driver's machine – to good effect. Devoid of chrome inside and out the ZT looks the part. Power initially comes from the 190 bhp V6 engine that gives the ZT sufficient poke, but for those wanting more there's more powerful rear-wheel-drive V8's under development. Make no mistake the ZT is a seriously good car.

Best all-rounder: MG ZT-T

NEW

MG ZS/Rover 45

Body styles: Hatchback, saloon
Engine capacity: 1.4, 1.6, 1.8, 2.0, 2.5V6, 2.0TD

Price from: £9,980
Manufactured in: England

Of all the cars in the current Rover line up the 45, is the most ignored. Seen as a model for the retirement market, it's a worthy if rather dull alternative to more competent, and youthful, rivals. Hardly the best basis for an 'outrageous fun for everyone' MG derivative, you might expect then. Of the three new MG models, however, it's this, the ZS, that has gained the most praise. While the add-on bodykit may not sit as well on its siblings; the ZS impresses most where it matters - behind the wheel. The chassis has been tuned to deliver sharp responses, while with the 180bhp V6 it outguns the current MG range topper - the ZT 190 – and delivers a suitably sporting rasp to add to the enjoyment. Impressive stuff indeed.

Best all-rounder: MG ZS 180.

NEW

Price from: £7,995

MG ZR/Rover 25

Body styles: Hatchback
Engine capacity: 1.1, 1.4, 1.6, 1.8, 2.0TD
Manufactured in: England

The Rover 25 has always been a popular model, despite a number of shortcomings – notably space. Its cheeky charm and neat lines gained enough approval for buyers to ignore this however - both as the 25 and as the 200 as it was previously badged. Now available 'MG-d' the 25 becomes the ZR in its sporty suit. The 25 is a tidy handler in its own right and the MG ZR builds on this. With the widest range of engines on offer in the MG range, the ZS is unsurprisingly the entry level sporting model, and hence the volume seller. It's a convincing package too, from the old school – delivering raw thrills that are hard to find among its contemporaries. That alone should win it sales.

Best all-rounder: MG ZS 180.

MG Rover MGF

Price from: £15,500

Body styles: Convertible
Engine capacity: 1.6, 1.8
Manufactured in: England

Until recently the MGF was the only car to feature the MG badge. Now joined by a range of sporting hatches and saloons the MGF gains a smaller 1.6 litre engine choice and the Sport Trophy model to increase its appeal. The addition of the Sport Trophy sees a hike in power, though it's stiffened ride ruins the delicacy of the sweet handling standard car. The 1.6-litre engine choice makes the MGF slower, only slightly, though opens the MGF to a wider market with its reduced entry-level price. Bigger changes are expected soon with a revised model waiting to be revealed, though the current mid-engined roadster still has the goods to compete well with newer competition.

Best all-rounder: MGF1.8VVC

MITSUBISHI

Reducing its prices in the UK market on what seems like a daily basis, the Japanese manufacturer is suffering from the lack of interest in its comprehensive, and competent, range of vehicles. Clever GDi technology and legendary names like the Shogun and Lancer EVO models have done little to increase brand awareness across the remainder of the model range. Additionally the tie up with DaimlerChrysler has, as yet, had little impact, though expect some shared technology throughout the ranges as the cash crisis continues. While only partially owned by the German/US conglomerate it looks like it will be swallowed up wholly in the future. Little in the way of new models, save for the EVO VII, which should also see a return to success for the rally team.

NEW

Mitsubishi Lancer Evo VII

Body styles: Saloon
Engine capacity: 2.0T
Price from: £na
Manufactured in: Japan

There's no denying the Evo VII looks the part. Huge wings, massive air intakes and striking alloy wheels all make the four-door Mitsubishi saloon look incredibly menacing. And the thing is, it's even more dramatic on the move. The 2.0-litre engine provides plenty of power, but it is the car's chassis that steals all the headlines. It is packed with clever gadgetry and electronic software, ensuring that it almost doesn't matter what speed you pile into corners – the car will drag you through in one piece, in a hugely thrilling and informative manner. So what if the interior is dull? It is a spacious family car with the ability to embarrass Ferraris – for a tiny fraction of the price. A true supercar bargain in disguise.

Best All-Rounder: Evo VII

Mitsubishi Colt

Price from: £7,960

Body styles: Hatchback
Engine capacity: 1.3, 1.5, 1.6
Manufactured in: Japan

Soon to be replaced, the Colt continues to offer plenty for the undemanding driver. The styling is reasonably smart, the interior adequately comfortable and well-equipped. The Colt is an unusual car to classify, for it is larger than most superminis, yet offers less space in the rear than many, and comes only in three-door guise. Supermini-rivalling prices make it look good value though, especially considering the driving experience. All controls are light, the engines are sweet and refined, and around town the Colt is an extremely easy car to drive. It lacks any real agility out on the open road, but it is not aimed at the sort of driver who would notice this; it is an easy-going driver's dream.

Best All-Rounder: Colt 1.6 GLX

Mitsubishi Carisma

Price from: £11,180

How misleading can you get? The Carisma has no charisma, for it is one of the dullest mid-size cars on the market. Forgettable styling houses an unadventurous interior which, although well-equipped, does not inspire in any way. The same could be said about the driving experience, which is fairly well-composed but uninvolving, while the ride is reasonable - making it a good motorway cruiser. The engines are its redeeming feature, especially the 1.8 GDI direct-injection petrol unit, which offers a choice between decent performance or diesel-like fuel economy. Interior packaging is just as sensible, with plenty of space front and rear, comfortable seats and a generously-sized boot.

Best All-Rounder: Carisma 1.8 GDI

Body styles: Hatchback, saloon
Engine capacity: 1.6, 1.8GDi, 1.9TD
Manufactured in: Netherlands

Mitsubishi Space Star

Price from: £9,960

Body styles: Compact MPV
Engine capacity: 1.3, 1.6, 1.8GDi, 1.9TD
Manufactured in: Netherlands

The clever Space Star is an often overlooked contender in the Renault Scenic mini-MPV class. The tall five-door body looks like a cross between a hatchback and an estate, but is ideally shaped to provide impressive interior space. Combined with a wide track, front and rear-seat passengers enjoy plenty of space, with a decently-sized boot too. Only a lack of flexibility lets it down in the mini-MPV stakes, for although the rear seat can be slid fore and aft, it can't be removed, and there aren't the neat touches found in other makes. It is good to drive though, with a comfortable chassis and smooth, economical engines. Competitive prices and high equipment levels also help its case.

Best All-Rounder: Space Star 1.8 GDI

Mitsubishi Galant

Price from: £15,995

The Galant is an excellent Audi A4 rival that is sadly ignored by the majority of UK buyers. Sharply styled, it is distinctive and imposing - but without the image of the German brands, success alludes it. This is a shame, for on the road, the Galant is impressive, with a sporty driving experience, fine refinement and superb range of engines; the 280bhp 2.5-litre V6 twin-turbo in the VR4 is simply astonishing. It is practical too, with comfortable seats, plenty of room and a particularly spacious estate load-carrier. Combine all this with plenty of gizmos and a list price far lower than many of its rivals, and the Galant's lack of impact in the UK is even more surprising.

Best All-Rounder: Galant 2.5 V6

Estate

Body styles: Saloon, estate
Engine capacity: 2.0, 2.4, 2.5V6, 3.0V6
Manufactured in: Japan

Mitsubishi Magna

Price from: $29,000(Aus)

Engine capacity: 3.0V6, 3.5V6

Manufactured in: Australia

The Magna competes in Australia's medium/large family car market, and is produced over there in both saloon and estate format. Like many large Mitsubishis, it is good-looking and quite imposing, with a sinister nose and small windows. A 3.0-litre V6 engine features as standard in the base Executive, with all other models gaining a 3.5-litre V6 – Sports and VR-X models get an uprated, 220bhp version, with the option of a Tiptronic-style five-speed automatic. However, although responsive, the V6 units are also fairly fuel-efficient, thanks to the light kerb weight that modern engineering brings. This lack of excess also means it rides and handles well; add in the spacious, well-equipped interior, and the Magna appears to offer a class-winning package.

Best All-Rounder: Magna 3.5 V6 Altera

Mitsubishi Space Wagon/Runner

Price from: £16,995/£na

One of the original MPVs, the latest incarnation of the Space Wagon was larger than its predecessor, and has become more of a Ford Galaxy competitor. Like many of its rivals, it offers three rows of seats and a very flexible interior, with plenty of storage space and equipment. The seats fold and slide, but a downside – common to MPVs – is a lack of luggage space for seven people. Behind the wheel it is comfortable, and the driving experience is very refined, with good ease-of-use and a smooth ride for passengers. The engines are refined and economical too. The smaller Space Runner is similar but smaller, with just two rows of seats and a 1.8-litre engine. Prices for both models are keen.

Best All-Rounder: Space Wagon 2.4

Body styles: MPV
Engine capacity: 2.0, 2.4, 3.0V6/1.8, 2.0, 2.4
Manufactured in: Japan

Mitsubishi FTO

Price from: £22,995

Body styles: Coupe
Engine capacity: 1.8, 2.0V6
Manufactured in: Japan

The dramatic curves, flared wheel arches and swoopy profile of the stylish FTO consistently turn heads, and if the interior is remarkably dull and boring in comparison, the driving experience soon makes up for it. The 2.0-litre V6 is the star, with variable valve timing giving it a Jekyll and Hyde character – ordinary below 6000rpm, manic at 8000rpm, where 200bhp is produced. Firm ride apart, the chassis is also very good, diving into corners with tremendous agility and composure. 1.8-litre and automatic versions are also available, offering slightly fewer thrills. The FTO's days are numbered, but it remains a great Japanese sports coupe.

Best All-Rounder: FTO 2.0 GPX

MITSUBISHI

Mitsubishi Eclipse

Price from: £na

Coupe

Body styles: Coupe, convertible
Engine capacity: 2.4, 3.0V6
Manufactured in: Japan

Hinted to be the FTO's successor, the US-built Eclipse is currently only sold in its country of manufacture. It was also styled by an American design team, which followed what was called a 'geo-mechanical' brief; that's lots of sharp edges blended with soft, round bits. It also has a reasonable interior, which is naturally very well-equipped. Under the sharp bonnet sits either a 2.4-litre four cylinder or 3.0-litre V6 engine – both are very smooth and refined, as well as impressively powerful. The handling is alert and chuckable, with precise steering and good ride quality. The convertible version adds open-air enjoyment to the package, which in either form is competitively-priced.

Best All-Rounder: Eclipse GT

Mitsubishi Space Gear

Price from: £na

Less of a people carrier, more of a bus – the Mitsubishi Space Gear is huge. Seating up to eight in comfort, the sliding doors and completely flat floor allows them to get in and move around easily, too. The Land Rover-style 'Alpine' roof windows allow plenty of light into the rear, creating quite a pleasant atmosphere. The front-mounted engines of various sizes drive the rear wheels in standard guise, though there is the option of a four-wheel-drive version using running gear from the Shogun 4x4 – an unlikely off-roader. Top versions feature electronically-controlled suspension. It is popular in Europe and Japan, and interestingly is sold in many countries as a Hyundai. One of the most commodious people carriers on sale.

Body styles: MPV
Engine capacity: 2.0, 2.4, 3.0V6, 2.5TD, 2.8TD
Manufactured in: Japan

Best All-Rounder: Space Gear 2.8TD

Mitsubishi Shogun Pinin

Price from: £12,495

5 - Dr

Body styles: Estate
Engine capacity: 1.8, 2.0
Manufactured in: Italy

The butch Shogun inspired a cute little relative, the Shogun Pinin, which has helped Mitsubishi belatedly compete in the booming recreational 4x4 sector. Built in Italy at a new Pininfarina factory, the Italian design house also styled the Japanese manufacturer's smallest 4x4. A switchable 4x4 system helps it hold its head high off-road, at the expense of some on-road comfort; the ride can be choppy, and the handling is sometimes a little lively, with imprecise steering and a fair degree of body roll. More disappointing is the packaging of the three-door version; both rear and luggage space are minimal, but the five-door model is far better. The Carisma's GDI engines are superb - overall the Pinin is a fine mini-4x4 with plenty of head-turning style.

Best All-Rounder: Shogun Pinin 2.0 5dr

Mitsubishi Shogun/Pajero

Price from: £19,000

Subtle it ain't. Huge wheel arches, rippled flanks and brash two-tone paintwork make no attempt to hide the Shogun's massive bulk, and it seems buyers like it best that way. Underneath all the glitz, however, the Shogun is surprisingly advanced – it dispenses with the traditional 4x4 separate chassis, preferring a car-like monocoque layout instead. This pays dividends in on-road refinement, and ride comfort, and also helps make the Shogun impressively agile and accurate through the corners. Seven-seat capacity boosts its practicality and there's plenty of equipment to play with. All engines are powerful, refined and torquey – if pretty thirsty. Still, even though it is about as discrete as a slap in the face, the Shogun remains a very desirable vehicle.

5 - Dr

Body styles: Estate
Engine capacity: 3.5V6, 3.2DiD
Manufactured in: Japan

Best All-Rounder: Shogun 3.5 V6 5dr

Mitsubishi Shogun Sport

Price from: £19,000

Body styles: Estate
Engine capacity: 3.0V6, 2.5TD
Manufactured in: Japan

As the Shogun has moved further and further up-market, so the gap below it in Mitsubishi's range has grown. The Shogun Sport fills it, offering lower-tech construction, far less luxuries and refinements, but a cheaper package. It is a true 4x4, with its no-compromise suspension set-up proving all-but unstoppable, even over the roughest terrains. This makes for a firm on-road ride over harsh surfaces, but it is all quite controlled. The handling is fairly composed too, but this is a large vehicle that few will push to its limits. In normal driving, it is the very plain dashboard that is disappointing, for it is not even particularly practical, though it is well-equipped. Best as a diesel, the well-built Sport is a fine budget Shogun.

Best All-Rounder: Shogun Sport 2.5 TD

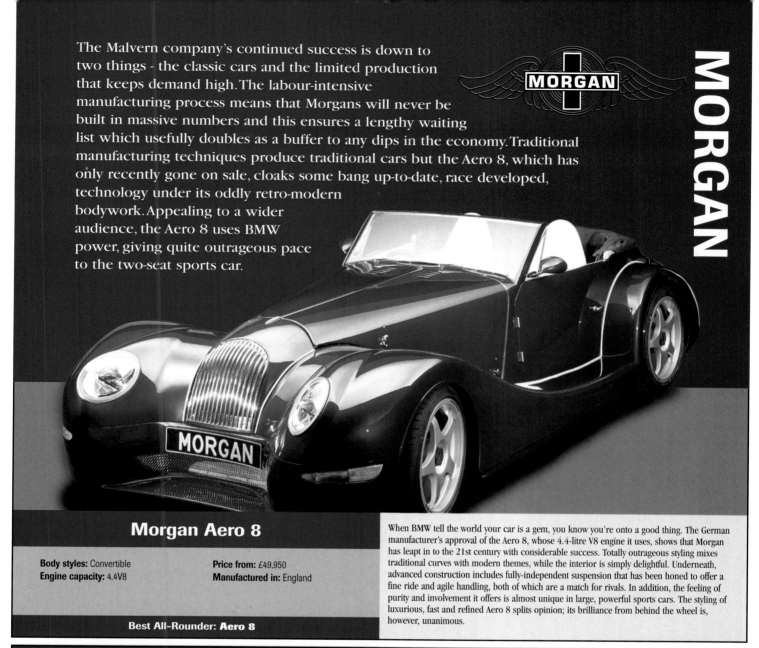

The Malvern company's continued success is down to two things - the classic cars and the limited production that keeps demand high. The labour-intensive manufacturing process means that Morgans will never be built in massive numbers and this ensures a lengthy waiting list which usefully doubles as a buffer to any dips in the economy. Traditional manufacturing techniques produce traditional cars but the Aero 8, which has only recently gone on sale, cloaks some bang up-to-date, race developed, technology under its oddly retro-modern bodywork. Appealing to a wider audience, the Aero 8 uses BMW power, giving quite outrageous pace to the two-seat sports car.

MORGAN

Morgan Aero 8

Body styles: Convertible
Engine capacity: 4.4V8

Price from: £49,950
Manufactured in: England

Best All-Rounder: Aero 8

When BMW tell the world your car is a gem, you know you're onto a good thing. The German manufacturer's approval of the Aero 8, whose 4.4-litre V8 engine it uses, shows that Morgan has leapt in to the 21st century with considerable success. Totally outrageous styling mixes traditional curves with modern themes, while the interior is simply delightful. Underneath, advanced construction includes fully-independent suspension that has been honed to offer a fine ride and agile handling, both of which are a match for rivals. In addition, the feeling of purity and involvement it offers is almost unique in large, powerful sports cars. The styling of luxurious, fast and refined Aero 8 splits opinion; its brilliance from behind the wheel is, however, unanimous.

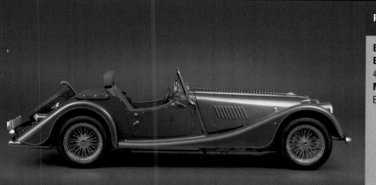

Price from: £31,948

Morgan Plus 8

Body styles: Convertible
Engine capacity: 4.0V8, 4.6V8
Manufactured in: England

All but identical to the 4/4, the Plus 8 features one major difference; its engine. Instead of the four-cylinder Ford unit, a rumbling great Rover V8 provides the power, and plenty of it. Available in 3.9-litre and 4.6-litre form, the latter produces 286bhp; in a car that is, in concept, over half a century old, this is certainly entertaining. Most drivers prefer to drive in a refined and relaxed manner, for the Plus 8 doesn't really like being pushed in the way more modern sports cars encourage. Enjoy the view down the long, graceful bonnet instead, as you effortlessly pilot your way around the English countryside, enjoying the admiring glances from all who you see. Off-beat and appealing, in an endearingly British way.

Best All-Rounder: Plus 8

Morgan 4/4

Price from: £21,590

The budget model in Morgan's range barely feels less special than its more expensive offerings, despite the presence of a 'lowly' four-cylinder engine under the curvaceous bonnet. The 1.8-litre Ford Zetec unit is fairly fast and refined, and surprisingly economical too. Of course, the rest of the Morgan is still from a bygone age, with the 'traditional' suspension offering classic-car levels of ride and handling. It is entertaining, but only true enthusiasts will realise that Morgans are about far more than driving dynamics. Character is the key, which even this 4/4 has by the bucket-load. The interior is unique, those sweeping curves cannot be found anywhere else, and in the eyes of true fans, the 4/4's competitive price makes it a real bargain.

Best All-Rounder: 4/4 1.8

Body styles: Convertible
Engine capacity: 1.8, 2.0
Manufactured in: England

NISSAN

The surprise take over by Renault in 2000 has seen little happen by way of shared models and technology between the Japanese and French concerns. Expect this to start changing soon with the next generation Micra sharing platforms and engines with the Clio's replacement. The new Primera is probably the most important new car, world-wide, for the firm in the near future, it at last adding attractive, even desirable, styling to its traditionally competent chassis. A new Skyline is also expected soon, both in luxury saloon form for its home market and as the technology-laden super coupe as it is best known in Europe. Allied to the new models, expect more technology sharing between Nissan and Renault, effecting better economies of scale and increasing profitability.

NEW

Nissan Primera

Body styles: Saloon
Engine capacity: 2.0, 2.5

Price from: £na
Manufactured in: England

The new Nissan Primera is a vast advance over the old model, not least because, for the first time, it is actually interesting to look at and sit in. The modern and sleek styling apes a concept car from a few years back, while the interior follows the same trend. Of course, the Primera always drove well, even if it didn't look as if it would, and the new model doesn't change this; engines are all smooth and powerful, and the handling is sharp without resulting in a harsh ride. The new interior is also very easy to use, and promises comfort for all shapes and sizes. Nissan may finally achieve the strong sales its Primera always deserved.

Best All-Rounder: Too soon to say

Nissan Micra

It may be a decade old, and have many superior rivals, but the Micra still offers a reasonable, good-value package. Fine 1.0-litre and 1.4-litre 16-valve engines are smooth, nippy and economical, and are mated to an easy-to-use clutch and gearbox. Indeed, the Micra's overall ease-of-use is where it really scores over rivals, but it is also refined, exceptionally reliable and well-built. Ride and handling are not quite as impressive, but the Micra offers a safe, fuss-free drive, and is in its element around town. It is only in space utilisation where the Micra's age really shows through - most of its rivals offer far more passenger and luggage room. A promising Renault co-developed replacement arrives in a year or two.

Best All-Rounder: Micra 1.0 GX

Price from: £7,250

Body styles: Hatchback
Engine capacity: 1.0, 1.4, 1.5D
Manufactured in: England

Price from: £9,995

Nissan Almera

5-Dr

Saloon

Body styles: Hatchback, saloon
Engine capacity: 1.5, 1.8, 2.2Di
Manufactured in: Japan

The sporty-looking Almera still lives under the shadow of its predecessor's dowdy image, which is a shame for it is an impressive step forward in most areas. The European designed interior is especially attractive, one of the best ever to grace a Japanese car ever. It is also practical and comfortable, with an almost-perfect driving position. On the move, all engines are adequately powerful and refined, and feature a brilliantly smooth gearchange. The handling is slick, just like the old model, though this is at the expense of a firmish ride. All of Nissan's traditional strengths remain, so build quality is exemplary, reliability is not an issue, and running costs should be low. Recent form suggests the image problem is being resolved, too.

Best All-Rounder: Almera 1.8 Sport

Nissan Almera Tino

Price from: £12,900

Based on the good-to-drive Almera, Nissan's Tino is a strong competitor for the market leader, Renault's Scenic. It too features five individual seats that slide, fold and can be removed, as well as a good-sized luggage bay and plenty of practical features. The overall design of the interior is one of Nissan's best, and is a very inviting and comfortable place to spend time in. It is also good to drive, with well-controlled handling, minimal body roll and a sporty but comfortable ride. All engines are useful, even the surprisingly effective 2.2-litre turbo-diesel, with the 2.0-litre being the preferable petrol option. The mini-MPV market is very competitive, but Nissan's able Almera Tino appears to be succeeding, no doubt thanks to that impressive interior.

Best All-Rounder: Almera Tino 2.2 TD

Body styles: Compact MPV
Engine capacity: 1.8, 2.0, 2.0Di
Manufactured in: Japan

Price from: £20,700

Nissan QX Maxima

Body styles: Saloon
Engine capacity: 2.0V6, 2.5V6, 3.0V6
Manufactured in: Japan

A new QX was introduced last year, but it was barely more imaginatively-styled than the previous Nissan range-topper. However, under the anonymous skin lies revised suspension and engines, as well as a stiffer structure to boost both ride and handling. The old car always drove well, and the new model is better still, especially with its super-smooth 2.0-litre and 3.0-litre V6 engines which are impressively powerful. But however good it is to drive, Nissan will never find European success with such a dull-looking car. Even the interior, though well-equipped, is completely lacking in interest. Arguably this doesn't matter – the QX is a hit in America, where it sells as a reliable family car, and in large numbers.

Best All-Rounder: QX 3.0 V6

Nissan Silvia

Price from: £na

A great-looking, very desirable Nissan that, sadly, is not available in the UK. Available in coupe and Varietta cabriolet form, the latter boasts a Mercedes SLK-style roof; flick a button, and the steel roof disappears to create a full, pillarless open-top car. Both versions are far more attractive than the dull-looking 200SX they replaced, though they do use a similar, high-performing 2.0-litre turbo-charged engine. They also use a rear-wheel-drive chassis, which is impressively agile and makes the Silvia feel far smaller than it really is. Overall, the Silvia is a very well-developed car, with the added attractions of plentiful equipment levels and an attractive list price. This is a smartly-styled, fast, good-handling Nissan. Why on earth is it not sold in the UK?

Best All-Rounder: Silvia Varietta

Body styles: Coupe, convertible
Engine capacity: 2.0
Manufactured in: Japan

NISSAN

Price from: £na

Nissan Serena

Body styles: MPV
Engine capacity: 1.6, 2.0, 2.3D
Manufactured in: Spain

It may well seat eight and be quite cheap to buy, but the Nissan Serena is a van, with only the smallest of design modifications to disguise this. The engine is mounted under the front seats, styling is unattractive, and on the road the Serena is embarrassed by more well-developed rivals. Only available in 2.3-litre diesel form, it approaches record breakingly-low performance, with plenty of noise and bad manners too. The ride is bouncy and corners are to be avoided, though the Serena is very easy to drive, like all Nissans. Inside, it is bleak and uninviting, and there isn't even plenty of equipment to make it more bearable. Now Nissan is part-owned by MPV experts Renault, expect the Serena to eventually fade away.

Best All-Rounder: Serena 2.3

Nissan Skyline

Price from: £54,000

The infamous Japanese monster continues to turn heads and intimidate wherever it prowls. Older variants may well have looked misleadingly timid, but this latest Skyline makes no attempt to hide its aggression, from the massive air intakes and menacing wheels, to the flared wheel arches and large rear spoiler. In the UK, those scoops feed the GT-R's 2.6-litre twin-turbo straight-six engine, that is just as fast as the Skyline's looks suggest; what's more, boosting power further is just a matter of swapping a computer chip. It is through the bends that the Skyline really scores though, for the four-wheel-drive, computer-controlled handling really is astonishing. Grip feels endless, clumsy manoeuvres are forgiven, and rapid driving is rewarded like few other cars. Simply awesome.

Best All-Rounder: Skyline GT-R

Body styles: Coupe, saloon
Engine capacity: 2.0, 2.5, 2.6
Manufactured in: Japan

NEW

Price from: £16,000

Nissan X-Trail

Body styles: Estate
Engine capacity: 2.0, 2.0T
Manufactured in: Japan

With the rugged Terrano, Nissan was one of the first entrants into the 'lifestyle' 4x4 market; it was probably too early. The Land Rover Freelander showed the world that a mix of 4x4 looks and a car-like driving style was what buyers wanted, and it is only now that Nissan can offer such a vehicle. The X-Trail is, therefore, big and butch-looking, but very easy-to-drive and refined out on the road. Both petrol and diesel engines are subdued, and although biased for the highway, it still offers plenty of ability off-road. Inside, Nissan's design revolution continues, with a stylish, plush and well-made interior that is also well-equipped. Only less-than head-turning exterior looks let the side down, for the X-Trail is a fine new 4x4.

Best All-Rounder: X-Trail 2.0 Sport

Nissan Terrano II

Price from: £16,150

Now the X-Trail 'recreational' 4x4 is here, the Terrano's appeal appears to be even more limited than it was. However, few other manufacturers still sell 'real' off-roaders for so little money, so it may still have a future. Its styling still has a certain charm, especially since its sister car, the original Ford Maverick, was ousted, and on the road it isn't outclassed, either. It has fair manners, and the 2.7-litre turbo-diesel engine is reasonably fast and refined. The rugged 4x4 drive-train helps it dust off its 'lifestyle' rivals off-road, though the three-door is better in the rough stuff than the bulkier five-door. Not taken seriously by true 'off-roaders', the Terrano is appealingly good value and still more than able.

Best All-Rounder: Terrano II 2.7TD

3-Dr

Body styles: Estate
Engine capacity: 2.4, 2.7TD
Manufactured in: Spain

Price from: £23,355

Nissan Patrol

Body styles: Estate
Engine capacity: 4.5, 2.8TD, 3.0Di, 4.2TD
Manufactured in: Japan

The huge Nissan Patrol is one of the largest, tallest, bulkiest 4x4s on sale in the UK. It has few rivals for on-the-road impact, allowing its drivers to easily tower above bus and van drivers. Naturally, it is almost unrivalled off-road, with a great ability to never get stuck, no matter how difficult the terrain. However, although this made earlier Patrols somewhat unrefined on-road, the latest model has a far smoother character. This is thanks in part to the 3.0-litre turbo-diesel engine, which is refined and extremely torquey. Handling is fairly stress-free, which is crucial in a vehicle this large. Inside, it borders on luxurious with plenty of equipment and plush trims, with the five-door model offering seven seats as standard.

Best All-Rounder: Patrol 5dr 3.0Di

America's oldest passenger car manufacturer, Oldsmobile has been a division of General Motors for nearly 100 years. It is a marque steeped in history, yet is to be phased out by 2003; hard-headed executives simply view it as an outdated brand, unable to generate sufficient sales. Heritage does not count for much when a division is losing money, and though GM appears unemotional, it is a simple business decision in an increasingly competitive market. The uproar in 'Olds' owners' circles is severe, especially when today's models are reasonably competitive against foreign rivals; the Bravada SUV is very effective. That, however, it is not enough to save the brand: Oldsmobile web site even shows a photo of the Silhouette driving into the sunset

Oldsmobile Bravada

Body styles: Estate
Engine capacity: 4.2

Price from: $32,200
Manufactured in: United States

Best All-Rounder: **Bravada**

The new Bravada is based on Chevrolet's Trailblazer, so it is larger than its too-small predecessor. The styling is also vastly improved, with the clean, modern lines helping to justify Oldsmobile's premium pricing. Inside, the interior is also extremely well appointed, with plenty of equipment and fine build quality. The new 4.2-litre straight-six engine is powerful, refined and very smooth, while the ride is also more composed, with a new five-link rear suspension and air-controlled springs. This is an important model for Oldsmobile, for it needs a strong competitor in the vital SUV market to assure its future. The Bravada is good enough to do well, with a pricing strategy that should also ensure good profits for GM's oldest car division.

Price from: $21,500

Oldsmobile Alero

Coupe

Convertible

Engine capacity: 2.4, 3.4V6
Manufactured in: United States

This Toyota Camry and Honda Accord rival is available as a very handsome and cleanly-styled four-door saloon, or an even neater two-door coupe. Offered with either a four-cylinder 2.4-litre engine or a 3.4-litre V6, punchy performance is assured. Handling is also sporty and precise, meaning there's plenty for the driver to enjoy. Passengers will appreciate the plentiful equipment too, which includes standard air conditioning, CD player and cruise control. It is the strength of foreign rivals that the Alero struggles against though; it is a fine car overall, but the Japanese makes are slightly better in key areas. The Alero sells well, but it could do so much better if it was developed further; even so, it is an important American saloon.

Best All-Rounder: **Alero GL**

Oldsmobile Aurora

Price from: $31,300

Oldsmobile's flagship model is still a fairly recent design, and develops its predecessor's strong style well. It is classy, elegant and sporty-looking, without being brash or tacky; a very desirable model. Behind the wheel, things are just as appealing, for both the 3.5-litre V6 and 4.0-litre V8 engines are cultured and powerful. They complement the stiff, sporty chassis well, which also offers a comfortable ride and a fine cruising ability. Inside there is a well-designed cockpit and excellent level of standard equipment, including ABS, air conditioning and CD player. Is that enough? If not, the Aurora also offers excellent build quality and an extremely low on-the-road price.

Best All-Rounder: **Aurora**

Body styles: Saloon
Engine capacity: 3.5V6, 4.0V8
Manufactured in: United States

PEUGEOT

Riding the crest of a wave, with its 206 model selling phenomenally well, Peugeot is aiming equally high with the 307. That car follows the trend in the family hatchback market of offering more versatility and space, though more enthusiastic drivers will lament the passing of the razor sharp responses of the 306. A new 106 is also long overdue, and the 406 replacement, the 407, is expected soon. Sales of the executive 607 model outside its native France are slow, though despite this, and in line with many other European manufacturers, Peugeot is developing a Mercedes S-Class, BMW 7 Series-sized competitor to ensure it has a model in every conceivable market sector. The 206 is likely to spawn estate and lifestyle 4x4 versions to join the popular hatch and cabriolet models.

NEW

Peugeot 307

5-Dr

Body styles: Hatchback
Engine capacity: 1.4, 1.6, 2.0, 1.4HDi, 2.0HDi
Price from: £10,860
Manufactured in: France

The 306 was always the prettiest car in the family car class, yet Peugeot has decided that its replacement, the 307, should be a more practical option, So, out go the flowing lines and in comes a mini-MPV style that is far taller and bulkier than its predecessor. It is to Peugeot's credit, then, that the 307 is an attractive car in its own right. It also has a good-quality interior that is reasonably spacious, if not to the extent suggested by the styling. Underneath, revised suspension offers a quieter drive, but not at the expense of ride and handling ability, which are both still excellent. Engines are similar to before, but equipment levels are boosted.

Best All-Rounder: 307 1.6 GLX

Peugeot 106

Price from: £6,495

It may be getting on a bit , but the Peugeot 106 remains an entertaining car to drive. Since the launch of the 206, it is now Peugeot's 'budget' offering, but it certainly doesn't drive like a budget car. A fine ride, eager and responsive handling and great steering feel all uphold the Peugeot reputation, especially in the terrific GTI performance model. Even the 1.1-litre and 1.4-litre models perform well, and the 1.5-litre diesel is economical. Its age shows in the compact interior, especially the impossibly tight pedals and cramped rear, the dash design too is also a little dated and cheaply-finished. The exterior still looks fresh though, which should help the 106 maintain its success until a replacement arrives.

Best All-Rounder: 106 1.6 GTI

Body styles: Hatchback
Engine capacity: 1.1, 1.4, 1.6, 1.5D
Manufactured in: France

Price from: £7,940

Peugeot 206

Convertible

Body styles: Hatchback, convertible
Engine capacity: 1.1, 1.4, 1.6, 2.0, 1.9D, 2.0HDi
Manufactured in: France, England, Argentina, Brazil

The success of the 206 continues. The 206CC, with its Mercedes SLK-style folding roof, has been a hit, and the British factory is struggling to keep up with UK demand. Good looks are part of the appeal, as is a spacious and comfortable interior, and feeling of solidity and good build. The way the 206 drives also attracts buyers, for it displays all the usual Peugeot flair – the ride is smooth, without compromising cornering ability. Few small hatches feel as mature as the 206, which is fine for the smaller-engined petrol and superb HDI turbo-diesel models, but a little disappointing in the 2.0-litre GTI. It is just too civilised. Overall though, the 206 is a worthy favourite for private buyers in the UK.

Best All-Rounder: 206 1.6 GLX

Peugeot Partner Combi

Price from: £9,095

Another van-based 'lifestyle' vehicle, all but identical to sister company Citroen's Berlingo Multispace. The French appear to love these cars, which take them back to their roots, but UK buyers are not quite as keen. They do sell reasonably well, due to their immense practicality. Featuring sliding doors there's huge interior room thanks to the high roof and boxy styling. Engines are basic, as are trim levels, but both are adequate and get the job done. It drives very well, with a supple ride and fun handling. Van drivers must have a blast behind the wheel, if this is what they enjoy every day. Good, cheap and practical fun.

Best All-Rounder: Partner Combi 1.4

Body styles: Estate
Engine capacity: 1.4, 1.8, 1.9D, 2.0HDi
Manufactured in: Spain, Portugal, Argentina

Price from: £13,480

Peugeot 406

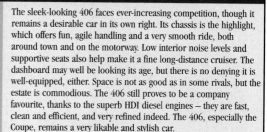

Estate

Coupé

Engine capacity: 1.8, 2.0, 2.2, 3.0V6, 2.0HDi, 2.2HDi
Manufactured in: France

The sleek-looking 406 faces ever-increasing competition, though it remains a desirable car in its own right. Its chassis is the highlight, which offers fun, agile handling and a very smooth ride, both around town and on the motorway. Low interior noise levels and supportive seats also help make it a fine long-distance cruiser. The dashboard may well be looking its age, but there is no denying it is well-equipped, either. Space is not as good as in some rivals, but the estate is commodious. The 406 still proves to be a company favourite, thanks to the superb HDI diesel engines – they are fast, clean and efficient, and very refined indeed. The 406, especially the Coupe, remains a very likable and stylish car.

Best All-Rounder: 406 HDI GLX

Peugeot 607

Price from: £18,195

Large, French cars have never really succeeded outside their home market, but the 607 is better qualified than most to do reasonably well. It is attractive for a start, with curvaceous lines housing neat detailing and a far more modern look than its boxy predecessor, the 605. And, although the chassis is actually related to the 605's, it is a very good base on which to work; the 607 handles well and rides very smoothly indeed. It is undemanding, and easy work over long distances. The engines are familiar Peugeot units, with the best all-rounder being the refined, economical 2.2-litre HDI. Like most non-prestige brands, the 607 comes loaded with equipment, and is also very comfortable; it lacks only the allure of a prestige badge.

Best All-Rounder: 607 2.2 HDI

Body styles: Saloon
Engine capacity: 2.0, 2.2, 3.0V6, 2.0HDi, 2.2HDi
Manufactured in: France

Price from: £17,920

Peugeot 806

Body styles: MPV
Engine capacity: 2.0, 2.0HDi
Manufactured in: France

It's old, awkward-looking and overshadowed by more talented rivals, but Peugeot's 806 still holds appeal to some. The sliding doors are a boon in tight supermarket car parks, whilst the practical interior is still quite spacious and comfortable. Best of all are the diesel engines - long a Peugeot strong point. The HDi common-rail units are smooth, powerful and very economical, and are far better than the thirsty petrol units. Its age shows on the road, where both ride and handling don't meet the high standards set by Ford's Galaxy and its derivatives. A new model aims to improve things though. Again developed with Fiat Group, it looks similar but will be far better to drive - just as a Peugeot should be.

Best All-Rounder: 806 HDi

PONTIAC

General Motors' most exciting brand, Pontiac, is most certainly not for shy and retiring types. As all US brands chase younger buyers, Pontiac can sit back, for most of its buyers are young, style conscious, not fussed with heritage and always looking out for new, unique and outlandish designs. Pontiac does not disappoint, whether it's the bewinged saloon Grand Am, striking Firebird or totally outrageous Aztec. The latter looks like no other car, which, judging by sales figures, is a bad thing; you can go too far, and the Pontiac image is suffering as a result. Other cars in Pontiac's range purvey the sporting image far more successfully, and it is these that make up the bulk of its not-insubstantial sales.

Pontiac Aztek

Body styles: Estate
Engine capacity: 3.4 V6

Price from: $22,000
Manufactured in: United States

One of America's most distinctive vehicles, the Aztek scares small children and attracts eager young drivers in equal measure. It is aimed specifically at the 'extreme sports' band, with plenty of space for surfboards and even the option of a detachable tent at the rear. The centre console houses a cool box, and there is plenty of rugged side mouldings to bash against mountain sides. Underneath, things are more ordinary, with the Montana minivan donating chassis and 3.4-litre V6 engines. So it does not drive as futuristically as its looks suggest, but it is quick enough for most drivers. A four-wheel-drive version is now on sale, making the Aztek a most capable sports utility - as long as you can live with the styling.

Best All-Rounder: Aztec 4WD GT

Pontiac Bonneville

Price from: $25,900

The Pontiac Bonneville was completely revised for the new millennium, gaining a far sportier and more dramatic look. Everything was enlarged; wheels, lights, even the air intakes, creating an aggressive air that the old model lacked. It is also better to drive, with a stiffer bodyshell providing sportier handling and a more controlled ride. The engine, a 3.8-litre V6, offers a choice of 205bhp or, in super-charged guise, 240bhp. The latter is especially rapid. Inside, there is also a very slick-looking interior, complete with racy red instrument graphics. The Bonneville name refers to the salt flats that were once a favourite for world speed record attempts; the Bonneville is no record breaker, but it is still a competitive mid-range sports saloon.

Body styles: Saloon
Engine capacity: 3.8 V6
Manufactured in:
United States

Best All-Rounder: Bonneville SLE

PONTIAC

Price from: $16,800

Pontiac Grand Am

Body styles: Saloon, coupe
Engine capacity: 2.4, 3.4V6
Manufactured in: United States

The Grand Am, like many Pontiacs, features a remarkable number of spoilers combined with swoopy styling. Big wheels, fog lamps and corrugated side panelling add further drama to what is otherwise a fairly standard-looking saloon or coupe shape. Still, it packs reasonable performance from its 2.4-litre four-cylinder and 3.3-litre V6 engines, helping make it Pontiac's best-selling model. Sales charts also show it to be one of America's best-selling 'compact' cars too; the Grand Am is an important model. That it doesn't really handle quite as well as its styling suggests is not important. It has plenty of equipment, and a keen list price. What's more, it perfectly fits Pontiac's brief of offering exciting, dramatic cars that are a little 'different'.

Best All-Rounder: Grand Am V6

Pontiac Grand Prix

Price from: $21,100

The Grand Prix is another Pontiac saloon and coupe line that features remarkably dramatic and sporty styling. Dubbed as the car that follows the 'Wider is Better' school, the Grand Prix is over six feet wide, and uses high drama to draw attention: massive wheels, exaggerated curves; even the wing mirrors look like aerodynamic aids. Fortunately, it is sporty to drive too, unlike some other Pontiacs. The 3.1-litre and 3.8-litre V6 engines provide plenty of power, especially in top-level 240bhp super-charged form. The front-wheel-drive chassis copes well with the power, with a stiff bodyshell allowing precise handling that doesn't object to being pushed hard. One of the sportiest saloon and coupe ranges sold in America, the Grand Prix is a worthy sales success.

Body styles: Saloon
Engine capacity: 3.1V6, 3.8V6
Manufactured in: United States

Best All-Rounder: Grand Prix GT

Price from: $19,400

Pontiac Firebird

Body styles: Coupe, convertible
Engine capacity: 3.8V6, 5.7V8
Manufactured in: United States

Incredibly, the Firebird is not a mad-looking concept car, but a real production model. Celebrating its 35th year, the one-time Mustang rival has been left behind in the development stakes, and is now a very dated, heavy and elderly-feeling car. Its aged dynamics make for interesting handling that can be fun in the right hands, but most will be discouraged from pushing it too hard – despite plentiful power from the powerful, roaring V6 and V8 engines. There's no denying it offers great value for money though, especially considering the huge list of standard equipment. Available in both coupe and convertible form, the Firebird may well be nearing the end of its life, but it retains a loyal following.

Best All-Rounder: Firebird

Pontiac Sunfire

Price from: $14,800

Pontiac's Sunfire is based on the Chevrolet Cavalier, GM's best-selling car. The cheapest Pontiac, it is marketed as a sporty, affordable car, which the dramatic styling confirms. Driving lamps, an aggressive nose and large alloy wheels all shout high performance, but this is only partly borne out behind the wheel. The engines, 2.2-litre or 2.4-litre four-cylinder units, are fairly brisk but quite gruff, while the chassis betrays its advancing years in a handling and ride package that is some way off the class best. As long as you don't push it, there is plenty to enjoy in the great-value Sunbird; the neat interior is well-equipped, and the Pontiac badge still commands respect and admiration.

Body styles: Saloon, Coupe
Engine capacity: 2.2, 2.4
Manufactured in: United States

Best All-Rounder: Sunfire SE

Price from: $25,000

Pontiac Montana

Body styles: MPV
Engine capacity: 3.4V6
Manufactured in: United States

The Montana used to be sold in the UK as the Vauxhall Sintra, so its looks should be familiar. A facelift last year added a new nose, but it is essentially the same as the vehicle that was sold in the UK during the 1990s. A single 3.3-litre V6 engine provides the power, and proves both refined and powerful on the road. Of course, as the Pontiac brand is GM's exciting, stylish division, the Montana is tuned to handle fairly sharply, with ride comfort remaining fine. Practicality is good, with sliding rear doors and the option of a long-wheelbase version; up to eight people can be accomodated. A surprisingly capable 'sports-MPV', that fits into the Pontiac range well.

Best All-Rounder: Montana

PORSCHE

Entering a completely new market soon with the Cayenne 4x4, Porsche is confident of increasing its sales, particularly in the US. More driver-orientated 4x4s may be just what the sports utility market needs, following the success of BMW's X5, but the Cayenne will need to be pretty special to avoid devaluing this highly respected brand. A revised 911 gets a new nose, better quality interior trim and most importantly more power, while the 911 cabriolet finally gets a glass rear screen. A coupe version of the Boxster is rumoured as the 911 becomes more of a GT, while the Carrera GT supercar is still a production possibility. More powerful derivatives are always under development to fulfil the insatiable demand for mega-performance, though the Boxster is kept in check to prevent it from taking sales from the more profitable 911 range. The continued independence of the marque remains refreshing in an industry awash with take-overs and mergers, though the Cayenne needs to succeed to ensure Porsche retains its autonomy.

Porsche Carrera GT

Body styles: Convertible
Engine capacity: 5.5 V10
Price from: £250,000 approx
Manufactured in: Germany

Best All-Rounder: Carrera GT

The supercar lives, and is in rude health. The race-car-inspired Carrera GT is big, fast and sensational in every respect, from its 550bhp, 40-valve V10 engine to its 15-inch ceramic composite disc brakes. Naturally, huge performance comes as standard; 0-125mph is expected to take less than 10 seconds, the Carrera GT continuing to accelerate onto a maximum speed of 205mph. It also shrugs off the corners you're slingshot into, thanks to huge tyres, wind-tunnel-developed wings and the engineering experience of some of the greatest minds in motorsport. Probably most important of all, though, is the stunning, near-revolutionary styling, that is unlike anything that has gone before. Production will only be confirmed once there's enough orders, but at an expected price of £250,000, it is, in supercar terms, a bargain.

Porsche 911 Turbo

The supercar icon. You may want a Ferrari, but you'll also want the 911 Turbo. It has always been one of the fastest cars you can buy, but today's version is also one of the best-handling, too. And, as modern standards are pretty high, this makes the 911 Turbo a driver's dream. Few will be able to comprehend the stupendous acceleration provided by the turbo-charged 3.6-litre flat-six engine, nor the retardation provided by the superb brakes. Grip and poise through corners are similarly sky-high, supported by modern technology and four-wheel-drive. The days of the skittish, unpredictable 911 Turbos are long gone; this latest model is even a model of civility around town. Supercars should redefine boundaries, and this one does, with dizzying conviction.

Price from: £86,000

Body styles: Coupe

Engine capacity: 3.6 Turbo

Manufactured in: Germany

Best All-Rounder: 911 Turbo

Porsche 911

Price from: £55,950

NEW

No sports car has a finer pedigree. The 911 has been around in various forms since the 1960s, and has thrilled on road and track ever since. It has got faster and even more capable over the years, but the basic profile has changed little, even with the launch of the all-new 996 variant in 1996. Underneath however, extensive development has made it better than ever. Handling is superb, steering feel excellent, and few cars feel as balanced or composed over challenging roads. Recent revisions mean it now looks less like the Boxster, while the flat-six engine has been enlarged to 3.6-litres, providing even more phenomenal performance. Rear or four-wheel drive, coupe, Targa or convertible, the 911 remains the definitive sports car.

Convertible

Body styles: Coupe, convertible
Engine capacity: 3.4, 3.6
Manufactured in: Germany

Best All-Rounder: 911 Carrera 4

Porsche Boxster

Price from: £31,450

Body styles: Convertible
Engine capacity: 2.7, 3.2
Manufactured in: Germany, Finland

The most affordable new Porsche is no less desirable than its illustrious 911 stable-mate. It uses similarly-delicious flat-six engines, a closely-related chassis design, and looks both fairly similar and completely different. The mid-engine layout means handling is alert and exquisitely-balanced, with superb steering and a great feeling of confidence. Early cars were even criticised for not having enough power to exploit it fully. This was later cured by an enlarged 2.7-litre engine, and the introduction of the 3.2-litre Boxster S version. The two-seat roadster also sports a superb electric roof system, making it a fine all-weather car. Superb to both look at and to drive, the Boxster is a sensible purchase that remains hugely desirable – understandably so to anyone who has enjoyed one.

Best All-Rounder: Boxster S

Having access, by virtue of ownership, to Lotus's talented engineers, the Proton range hides a few genuine surprises. While recognised as a budget brand, it intends to launch a sports car utilising the platform from the stillborn Lotus M250 project. Such a move has been typical of Proton's until now - the current Wira and Satria are old Mitsubishi models, tweaked and build it in Malaysia. But the new Impian has received acclaim, particularly for its ride and handling, and it is all-Proton. A range of new engines will join the line-up later this year, firstly in the Impian, eventually being used in new models that are under development to replace the ageing Wira and Satria ranges. Meanwhile the Satria GTi will continue as a sporting flagship to inject some youthful appeal into the largely ignored marque.

NEW

Proton Impian

Body styles: Saloon
Engine capacity: 1.6

Price from: £12,000
Manufactured in: Malaysia

Proton's first car to be designed entirely in-house, the Impian marks a big step forward for the young Malaysian company. Importantly, it has sought assistance from 'outside' engineering firms, most notably from Lotus for suspension development. Styling is modern if undramatic, and the interior is a vast improvement on previous dull designs. It is also very well-equipped, and surprisingly spacious. The engine is sourced from Mitsubishi and offers average performance, but very good fuel economy. However, it is from behind the wheel where the Impian really scores. Handling is entertaining, the ride is smooth and the steering set-up excellent; the Lotus input really shows. The great-value Impian is good enough to compete on ability as well as price; an important and impressive model.

Best All-Rounder: Impian 1.6 X

Price from: £6,999

Proton Satria

Body styles: Hatchback
Engine capacity: 1.3, 1.5, 1.6, 1.8
Manufactured in: Malaysia

Basically a rebadged previous-generation Mitsubishi, the Satria was, prior to the launch of the Impian, Proton's youngest design; it was first released as the Colt in the early 1990s. This means the styling is still fairly modern, and the dynamics are not too far off the pace of modern designs. Larger than a supermini but smaller than family hatches, the Satria is an 'in-between' car, however space is surprisingly tight in the rear, even when compared to some smaller hatchbacks. The dashboard looks dated, but is well-equipped. Dynamically it is average, except the Lotus-developed GTI, which is a superb hot hatch. Its engine may not be the most refined, like all Satrias, but twisty roads are a joy. Great value too, like all Protons.

Best All-Rounder: Satria GTI

Proton Wira

The Wira range is fairly extensive, featuring hatchback, saloon and coupe variants, though the latter is more of a three-door hatch than a true sleek sports car. There is also a large range of engines, including a strong 1.8-litre twin-cam and economical 2.0-litre turbo-diesel. The lowly 1.3-litre is best avoided if easily maintaining pace is important. The Wira is an aged design, that sells above all on its competitive price and equipment levels. It has been around since the early 1990s, and was sold as a Mitsubishi before that, so the fact that it is still reasonably good to drive is a surprise. Handling is good, and the Wira is an extremely easy, effortless car to use, and is handily spacious, too.

Price from: £7,499

Body styles: Hatchback, saloon, coupe
Engine capacity: 1.3, 1.5, 1.6, 1.8, 2.0D, 2.0TD
Manufactured in: Malaysia

Best All-Rounder: Wira 1.8 Lux

Claiming to offer some of the cheapest models available in the UK market, Perodua is a little brand that is known to few. Those after cheap and simple transport could do worse than looking at the small car range from Malaysia. Honest and basic transportation, the range, like that of many budget manufacturers, utilises cast-offs from other manufacturers - Peroduas are based on old Daihatsu models. The popular exports are the Nippa (Kancil in Malaysia) which is the old Daihatsu Cuore or Mira, largely unchanged. The newer Kenari takes the same mechanical package and puts it into a (slightly) more stylish body. The Kembara and Rusa are not exported to Europe and based on Daihatsu's Terios micro 4x4 and Hijet mini-MPV respectively.

Perodua Kenari

Body styles: Hatchback
Engine capacity: 1.0

Price from: £6,175
Manufactured in: Malaysia

Even the Kenari, Perodua's most expensive export, is cheaper than most manufacturer's base-level models. It takes the 'upright' style of most eastern designs to an extreme, but this pays dividends with interior space; considering the tiny dimensions, interior room is remarkably generous. It is also very well-equipped, with power steering, twin airbags, electric windows and a CD player. Within the city, the Kenari is a fine performer too, with light steering and great ease-of-use. Its limits are soon found on the open road though, despite an eager three-cylinder engine. Still, this one-time Daihatsu Move is cheap to buy and well-equipped, economical to run and even quite 'individual'; the twin-headlights and chrome grille may not be to everyone's tastes, but at this price, who really minds?

Best All-Rounder: Kenari GX

Perodua Nippa

Price from: £4,624

Body styles: Hatchback
Engine capacity: 0.85
Manufactured in: Malaysia

Still Britain's cheapest car, the Nippa is also very cheerful, too. The 'smiley' face heads a five-door bodyshell that disguises well the fact that the Nippa is tiny. It was once known as the Daihatsu Mira years ago, and was designed to meet Japanese small-car regulations. Surprisingly spacious inside it also offers decent luggage space. However, few cars are as basic, for hard plastics and bare metals abound, and you don't even get an airbag or power steering. But it is economical, the sweet three-cylinder 850cc engine returning great fuel economy, and performance that isn't as bad as you'd expect. It isn't a car that encourages fast driving, but keep it around town, and the Nippa is a surprisingly likeable car.

Best All-Rounder: Nippa EX

Adventurous as ever the French firm has reinterpreted what customers are looking for in executive models. The Vel Satis looks well specified, well priced and well – strange, while the Avantime luxury MPV coupe is a bold idea that has yet to be proven. You have to admire Renault's bravery, gambling that, in the German dominated executive market, the only way to make any impact is to be different. Safety, too, has become a real issue, Renault boasting the first ever five star rating in the Euro NCAP test with the Laguna, with the remainder of the range also producing excellent crash-worthiness results. Platform and power-train sharing between recent acquisition, Nissan, should see a reduction in production and development costs, and Renault coping well against the heavy-weight competition.

NEW

Renault Avantime

Body styles: Hatchback
Engine capacity: 2.0T, 3.0V6

Price from: £24,000
Manufactured in: France

Still fancy a BMW 5-Series or Mercedes E-Class? Renault is aiming to succeed where it has always been weak; the Avantime is a bold new executive car from Europe's most innovative manufacturer. And for those who doubt the concept of a coupe-MPV-luxury car, seeing it in the flesh confirms that this is one of the most dramatic and innovative new cars in years. The interior is equally brilliant, with entry into the four full-size leather armchairs aided by clever double-hinged doors. There are no central pillars to impede entry, so lowering the windows and opening the panoramic glass sunroof creates an effect more akin to a cabriolet. Totally unique and extremely stylish, the Avantime makes a massive impact and should affirm Renault's luxury car credentials.

Best All-Rounder: Avantime 3.0 V6 Privilege

Price from: £na

Renault Twingo

Body styles: Hatchback
Engine capacity: 1.2
Manufactured in:
France, Spain, Columbia, Uruguay

Back in the early 1990s, the Twingo was the first sign of Renault's resurgence in innovation and stylish design. One of the original European city cars, it beat Ford's Ka to the market by years, yet the 'one-box' style means it remains innovative today. Small exterior dimensions house remarkable space inside, which can be fully utilised thanks to the sliding rear seat. The interior design is just as attractive as the exterior too, and it is only really on the road that the Twingo shows its age. A comfy ride results in plenty of lean through corners, and the single 1.2-litre engine option is no ball of fire. It is fun though, and surprisingly refined when cruising. Still appealing, the Twingo is a true modern classic.

Best All-Rounder: Twingo 1.2

Renault Clio

Price from: £7,495

NEW

The Clio was facing stiff competition from newer rivals, so it has received an early and very thorough facelift. The new nose is more distinctive, there is a better interior and engine line-up, but the real headline is the knock-out standard specification level – by far the best in the supermini class. It should further boost sales of an already popular car that is both stylish and enjoyable to drive. An extensive range includes the tremendous mid-engined V6, which is a real supercar and a total contrast to the all-new, very economical common-rail diesel model. There is something for most buyers, which competitive pricing puts in the reach of many, too. Combined with a fine ride, good handling and low running costs, the Clio remains a very attractive package.

Best All-Rounder: Clio 1.2 Expression +

5-DR

V6

Engine capacity: 1.2, 1.4, 1.6, 2.0, 3.0V6, 1.5dCi, 1.9D, 1.9TD
Manufactured in:
Worldwide

RENAULT

Price from: £14,255

Renault Laguna

Estate

Body styles: Hatchback, estate
Engine capacity: 1.6, 1.8, 2.0, 3.0V6, 1.9dCi, 2.2dCi
Manufactured in: France

Whereas most manufacturers like to take a 'sporting' slant, Renault prefers to emphasise the dignity of its cars. So the new Laguna is marketed as a smooth, elegant and refined mid-range car, which is borne out by the driving experience. Few rivals ride so well, or are as refined, or come equipped so well. This does not mean the handling is unengaging – far from it – but the Laguna feels more of a car to cruise in rather than to race. The familiar engines bear this out, and are very hushed at most speeds. Styling is classy and distinctive, with the Sport Tourer estate appearing especially attractive and desirable; it looks far more expensive than it is. A quality car, that is appealingly different from its rivals.

Best All-Rounder: Laguna 1.8 Dynamique

Renault Kangoo

Price from: £8,850

If you remember the Renault 4, you'll be familiar with the concept behind the Kangoo. It is huge inside, thanks to its van origins, with bags of front and rear space, a huge boot and loads of headroom. And although the Kangoo is distinctly utilitarian in style, the benefit comes in prices that start well under £10,000. This does not mean it is basic to drive, though. A soft, comfortable ride absorbs most bumps, whilst the handling is fun, and easily copes with the limited power from the engines. All controls are easy, and fine visibility makes it simple to drive. New Trakka 4x4 versions add further practicality and added style, but in either form, the Kangoo remains sensible, easy-going transport.

Best All-Rounder: Kangoo 1.4

Body styles: Estate
Engine capacity: 1.2, 1.4, 1.9D, 1.9TD
Manufactured in: France, Argentina, Morocco

Price from: £10,265

Renault Megane

Convertible

Coupe

Engine capacity: 1.4, 1.6, 1.8, 2.0, 1.9dTi, 1.9dCi
Manufactured in: Worldwide

It may be getting on a bit now, but the Megane remains a popular family buy. This is no doubt helped by its admirable safety record, showing it to be one of the safest cars in its class. Equipment levels are also high, and low prices make the Megane notably good value, with the huge range offering endless choices. On the road, it is competent but not up with the best; ride comfort is fine, but at the expense of agility. Engines are also largely undramatic, though the new 2.0-litre direct-injection petrol unit is impressive, combining low economy and emissions with good performance and refinement. Interior space is the Megane's biggest drawback though, proving particularly cramped in the rear, and compromised for tall drivers, too.

Best All-Rounder: Megane 1.6 Expression +

Renault Scenic

Price from: £12,400

The pioneer remains a best-seller, but nowadays faces increasingly stiff competition. So, following last year's facelift, Renault has revised the model groupings and boosted standard equipment. It is now one of the most comprehensively-equipped mini-MPVs, and remains one of the most desirable. The interior is very well thought-out, and has plenty of space for five adults and their luggage. The three individual rear seats can be slid fore and aft, and also completely removed – just one of the Scenic's many clever and practical touches. To drive, it feels similar to the Megane upon which it is based, so expect a good ride and reasonable engine range. Most interesting is the semi off-road RX4, but the standard models remain the best-value, most sensible choices.

Best All-Rounder: Scenic 1.9 dCi Expression

Body styles: Compact MPV
Engine capacity: 1.4, 1.6, 1.8, 2.0, 1.9D, 1.9dTi, 1.9dCi
Manufactured in: France, Mexico

Price from: £19,350

Renault Espace

Body styles: MPV
Engine capacity: 2.0, 3.0V6, 1.9TD, 2.2dCi
Manufactured in: France

The first European MPV is nowadays one of the first executive people carriers. A great image means Renault has been able to successfully move the Espace upmarket, while maintaining its strong sales. The luxury credentials are clear, thanks to the seven individual and very comfortable seats that can be moved around almost at will. Impressive room is boosted further in the Grand Espace, which offers plenty of luggage space – rare in many MPVs. The driver enjoys a futuristic, swooping dashboard, while all around the cabin there are ingenious features and storage areas. To drive, size is the biggest hindrance, for otherwise the Espace is very easy to control, and often quite fun. Powerful engines complete the picture of great refinement and feeling of luxury.

Best All-Rounder: Espace 2.2 dCi Expression

ROLLS-ROYCE

Finally splitting from Bentley, Rolls-Royce has now had planning permission granted for its new Goodwood production facility. The painful separation sees VW take Bentley, the customer database and the production capacity for the Seraph and Corniche with it. Roll-Royce owner BMW has a car in the pipeline but it looks like the first models will have to be constructed in Germany, as the British factory is unlikely to be completed in time. With Mercedes re-introducing Maybach and Bentley being the more dynamic luxury badge, BMW will have a job convincing customers that a Rolls-Royce is the car for them. Initial reports suggest that the new Rolls will be a behemoth, giving the car serious presence, while the super luxurious interior and scope for personalisation will continue to customers' demands. It will be fascinating to see how the marque fares in the next few years.

Rolls-Royce Silver Seraph

Body styles: Saloon
Engine capacity: 5.4V12

Price from: £159,000
Manufactured in: England

Even though the Mercedes S-Class and new BMW 7 Series are the most crushingly effective luxury cars, they still can't match a Rolls-Royce for sheer upper-class luxury. Of course, the Silver Seraph is a fine car in its own right too, with a modern chassis design and powerful BMW V12 engine behind the famous Rolls-Royce grille. It is very swift and refined, with surprisingly capable handling and, of course, hugely impressive ride comfort. Lavish trappings feature inside, with plenty of real wood and top-quality leather, as well as modern electronics to increase modern appeal, too. The head may say German, but there is only one luxury car to really appeal to the heart; the British-built, German-owned, Rolls-Royce Silver Seraph.

Best All-Rounder: Silver Seraph

Rolls-Royce Corniche

Price from: £250,000

Is there a better car for the rich and famous than the Rolls-Royce Corniche? Cruising in the south of France, basking in the sun and admiring glances, is surely the ultimate expression of style and panache; no car tells the world that you've made it more formidably. Built by hand, the Corniche is equipped to the customer's own specification, though Wilton carpets, wood veneers and hand-stitched leather upholstery inevitably all feature. Adequate performance is provided by Rolls-Royce's own turbo-charged V8 engine, which is a massive 6.75 litres in size. Handling is easy but not really an issue, for the smooth ride and ease of use are of far more importance. Hugely desirable, very expensive, and an ultimate motoring expression of wealth and importance.

Body styles: Convertible
Engine capacity: 6.8V8
Manufactured in:
England

Best All-Rounder: Corniche

SAAB

The revised 9-5 is the first of a number of new models expected from the Swedish marque. The revisions to that car are largely cosmetic, though a diesel joins the range, and the interior is significantly updated. Despite these changes the 9-5 and 9-3 need replacing soon, for both are based on ancient GM platforms. Using old technology hasn't detracted much from their appeal until now, Saab having a perceived quality and cachet higher in some buyers' eyes than BMW. Its safety record is impeccable too, with both models scoring highly in independent crash tests. A smaller sports coupe model, to rival the likes of Audi's TT, is expected soon, adding another model to the rather small range. But of all the premium brands it is Saab that has the most serious credibility in the image stakes. These need to be addressed, and quickly.

Saab 9-5

Body styles: Saloon, estate
Engine capacity: 2.0T, 2.3T, 3.0V6, 3.0TiD

Price from: £21,395
Manufactured in: Sweden

Discrete styling disguises a very accomplished car. The 9-5 will turn no heads with its mature lines and Saab family style, but owners don't seem to mind. They're attracted to near faultless build quality, competitive prices and high specification levels, as well as a class-competitive driving ability. It may be comfort-orientated, but the 9-5 is still a very responsive car to drive, and proves immensely relaxing on long motorway trips. The interior, with its Jaguar-like ambience of luxury, certainly helps, as do some of the best seats in the business. Individuality is added by the superb, all-turbo engine range; even the 3.0-litre V6 is turbo-charged, and every version is responsive and powerful, as well as environmentally 'clean'. A huge estate caps an impressive range of recently-face-lifted cars.

Best All-Rounder: Saab 9-5 2.3t SE

Saab 9-3

Price from: £16,795

The good-looking 9-3 is getting on a bit nowadays, and struggles to compete against newer rivals. It is essentially a mildly-reworked 900, which was based on 1988's Vauxhall Cavalier. However, considering the age of the hardware, Saab's engineers have done a fine job to make the 9-3 ride and handle reasonably well. It is no class-leader, but on a long journey, few cars are more relaxing. The smooth all-turbo engine range helps, as do superb seats in the faultless interior, which ergonomically is among the best on the market. There is an extremely high level of safety too, as well as a great sense of satisfaction from the trend-setting Convertible. A new model is on the way, which Saab hopes will challenge the class leaders.

Body styles: Hatchback, convertible
Engine capacity: 2.0T, 2.2TiD
Manufactured in: Sweden

Best All-Rounder: Saab 9-3 2.0t SE

SATURN

GM's youngest brand, Saturn, is around a decade old, and already has carved its own niche. Offering fuss-free, reliable cars with excellent warranties and standard specification, the dealers rate customer service even higher than the already-high American norm. The no-haggle prices are reasonable considering the package, which features dent-free plastic body panels for an assured long life. However, this marketing focus today seems outdated in the youth-obsessed US, so Saturn is making great efforts to change its image. If it can guarantee investment and interest from GM, and produce more interesting cars that still benefit from Saturn's impressive sales package, it could still have a place in today's market.

Saturn SC Coupe

Engine capacity:
1.9

Price from: $14,100
Manufactured in: United States

Like the SL saloon upon which it is based, Saturn's SC coupe is getting on a bit. Last year came a redesigned interior and new-look plastic body panels, but all the basics were pretty much the same as before. The engines, either 8-valve or 16-valve 1.9-litre units, provide zippy and willing performance, just as they do in the saloons, but the handling is also similar to its sisters – safe but dull. It does not drive in the fun manner expected of a coupe – but then, Saturn buyers are not likely to drive in that way, anyway. Their demands of reliability, value, ease of use and fuss-free driving are met, with an added dose of style to make them feel good, too.

Best All-Rounder: SC Coupe

Saturn L Series

Price from: $16,800

Body styles: Saloon, estate
Engine capacity: 2.2, 3.0V6
Manufactured in: United States

Based on the platform of the Vauxhall Vectra, the Saturn L Series uses a larger, wider bodyshell to cater for American demands. There are two excellent Vauxhall engines – either the new 2.2-litre 4-cylinder or the 3.0-litre V6 unit – making the L Series a keen performer. Available in LS saloon or LW estate form, the L Series also handles and rides well; it is softer than the Vectra, benefiting ride, but still offers handling that is sharp and informative compared to the American norm. It is also well-equipped, and is styled in a discrete and refined way. All body panels are composite too - meaning an L Series will remain dent and rust-free throughout its life. A fine Honda Accord or Toyota Camry alternative.

Best All-Rounder: Saturn LS1 four-door

Saturn S Series

Price from: $11,000

The ageing S Series range of cars still offers fine value for the undemanding driver. Available in saloon and estate form, the trademark plastic body panels feature, as does the fine value and good customer loyalty. There is a single 1.9-litre engine option, with either 100bhp or 124bhp. Both are lively and eager on the road, and settle down well to a refined cruise. The handling is uninvolving, proving soggy and discouraging through the corners; the pay-off is a supple ride, though even this is some way off the best of the class leaders. Saturn's S Series is a car overdue for major revisions, but for the value-seeking buyer, it can still attract.

Best All-Rounder: S Series SL1 four-door

Body styles: Saloon, coupe, estate
Engine capacity: 1.9
Manufactured in: United States

Having cast aside its low-rent image, Skoda is now a strong brand in its own right. By raiding the Volkswagen parts bin the Skoda range has been the biggest winner its parent company's platform sharing strategy, borrowing components from both VW and Audi models. Solidity and quality are the result, Skoda shaming many more expensive manufacturers with its simple, though stylish, cars at extremely attractive prices. More powerful sporting versions and estate and saloon Fabias have all been introduced this year; the company also looking at more luxurious models. Witty advertising and a strengthening image has seen sales rocket in the past few years, the current range still relatively young meaning new models, except the Superb, are unlikely in the foreseeable future.

SKODA

Skoda Fabia

5-Drs Estate

Body styles: Hatchback, saloon, estate
Engine capacity: 1.0, 1.4, 2.0, 1.9SDi, 1.9TD

Price from: £7,685
Manufactured in: Czech Republic

Best All-Rounder: Fabia 1.4 16v

Cheaper than many of its rivals, the award-winning Skoda Fabia is also one of the most advanced superminis on sale. Debuting the next-generation Polo chassis, which is still not yet on sale as a VW, meant Skoda scored an immense coup for its first-ever supermini - it immediately leapt to the top of the class. Attractive styling hides a simple but well-built, well-equipped interior that is spacious and comfortable both front and rear. It is also impressive on the move, with a smooth ride, sharp handling and good power steering – long distances are a breeze, even though the engines are hardly the last word in ultimate performance. All are commendably refined and unintrusive though, helping make this a great 'Millennium car'.

Skoda Octavia

Price from: £9,765

Skoda's renaissance started here. Based on the excellent Golf chassis but almost Ford Mondeo-sized, the Octavia kicked off the current European boom in Skoda sales, and with good reason. It is attractive, hugely practical (especially in estate form) and very comfortable and able. Engines include many of VW's best, from economical diesels to very high-performance turbo petrol units. There is also plenty of VW build quality evident, giving the Octavia a very solid feel. Space in the rear may be a little tight, but compensation is the huge boot, whether in saloon-like hatch or stylish estate. It drives well on the road, and is particularly impressive in hot RS guise – a great performance car that should further boost the Octavia's image.

Best All-Rounder: Octavia 1.9 TDI 110

Estate

Body styles: Saloon, estate
Engine capacity: 1.4, 1.6, 1.8T, 2.0, 1.9SDi, 1.9TD
Manufactured in: Czech Republic

SEAT

Of all the VW-owned brands, Seat is perhaps the busiest at the moment with a number of new models expected within the next year. A Leon-based cabriolet has been spotted and the Ibiza is certain for replacement in 2002. That new car should also spawn a mini-MPV model to rival models like the Renault Scenic. Creating a performance-orientated brand is high on the priority lists, a wider and wilder range of models being rumoured – including a 2.8 V6 four-wheel-drive version of the Leon. With an extensive range of engine and transmission choices available to them from VW, Seat can cherry pick the best bits and build on its sporting image, all at a fraction of the cost of competitors.

Seat Arosa

Body styles: Hatchback
Engine capacity: 1.0, 1.4, 1.4TDi, 1.7D
Price from: £6,695
Manufactured in: Germany

A recent facelift helped make the Arosa just as distinctive as the mechanically identical Volkswagen Lupo. But whereas in Germany the style is cute and refined, over in Spain, cute and sporty is the key. The interior also received a makeover, and now displays the same great stylish and trendy feel as the more expensive Lupo. Under the skin the modified VW Polo chassis keeps the same line-up of engines, with a new addition - a superb 1.4-litre turbo-diesel. It is very safe and easy to drive, with the 1.4 S also proving quite sporty, but it is refinement that really is the Arosa's strong point; it is excellent, making it a very strong city-car competitor.

Best All-Rounder: Arosa 1.4 S

Seat Ibiza

Price from: £7,960

The stylish Ibiza looks far younger than it actually is, thanks to a very successful facelift in 2000. A sporty nose and tail were added, as well as a far funkier and more interesting dashboard. Under the skin, though, it is still closely related to the VW Polo-based 1993 original, with a revised line-up of engines. However, although it has always been marketed as a supermini, the Ibiza is larger than most such models, so benefits from some notably more powerful engines – including 156bhp and 180bhp versions of the 1.8-litre turbo unit, for very swift performance. Sportier models also have a firmer, more focused ride and handling set-up, but milder versions exhibit a more comfortable overall feel. Low prices make the Ibiza a particularly attractive supermini.

Best All-Rounder: Ibiza 1.4 S

5-Door

Body styles: Hatchback
Engine capacity: 1.0, 1.4, 1.6, 1.8T, 1.9D, 1.9TDi
Manufactured in: Spain

Price from: £na

Seat Cordoba

Coupe

Body styles: Saloon, coupe, estate
Engine capacity: 1.4, 1.6, 1.8T, 1.9D, 1.9TDi
Manufactured in: Spain

For many years largely ignored in the UK, the Cordoba is once again a Europe-only model. It has a far higher profile abroad, where the model range includes sporty 180bhp Cupra models, but here, the estate, saloon and saloon-look 'coupe' models never caught on. Under the dull styling sits the chassis of the Ibiza, so it does at least drive in a sporty manner. Engines are smooth, handling is keen, and although this results in a firmish ride, it fits in well with SEAT's racy image. The Cordoba World Rally Car was also a good way to boost the image of the range – but again, this only really worked in Europe. Models such as the Leon and Arosa offer far more appeal to UK buyers.

Best All-Rounder: Cordoba 1.9 TDi

Seat Leon

Price from: £9,960

Based on the VW Golf, SEAT'S Leon offers a particularly attractive blend of qualities. The vibrantly-styled exterior is attractive, while it uses a similar interior to the acclaimed Audi A3. It is fairly spacious, well-equipped and excellent value for money. Best of all, it drives well, with good composure and comfort, even over long distances. The sweetest-handling version is the sporty Cupra, which also offers impressive performance thanks to its 180bhp engine and six-speed gearbox. Lower-range models are good though, especially the TDI turbo-diesel and 1.6-litre versions, with a more focused feel than the comfort-orientated Golf. Only tight rear passenger space blots the copybook, for this is a stylish, well-built hatch which, considering the list prices, is something of a bargain.

Best All-Rounder: Leon Cupra

Body styles: Hatchback
Engine capacity: 1.4, 1.6, 1.8, 1.8T, 2.8V6, 1.9D, 1.9TDi
Manufactured in: Spain

Price from: £14,495

Seat Toledo

Body styles: Saloon
Engine capacity: 1.6, 1.8, 2.3V5, 1.9TDi
Manufactured in: Spain

The Toledo saloon was launched before its hatchback relative, the Leon, but nowadays is comprehensively outsold by the more stylish hatch. It is basically the same car though, which means the interior is just as attractive, ride and handling display similar characteristics, and comfort levels are the same. The Toledo has a bigger boot, however, as well as a more upmarket trim line-up, reflected by the higher prices. It also has an extra engine, a 2.3-litre V5, which is extremely smooth, refined and powerful – and has a great soundtrack. SEAT would like to see the Toledo as a Peugeot 406 competitor, but it is simply not big enough to compete, especially in the rear. It makes a fine budget executive saloon, though.

Best All-Rounder: Toledo 2.3 V5

Seat Alhambra

Price from: £16,995

SEAT's value-for-money values are clearly evident in the Alhambra, its clone of the Ford Galaxy and VW Sharan. Despite looking just as good as the class-leading Ford and VW, it costs many £1000s less, yet does not stint on equipment either. Air conditioning is standard on all models, as is a six-speed manual gearbox. The interior is just as flexible as rivals, with a car-like driving position and excellent interior design pleasing the driver. The sporty drive will also find praise, with the stiff suspension keeping body roll well in check. The engines are also universally good, with the 2.8-litre V6 and TDI turbo-diesel engines gaining particular praise. Dashes of sporty SEAT flair are the finishing touches to a competitive package.

Best All-Rounder: Alhambra TDi 115

Body styles: MPV
Engine capacity: 1.8T, 2.0, 2.8V6, 1.9TDi
Manufactured in: Portugal

SUBARU

It was always going to be difficult to successfully replace the iconic Impreza. Subaru has just about managed it with the new car, though it's bug-eyed looks have caused controversy. It is the Impreza that has firmly established Subaru as a performance car maker, and the evolutionary process has already started on the new Impreza, developing faster, more extreme, versions through its STi tuning operation and also Prodrive in the UK. With the Impreza appealing to performance aficionados, the Legacy is aiming to compete with more luxurious rivals and it now comes with the option of a six-cylinder engine. The Forester bridges the gap between conventional estates and sports utility vehicles. It should sell in greater numbers given the increasing popularity of this growing market segment, but it remains a relatively rare sight on UK roads.

Subaru Impreza

Estate

Body styles: Saloon, estate
Engine capacity: 1.5, 1.6, 2.0, 2.0T

Price from: £15,750
Manufactured in: Japan

The icon of the 1990s has been replaced by an all-new, even more able model. The styling for both saloon and hatchback is certainly more distinctive, though the bug-eyed front seems to divide opinion like few other cars. Inside, things are more decisive; a vast improvement on the old model, in both design and build quality. Of course, most only have eyes for the turbo-charged WRX model, and on the road this is a big improvement, too. It may not be as ultimately involving, but it is more composed, refined, and easier to drive very fast. The ride over rough roads is now much smoother, aiding pace. The same is true for the lower-powered versions, but you'll be going a lot slower, of course.

Best All-Rounder: Impreza WRX

Subaru Pleo

Price from: £na

Not available in the UK, this Daewoo Matiz-rivalling city car is a replacement for the Vivio. More normal-looking than many city cars, it is still designed to be tall, allowing maximum interior room for the tightest exterior dimensions. It has five doors, with just enough room for four adults – impressive. It is fairly basic inside - though there are plenty of options and trims available - and on the face of it the 650cc engine appears quite weedy. However, turbo-charged and super-charged versions are also available, as well as a CVT automatic transmission with the option of seven steering wheel-controlled 'manual' gears. It is best kept around town, where the compact dimensions pay dividends, but the plentiful power won't leave it embarrassed on the motorway, either.

Body styles: Hatchback
Engine capacity: 0.7
Manufactured in: Japan

Best All-Rounder: Pleo

SUBARU

Price from: £8,995

Subaru Justy

Body styles: Hatchback
Engine capacity: 1.3
Manufactured in:
Hungary

The idea of a four-wheel-drive small hatchback from rally experts Subaru sounds appealing, until you see that it is based on the Suzuki Swift, one of the sector's most elderly competitors. Built in Hungary, its days are numbered, so don't expect to see it in showrooms for much longer. For those who are interested, the four-wheel-drive system is certainly useful in icy weather, or in hilly, snow-covered parts, but practical benefits are otherwise limited, thanks to the weedy engine. The gearchange is also reluctant, whilst the sloppy steering and bouncy ride do little to attract. The cabin is dated, but space is generous, thanks to the reasonable exterior dimensions. It is an old car though, that few will miss when it does finally disappear.

Best All-Rounder: Justy 1.3 GX

Subaru Forester

A mini off-road estate car, the Forester is tall and high enough to offer more ground clearance than the Jeep Cherokee, an impressive feat. The permanent four-wheel-drive platform is derived from the Impreza, and power comes from a range of four-cylinder boxer engines. All are fine, with the 2.0-litre turbo offering a truly impressive 174bhp. They also offer a distinctive engine note. To drive, the Forester feels very similar to the legendary Impreza, with huge reserves of grip and an extremely well-controlled feel. Ride quality is also good – important when crossing bumpy fields. Inside, there is plenty of space all-round, as well as a good-sized boot. Sport utility vehicles rarely come more able, though many are more stylish.

Best All-Rounder: Forester 2.0 Turbo

Body styles: Estate
Engine capacity: 2.0, 2.0T, 2.5
Price from: £15,495
Manufactured in: Japan

Price from: £14,995

Subaru Legacy

Body styles: Saloon, estate
Engine capacity: 2.0, 2.0T, 2.5, 3.0
Manufactured in: Japan

The understated and attractive new Legacy is Subaru's strong competitor to the BMW 3-Series, though few buyers appear to see it as such. It seems it just doesn't appear as dynamic as rivals, though on the road it can show many of them a trick or two. The four-wheel-drive chassis is very grippy and relaxing over long distances, in all weathers, while the engines are all smooth and refined. They may not be the last word in performance, but get the job done with minimal fuss. The interior is less impressive though. It is dull and questionably-trimmed in places, though the overall design is ergonomically sound and spacious enough. The Legacy is a sensible car that's eager to please; shame its image doesn't reflect this.

Best All-Rounder: Legacy 2.5 Estate

Subaru Legacy Outback

Price from: £26,995

For those who find the Forester simply too dull and gawky-looking, Subaru offers the lifestyle-focused Outback. The toughened estate bodyshell is rugged enough to handle mild off-road conditions, while the 3.0-litre 'H6' flat-six engine produces over 200bhp for very impressive performance, and a unique soundtrack. It handles as well as most four-wheel-drive Subarus, with seemingly limitless grip and a very eager nature through the corners. It also uses the same dull interior of the Legacy, which harms its lifestyle credentials a little, though plusher trims and other details do lift it over the standard car. There are also plenty of exterior additions to make it look more expensive, but some colour schemes are questionable. An interesting lifestyle car, that Subaru hopes will prove popular.

Best All-Rounder: Outback

Body styles: Estate
Engine capacity: 3.0
Manufactured in: Japan

SUZUKI

In the UK Suzuki is known for its cars and motorcycles. In its home market, however, a trip to your Suzuki dealer could see you buying a new home, the Japanese manufacturer listing prefabricated houses among its varied products. New models, cars that is, this year include the Liana and the Grand Vitara XL-7. The Liana is an adventurous move into the family hatchback market while the Grand Vitara XL-7 is a seven-seat 4x4 that's only slightly smaller than a Land Rover Discovery. Despite these new, larger models, Suzuki is still an attractive ally to manufacturers wanting a quick means of producing a city car; Suzuki still regarded as the expert in this growing market.

NEW

Suzuki Liana

Body styles: Hatchback
Engine capacity: 1.5
Price from: £9,995
Manufactured in: Japan

Complementing the tedious Baleno is the far more interesting Liana, or 'Life In A New Age' as Suzuki insist on referring to it as. Silly name apart, it offers an interesting alternative in the budget family car sector, with its Honda Civic-like style housing a spacious interior. The interior is also well-designed and attractive, something of a revolution for Suzuki. Comfort is good, too. On the move, the 1.6-litre engine is refined, while the supple ride is very relaxing. It is not a sports car, but provides a smooth and confident drive. As ever, equipment levels are high and prices competitive, making the Liana an interesting car. It has the looks and ability to do well.

Best All-Rounder: Liana 1.6 GLX

Suzuki Wagon R

Price from: £7,940

Body styles: Hatchback
Engine capacity: 1.0, 1.0T, 1.3
Manufactured in: Japan, Hungary

Believe it or not, the Wagon R, which barely registers on sales charts over here, is Japan's best-selling car – a sign of the popularity of these strange-looking high-rise city cars. The latest version was developed with General Motors, and is also sold in the UK as the Vauxhall Agila. Compared to its box-like predecessor, the new model is far more rounded, though still unmistakably a Wagon R, and now features a far more attractive interior. There is also surprising room inside, with great ease of entry and exit for the less mobile. On the road, it is perfect in town, thanks to its ease of use and tight dimensions, and it has just enough power not to get swallowed up on the open road.

Best All-Rounder: Wagon R 1.3 GL

Suzuki Ignis

Price from: £6,940

Suzuki always seems to do things a little differently – witness its latest supermini competitor, the Ignis. It does not simply follow the usual hatchback theme, for it has a style all of its own – part mini-off-roader, part mini-MPV. It is tall, rugged, and not unattractive. Inside, things are a little more ordinary, which is a slight disappointment, as is the lack of flexibility compared with some rivals. Still, it is spacious and commendably well-equipped. It is fair to drive on the road too, the slightly higher position aiding in-town manoeuvrability and ease of use. The engine is a little noisy when extended, but it is quiet enough in the city, too. For many, the Ignis's extra dose of individuality may just swing things.

Body styles: Hatchback
Engine capacity: 1.3
Manufactured in: Japan

Best All-Rounder: Ignis 1.3 GL

Price from: £6,300

Body styles: Hatchback
Engine capacity: 0.7, 0.7T, 1.0
Manufactured in: India

Suzuki Alto

Suzuki's cheapest model competes in the micro city-car sector that the Japanese are famous for. The styling is a little more rounded than the usual fare, though it is still a full five-door hatch, with reasonable space to squeeze four adults inside. It is also quite comfortable and well-built, with a solid feel that helps justify a price higher than some rivals. Equipment is minimal however, which is a sign of where costs have been cut. The Indian-built Alto is enjoyable to drive within its natural habitat however, with a free-revving engine that, although of small capacity, offers reasonably nippy performance. It may not be the most distinctive-looking city car, but the Alto is a reasonable choice for those seeking reliable, well-built budget transport.

Best All-Rounder: Alto 1.0

Suzuki Swift

Price from: £6,845

The Swift is certainly elderly nowadays, but Suzuki doggedly sticks with it. Now marketed as a budget car, it is built in Hungary alongside the four-wheel-drive but otherwise identical Subaru Justy. It is available in three-door and longer five-door variants, with space being especially good in the latter model. It also rides fairly well, doesn't handle too unencouragingly, and is quite well built too – well up to normal Japanese standards, even if the engines are hardly the last word in performance. It has no hope of competing with more recent European and Japanese competitors, however, so its true role is as a very cheap and spacious budget model for developing markets.

Best All-Rounder: Swift 1.3

Estate

Body styles: Hatchback
Engine capacity: 1.0, 1.3
Manufactured in: Hungary

Price from: £11,585

Body styles: Hatchback, saloon, estate
Engine capacity: 1.3, 1.6, 1.8, 1.9TD
Manufactured in: Japan

Suzuki Baleno

Never a great car in its prime, the Baleno is now close to the end of its life, replaced by the thoroughly modern Liana. The Baleno's willing engines have always offered fine performance, however, and equipment levels are naturally high. But use the engines fully and the limitations of the chassis are soon discovered, while compact interior dimensions mean taller passengers find the Baleno a bit of a squeeze, especially in the rear. The interior design is a little more interesting than the exterior, and build quality is good with reliability sure to be reassuring. The three-door hatch tries to offer slightly more interesting styling, but only succeeds to a certain degree.

Best All-Rounder: Baleno 1.6

Suzuki Grand Vitara/XL/7

Price from: £12,495

Suzuki should be pleased, for its Land Rover Freelander competitor highlights just what a bargain the Grand Vitara is. Even the range-topping 2.7-litre V6 model is only £500 more than the base Freelander, yet the Suzuki is barely less capable. It is smooth and refined at all speeds, especially with the silky V6 which also offers impressive performance. It is almost a 'driver's 4x4' especially with its comfortable and supportive seats. It is only really with interior space that attracts criticism though the new XL/7 long wheelbase model answers that with its seven-seat body. The range is wide, also encompassing three-door hard top and convertible as well as the standard five-door "Grand".

Best All-Rounder: Grand Vitara 2.5 V6

5-Dr

Body styles: Estate, convertible
Engine capacity: 1.6, 2.0, 2.5V6, 2.7V6, 2.0TD
Manufactured in: Japan, Canada, Spain

Price from: £9,980

Body styles: Estate, convertible
Engine capacity: 0.7, 1.3
Manufactured in: Japan, Spain

Suzuki Jimny

Suzuki's smart-looking budget hard or soft-top 4x4 is the cheapest 'proper' off-roader you can buy. It may well be tiny, but it offers surprising off-road pace, just like the models that went before it. It is also practical, making good use of the compact dimensions to offer reasonable comfort, although the boot is very small. Fidgety ride apart, it is best around town, thanks to the compact dimensions, easy controls and high seating position that gives great all-round visibility. But raise the pace, and the Jimny struggles; it doesn't feel composed enough in fast driving, though admittedly it was not designed for this. As a city car with a difference, it is an interesting buy, but there are better all-rounders out there.

Best All-Rounder: Jimny 1.3

TOYOTA

With such an extensive model range there is an almost constant stream of new models from the Japanese manufacturer. The 'Verso' name, denoting a versatile MPV-like derivative, will become a more familiar sight with Corolla and Avensis versions hitting the UK market soon. The Avensis Verso debuts a new platform, which will be used by the new Avensis saloon and hatch, though not for a couple of years. Toyota has also developed a simplified petrol/battery hybrid system that features on the Prius. The new system should be fitted to Japanese models soon, the US and European markets expected to get the emission-reducing technology after it's been fully tested at home.

NEW

Toyota Avensis Verso

Body styles: Hatchback, saloon, estate
Engine capacity: 1.6, 1.8, 2.0, 2.0D4-D

Price from: £12,980
Manufactured in: England

Replacing the largely-ignored Picnic, the new Avensis Verso continues to be an 'in-between' MPV – larger than the Renault Scenic, but smaller than the Espace. Toyota reckons it is the ideal compromise, for the Verso offers seven-seat capacity, with decent amounts of room for passengers – and crucially, some of their luggage, too. The interior is also very neat and well-equipped. As it is based on the all-new platform of the forthcoming Avensis saloon, the Verso drives very well indeed, with good handling and ride quality. Refinement is fine too, with little wind noise or grumbles from the smooth drive-train. And importantly, it looks more 'normal' than the outlandish Previa which, along with lower prices, may make it a popular new alternative.

Best All-Rounder: Avensis Verso 2.0 VVT-i GS

Toyota Yaris

Price from: £6,995

Toyota undertook a massive development program when designing the Yaris, and its sales success shows that this has paid off. Great effort was made to offer class-leading interior room, so the Yaris is extremely spacious both front and rear, with the sliding rear seat boosting luggage space when necessary, too. The Yaris Verso takes this further with rear seats that fold into the floor, but its looks may put some off. Both versions use the same futuristic cabin design, with centrally-mounted digital instruments, and it works very well. Engines are also fine – and very economical – as is the chassis that is both comfortable and fairly engaging through the bends. It is extremely easy to drive too, making the Yaris a great overall package.

Best All-Rounder: Yaris 1.3 CDX

Estate

Body Styles: Hatchback, estate
Engine capacity: 1.0, 1.3, 1.5
Manufactured in: Japan

Price from: £8,960

Toyota Corolla

Estate

Body styles: Hatchback, saloon, estate
Engine capacity: 1.3, 1.5, 1.8, 2.2TD
Manufactured in: Japan, England

Corollas used to be as dull as household appliances, but this model, though soon to be replaced, shows a little more effort. The smiling face, sharp headlights and sporty trim are all improvements over anonymous older models, even though things underneath are essentially the same. Smooth engines perform reasonably in any of the four body styles - three and five-door hatchbacks, saloon and estate. The cabin is also fair, proving both comfortable and well-equipped, but space is lacking compared to newer models. It's dull too, but few interiors are as user-friendly, which also sums up the driving experience. The Corolla doesn't inspire, but won't intimidate, either. However, Toyota realises that this isn't enough, so the new model will be far more dynamic…but just as reliable.

Best All-Rounder: Corolla 1.3 GS

Toyota Avensis

Price from: £12,980

The brilliantly-built, utterly reliable Avensis is one of the UK's most hassle-free cars to own. Nothing goes wrong, it does everything its drivers ask of it, and it will carry on doing so without complaint for years. Such qualities may not grab headlines, but they count in the long-term far more than zippy performance or great handling. The Avensis is dynamically competent too though – again, it'll never inspire like more racy rivals, but it is still acceptable, and very refined too. Engines are powerful and smooth, while plenty of space in the neat interior mean long-distance comfort is not lacking, either. Revisions last year gave it a little more visual impact; this is not a car to arouse emotions, but is nevertheless a worthy competitor.

Best All-Rounder: Avensis 1.8 GS

Estate

Body styles: Hatchback, saloon, estate
Engine capacity: 1.6, 1.8, 2.0, 2.0D4-D
Manufactured in: England

Price from: £20,180

Toyota Camry

Body styles: Saloon
Engine capacity: 2.0, 3.0V6
Manufactured in: England

Almost completely devoid of identity, the Camry disguises its 'cheap Lexus' status far too well. It is, after all, a very refined and able saloon that is well-equipped and impressive to drive. Americans have cottoned on, which is why it is the best-selling car over there, but UK buyers can't see further than the badge. This is a shame, for although it is plain – both inside and out – the Camry has much to appeal to British drivers. The chassis handles keenly while both engines are smooth and powerful – the V6 is very rapid indeed, and makes a great noise. Standard equipment is extensive, and build quality is superb. As a Lexus, it would sell very well indeed – but as a Toyota, it's a bargain.

Best All-Rounder: Camry V6

Toyota Previa

Price from: £19,950

Some manufacturers build MPVs that look like buses; Toyota prefers to model its people carrier on space ships. Swoops, curves and hard-edged slashes abound, making the latest version just as distinctive as its predecessor. Things are more conventional underneath, with a front-wheel drive chassis driven by powerful and refined engines. The Previa is very easy to drive, only its size hindering progress. Ride quality is good, and fine handling keeps things on an even keel through bends, too. But an MPV also needs to offer great interior practicality, and here the Previa is a little less strong. Seating flexibility and luggage space are not as good as the class leaders, even though passenger space is admirably up there with the best.

Best All-Rounder: Previa 2.0 D-4D GLS

Body styles: MPV
Engine capacity: 2.4, 3.0V6, 2.0 D4-D
Manufactured in: Japan

Price from: £16,980

Toyota Celica

Body styles: Coupe
Engine capacity: 1.8
Manufactured in: Japan

One of the world's longest-running series of coupes, the latest Celica is a far better car than its fussy and bulky predecessor. Styling is funky, with both drama and beauty in equal measure, whilst inside it is also slick, though too much plastic lets things down a little. It is comfortable though, and the Celica is as easy as any Toyota to drive. Except this Toyota is also very sporty, with responsive steering, very sharp and fluid handling, and a ride quality that is never harsh or crashy. It is so good, in fact, that the standard engine feels under powered; the dramatic 190 VVT-i model answers such criticism brilliantly, with a very high-revving engine providing great power and sound effects. Impressive in every respect.

Best All-Rounder: Celica 190

TOYOTA

Price from: £16,495

Toyota Prius

Body styles: Saloon
Engine capacity: 1.5
Manufactured in: Japan

The clever Prius really is a 'car of the future'. It is the world's first production hybrid vehicle, and uses a 1.5-litre petrol engine which is boosted by an electric motor. It switches between the two seamlessly, thus dramatically cutting fuel consumption and emissions output. There are few compromises in performance though, making the Prius an entirely viable everyday proposition. It is also easy to drive, and the chassis is more than competent overall. Good levels of space and high equipment levels also feature, along with a brilliant digital 'economy centre' in the dash. Only the styling may put people off, for it is the only area where the Prius stands out. Otherwise, it is an effortless way to 'do your bit' for the environment.

Best All-Rounder: Prius 1.5

Toyota MR2

Price from: £17,980

Like with the Celica, Toyota stripped the MR2 of all excess fripperies when it was replaced last year. The latest model is thus smaller, lighter and far more engaging than the cumbersome old model – and for the first time with a convertible roof, too. Its new-found eagerness is apparent in the handling, which is very agile and quick to respond, and well-balanced too thanks to the rear-wheel-drive chassis. The 1.8-litre engine produces 140bhp, and is an impressive performer thanks to the MR2's light weight. Its smooth and eager nature is delightful – as is the great gearchange, though a Formula 1-style paddle-shift semi-auto is also available. It is comfortable inside, and although it lacks luggage space, the MR2 is a great car overall.

Best All-Rounder: MR2

Body styles: Convertible
Engine capacity: 1.8
Manufactured in: Japan

Price from: £13,480

Toyota Rav 4

Body styles: Estate
Engine capacity: 1.8, 2.0, 2.0D4-D
Manufactured in: Japan

Arguably the world's first 'soft roader', Toyota's RAV4 continues to offer 4x4 looks with a hot-hatch driving style. This all-new model has clearly been derived from the old one, but is improved in every way, not least in interior room and practicality. It is still available in three and five-door format, in both two and four-wheel-drive format, and offers a similar range of engines. Its handling remains great fun too, offering GTI-like agility that seems at odds with the rugged looks and tall construction. Ride and refinement are also impressive, as is the new-found interior room and flexibility. The dash design is pleasant, and it is well-equipped and very well-built. It may have many more rivals nowadays, but Toyota's RAV4 remains a strong choice.

Best All-Rounder: RAV4 2.0 NV 5dr

Toyota Land Cruiser Colorado

Price from: £23,800

For those who find the Amazon simply too huge, Toyota offers the smaller – but still big – Land Cruiser Colorado, its Land Rover Discovery rival. It is just as rugged, almost as imposing, and pretty impressive off-road too. However, on-road comfort is also fine, which in reality is where most are used. Here, the high driving position and ease of use really score, as does the impressive pulling power from the petrol and diesel engines. Body roll and ride quality are both well-controlled on the move, too. The interior may be plain but it is well-equipped, and the larger five-door version offers the practicality of seven seats. Throw in the assurance of Toyota build quality, and the capable Colorado appears an attractive choice.

Best All-Rounder: Land Cruiser Colorado GX

Body styles: Estate
Engine capacity: 2.7, 3.4V6, 3.0D4-D
Manufactured in: Japan

Price from: £34,000

Toyota Land Cruiser Amazon

Body styles: Estate
Engine capacity: 4.7V8, 4.2TD
Manufactured in: Japan

You expect it to be big, but the Amazon's sheer bulk still takes you by surprise when you first see one. This means its drivers enjoy a tremendous feeling of security, though this is replaced by stress when manoeuvring in tight spaces. Find an open road though, and the Amazon's bulk disappears. It handles well, with little of the typical 4x4 body roll, and always feels very well balance and composed. Large engines provide impressive performance, though both are also refined and smooth. Of course, the Amazon was designed as an off-roader, and here it is supreme. It is rarely challenged, and can truly be called a 'go-anywhere' vehicle – with the benefit of an extremely luxurious and comfortable interior as well.

Best All-Rounder: Land Cruiser Amazon VX TD

One of India's largest car makers, Tata has been selling the
Safari 4x4 vehicle, as well as a number of commercials, in the
UK market for some time now. Rarer than some supercars,
you're unlikely to have ever seen one. A Safari maybe crude by
western standards but it does come well specified by way of an apology. The Indica hatchback
has been on the motor show circuit for some time now but there has been little news of an on-
sale date in Western markets. Also competing for space on the Tata motor show stands has
been the Aria sports coupe. Looking like quite a convincing little car whether it will reach
production, or be able to compete in this already busy market sector, remains to be seen.

TATA

Tata Indica

Body styles: Hatchback
Engine capacity: 1.4, 1.4D

Price from: £na
Manufactured in: India

The Indian manufacturer has high hopes for this Fiesta-sized five-door hatchback. Sales are
due to commence in Europe, where its Italian IDEA-designed lines may well find favour. It is a
neat car, with an impressively spacious and well-designed interior. Even equipment levels are
commendable. The Tata should be reasonable to drive, thanks to all-independent suspension
and power-assisted steering. The French designed 1.4-litre petrol and diesel engines have a
good pedigree, though only the petrol unit looks to offer adequate performance. It is
currently a huge seller in a rapidly-expanding Indian market, so European sales will only add
to the growth of this increasingly comprehensive manufacturer.

Best All-Rounder: Indica 1.4

Tata Safari

Price from: £14,995

The Safari is Indian manufacturer Tata's first true passenger car,
and offers Land Rover Discovery-rivalling space for less than the
cost of a Freelander. It is very well-equipped too, and comes with
the assurance of a comprehensive warranty. Drawbacks? Sadly,
there are many. On the road, the diesel engine is noisy, slow and
not particularly economical, whilst the chassis lacks the on-road
ability and refinement of every other competitor. Build quality is
not great, and trim quality is poor, too. However, take the Safari
off-road, and it is far more competitive, with the four-wheel-drive
system providing great traction and grip over most terrains. As a
basic off-road wagon with an attractive amount of equipment, the
Safari makes sense; far more so than as a road car.

Body styles: Estate
Engine capacity: 2.0TD
Manufactured in: India

Best All-Rounder: Safari TDi

TVR

Independent in every meaning of the word, TVR is a two-fingered salute to the rest of the world's sports car manufacturers. Making virtually all its own components, including engines, TVR produces cars with performance to match the looks – outrageous. The past year has seen the end of production of the Griffith - the car that was responsible for the turn around of fortunes of the Blackpool based manufacturer. Overseas production ventures have proved unsuccessful, home production also being hit by a dip in the market. The Tamora joins the range as a replacement for the Griffith, while the Tuscan is now available in even more extreme racing variants. Heavily reliant on sales in its home market, TVR's blend of incredible power and jaw dropping design would undoubtedly sell well in the USA, though, sadly, getting their cars through tough approval laws would prove a prohibitively expensive hurdle.

NEW

TVR Tamora

`Engine capacity:` 3.6

Price from: £36,500

Manufactured in: England

Best All-Rounder: Tamora

TVR's new roadster has been designed to be smaller, cheaper and more accessible than its other models – though being a TVR, it is also innovative, uniquely-designed and, really, just 'different' from other rivals. It is based on the Tuscan chassis, and uses a 3.6-litre version of its straight-six engine. Performance is more than adequate, and the noise it makes has to be among the best of any road car. The interior is also great, with modern styling making it more of a work of art than a mere cockpit. From the outside, it is instantly recognisable as a TVR, with simple lines that portray the model's power well. It is sure to be a highly successful addition to TVR's increasingly comprehensive and desirable range.

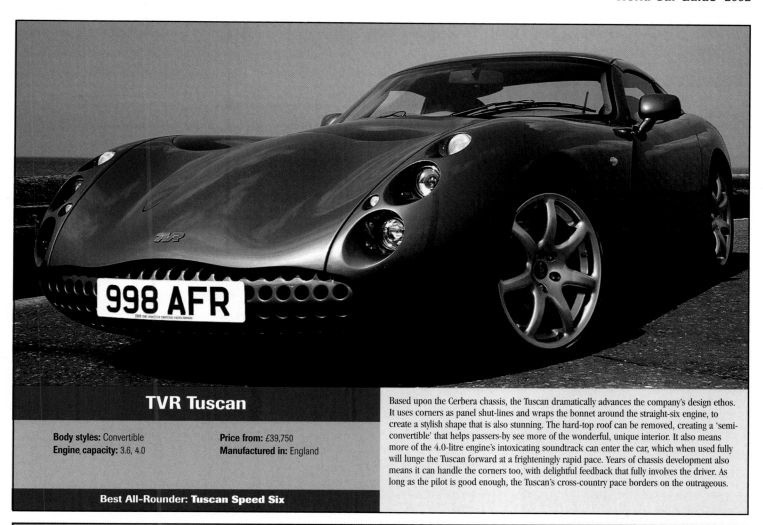

TVR Tuscan

Body styles: Convertible
Engine capacity: 3.6, 4.0

Price from: £39,750
Manufactured in: England

Best All-Rounder: Tuscan Speed Six

Based upon the Cerbera chassis, the Tuscan dramatically advances the company's design ethos. It uses corners as panel shut-lines and wraps the bonnet around the straight-six engine, to create a stylish shape that is also stunning. The hard-top roof can be removed, creating a 'semi-convertible' that helps passers-by see more of the wonderful, unique interior. It also means more of the 4.0-litre engine's intoxicating soundtrack can enter the car, which when used fully will lunge the Tuscan forward at a frighteningly rapid pace. Years of chassis development also means it can handle the corners too, with delightful feedback that fully involves the driver. As long as the pilot is good enough, the Tuscan's cross-country pace borders on the outrageous.

Price from: £34,980

TVR Chimaera

Body styles: Convertible
Engine capacity: 4.5V8, 5.0V8
Manufactured in: England

Even the cheapest model in TVR's range, the 'entry-level' Chimaera, packs a high-capacity V8 engine. Available in various states of tune, even the basic version is more than powerful enough; it's a case of just how fast you want to go. All make a great noise when worked hard, deep and throbbing and beastly. Surprisingly, refinement is good on motorways, too. Handling can be entertaining, especially in the wet, but the rear-wheel-drive chassis is generally well-behaved, and very sporting in feel. The cockpit is also traditionally racy, with superb leather bucket seats and a distinctive wood-trimmed dashboard. It may show its age when sat next to the Tuscan and Tamora, but the Chimaera is still brilliant fun.

Best All-Rounder: Chimaera 5.0

TVR Cerbera

Price from: £41,100

Body styles: Coupe
Engine capacity: 4.0V8, 4.2V8, 4.5V8
Manufactured in: England

The Cerbera coupe looks like a sleek sports car, which it is, but it is a four-seater too, though admittedly the rear two are tiny. It is extremely low and long, which makes for a stunning presence on the road. Inside, things are just as stylish, with the dash being extremely innovative in its design and materials. Ahead is either a V8 or straight-six engine, providing supercar-like power and the ability to make all the right noises. The Speed Six, with that straight-six engine, is especially desirable, and its softer suspension settings create more of a 'British' feel, too. Any Cerbera will offer a driving challenge, thanks to all that power and the rear-wheel-drive set-up. Mastering it is all part of the appeal.

Best All-Rounder: Cerbera Speed Six

VAUXHALL/OPEL

The European arm of the GM empire has oft been criticised for producing lacklustre cars, average in every way without much in the way of driver appeal. In the past there have been flashes of inspiration, rebellion even, though until recently the range continued to offer transportation at its most dull. Thankfully things have changed for the better, the current model line up being far more appealing than their predecessors, some even up there with the class leaders. The indifferent Euro NCAP performance of the otherwise excellent Zafira was a surprise, and given the importance buyers are now placing on safety a serious oversight. The most important car to debut this year is the new Vectra which should, if the Astra and Corsa are measures, prove to be a giant leap forward in every way from the current car – it needs to be.

Vauxhall/Opel VX220

Body styles: Convertible
Engine capacity: 2.2
Price from: £22,995
Manufactured in: England

A Vauxhall roadster that can outrun a Porsche? You'd better believe it, for the VX220 is the most dramatic car to sport the Griffin badge since the outrageous Lotus Carlton. Fittingly, Lotus engineering is present here too, as the VX220 is built by the British specialist, on an adapted version of the Elise chassis. This means it is very light, very strong, and handles just as well as a race car. Feedback and agility are superb, making it a real pleasure to drive. It is also very fast, the 150bhp 2.2-litre engine combining with the light weight to offer superb performance; ABS-supported brakes slow things down well, too. It is basic inside, but when it drive this well, who cares? Brilliant fun, and affordable too.

Best All-Rounder: VX220 2.2

Vauxhall/Opel Agila

Price from: £6,995

Body styles: Hatchback
Engine capacity: 1.0, 1.2
Manufactured in: Hungary

The recent city car explosion caught Vauxhall unawares. As a market leader, such a hole in its range was unacceptable, so owners General Motors stepped in with assistance. Thus, a reworked Suzuki Wagon R now sports the Vauxhall 'V' grille and an Agila badge at the rear. Built at a new plant in Hungary, the Agila is a little more distinct underneath, using Vauxhall's own, excellent 1.0-litre three-cylinder and 1.2-litre four-cylinder engines. They help make the Agila surprisingly good to drive, though interior practicality is likely to be a bigger selling point. The tall body means there is plenty of room for four adults, if not all of their luggage, and there's fair amount of equipment. Only style is lacking, which is where its rivals score.

Best All-Rounder: Agila 1.2 16v

Vauxhall/Opel Corsa

Price from: £7,495

As good as the old model was poor, Vauxhall's Corsa is now a far more appealing proposition. The styling may look similar to before, but underneath, the all-new chassis is far more capable. Ride and handling are now well up with the class leaders, while refinement and safety are also very impressive. Engines are similar to before, but this is fine as they were always a highlight of the old Corsa. The high levels of interior space also remain, with added build quality and comfort, too. However, whereas three and five-door models used sport distinct styles, they now look the same, to boost previously disappointing sales of the more practical version. Far better in every way, the Corsa remains a UK best-seller.

Body styles: Hatchback
Engine capacity: 1.0, 1.2, 1.4, 1.8, 1.7Di, 1.7DTi
Manufactured in: Portugal, Spain

Best All-Rounder: Corsa 1.4 Elegance

Vauxhall/Opel Astra

Price from: £10,580

Estate

Convertible

Engine capacity: 1.2, 1.4, 1.6, 1.8, 2.0, 2.0T, 2.2, 1.7DTi, 2.0Di, 2.0DTi
Manufactured in: Eng

The Astra marked a turnaround in Vauxhall's philosophy. Dull dynamics and a clumpy ride quality were out, to be replaced by a genuinely pleasurable experience that is still in many ways class-leading. The handling is superb, with great composure and security boosted by very precise steering. The ride quality is also excellent, especially over poor-quality surfaces, and reinforces the fine levels of refinement; the Astra makes a good long-distance cruiser. There is a large engine range, and few are less than excellent – the star is the new 2.2-litre unit. The interior offers a generous amount of space, though the dashboard design is extremely unimaginative, and is by far the Astra's weakest area. Otherwise, the extensive Astra range is competitive, making it a genuinely desirable family car contender.

Best All-Rounder: Astra 1.6 16v SXi

Vauxhall/Opel Vectra

Price from: £13,235

Despite all the criticism, Vauxhall's Vectra continues to be a best seller, proving that it can't all be bad. Sure enough, it has many strengths, not least a superb range of engines. The 2.2-litre unit is a gem, though even the entry 1.6-litre is fairly quick and refined. Equipment levels are also reasonable, and there is a fair amount of interior space. On the road, motorways are the Vectra's forte, where it is as refined and relaxing as any rival. It is when you travel on other roads that the flaws are revealed; the ride can be choppy, and the handling is unengaging, though it is far better than it was.

Best All-Rounder: Vectra 2.2DTi

Estate

Body styles: Hatchback, saloon, estate
Engine capacity: 1.6, 1.8, 2.2, 2.6V6, 2.0DTi, 2.2DTi
Manufactured in: England

Vauxhall/Opel Omega

Price from: £18,195

Estate

Body styles: Saloon, estate
Engine capacity: 2.0, 2.2, 2.6V6, 3.2V6, 2.2DTi, 2.5TD
Manufactured in: Germany

One of the few mass-manufacturer executive cars to really succeed, Vauxhall's Omega continues to offer an appealing package. The rear-wheel-drive chassis is well balanced, indulging the keen driver without sacrificing ride comfort or composure; the Omega is great on motorways, but good on twisty back roads, too. It is powered by a fine engine range, that includes pleasant V6 units and Vauxhall's current star, the 2.2-litre four-cylinder powerplant, which is fast and refined, but economical too. Also, there is more than enough space in the comfortable interior, which is very well designed thanks to revisions in 1999. It may be familiar, but the Omega is still an attractive proposition, especially considering Vauxhall's competitive prices and extensive support network.

Best All-Rounder: Omega 2.2 GLS

Vauxhall/Opel Zafira

Price from: £13,995

It may have arrived a few years later than the car that inspired it, Renault's Scenic, but the Zafira has quickly established itself as a class leader. This sales success is due mainly to one key advantage over the Renault – seven seats. The rear two fold flat into the floor, too, meaning luggage space is not compromised when they're not in use – clever. As it is based on the Astra, the Zafira drives well, and has even spawned a rapid turbo-charged version which is great fun to drive. The ride is perhaps a little firm around town, but this pays dividends on the motorway, where the Zafira is composed. Sadly, the Astra's dull dashboard also remains, but otherwise it is a well-deserved sales success.

Best All-Rounder: Zafira 1.8 Comfort

Body styles: Compact MPV
Engine capacity: 1.6, 1.8, 2.2, 2.0DTi
Manufactured in: Germany

Vauxhall/Opel Frontera

Price from: £15,495

5-DR

Body styles: Estate
Engine capacity: 2.2, 3.2V6, 2.2DTi
Manufactured in: England

The success of the Land Rover Freelander has, ironically, highlighted just what good value the Frontera is. Few small 4x4s offer such space, equipment and off-road ability for so little, with the added bonus of rugged good looks, too. A strong engine range includes a very smooth and powerful 3.2-litre V6, though the best overall bet is probably the refined 2.2-litre turbo-diesel. All are fine on-road performers, but are let down by the chassis; it is not as smooth or composed as many rivals, a legacy of the great off-road ability. It is certainly tough though, and will easily take rough driving conditions in its stride. The interior is also comfortable and practical, and overall the Frontera is a stylish but sensible buy.

Best All-Rounder: Frontera 2.2 TD Estate

VOLKSWAGEN

The ambitious plans of VW seem to be working: the Golf/Bora is one of the world's best selling cars. Moving ever-more upmarket, the VW range is complemented by its sub-brands Skoda and Seat while it's encroaching on Audi territory with many of its models. Not only does it have the volume car market sewn up: VW's ownership of Bugatti, Lamborghini (through Audi) and Bentley give it the sort of scope unrivalled by any other manufacturer. In spite of this, rumours of a Ford take-over have been circulating, but seem unlikely. New models introduced this year should include an as yet unnamed 4x4, which it shares with Porsche, and the D1 luxury car. The concept microbus is also under consideration for production, a model that would appeal to both US and European buyers alike.

NEW

Volkswagen Micobus

Engine capacity: 3.2 V6

Price from: £na

Manufactured in: na

Best All-Rounder: To early to say

Like the original New Beetle concept, Volkswagen's Microbus concept brilliantly brings the '60s icon bang up-to-date – and it too looks set for production. Few vehicles are as desirable, and no six-seat MPV is as stylish as this imposing all-new 'Combi'. It's a similar story inside, where the original interior has been combined with 21st-century design, sending 'wantability' right off the scale. Meanwhile, a 3.2-litre V6 engine offers smooth-running power, which the chassis should cope well with; it's based on the forthcoming VW 4x4. On a practical front, there's plenty of space for six passengers – who enjoy cosseting aircraft-style seats – and overall comfort levels are boosted by a wealth of futuristic gadgets. For around £30,000 it is sure to be popular; get your order in now!

Volkswagen Lupo

Price from: £7,195

The cute Lupo is the city car sector's highest-quality entrant. From the flawless paint finish to the extremely high-quality interior that wouldn't look out of place in a £50,000 car, the Lupo exudes expense. So the fact that it is competitively-priced is even more surprising, especially when the equipment level shows no evidence of cost-cutting. A wide engine range means there is a model for most needs, topped by the fun GTi's 1.6-litre unit. All Lupos drive with a confident and mature feel, though only the GTi could be called sporting. Refinement in all models is excellent, and it is only in rear passenger and boot space where the Lupo is not so good. Otherwise, a fine and very desirable city car front-runner.

Body styles: Hatchback
Engine capacity: 1.0, 1.4, 1.6, 1.2TD, 1.4TD, 1.7D
Price from: £7,195
Manufactured in: Germany

Best All-Rounder: Lupo 1.4 S

NEW

Volkswagen Polo

Price from: £9,000 (est)

Body styles: Hatchback
Engine capacity: 1.2, 1.4, 19D, 1.4 TDi, 1.9 TDi
Manufactured in: Germany

Each incarnation of the Polo gets bigger than before, so this all-new model is now pretty much the same size as the original Golf. It takes on the cheeky nose of the smaller Lupo, but otherwise it's a plain, workmanlike design from the house of Volkswagen. The chassis is similar to that of the award-winning Skoda Fabia, so there is plenty of promise there. Engines are a mix of the familiar and new – an interesting model will be the new 3-cylinder 1.2-litre petrol model. Initially the only other petrol engine will be a 1.4, but there will be a host of diesels to keep frugal drivers happy. Safety levels are vastly improved. All Polos get ABS brakes, four airbags and four head restraints.

Best All-Rounder: Too soon to say

Volkswagen Golf

Price from: £10,715

The icon of modern-day Volkswagen. The Beetle may have helped the Group grow, but it is the Golf that keeps it prospering, thanks to a peerless image and unsurpassable quality. It really is quite brilliantly well-built, with a feeling of quality that even some Mercedes now lack. It is also spacious and very comfortable too, with room for four passengers and all of their luggage. On the road, a large engine range offers plenty of choice in power, but all are refined and smooth. In any guise, the Golf drives with supreme refinement, and is also comfortable and confident across most surfaces. Only the sporty versions really handle with true driver involvement, though. Overall, a deserved object of much desire.

Best All-Rounder: Golf TDI 115

Estate

Convertible

Body styles: Hatchback, saloon, convertible, estate
Engine capacity: 1.4, 1.6, 1.8T, 2.0, 2.3V5, 2.8V6, 1.9SDi, 1.9TD
Manufactured in: Germany

Volkswagen Bora

Price from: £13,035

Body styles: Saloon
Engine capacity: 1.4, 1.6, 1.8T, 2.0, 2.3V5, 2.8V6, 1.9TD
Manufactured in: Germany

Far more of a junior executive saloon than its predecessors, few now see the Bora as merely a 'booted' Golf. The unique and attractive nose helps, though the middle section, chassis and interior are identical to its illustrious sister. This means comfort and refinement are excellent, and higher specification levels add further attraction, too. To make the Bora drive as a sporty car should, the suspension has been stiffened over the Golf's set-up, providing a keener cornering stance with less roll. This means the ride is firmer, but it is a good compromise – especially with some of the attractive large alloy wheel options. The engine range is smaller than the Golf's but features more of its upper-range units. A good-value Audi and BMW alternative.

Best All-Rounder: Bora 2.3 V5

Volkswagen Passat

Price from: £14,495

Facelifted last year, the Passat remains one of the Mondeo class's largest and most mature competitors; the estate version is particularly spacious. It is also imposing but attractive to look at, with swooping curves and a wide-tracked stance. Inside, it is comfortable and relaxing, with a simple and clean dash design that is very easy to use. A huge engine range is offered, from lowly 1.6-litre to powerful 2.8-litre V6 petrol units, though it is the diesel units that are the stars of the show. All provide effortless performance, that fits in well with the Passat's relaxed, refined nature. It may not handle like a BMW, but it provides a long-distance motorway comfort that few others can match. Still a worthy choice.

Best All-Rounder: Passat TDI 130

Estate

Body styles: Saloon, estate
Engine capacity: 1.6, 1.8T, 2.0, 2.3V5, 2.8V6, 1.9TD, 2.5TD
Manufactured in: Germany

VOLKSWAGEN

Price from: £18,395

Volkswagen Sharan

Body styles: MPV
Engine capacity: 1.8T, 2.0, 2.8V6, 1.9TDi
Manufactured in: Portugal

Now looking, along with its Galaxy and Alhambra friends, a little more distinct and stylish, the Sharan remains the quality MPV of choice. It is, of course, all but identical to the Ford and SEAT, but the trims and image of the Volkswagen seem that bit more expensive than the other two. The dash and interior design is just as attractive and versatile though, making this a justifiably popular practical MPV. The wide engine range includes powerful V6 and impressively economical TDI diesel units, with the option of six-speed manual and automatic transmissions; there is also a four-wheel-drive option. Well equipped too, the practical Sharan remains a comfortable MPV that is also one of the most stylish on the market.

Best All-Rounder: Sharan TDI 115

Volkswagen Beetle

Price from: £13,000

It is surely the most recognisable profile in the world – the big-wheelarched, hoop-roofed original is the world's best-selling car, and is still loved by millions across the globe. Keen to commemorate this, Volkswagen has thus brought us the New Beetle; unmistakably retro, and stylish like few other cars. Underneath sits the chassis of a Golf, which means the front-engined, front-wheel-drive Beetle drives with composure, though many won't find it as fun as the original. Engines are also either unremarkable or expensive to fuel – with the exception of the acclaimed TDI turbo-diesel. Inside, the interior is just as stylish, though a little cramped in the rear. It faces stiff competition against the new MINI, but VW's New Beetle is accomplished enough to compete.

Best All-Rounder: Beetle TDI

Body styles: Hatchback
Engine capacity: 1.6, 1.8T, 2.0, 2.3V5, 1.9TD
Manufactured in: Mexico

Price from: £12,380

Volkswagen Beetle

Body styles: Saloon
Engine capacity: 1.6
Manufactured in: Mexico

The longest-running car in the world remains on sale, and incredibly is also still available in the UK. Built in Mexico, shrewd importers have responded to the 'New Beetle' hype with their own 'new Beetle', a modern classic in every sense of the word. However, it has disc brakes, a fuel-injected version of the famous flat-four engine and even a catalytic converter; everyday motoring in modern conditions is certainly viable. Don't expect modern levels of comfort or convenience inside though, for there haven't really been any modifications since VW stopped making them in the 1970s – it's all part of the charm. For many only the look and thrummy sound of the rear-engined original will do; it still makes sense, even now.

Best All-Rounder: Beetle 1.6i

Volkswagen Gol

Price from: £na

It is not missing an 'f' – Gol is Portuguese for goal, and Volkswagen has certainly 'struck' with its car for South America. Built using local labour, it has certainly been an answer to the flood of European-built hatches which have gained a strong footing in the open Brazilian market. It is a true Brazilian design too, merely taking styling cues from Volkswagen Europe, not direction or manpower. It is a very appealing model, with an eager range of engines that is topped by the impressive 145bhp GTi. The well-built Volkswagen feel carries across onto the road too, with the Gol displaying a very mature stance in rough conditions. Also available as an estate, this is an impressive car for a rapidly-growing market.

Best All-Rounder: Gol 2.0 GTi 16v

Body styles: Hatchback, estate
Engine capacity: 1.0, 1.2, 1.6, 1.8, 2.0
Manufactured in: Brazil

Now owned by Ford, Volvo is set to spearhead the blue oval's attack on the executive car market, with a blend of Swedish style and accomplished dynamics. The attractive S60 is gaining recognition as a true BMW 3-Series alternative, while the much-improved S/V40 range is posting reasonable sales at the lower end. Future models include rivals to the Audi A3 hatchback and Allroad semi-off-roader – dubbed SCC and ACC – while enthusiasts will be encouraged by the imminent launch of the high-performance S60 model. Volvo traditions also remain, not least the admirable crash safety record and reassuringly solid build quality; while class-competitive style is a more recent addition, Volvo appears to do that just as well, too.

VOLVO

Volvo SCC

Engine capacity:
not known

Price from: £na

Manufactured in: unconfirmed

Best All-Rounder: Too soon to say

Shown as a concept at the 2001 Geneva Motor Show, the Safety Concept Car provides a strong pointer to Volvo's future. The Golf-sized hatchback features a very attractive style with plenty of references to Volvo's past, and enough style to place it at the head of the fashion-conscious set. As the name indicates, there are plenty of innovative safety features, many of which will hopefully make it into production. Harder to gauge are the SCC's mechanicals; a shortened version of the S/V40 chassis has been suggested, possibly with engines derived from the extensive range of Ford units. Not due until 2003 at the earliest, the SCC is the model intended to boost Volvo sales by a third; its success is vital.

Volvo S/V40

Price from: £14,480

Today's smallest Volvos have come a long way from their Mitsubishi Carisma roots. Despite being produced in the same Netherlands factory, both S40 saloon and V40 estates offer a superior drive that is far better than the first models. Last year, a lengthened wheelbase and widened track improved ride quality and stability, and handling was also sharpened through influence from new owners Ford. A mildly revised dash improved quality, though good design and reasonable equipment levels have always been a factor. A powerful, if slightly gruff, range of engines provide adequate pace, which borders on sports-car quick in the 200bhp turbo-charged T4. Best in practical V40 form, both Ford and Volvo will be hoping their considerable efforts result in improved sales figures.
Best All-Rounder: V40 2.0 T

Estate

Body styles: Saloon, estate
Engine capacity: 1.6, 1.8, 1.8GDi, 2.0, 2.0T, 1.9TD
Manufactured in: Netherlands, South Africa

ROY 780

VOLVO

Price from: £19,995

Volvo S60

Body styles: Saloon
Engine capacity: 2.0T, 2.3T, 2.4, 2.4T, 2.4D5
Manufactured in: Sweden

The much-praised S60 is slowly gaining recognition in the compact executive market, due in no small part to its distinctive styling. The pronounced waistline runs from the front grille to the bootlid, which itself sweeps forward into a coupe-like rear profile. It is clever and unique, as is the roomy and practical interior, which, in the Volvo tradition, is ergonomically superb. Power is provided by a range of turbo-charged five-cylinder engines, all with power outputs and refinement that put them near the top of their class. The S60 also handles with flair, despite the limitations of a front-wheel-drive chassis, and ride comfort is fine over most surfaces. For those who want something that's stylish and different, Volvo's S60 offers a commendable package.

Best All-Rounder: S60 2.0T

Volvo V70

Price from: £20,500

Not an S80 estate, the similarities between the stylish V70 and Volvo's largest saloon seem obvious. It is a stand-alone model though, and uses a reworked version of the S80 chassis that is optimised for estate-car use. The interior is also similar but the biggest news is behind the rear seats – few manufacturers offer such practicality or sheer volume. Safety is also traditionally high, with a multitude of airbags and good Euro NCAP crash test results – but unlike older Volvos, it is also pleasant from behind the wheel. In its element on motorways, the V70 is also good over twisty B-roads, with plenty of power from the turbo-charged range of five-cylinder engines and fine, smooth-running comfort.

Best All-Rounder: V70 2.4T

Body styles: Estate
Engine capacity: 2.0T, 2.3T, 2.4, 2.4D5
Manufactured in: Sweden, Belgium

Price from: £20,640

Volvo S80

Body styles: Saloon
Engine capacity: 2.0T, 2.4, 2.4T, 2.8T, 2.9, 2.4D5
Manufactured in: Sweden

The largest Volvo saloon was a big step forward over its boxy, style-free predecessors. A new design with a distinctive waistline set the theme for future models, and was strong enough to be attractive in its own right – without copying the dominant Germans. Inside, typically efficient Swedish design offers a very comfortable environment, with plenty of room for passengers. The S80 is fine to drive too, with a very safe feel and impressive ride quality. The front-wheel-drive chassis is not tuned for handling supremacy, but over long distances in bad weather, few cars feel as secure or composed. Safety kit is also unsurpassed, and combined with responsive, powerful engines, the S80 appears a good choice for those who cover huge mileages.

Best All-Rounder: S80 2.9

Volvo C70

Price from: £22,860

This was the car that showed the world that things at Volvo were changing. Safety would always be on the menu, but future models would add simple, elegant Swedish style too; unarguably present in the luxuriously sporting C70. They would also be good to drive, in the manner debuted by the C70 – plenty of refinement and pace, and secure, reasonably sharp handling. Cross-country enjoyment may not be up there with the best, but the overall speed available is very impressive indeed. Inside, comfort levels are high, and one of the best stereo systems in the business is available as an option. Stylish in coupe form and elegant as a cabriolet, the C70 is an endearing, low-volume alternative to BMW's smaller 3-Series coupe.

Best All-Rounder: C70

Convertible

Body styles: Coupe, convertible
Engine capacity: 2.0T, 2.3T, 2.4T
Manufactured in: Sweden

TRACK DAYS

Ever fancied not just sitting in front of the TV, watching Schumacher and Coulthard battle it out, but actually having a go yourself? Ironically, thanks to ever-increasing speed and safety regulations, combined with increasingly more capable cars, a whole new industry has formed that allows drivers to use their cars harder than ever: the booming industry of track days.

The world-wide increase in track day popularity means that almost every famous circuit now opens its gates to the paying public, giving them the opportunity them to push their cars to the maximum around the famous twists and turns. Forget TV, but the only way to really experience a circuit is to actually drive on it yourself – true interaction!

In its simplest form, a track day is exactly that – a day at the track. Just turn up in your road car, arrange your allocated sessions, and you are then basically free to drive as fast as you want. There are no speed limits, no traffic-calming measures, absolutely nothing to hinder you from pushing you and your car to the limit.

So how does it pan out in practice? The majority of organisers work to a session format – usually half-hour blocks where groups of cars are allowed out onto the circuit. This ensures there is no overcrowding, and most also try to group cars of similar performance and drivers of similar experience, further reducing congestion on the circuit.

You are free to stay out in your session for as long as you want, pushing harder and harder each time round, as you discover what your car can really do and just where its limits lie. Just try not to spin, or overheat your brakes or engine; both will bring your day to a premature end.

Even when you're not driving there's plenty to see and do. Watching other cars on the track is

great fun, as is the camaraderie in the pit lane with other car owners. If you own a popular model, you'll be chatting all day long, and will probably also pick up a few tips on how to improve your car. You really get involved, and may even make new friends to attend future days with, too.

You are also driving on the same tarmac as the greats. Whereas before, the only way you could actually drive on the circuits was if you were racing or taking part in an expensive 'experience' day, now all you need is your road car and a few hundred pounds. As long as you compensate for additional tyre and brake wear – and consider taking out extra track-only insurance, which is relatively inexpensive – you'll have a truly affordable experience that will be raved about for weeks.

Believe it or not, there is even a safety benefit once you're back on the highway, too. Familiarity with on-the-limit handling characteristics on the track means that, should an emergency situation arise on the road, you'll have far more knowledge and confidence in your car to avoid it. And, should your car 'bite' on the limit, you'll be aware of it and know what to do, too.

Almost every new car on sale makes a viable track day car. If you're pushing it to the limit, overall power is immaterial; the sheer thrill of driving a car flat-out is often enough; a supermini can be just as much fun as a high-performance sports car. As actual racing is discouraged at track days, if someone else has a faster car, so what? You don't need to beat them to have fun.

Of course, many have preferences for high-performance cars. However, a small hot hatch can often be more fun than such expensive machinery, meaning you can buy a very focused brand-new track day machine often for less than £15,000. Second-hand cars are even less; a £1000 1980s hot hatch is just as thrilling, without the heartbreak should you 'push the limits' a little too far…

This affordability really is the best part of track days. Buying and running a race car is extremely expensive, putting it out of the reach of all but a select few. Even if you enter just a few races a year, you could quite easily be looking at five-figure sums.

However, a track day allows you to run at Silverstone, Monza, the Nurburgring and other famous circuits for a comparative pittance. Even the most prestigious events don't cost much more than £300, whilst an average event will give you a day's running for the price of a few tanks of fuel. And you can do it all in your standard road car.

This means track days are open to us all. They are huge fun, they allow a car's limits to be experienced in safety, and they teach you how to control extreme situations on the public highway. Anyone who says that modern motoring isn't any fun only needs to visit one, for a blast unlike any they've had in years. Schumacher, watch out!

AND THE REST...

While we strive to make the World Car Guide as comprehensive as possible there's a number of smaller manufacturers around the world that are little known to all but a select few. Here's just a few of the many small manufacturers that plug the holes left by the bigger manufacturers, offering cars that are ideal for their particular market conditions, be it rough third world roads or sweeping unrestricted autobahns.

Pagani Zonda

The Zonda represents the current pinnacle of supercar manufacture. Built by an independent concern, Pagani Cars, the Zonda C12 rocked the supercar establishment when it was launched to a wide-eyed public. Awesome looks clothe an immensely strong structure featuring carbon construction with massive Mercedes firepower in the form of a tweaked V12 engine. All this gives the C12 shattering performance, being the fastest supercar of the moment, which while unable to breach the lofty heights of the McLaren F1, is about as close as you'll get in any current production car. All this, and the attention to detail inside and out, makes the C12 one of the most complete cars of its type - ever. Expect it to become a household name.

Ascari Ecosse

The Ecosse is the dream creation of one man Klauss Zwart – a Dutch businessman living in Scotland – hence the name. Made in tiny numbers, the Ecosse is one of only a handful of cars that can credibly claim to be a 200mph machine. Its power comes from a Hartge-tuned 4.7-litre V8 engine, sourced from BMW, allowing the Ecosse to sprint to 60mph in around 4 seconds. Designed to give a real racecar for the road feel, the Ascari is an accomplished supercar. Add in individual good looks, exclusivity and a pricing that makes the more established manufacturers look expensive and the Ecosse has desirability written all over it.

Bristol Blenheim

Bristol has a long and illustrious history producing fine automobiles for customers that are more discerning than the average motorist. Despite the odd proportions, the Blenheim is a comfortable four-seater with the sort of performance that both the customers and company would describe as 'adequate'. An all-new car is expected soon – the Fighter – certain to offer 200+mph capability and outstanding comfort for its occupants. Firm orders for the first year's production have been taken, the quiet British firm offering peerless cars without the need to shout about it. Singular in its approach to everything, Bristol maintains the majority of its customer's cars, constantly improving all its models, not just the newer versions. A unique car maker that is one of Britain's treasures.

Westfield

Creating thrilling sports cars for a band of loyal customers, the Midlands-based manufacturer may be a small concern in the world of car manufacture but offers other-worldly performance from its range of machines. Compact and lightweight, the cars can be bought either full assembled or as a kit. Obviously the latter route is the way to go for a cheaper car, and taken by many, but either way customers will get a car of immense ability. A wide range of engines are available, from a wild V8 to more tame four-cylinder units, but for really manic thrills there's the option of superbike-engined versions. Whatever the choice, faithful steering, entertaining handling and pin-sharp responses ensure that you'll always have an exhilarating drive. Totally impractical – but then that's not the point, is it?

Lada

The butt of many a joke, the Russian manufacturer is still producing cars to this day for its home market. Basic and utilitarian, the range is suited to the harsh conditions it faces in Russia - but it left Britain back in 1990. The Niva 4x4 is an off-roader of exceptional ability, while the saloon 110 and Samara offer motoring that's about as far removed from Western vehicles as imaginable. Producing arguably one of the world's cheapest cars – the Oka – retailing at the equivalent of £1,000, it's a hugely basic means of transport. Safety and emission legislation prevent them being sold over here, thankfully, its survival, even in its home market, being one of the mysteries of the automotive industry.

Grinall

Creators of the oddball Scorpion three wheeler, Grinall has gotten sensible and is looking to produce a four-wheeled version. Not that the three-wheel Scorpion was the joke that the majority of three-wheeled vehicles tend to be, offering a spectacularly entertaining drive with its single driven rear wheel and BMW motorcycle power. The four-wheeled version gains a car engine as well as the extra wheel, this time power being Fiat sourced, utilising the turbo-charged five-cylinder 2.0-litre unit that used to power the now defunct coupe model. Fortunately Grinall has decided to stick to the styling of the Scorpion. The new car is certain to be a hit among the growing band of track day enthusiasts who seek increasingly outrageous performance machines to get their thrills.

Jensen

The gestation period for the S-V8 has been a lengthy process - the car was first shown back in 1998. Good news for Jensen fans, though, is that the first cars are now being delivered to the new nation-wide (UK) dealership network. Offering styling that harks back to Jensen models of yesteryear it's a distinctive looking machine. Using a Ford-sourced 4.6-litre 325bhp V8 engine, the performance is sure to be impressive, much effort being paid to the suspension settings to ensure both a cosseting ride and high levels of grip and driver involvement. The 155mph roadster will be joined by a coupe version, the C-V8 sometime next year, which arguably looks better than the roadster version upon which it is based.

Hindustan

If you ever wondered what happens to old cars once manufacturers have finished with them then Hindustan offers an insight. Rather than scrap expensive tooling for obslolete models, manufacturers often sell production equipment, resulting in old models cropping up in far-flung markets under unusual badging. This is the case with Hindustan, which produces the Ambassador, amazingly an Indian version of the 1950's Morris Oxford. It's not the only car they produce, but one of the most popular, with its simple construction and rugged character suited to the conditions in India. Recently a license agreement with Mitsubishi gives Hindustan the ability to produce old Lancers, but the Ambassador continues to be a hugely popular vehicle.

Mahindra

Sold for a short time to British buyers, the CJ was seen as a cheap and cheerful route to obtaining a rugged looking off-roader. Sadly the reality was an incredibly crude vehicle that had some semblance of cool with its Willy's Jeep roots. While inappropriate for European roads in its home market of India the CJ is a highly desirable vehicle. Its crudeness and off-road ability means it's perfectly suited to the rough driving conditions encountered in India – where Tarmac roads are often in a poor state of repair. A wide range of body styles and wheelbases are offered making the CJ the most practical of vehicles, power comes from a range of Peugeot-sourced diesels.

Strathcarron

Like a number of specialist manufacturers Strathcarron has opted to power its lightweight roadster with a motorcycle engine – a 1,200cc Triumph engine mated to a sequential gearbox. Featuring a lightweight chassis developed by the legendary racecar manufacturer Reynard, the Strathcarron is a flyweight contender with serious performance appeal. There are no concessions to practicality – with no doors or even a roof – the Strathcarron intended to be used as a toy rather than day-to-day proposition. While that may seem like an oversight, the increasing popularity of track days means there's a growing number of customers wanting a fun car, Strathcarron claiming it can hardly keep up with the growing demand.

Noble

Noble Moy Automotive may only be a few years old but in its short existence it's managed to upset a few established manufacturers with its offerings. First to upset the natural order was the M10 which took on the acclaimed Lotus Elise and beat it at its own game. The latest car is the M12 GTO that since being introduced last year has proven to be one of the most enjoyable sportscars ever. Powered by a 2.5-litre mid mounted V6 engine, the M12 GTO has gained praise from all who have driven it, impressing with an incredible combination of performance, fantastic handling and incredible value. Considering the short gestation period what Noble Moy has achieved is phenomenal. Customers recognise this with full order books for the next full year of production.

TECHNICAL DATA

The table on the next few pages outlines the technical background to cars listed in the Guide. With close to 1400 versions listed, it is the most comprehensive guide you'll find.

By and large we have used the car manufacturers' own figures, so in places where they are unable or unwilling to release the information we have placed a dash. Engine capacity is given in cubic centimetres, power in bhp, although the common metric power unit, PS, gives much the same result. Fuel type is denoted by P for petrol, D for diesel. Engine configuration is a combination of the layout and the number of cylinders – S equates to straight (or in-line), F for flat (or horizontally opposed) V is self explanatory; the number of cylinders follows. The driven wheels are noted, Front, Rear or 4 wheel drive. Top speed and acceleration from rest to 60 mph are the two universally popular measures of a car's performance. Just one fuel consumption figure is given, the combined cycle, as this is arguably the most realistic of the statutory tests. The insurance group is the standardised rating system used in the UK, on a scale of 1 to 20. Groups cannot be given for cars not sold in the UK, or the very latest models which have yet to be rated. Length and width are for the saloon or hatchback version. Figures for estate cars are not included, and the weight, in kilograms, is for the lightest version in each range.

Finally, not all the cars listed will be available for sale in the UK. Check the new price tables later on for the definitive list of availability, then cross refer back to this list. Remember that some cars are sold only in a restricted model range in the UK, and different examples are available elsewhere – the data table is as complete as we can make it.

	Engine – CC	Power – bhp	Fuel	Engine config.	Driven wheels	Top speed – mph	0–60 mph – secs	mpg – average	Insurance group	Length – mm	Width – mm	Weight – Kg
AC												
Cobra												
5.0	4942	228	P	V8	R	145	5.3	–	20	4200	1746	1050
3.5	3506	354	P	V8	R	–	4.0	–	20	4200	1746	900
Mamba												
3.5	3506	354	P	V8	R	–	–	–	–	4200	1746	–
4.0	3984	232	P	V8	R	–	–	–	–	4200	1746	–
4.0 LPG	3506	193	LPG	V8	R	–	–	–	–	4200	1746	–
ALFA ROMEO												
147												
1.6 Twin Spark	1598	104	P	S4	F	115	11.3	35	–	4170	1730	1190
1.6 Twin Spark	1598	118	P	S4	F	121	10.6	34	12	4170	1730	1200
2.0 Twin Spark	1969	148	P	S4	F	129	9.3	32	14	4170	1730	1250
1.9 JTD	1910	108	P	S4	F	117	10.5	50	–	4170	1730	1270
156												
1.6 Twin Spark	1598	118	P	S4	F	124	10.5	34	11	4430	1745	1240
1.8 Twin Spark	1747	138	P	S4	F	129	9.4	33	13	4430	1745	1250
2.0 Twin Spark	1969	148	P	S4	F	133	8.8	32	14	4430	1745	1250
2.5 V6	2492	189	P	V6	F	143	7.3	24	16	4430	1745	1320
1.9 JTD	1910	104	D	S4	F	117	10.5	49	–	4430	1745	1270
2.4 JTD	2387	138	D	S5	F	127	9.4	42	14	4430	1745	1350
166												
2.0 Twin Spark	1970	148	P	S4	F	131	9.8	29	15	4720	1815	1420
2.0 Turbo	1997	202	P	V6	F	147	8.1	24	–	4720	1815	1495
2.5 V6	2492	185	P	V6	F	140	8.4	24	16	4720	1815	1490
3.0 V6	2959	217	P	V6	F	149	7.9	23	17	4720	1815	1510
2.4 JTD	2387	138	D	S5	F	126	9.9	37	–	4720	1815	1490
Spider												
1.8 Twin Spark	1747	142	P	S4	F	127	9.3	32	–	4285	1780	1350
2.0 Twin Spark	1969	148	P	S4	F	130	8.5	31	17	4285	1780	1370
2.0 Turbo	1997	199	P	V6	F	141	7.7	26	–	4285	1780	1430
3.0 V6	2959	189	P	V6	F	140	7.3	24	–	4285	1780	1420
3.0 V6	2959	215	P	V6	F	146	6.8	24	19	4285	1780	1415
GTV												
1.8 Twin Spark	1747	142	P	S4	F	130	9.2	32	–	4285	1780	1350
2.0 Twin Spark	1969	148	P	S4	F	133	8.5	31	17	4285	1780	1370
2.0 Turbo	1997	199	P	V6	F	146	7.4	26	–	4285	1780	1430
3.0 V6	2959	215	P	V6	F	150	6.5	24	19	4285	1780	1415
ASTON MARTIN												
DB7												
6.0 V12	5935	414	P	V12	R	185	5.0	15	20	4665	1830	1780
Vanquish												
6.0 V12	5935	460	P	V12	R	190	4.6	–	20	4665	1998	1835
AUDI												
A2												
1.4	1390	74	P	S4	F	107	12.0	47	5	3825	1675	895
1.2 TDi	1191	60	D	S3	F	104	14.8	94	–	3825	1675	825
1.4 TDi	1422	74	D	S3	F	107	12.3	66	5	3825	1675	990
A3												
1.6	1595	101	P	S4	F	117	10.9	42	9	4150	1735	1090
1.8	1781	123	P	S4	F	125	9.7	36	11	4150	1735	1160
1.8 Turbo	1781	150	P	S4	F	135	8.2	36	14	4150	1735	1175
1.8 Turbo	1781	150	P	S4	4x4	133	8.2	32	–	4150	1735	1290
1.8 Turbo	1781	180	P	S4	F	141	7.6	36	–	4150	1735	1180
1.8 Turbo	1781	180	P	S4	4x4	140	7.5	30	15	4150	1735	1305
1.8 S3 Turbo	1781	209	P	S4	4x4	148	6.9	31	17	4150	1735	1420
1.9 TDi	1896	90	D	S4	F	112	12.4	58	11	4150	1735	1185
1.9 TDi	1896	110	D	S4	F	120	10.5	58	11	4150	1735	1190
A4												
1.6	1595	101	P	S4	F	118	12.5	38	–	4545	1765	1265
1.8 Turbo	1781	150	P	S4	F	137	8.9	34	15	4545	1765	1375
2.0	1984	130	P	S4	F	131	9.9	36	13	4545	1765	1375
3.0 V6	2976	220	P	V6	F	152	6.9	30	–	4545	1765	1425
3.0 V6 quattro	2976	220	P	V6	4x4	151	6.9	30	17	4545	1765	1430
1.9 TDi 130	1896	130	D	S4	F	128	9.9	51	13	4545	1765	1395
2.5 TDi V6quattro	2496	180	D	V6	4x4	140	8.6	37	15	4545	1765	1590
A6												
1.8 Turbo	1781	150	P	S4	F	134	9.7	34	–	4796	1810	1430
1.8 Turbo quattro	1781	150	P	S4	4x4	133	9.8	30	–	4795	1810	1540
2.0	1984	130	P	S4	F	127	10.5	34	–	4796	1810	1395
2.4 V6	2393	170	P	V6	F	139	9.3	29	–	4795	1810	1480
2.4 quattro V6	2393	170	P	V6	4x4	137	9.4	26	–	4795	1810	1585
2.7 Turbo quattro V6	2671	250	P	V6	4x4	154	6.8	24	–	4795	1810	1660
3.0 V6	2976	220	P	V6	F	151	7.5	29	–	4795	1810	1480
3.0 V6 quattro	2976	220	P	V6	4x4	149	7.6	25	–	4795	1810	1590
4.2 quattro V8	4172	300	P	V8	4x4	155	6.9	22	–	4795	1810	1750
4.2 quattro V8 S6	4172	340	P	V8	4x4	155	6.7	20	–	4795	1810	1760
1.9 TDi 130	1896	130	D	S4	F	126	10.5	50	–	4795	1810	1480
2.5 TDi V6	2496	155	D	V6	F	136	9.7	41	–	4795	1810	1560
2.5 TDi V6	2496	180	D	V6	F	137	8.9	35	–	4795	1810	1595
2.5 TDi quattro V6	2496	180	D	V6	4x4	139	8.9	35	–	4795	1810	1675
A8												
2.8 V6	2771	193	P	V6	F	146	8.4	26	–	5035	1880	1540
2.8 quattro V6	2771	193	P	V6	4x4	144	10.1	24	18	5035	1880	1580
3.7 V8	3697	260	P	V8	F	155	8.1	25	–	5035	1880	1645
3.7 quattro V8	3697	260	P	V8	4x4	155	8.6	23	19	5035	1880	1725
4.2 quattro V8	4172	310	P	V8	4x4	155	6.9	22	20	5035	1880	1750
4.2 quattro V8 S8	4172	360	P	V8	4x4	155	5.4	21	20	5035	1880	1730
6.0 quattro W8	5998	420	P	W8	4x4	155	5.8	–	–	5165	1880	1980
2.5 TD V6	2496	180	D	V6	F	141	8.8	39	–	5035	1880	1630
2.5 TD V6 quattro	2496	180	D	V6	4x4	138	9.9	32	–	5035	1880	1735
3.3 TD quattro V8	3328	224	D	V8	4x4	150	8.2	–	–	5035	1880	1860
TT												
1.8 T Roadster	1781	150	P	S4	F	133	8.9	34	–	4040	1765	1340
1.8 T	1781	180	P	S4	F	141	7.8	35	–	4040	1765	1280
1.8 T quattro	1781	180	P	S4	4x4	140	7.4	30	18	4040	1765	1410
1.8 T quattro	1781	225	P	S4	4x4	151	6.6	30	18	4040	1765	1465
1.8 T Roadster	1781	180	P	S4	F	138	8.1	34	–	4040	1765	1340

Model	Engine – CC	Power – bhp	Fuel	Engine config.	Driven wheels	Top speed – mph	0–60 mph – secs	mpg – average	Insurance group	Length – mm	Width – mm	Weight – Kg
1.8 T quattro Roadster	1781	180	P	S4	4x4	136	8.2	30	18	4040	1765	1340
1.8 T quattro Roadster	1781	225	P	S4	4x4	147	6.7	30	18	4040	1765	1515
BENTLEY												
Arnage V8	6750	405	P	V8	R	154	5.9	15	20	5390	1930	2580
Continental R V8	6750	400	P	V8	R	155	6.0	15	20	5340	1880	2450
Continental T V8	6750	420	P	V8	R	167	5.8	15	20	5220	1920	2450
Azure V8	6750	400	P	V8	R	155	6.3	16	20	5340	1880	2610
BMW												
3-Series Compact												
316ti	1796	116	P	S4	R	125	10.9	41	-	4261	1739	1300
325ti	2494	192	P	S6	R	147	7.1	32	-	4261	1739	1405
3-Series												
316i	1895	105	P	S4	R	124	12.4	37	11	4470	1740	-
318i	1895	118	P	S4	R	128	10.4	36	12	4470	1740	1285
320i	2198	170	P	S6	R	140	8.3	32	15	4470	1740	1390
325i	2494	192	P	S6	R	149	7.2	31	15	4470	1740	1410
330i	2979	231	P	S6	R	155	6.5	31	16	4470	1740	1430
320d	1951	136	D	S4	R	128	9.9	50	12	4470	1740	1375
330d	2926	184	D	S6	R	141	7.8	42	15	4470	1740	1520
5-Series												
520i	2171	170	P	S6	R	140	9.1	31	15	4775	1800	1495
525i	2494	192	P	S6	R	148	8.1	30	16	4775	1800	1500
530i	2979	231	P	S6	R	155	7.1	30	17	4775	1800	1540
535i V8	3498	235	P	V8	R	155	6.9	24	17	4775	1800	1610
540i V8	4398	286	P	V8	R	155	6.2	23	18	4775	1800	1630
M5 V8	4941	400	P	V8	R	155	5.3	20	20	4775	1800	1720
520d	1951	136	D	S4	R	128	10.6	48	-	4775	1800	1490
525d	2497	163	D	S6	R	136	8.9	40	-	4775	1800	1595
530d	2926	193	D	S6	R	143	7.8	40	15	4775	1800	1625
7-Series												
735i	3600	272	P	V8	R	155	7.5	26	-	5029	1902	1935
745i	4398	333	P	V8	R	155	6.3	26	-	5029	1902	1945
Z8												
4.9	4941	400	P	V8	R	155	4.7	19	20	4400	1830	1615
Z3												
1.9	1895	118	P	S4	R	122	10.4	36	14	4050	1740	1220
2.2	2171	168	P	S6	R	139	7.9	31	16	4050	1740	1270
2.5	2494	194	P	S6	R	140	7.5	-	-	4050	1740	1270
3.0	2979	228	P	S6	R	149	6.0	30	18	4050	1740	1285
M	3246	321	P	S6	R	155	5.3	25	19	4050	1740	1350
X5												
3.0	2979	228	P	S6	4x4	128	8.5	22	17	4667	1872	1990
4.4 V8	4400	282	P	V8	4x4	128	7.5	20	19	4667	1872	2095
3.0d	-	184	D	S6	4x4	124	10.5	29	-	4667	1872	1990
BRISTOL												
Blenheim	5898	354	P	V8	R	155	6.8	-	20	4825	1765	1740
BUICK												
Century 3.1 V6	3100	175	P	V6	F	121	-	29	-	4940	1845	1530
Regal												
3.8 V6 S'charged	3791	200	P	V6	F	121	-	30	-	4985	1845	1560
3.8 V6 S'charged	3791	240	P	V6	F	136	-	28	-	4985	1845	1605
Le Sabre – 3.8 V6	3791	205	P	V6	F	124	-	30	-	5080	1865	1620
Park Avenue												
3.8 V6	3791	205	P	V6	F	121	-	28	-	5250	1900	1715
3.8 V6 S'charged	3791	240	P	V6	F	136	-	27	-	5250	1900	1760
Rendevous												
3.4	3350	188	P	V6	4x4	112	-	-	-	4740	1870	1825
CADILLAC												
Catera	2962	203	P	V6	R	124	8.5	26	-	4930	1790	1710
Seville												
4.6	4565	279	P	V8	F	127	7.8	21	-	4995	1900	1800
4.6 STS	4565	305	P	V8	F	149	7.8	20	19	4995	1900	1815
Escalade	5733	258	P	V8	4x4	110	10.5	18	-	5110	1955	2530
Eldorado												
4.6	4565	279	P	V8	F	112	7.4	26	-	5095	1920	1730
4.6	4565	305	P	V8	F	148	7.5	26	-	5095	1920	1760
Deville												
4.6	4565	279	P	V8	F	112	8.0	26	-	5260	1890	1805
4.6	4565	301	P	V8	F	130	7.3	26	-	5260	1890	1835
CATERHAM												
Seven												
1.1 Fireblade	1100	130	P	-	R	-	-	-	-	3380	1580	-
1.1 Superlight	1100	170	P	-	R	132	3.9	-	-	3380	1580	-
1.6 K-Series	1588	113	P	S4	R	112	6.2	38	-	3380	1580	550
1.6 Superlight	1588	131	P	S4	R	129	4.6	-	-	3380	1580	470
1.8 K-Series	1795	122	P	S4	R	118	5.8	36	-	3380	1580	550
1.8 VVC	1795	150	P	S4	R	126	4.9	36	-	3380	1580	550
1.8 Superlight R	1796	190	P	S4	R	140	4.0	-	-	3380	1580	460
1.8 Superlight R500	1796	230	P	S4	R	146	3.4	-	-	3380	1580	460
CHEVROLET												
Camaro												
3.8	3791	203	P	V6	R	125	8.5	27	13	4900	1880	1500
5.7	5665	310	P	V8	R	157	5.5	21	18	4900	1880	1570
Prizm												
1.8	1794	126	P	S4	F	118	-	-	-	4430	1695	1090
Cavalier												
2.2	2190	116	P	S4	F	105	10.0	-	-	4595	1725	1215
2.4	5665	310	P	S4	F	118	8.0	-	-	4595	1725	-
Monte Carlo												
3.4	3350	182	P	V6	F	112	10.0	-	-	5025	1845	1515
3.8	3791	203	P	V6	F	124	8.5	-	-	5025	1845	-
Corvette												
5.7	5665	339	P	V8	R	174	4.5	22	20	4565	1870	1455
Malibu												
3.1	3135	173	P	V6	R	112	8.5	28	-	4835	1760	1395

Model	Engine – CC	Power – bhp	Fuel	Engine config.	Driven wheels	Top speed – mph	0–60 mph – secs	mpg – average	Insurance group	Length – mm	Width – mm	Weight – Kg
Impala												
3.4	3350	182	P	V6	F	112	10.0	25	-	5080	1855	1540
3.8	3791	203	P	V6	R	124	8.5	25	-	5080	1855	1560
Tracker												
2.0	1995	129	P	S4	4X4	99	-	-	-	3850	1710	1220
2.5	2494	156	P	V6	4X4	106	-	-	-	3850	1710	1300
TrailBlazer												
4.2	4157	273	P	S6	4X4	117	9.0	-	-	4870	1895	2015
Blazer												
4.3	4300	193	P	V6	4X4	112	10.1	21	-	4650	1830	1665
Tahoe												
4.8	4806	280	P	V8	4X4	99	-	-	-	5050	2005	2345
5.3	5327	290	P	V8	4X4	105	9.8	19	-	5050	2005	2345
6.0	5967	305	P	V8	4X4	105	-	-	-	5050	2005	2345
Venture												
3.4	3350	187	P	V6	F	116	11.2	24	-	4760	1830	1680
CHRYSLER												
Neon												
2.0	1996	133	P	S4	R	124	10.8	35	11	4390	1715	1250
2.0	1996	150	P	S4	R	132	9.6	34	12	4390	1715	1250
LHS – 3.5	3518	257	P	V6	F	130	9.0	27	-	5275	1890	1625
Concorde												
2.7	2736	203	P	V6	F	124	10.5	26	-	5310	1895	1580
3.2	3231	228	P	V6	F	130	9.5	26	-	5310	1895	1580
300M												
2.7	2736	203	P	V6	F	130	10.5	28	-	5000	1920	1610
3.5	3518	254	P	V6	F	143	8.8	27	-	5000	1920	1660
Sebring												
2.0	1996	141	P	S4	F	127	11.0	27	-	4845	1790	1450
2.4	2429	152	P	S4	F	124	11.0	-	-	4845	1790	1475
2.7	2736	203	P	V6	F	134	10.5	27	-	4845	1790	1535
Prowler – 3.5 V6	3518	255	P	V6	R	130	6.5	25	-	4200	1945	1295
PT Cruiser												
2.0	1996	141	P	S4	F	118	9.6	33	12	4290	1705	1425
2.4	2429	152	P	S4	F	105	8.3	-	-	4290	1705	1425
Voyager												
2.4	2429	150	P	S4	F	113	15.8	24	14	4805	1995	1750
3.3	3301	174	P	V6	F	111	11.7	22	15	4805	1995	1800
3.8	3778	218	P	V6	F	112	11.0	21	-	4805	1995	1800
2.5 CRD	2499	141	D	S4	F	115	12.6	37	14	4805	1995	1850
Jeep Wrangler												
2.5	2464	122	P	S4	4x4	88	14.8	24	-	3885	1695	1405
4.0	3964	193	P	S6	4x4	108	9.4	24	14	3885	1695	1590
Jeep Liberty												
2.4	2429	156	P	S4	4x4	105	12.0	-	-	4355	1820	1370
3.7	3709	214	P	V6	4x4	112	10.0	-	-	4355	1820	1750
2.5 CRD	2499	116	D	S4	4x4	105	12.0	-	-	4355	1820	1880
Jeep Grand Cherokee												
4.0	3956	197	P	S6	4x4	112	10.9	19	16	4610	1840	1710
4.7	4701	220	P	V8	4x4	124	8.3	18	17	4610	1840	1825
3.1 TD	3124	140	D	S5	4x4	105	13.5	24	16	4610	1840	1980
CITROEN												
Saxo												
1.1	1124	60	P	S4	F	100	14.9	46	3	3720	1595	805
1.4	1361	75	P	S4	F	109	12.9	46	5	3720	1595	840
1.6 8v	1587	98	P	S4	F	120	11.4	42	7	3740	1620	920
1.6 16v	1587	118	P	S4	F	127	8.7	33	14	3740	1620	935
1.5 D	1527	57	D	S4	F	98	18.3	41	4	3720	1595	890
Xsara												
1.4	1361	75	P	S4	F	107	14.8	42	5	4190	1705	1020
1.6	1587	109	P	S4	F	121	10.9	41	8	4190	1705	1135
2.0	1998	136	P	S4	F	130	9.6	37	13	4190	1705	1175
2.0	1998	163	P	S4	F	136	8.7	30	16	4190	1705	1220
1.9 Diesel	1868	71	D	S4	F	100	18.0	46	-	4190	1705	1150
2.0 HDi	1997	90	D	S4	F	112	13.1	52	8	4190	1705	1200
2.0 HDi	1997	110	D	S4	F	119	10.3	54	8	4190	1705	1200
C5												
1.8 16v	1749	117	P	S4	F	122	11.1	37	8	4618	1770	1290
2.0 16v	1997	138	P	S4	F	129	9.8	34	9	4618	1770	1318
2.0 HPi	1997	143	P	S4	F	130	9.6	38	10	4618	1770	1325
3.0	2946	210	P	V6	F	144	9.7	28	14	4618	1770	1520
2.0 HDI	1997	90	D	S4	F	112	13.1	50	7	4618	1770	1360
2.0 HDI	1997	110	D	S4	F	119	11.3	50	8	4618	1770	1385
2.2 HDI	2179	136	D	S4	F	127	10.2	44	10	4618	1770	1485
Berlingo Multispace												
1.4	1361	75	P	S4	F	93	14.0	40	4	4110	1720	1125
1.6	1587	109	P	S4	F	107	12.7	38	5	4110	1720	1170
1.9 Diesel	1868	71	D	S4	F	88	16.3	41	5	4110	1720	1175
2.0 HDi	1997	90	D	S4	F	98	15.3	49	-	4110	1720	1280
Picasso												
1.6	1587	95	P	S4	F	106	15.0	38	5	4275	1750	1240
1.8	1749	115	P	S4	F	118	12.2	37	8	4275	1750	1245
2.0 HDi	1997	90	D	S4	F	109	14.5	40	6	4275	1750	1300
Synergie												
2.0	1997	136	P	S4	F	115	11.9	31	11	4455	1820	1525
2.0 HDi	1997	110	D	S4	F	109	15.8	41	11	4455	1820	1595
DAEWOO												
Matiz												
0.8	796	52	P	S3	F	89	17.0	44	2	3495	1495	725
Lanos												
1.4	1349	75	P	S4	F	103	15.0	36	4	4075	1680	1005
1.5	1498	86	P	S4	F	107	12.5	33	-	4075	1680	1010
1.6	1598	106	P	S4	F	112	11.5	34	6	4075	1680	1050
Nubira												
1.5	1500	110	P	S4	F	115	11.0	32	-	4495	1700	1080
1.6	1598	106	P	S4	F	115	11.0	36	7	4495	1700	1080
1.8	1800	136	P	S4	F	121	9.0	30	-	4495	1700	1230
2.0	1998	136	P	S4	F	121	9.0	33	11	4495	1700	1230

Model	Engine – CC	Power – bhp	Fuel	Engine config.	Driven wheels	Top speed – mph	0–60 mph – secs	mpg – average	Insurance group	Length – mm	Width – mm	Weight – Kg
Leganza												
1.8 8v	1796	95	P	S4	F	112	13.5	28	–	4670	1780	1220
2.0 8v	1998	116	P	S4	F	116	12.2	30	–	4670	1780	1220
2.0 16v	1998	136	P	S4	F	128	10.2	31	11	4670	1780	1370
2.2 16v	2198	136	P	S4	F	128	9.9	30	–	4670	1780	1400
Tacuma												
1.8	1796	101	P	S4	F	105	12.0	31	8	4350	1755	1230
2.0	1998	105	P	S4	F	113	-	-	-	4350	1755	1260
2.0 16v	1998	121	P	S4	F	117	10.5	29	10	4350	1755	1270
Korando												
2.0	1995	128	P	S4	4x4	95	–	22	–	4260	1840	1755
2.3	2295	140	P	S4	4x4	102	12.5	28	12	4260	1840	1755
3.2	3199	220	P	S6	4x4	133	10.9	22	–	4260	1840	1830
2.3 D	2299	80	D	S4	4x4	78	25.0	34	–	4260	1840	1750
2.9 D	2874	98	D	S5	4x4	87	19.0	29	–	4260	1840	1750
2.9 TD	2874	100	D	S5	4x4	87	19.8	29	12	4260	1840	1780
Musso												
2.0	2000	129	P	S4	4x4	104	–	–	–	4655	1860	1890
2.3	2295	140	P	S4	4x4	109	12.5	23	14	4655	1860	1890
3.2	3199	220	P	S6	4x4	118	10.2	20	–	4655	1860	1910
2.3 D	2299	77	D	S4	4x4	84	25.0	30	–	4655	1860	1795
2.9 D	2874	98	D	S5	4x4	89	19.0	29	–	4655	1860	1850
2.9 TD	2874	120	D	S5	4x4	99	16.0	31	14	4655	1860	1850
DAIHATSU												
Cuore												
0.7	659	45	P	S3	F	74	–	55	–	3410	1475	690
1.0	989	56	P	S3	F	87	12.8	53	3	3410	1475	720
Move												
1.0	989	56	P	S3	F	87	15.0	50	-	3410	1475	815
YRV												
1.0	989	64	P	S4	F	93	-	-	-	3765	1620	870
1.3	1298	87	P	S4	F	109	11.2	47	6	3765	1620	890
1.3 Turbo	1298	140	P	S4	F	-	-	-	-	3765	1620	890
Sirion												
1.0	989	56	P	S3	F	90	15.1	51	5	3675	1595	810
1.3	1298	102	P	S4	F	112	9.6	50	8	3765	1620	850
Grand Move												
1.5	1499	90	P	S4	F	102	13.3	-	-	4100	1640	1010
1.6	1590	91	P	S4	F	102	11.7	37	-	4100	1640	1040
Terios – 1.3	1298	86	P	S4	4x4	90	16.6	37	-	3845	1555	1045
Fourtrak												
2.2	2237	91	P	S4	4x4	81	–	25	–	3840	1690	1380
2.8 D	2765	73	D	S4	4x4	81	18.1	30	–	3840	1690	1620
2.8 TD	2765	98	D	S4	4x4	84	18.1	30	8	3840	1690	1620
FERRARI												
360M	3586	400	P	V8	R	183	4.5	16	20	4475	1920	1400
550M	5474	485	P	V12	R	198	4.4	12	20	4550	1935	1690
456M GT	5474	442	P	V12	R	186	5.2	13	20	4765	1920	1790
FIAT												
Seicento												
0.9	899	39	P	S4	F	87	18.0	46	-	3335	1510	730
1.1	1108	52	P	S4	F	93	14.2	52	1	3335	1510	730
Palio												
1.0 8v	994	55	P	S4	F	93	16.3	-	-	3740	1610	905
1.0 16v	994	70	P	S4	F	99	14.0	-	-	3740	1610	905
1.2 8v	1241	60	P	S4	F	99	12.9	42	-	3740	1610	970
1.2 16v	1241	80	P	S4	F	104	12.2	-	-	3740	1610	970
1.6	1581	106	P	S4	F	117	9.5	-	-	3740	1610	1005
1.7 TD	1698	69	D	S4	F	102	14.9	-	-	3740	1610	925
Punto												
1.2	1242	60	P	S4	F	96	14.3	50	3	3835	1660	860
1.2 16v	1242	80	P	S4	F	107	11.4	47	6	3835	1660	920
1.8 HGT	1747	131	P	S4	F	127	8.6	34	14	3835	1660	1020
1.9 D	1910	60	D	S4	F	96	15.0	50	3	3835	1660	-
1.9 JTD	1910	80	D	S4	F	105	12.2	58	6	3835	1660	1040
Stilo												
1.2 16v	1242	80	P	S4	F	107	13.4	45	-	4182	1784	-
1.6 16v	1596	103	P	S4	F	115	10.5	39	-	4182	1784	-
1.8 16v	1747	133	P	S4	F	125	9.9	35	-	4182	1784	-
2.4 20v	2446	170	P	S4	F	133	8.5	29	-	4182	1784	-
1.9 JTD	1910	115	D	S4	F	119	10.3	53	-	4182	1784	-
1.9 JTD	1910	80	D	S4	F	107	12.9	52	-	4182	1784	-
Marea												
1.6	1581	103	P	S4	F	116	10.7	35	10	4390	1740	1140
1.8	1747	113	P	S4	F	121	10.6	34	10	4390	1740	1195
1.8	1747	132	P	S4	F	123	9.6	-	-	4390	1740	1255
2.0	1998	155	P	S5	F	129	8.6	29	14	4390	1740	1255
2.0 Turbo	1998	182	P	S5	F	141	7.4	-	-	4390	1740	1310
2.4	2446	160	P	S5	F	130	8.6	-	-	4390	1740	1300
1.9 JTD	1910	110	D	S4	F	116	10.8	52	10	4390	1740	1215
2.4 TD	2387	130	D	S5	F	122	10.0	42	-	4390	1740	1280
barchetta – 1.8	1747	131	P	S4	F	124	8.9	34	16	3915	1640	1060
Doblo												
1.2	1242	65	P	S4	F	88	18.9	37	3	4160	1715	1220
1.6	1581	103	P	S4	F	105	-	-	-	4160	1715	-
1.9 D	1910	63	D	S4	F	87	20.9	39	-	4160	1715	1290
1.9 JTD	1910	101	D	S4	F	105	-	-	-	4160	1715	1290
Multipla												
1.6	1581	103	P	S4	F	105	12.6	33	7	3995	1870	1300
1.9 JTD	1910	110	D	S4	F	107	12.2	44	8	3995	1870	1370
Ulysse												
2.0	1998	136	P	S4	F	115	10.9	31	11	4455	1830	1510
2.0 JTD	1997	109	D	S4	F	109	13.9	40	11	4455	1830	1740
FORD												
Ka												
1.3	1299	60	P	S4	F	96	15.4	45	2	3620	1640	890

Model	Engine – CC	Power – bhp	Fuel	Engine config.	Driven wheels	Top speed – mph	0–60 mph – secs	mpg – average	Insurance group	Length – mm	Width – mm	Weight – Kg
Fiesta												
1.3	1297	68	P	S4	F	99	16.0	49	-	3917	1683	-
1.4	1388	80	P	S4	F	103	13.5	46	-	3917	1683	-
1.6	1596	100	P	S4	F	115	10.8	43	-	3917	1683	-
1.4TDCi	1399	68	D	S4	F	68	14.8	63	-	3197	1683	-
Focus												
1.4	1388	75	P	S4	F	106	14.3	43	4	4150	1700	1060
1.6	1596	101	P	S4	F	115	10.9	40	5	4150	1700	1060
1.8	1796	116	P	S4	F	123	10.2	37	6	4150	1700	1125
2.0	1988	131	P	S4	F	125	9.2	33	8	4150	1700	1145
1.8 TDdi	1753	91	D	S4	F	114	12.4	52	5	4150	1700	1175
Mondeo												
1.8i	1798	110	P	S4	F	120	11.6	37	-	4730	1810	1300
1.8i	1798	125	P	S4	F	127	10.8	36	8	4730	1810	1300
2.0i	1999	145	P	S4	F	133	9.8	35	9	4730	1810	-
2.5i	2495	170	P	V6	F	140	8.7	29	15	4730	1810	1385
2.0 D	1998	90	D	S4	F	112	13.1	48	-	4730	1810	1410
2.0 D	1998	116	D	S4	F	121	10.6	48	8	4730	1810	1415
Puma												
1.6	1596	103	P	S4	F	118	10.4	39	10	3895	1675	1035
1.7	1679	125	P	S4	F	126	9.2	38	12	3895	1675	1040
Galaxy												
2.0	1998	116	P	S4	F	110	15.4	28	-	4640	1810	1575
2.3	2295	145	P	S4	F	122	12.3	28	11	4640	1810	1605
2.8	2792	204	P	V6	F	135	9.9	26	15	4640	1810	1625
1.9 TD	1896	90	D	S4	F	103	17.2	43	11	4640	1810	1590
1.9 TD 115	1896	115	D	S4	F	112	13.7	43	11	4640	1810	1665
Maverick												
2.0	1988	132	P	S4	4x4	103	13.5	29	9	4395	1780	1470
3.0	2967	203	P	V6	4x4	118	10.5	22	12	4395	1780	1570
Explorer												
4.0	3996	213	P	V6	4x4	112	10.0	-	-	4810	1830	1965
4.6	4601	242	P	V8	4x4	115	-	-	-	4810	1830	-
FORD USA												
ZX2												
2.0	1988	132	P	S4	F	118	-	-	-	4450	1710	1125
Taurus												
3.0	2986	156	P	V6	F	112	-	27	-	5020	1855	1510
3.0-24v	2967	203	P	V6	F	130	-	30	-	5020	1855	-
Crown Victoria												
4.6	4601	223	P	V8	R	124	-	-	-	5385	1985	1775
Mustang												
3.8	3813	193	P	V6	R	112	-	30	-	4655	1855	1390
4.6	4601	264	P	V8	R	133	-	27	-	4655	1855	1470
4.6	4601	324	P	V8	R	149	5.5	-	-	4655	1855	1555
5.4	5403	390	P	V8	R	170	4.5	-	-	4655	1855	1630
Thunderbird												
4.0	3950	256	P	V8	R	136	7.0	-	-	4735	1830	1700
Suburban												
5.3	5328	285	P	V8	4X4	-	-	-	-	5570	2004	-
6.0	5967	320	P	V8	4X4	-	-	-	-	5570	2004	-
8.1	8128	340	P	V8	4X4	-	-	-	-	5570	2004	-
Windstar												
3.8	3797	203	P	V6	F	105	-	25	-	5100	1915	1710
Expedition												
4.6	4601	218	P	V8	4X4	105	11.0	-	-	5195	2000	2220
5.4	5403	264	P	V8	4X4	112	10.0	-	-	5195	2000	2290
FORD Australia												
Falcon/Fairmout												
4.0	3987	213	P	S6	R	130	8.0	23	-	4910	1870	1515
4.0	3987	234	P	S6	R	-	-	-	-	4910	1870	1515
4.9	4942	238	P	V8	R	136	-	23	-	4910	1870	1515
4.9	4942	252	P	V8	R	136	-	23	-	4910	1870	1515
HINDUSTAN												
Ambassador												
1.8	1817	75	P	S4	R	87	-	-	-	4325	1660	1105
2.0D	1995	55	D	S4	R	81	-	-	-	4325	1660	1200
Contessa Classic												
1.8	1817	75	P	S4	R	99	-	-	-	4590	1700	1200
2.0D	1995	55	D	S4	R	81	-	-	-	4590	1700	1270
HOLDEN												
Commodore/Calais												
3.8	3791	207	P	V6	R	124	9.0	27	-	4890	1840	1525
3.8	3791	233	P	V6	R	130	8.5	21	-	4890	1840	1600
5.7	5665	306	P	V8	R	149	6.0	-	-	4890	1840	1599
HONDA-ACURA												
Civic												
1.4	1396	90	P	S4	F	109	11.8	42	4	4285	1695	1130
1.6	1590	110	P	S4	F	116	10.2	41	6	4285	1695	1145
1.7	1668	116	P	S4	F	115	11.1	42	11	4285	1695	1100
Insight												
1.0	995	68	P	S3	F	112	12.0	83	12	3945	1695	820
Inspire												
2.5	2495	200	P	V6	F	130	-	-	-	4840	1785	1500
3.2	3210	225	P	V6	F	136	-	-	-	4840	1785	1575
Avancier												
2.3	2254	150	P	S4	F	112	-	-	-	4700	1790	1500
3.0	2997	215	P	V6	F	112	-	-	-	4700	1790	1600
Accord												
1.6	1590	116	P	S4	F	118	12.1	34	-	4595	1750	1275
1.8	1850	136	P	S4	F	127	10.9	33	8	4595	1750	1380
2.0	1997	147	P	S4	F	130	10.4	32	10	4595	1750	-
2.2 Type R	2157	212	P	S4	F	141	6.9	29	16	4595	1750	1345
3.0	2997	200	P	V6	F	130	8.0	26	17	4595	1750	1485
2.0 TD	1994	105	D	S4	F	115	-	44	-	4595	1750	-
Legend – 3.5	3474	205	P	V6	F	133	9.1	23	17	4995	1820	1675
S 2000 – 2.0	1997	241	P	S4	R	149	6.2	29	20	4135	1750	1250

Model	Engine – CC	Power – bhp	Fuel	Engine config.	Driven wheels	Top speed – mph	0–60 mph – secs	mpg – average	Insurance group	Length – mm	Width – mm	Weight – Kg
NSX												
3.0	2977	252	P	V6	R	161	7.5	24	-	4430	1810	1430
3.2	3179	280	P	V6	R	167	5.7	24	20	4430	1810	1410
Stream												
1.7	1668	131	P	S4	F	118	11.1	37	9	4570	1695	1310
2.0	1590	125	P	S4	F	127	9.4	33	12	4570	1695	1590
HR-V												
1.6	1590	105	P	S4	4X4	102	11.2	34	8	4010	1695	1125
1.6 VTEC	1590	125	P	S4	4X4	105	10.7	33	9	4010	1695	1185
CR-V												
2.0	1973	147	P	S4	4X4	110	10.5	29	9	4420	1750	1490
MDX												
3.5	3471	243	P	V6	4X4	-	-	-	-	4790	1940	1965
HYUNDAI												
Atoz/Amica – 1.0	999	56	P	S4	F	88	15.1	45	3	3495	1495	810
Matrix												
1.6	1600	107	P	S4	F	105	-	-	-	4025	1740	1200
1.8	1796	132	P	S4	F	112	-	-	-	4025	1740	-
1.5 TD	1493	76	D	S4	F	90	-	-	-	4025	1740	-
Accent												
1.3	1341	60	P	S4	F	-	-	38	-	4200	1670	935
1.3	1341	75	P	S4	F	-	-	38	-	4200	1670	935
1.3	1341	84	P	S4	F	105	14.7	44	4	4200	1670	935
1.5 12v	1495	90	P	S4	F	107	11.5	40	-	4200	1670	-
1.5 16v	1495	99	P	S4	F	112	10.5	37	5	4200	1670	970
Elantra												
1.6	1600	107	P	S4	F	112	11.0	38	8	4495	1720	1175
1.8	1796	132	P	S4	F	118	9.7	-	-	4495	1720	-
2.0	1975	141	P	S4	F	128	9.1	34	13	4495	1720	1300
2.0 TD	1991	112	D	S4	F	118	11.7	44	-	4495	1720	-
Sonata												
2.0	1997	136	P	S4	F	124	9.6	32	10	4710	1820	1320
2.4	2351	150	P	S4	F	118	-	31	-	4710	1820	1320
2.5	2494	160	P	S4	F	136	9.3	28	12	4710	1820	1320
XG												
2.5	2494	160	P	V6	F	135	9.3	23	-	4865	1825	1640
3.0	2972	182	P	V6	F	140	8.9	26	16	4865	1825	1670
Coupe												
1.6	1600	114	P	S4	F	120	11.2	38	9	4345	1730	1235
1.8	1796	132	P	S4	F	118	-	32	-	4345	1730	1165
2.0	1975	139	P	S4	F	125	8.6	32	12	4345	1730	1250
Trajet												
2.0	1997	139	P	S4	F	111	13.1	30	10	4695	1840	1645
2.7	2657	173	P	V6	F	119	11.5	25	12	4695	1840	-
2.0 TD	1991	112	D	S4	F	105	15.7	30	10	4695	1840	-
Santa Fe												
2.0	1997	136	P	S4	4X4	108	12.2	29	-	4500	1820	1675
2.4	2351	150	P	S4	4X4	105	12.5	30	12	4500	1820	-
2.7	2657	170	P	V6	4X4	112	11.6	25	13	4500	1820	-
2.0 TD	1991	112	D	S4	4X4	103	14.9	37	11	4500	1820	-
ISUZU												
Vehi-Cross – 3.2	3165	215	P	V6	4x4	105	-	22	-	4130	1790	1750
Trooper												
3.5 V6	3494	215	P	V6	4x4	112	9.6	19	15	4365	1835	1990
3.0 TD	2999	159	D	S4	4x4	99	15.8	26	14	4365	1835	1990
Axiom												
3.5 V6	3494	233	P	V6	4x4	118	-	20	-	4640	1795	1780
JAGUAR												
X-Type												
2.5	2495	197	P	V6	4x4	139	8.3	29	15	4670	1790	1555
3.0	2967	234	P	V6	4x4	145	7.0	27	16	4670	1790	-
S-Type												
3.0	2967	238	P	V6	R	146	7.5	28	15	4860	1820	1670
4.0	3996	276	P	V8	R	149	6.6	23	17	4860	1820	1750
XJ8												
3.2	3253	237	P	V8	R	140	8.5	24	16	5025	1800	1710
4.0	3996	284	P	V8	R	149	7.3	24	17	5025	1800	1710
4.0 S'charged XJR	3996	363	P	V8	R	155	5.6	22	19	5025	1800	1775
XK8												
4.0	3996	284	P	V8	R	155	6.7	25	18	4760	1830	1615
4.0 S'charged XKR	3996	363	P	V8	R	155	5.4	23	20	4760	1830	1640
JENSEN												
S-V8												
4.6	4601	330	P	V8	R	155	4.8	25	-	4160	1760	1250
KIA												
Rio												
1.3	1343	84	P	S4	F	107	14.3	40	-	4215	1675	925
1.5	1493	103	P	S4	F	115	11.6	39	-	4215	1675	940
Shuma												
1.6	-	-	P	S4	F	-	-	-	-	-	-	-
Rio												
1.3	1343	84	P	S4	F	107	14.3	40	-	4215	1675	925
1.5	1493	103	P	S4	F	115	11.6	39	-	4215	1675	940
Magentis												
2.0	1997	136	P	S4	F	128	-	-	-	4720	1815	1320
2.5 V6	2494	168	P	V6	F	133	-	-	-	4720	1815	1420
Carens												
1.8	1793	109	P	S4	F	115	13.1	31	8	4440	1710	1115
Sedona												
2.5 V6	2495	165	P	V6	F	115	13.8	25	10	4890	1900	1735
2.9 TD	2903	126	P	S4	F	104	17.3	34	10	4890	1900	1855
Sportage												
2.0	1998	95	P	S4	R	99	-	24	-	3760	1730	1420
2.0 16v	1998	128	P	S4	R	107	14.7	24	9	3760	1730	1440
2.0 TD	1998	83	D	S4	R	90	20.5	31	-	3760	1730	1540

Model	Engine – CC	Power – bhp	Fuel	Engine config.	Driven wheels	Top speed – mph	0–60 mph – secs	mpg – average	Insurance group	Length – mm	Width – mm	Weight – Kg
LADA												
Samara												
1.1	1100	53	P	S4	F	87	16.0	35	-	4010	1620	900
1.1	1100	58	P	S4	F	-	-	33	-	4010	1620	900
1.3	1288	67	P	S4	F	93	14.5	35	-	4010	1620	920
1.3	1288	73	P	S4	F	-	-	-	-	4010	1620	920
1.5	1500	71	P	S4	F	97	14.0	37	-	4010	1620	920
1.5	1500	79	P	S4	F	96	13.0	36	-	4010	1620	940
1.5-16v	1500	90	P	S4	F	112	12.0	-	-	4010	1620	-
Niva												
1.7	1690	80	P	S4	4x4	85	22.0	24	-	3720	1680	1210
1.8	1774	99	P	S4	4x4	87	20.0	-	-	3720	1680	1210
1.9 TD	1905	75	D	S4	4x4	82	21.3	29	-	3720	1680	1240
1.5 TD	1524	65	D	S4	4x4	78	25.0	35	-	3720	1680	1250
110												
1.5	1500	76	P	S4	F	105	14.0	40	-	4265	1680	1040
1.5 16v	1500	94	P	S4	F	115	11.5	39	-	4265	1680	1080
1.6	1596	102	P	S4	F	112	13.0	-	-	4265	1680	1080
2.0	1998	150	P	S4	F	128	9.0	27	-	4265	1680	1100
LAMBORGHINI												
Diablo												
5.7 V12	5707	530	P	V12	4x4	207	3.8	11	-	4470	2040	1625
6.0 V12	5992	550	P	V12	4x4	204	3.8	12	20	4470	2040	1625
6.0 V12 GT	5992	575	P	V12	R	202	3.8	12	-	4430	2040	1460
LANCIA												
Y												
1.1	1108	54	P	S4	F	93	15.5	45	-	3740	1690	850
1.2	1242	60	P	S4	F	99	14.1	50	-	3740	1690	860
1.2	1242	80	P	S4	F	108	11.2	47	-	3740	1690	910
Lybra												
1.6	1581	103	P	S4	F	115	11.3	34	-	4465	1745	1175
1.8	1747	131	P	S4	F	125	10.3	34	-	4465	1745	1225
2.0	1998	150	P	S4	F	130	9.6	29	-	4465	1745	1275
1.9 JTD	1910	110	D	S4	F	115	11.3	48	-	4465	1745	1235
2.4 JTD	2387	134	D	S4	F	127	9.5	42	-	4465	1745	1295
Z												
2.0	1997	136	P	S4	F	115	10.9	27	-	4470	1835	1600
2.0 JTD	1997	109	D	S4	F	109	14.8	42	-	4470	1835	1670
LAND ROVER												
Freelander												
1.8	1795	117	P	S4	4x4	106	11.8	27	10	4380	1805	1425
2.5 V6	2499	177	P	V6	4x4	113	10.1	23	12	4380	1805	1520
2.0 Td4	1950	112	D	S4	4x4	102	13.2	37	10	4380	1805	1540
Defender												
2.5 Td5	2495	122	D	S5	4x4	88	15.4	28	9	3880	1790	1695
4.0	3947	182	P	V8	4x4	87	-	18	-	3880	1790	1630
Discovery												
2.5 Td5	2496	138	D	S5	4x4	98	14.2	30	12	4710	2190	2075
4.0	3947	185	D	V8	4x4	106	10.9	17	14	4710	2190	2020
Range Rover												
4.0	3947	185	P	V8	4x4	116	11.4	19	13	4715	2228	2090
4.6	4552	218	P	V8	4x4	122	9.6	17	15	4715	2228	2120
2.5 TD	2497	136	D	S6	4x4	105	14.3	27	13	4715	2228	2070
LEXUS												
IS200												
2.0	1988	155	P	S6	R	133	9.5	29	12	4400	1720	1400
2.0	1988	186	P	S6	R	133	8.0	-	-	4400	1720	1450
3.0	2997	218	P	S6	R	143	7.1	-	-	4400	1720	1480
GS300	2997	228	P	S6	R	143	8.2	24	15	4810	1800	1690
GS430	4293	283	P	V8	R	155	6.3	23	17	4810	1800	1720
ES 300	2995	213	P	V6	F	140	7.7	-	-	4830	1790	1520
SC430	4293	228	P	V8	R	155	7.0	-	-	4515	1825	1750
LS430	4293	281	P	V8	R	155	6.7	24	17	5005	1830	1875
RX300	2995	201	P	V6	4x4	112	8.8	22	15	4575	1815	1815
LX470	4664	234	P	V8	4x4	109	9.9	-	-	4890	1940	2450
LINCOLN												
Continental	4601	279	P	V8	F	133	-	25	-	5260	1870	1760
Town Car	4601	223	P	V8	R	112	-	25	-	5470	1985	1835
Navigator												
5.4 V8	5403	304	P	V8	4x4	118	-	-	-	5200	2030	2445
LS												
3.0	2967	213	P	V6	R	124	-	-	-	4925	1860	1630
4.0	3950	256	P	V8	R	136	-	-	-	4925	1860	-
LOTUS												
Elise												
1.8	1795	122	P	S4	R	124	5.7	39	19	3785	1720	755
Exige												
1.8	1795	179	P	S4	R	135	4.7	-	-	-	-	780
Esprit – 3.5	3506	354	P	V8	R	175	4.9	21	20	4370	1885	1340
MASERATI												
3200 GT – 3.2 V8	3217	370	P	V8	R	174	5.1	17	20	4510	1820	1590
MAZDA												
Demio												
1.3	1324	63	P	S4	F	94	14.0	40	3	3815	1670	1030
1.5	1498	75	P	S4	F	99	13.0	39	4	3815	1670	1035
323												
1.3	1324	73	P	S4	F	104	14.2	38	6	4200	1705	980
1.6	-	-	P	S4	F	-	-	-	-	4200	1705	1010
2.0	-	-	P	S4	F	-	-	-	-	4200	1705	1105
2.0 TD	1998	90	D	S4	F	110	12.2	55	7	4200	1705	1160
Premacy												
1.8	1840	100	P	S4	F	108	11.8	31	6	4295	1710	1250
1.8	1840	115	P	S4	F	112	11.4	34	7	4295	1710	1250
2.0TD	1998	90	D	S4	F	105	12.9	50	6	4295	1710	1340

Model	Engine – CC	Power – bhp	Fuel	Engine config.	Driven wheels	Top speed – mph	0–60 mph – secs	mpg – average	Insurance group	Length – mm	Width – mm	Weight – Kg
MPV												
2.0	1991	136	P	S4	F	105	14.2	28	11	4750	1830	1600
2.5 V6	2495	170	P	V6	F	115	11.0	-	-	4750	1830	-
626												
1.8	1840	90	P	S4	F	112	12.6	37	8	4575	1710	1185
2.0	1991	116	P	S4	F	123	9.9	36	10	4575	1710	1185
2.0	1991	136	P	S4	F	129	9.6	35	12	4575	1710	1175
2.5	2497	200	P	V6	4x4	136	–	26	–	4575	1710	1500
2.0 TD	1998	101	D	S4	F	115	11.5	54	9	4575	1710	1275
Xedos 9												
2.0	1995	143	P	V6	F	125	11.5	32	–	4825	1770	-
2.3	2255	211	P	V6	F	143	9.4	29	17	4825	1770	1500
2.5	2497	163	P	V6	F	128	11.0	26	-	4825	1770	1570
MX-5												
1.6	1598	110	P	S4	R	118	9.7	35	11	3975	1680	1035
1.8	1840	140	P	S4	R	128	8.4	32	12	3975	1680	1065
Tribute												
2.0	1988	124	P	S4	4x4	103	13.7	29	-	4395	1800	1420
3.0	2967	197	P	V6	4x4	118	11.8	22	-	4395	1800	1510
MCC Smart												
0.6	599	45	P	S3	R	84	18.9	57	–	2500	1515	720
0.6	599	54	P	S3	R	85	17.2	57	–	2500	1515	720
0.6	599	61	P	S3	R	85	16.8	57	–	2500	1515	720
0.8 CDi	799	40	D	S3	R	84	19.8	67	–	2500	1515	730
MERCEDES-BENZ												
A-Class												
A140	1397	82	P	S4	F	105	12.9	40	5	3575	1719	1020
A160	1598	102	P	S4	F	113	10.8	39	6	3575	1719	1040
A190	1898	125	P	S4	F	123	8.8	37	8	3575	1719	1080
A170 CDi	1689	60	D	S4	F	96	17.6	63	–	3575	1719	1080
A170 CDi	1689	90	D	S4	F	109	12.5	58	6	3575	1719	1100
C-Class												
C180	1998	129	P	S4	R	130	11.0	30	12	4526	1728	1380
C200 K S'charged	1998	163	P	S4	R	143	9.3	29	13	4526	1728	1415
C240 V6	2597	170	P	V6	R	146	9.2	25	15	4526	1728	1460
C320 V6	3199	218	P	V6	R	152	7.8	26	17	4526	1728	1490
C320 V6 AMG	3199	354	P	V6	R	155	5.2	-	-	4526	1728	1560
C200 CDi	2148	116	D	S4	R	126	12.1	46	–	4526	1728	1430
C220 CDi	2148	143	D	S4	R	136	10.3	46	13	4526	1728	1445
C270 CDi	2685	170	D	S4	R	143	8.9	42	15	4526	1728	1510
E-Class												
E200	1998	163	P	S4	R	138	9.7	32	14	4818	1799	1465
E240 V6	2597	170	P	V6	R	142	9.3	26	15	4818	1799	1515
E280 V6	2799	204	P	V6	R	143	8.9	26	15	4818	1799	1535
E320 V6	3199	224	P	V6	R	148	7.9	27	16	4818	1799	1555
E430 V8	4266	279	P	V8	R	155	6.6	26	17	4818	1799	1605
E55 AMG V8	5439	354	P	V8	R	155	5.7	23	19	4818	1799	1695
E200 CDi	2148	116	D	S4	R	123	12.5	46	–	4818	1799	1515
E220 CDi	2148	143	D	S4	R	132	10.4	46	14	4818	1799	1515
E270 CDi	2685	170	D	S5	R	140	9.0	41	-	4818	1799	1555
E320 CDi	3224	197	D	S6	R	143	8.3	36	16	4818	1799	1585
S-Class												
S280	2799	204	P	V6	R	143	9.5	26	15	5038	1855	1695
S320	3199	224	P	V6	R	149	8.2	25	16	5038	1855	1695
S430	4266	279	P	V8	R	155	7.3	23	18	5038	1855	1780
S500	4966	306	P	V8	R	155	6.5	21	19	5038	1855	1780
S600	5786	367	P	V12	R	155	6.3	21	20	5038	1855	1960
S320 CDI	3222	197	D	S6	R	143	8.8	35	16	5038	1855	1830
S400 CDI	3996	250	D	V8	R	155	7.8	29	-	5038	1855	1895
CL-Coupe												
500	4966	306	P	V8	R	155	6.5	21	20	4989	1840	1790
55 AMG	5439	360	P	V8	R	155	6.0	21	20	4989	1840	-
600	5786	367	P	V12	R	155	6.1	21	20	4989	1840	1880
CLK												
2.0 Kompressor	1998	163	P	S4	R	138	9.1	30	14	4567	1722	1340
2.3 Kompressor	2295	197	P	S4	R	146	7.9	29	15	4567	1722	1370
3.2	3199	218	P	V6	R	149	7.4	28	16	4567	1722	1420
4.3	4266	279	P	V8	R	155	6.3	25	18	4567	1722	1480
5.5 AMG	5439	347	P	V8	R	155	5.4	24	20	4567	1722	1545
SLK												
200 K	1998	163	P	S4	R	138	8.2	29	16	3995	1715	1290
230 K S'charged	2295	197	P	S4	R	149	7.2	29	17	3995	1715	1310
320 V6	3199	218	P	V6	R	152	6.9	25	18	3995	1715	1330
320 V6 AMG	3199	354	P	V6	R	152	6.9	-	-	3995	1715	1370
SL												
500	4966	306	P	V8	R	155	6.3	22	-	-	-	-
V-Class												
2.3	2300	143	P	S4	R	108	15.1	25	14	4659	1880	-
2.8	2800	174	P	S4	R	117	12.7	21	16	4659	1880	-
2.2 CDi	2200	122	D	S4	R	103	17.5	38	14	4659	1880	-
M-Class												
ML320	3199	218	P	V6	4x4	121	9.5	22	16	4590	1830	2170
ML500	4966	292	P	V8	4x4	138	7.7	19	-	4590	1830	2210
ML55 AMG	5439	347	P	V8	4x4	144	6.9	20	20	4590	1830	2300
ML270 CDI	2688	163	D	S5	4x4	115	11.7	30	16	4590	1830	2175
ML400 CDI	3996	250	D	V8	4x4	132	8.1	26	-	4590	1830	2335
G-Class												
320	3199	215	P	V6	4x4	107	10.9	18	-	4680	1760	2165
5.0	4966	296	P	V8	4x4	118	9.7	17	-	4680	1760	2300
2.9 TD	2874	120	D	S5	4x4	86	16.0	26	-	4680	1760	2060
4.0 CDI	3996	250	D	V8	4x4	112	10.3	22	-	4680	1760	2400
MERCURY												
Sable												
3.0	2986	157	P	V6	F	118	–	29	–	5070	1850	1535
3.0	2967	203	P	V6	F	124	–	27	–	5070	1850	1535
Grand Marquis – 4.6	4601	203	P	V8	R	118	–	25	–	5380	1980	1795
Cougar												
2.0	1988	126	P	S4	F	130	10.0	-	-	4700	1770	1300
2.5	2544	173	P	V6	F	140	8.5	-	-	4700	1770	1370
Villager – 3.3	3275	173	P	V6	F	109	11.0	25	-	4950	1900	1815
Mountaineer												
4.0	3996	213	P	V6	4X4	105	10.2	-	-	4845	1830	2000
4.6	4601	243	P	V8	4X4	112	8.6	-	-	4845	1830	2000
MG ROVER												
25												
1.1	1113	60	P	S4	F	100	13.5	42	3	3990	1690	985
1.4	1396	84	P	S4	F	109	11.8	43	4	3990	1690	1020
1.4 16v	1396	103	P	S4	F	112	10.2	43	6	3990	1690	-
1.6	1588	109	P	S4	F	115	9.5	43	7	3990	1690	1030
1.8	1795	117	P	S4	F	115	9.5	34	-	3990	1690	1060
1.8 vi	1795	145	P	S4	F	124	7.8	38	14	3990	1690	1090
1.8 MG ZR	1795	160	P	S4	F	130	7.5	38	-	3990	1690	1100
2.0 D Turbo	1996	101	D	S4	F	113	9.9	55	7	3990	1690	1130
45												
1.4	1396	103	P	S4	F	115	11.2	41	8	4360	1700	1105
1.6	1588	109	P	S4	F	118	10.3	41	10	4360	1700	-
1.8	1795	117	P	S4	F	121	9.3	40	11	4360	1700	1155
1.8 MG ZS	1795	117	P	S4	F	122	9.0	39	-	4360	1700	-
2.0	1991	150	P	V6	F	124	9.5	30	12	4360	1700	1265
2.5 MG ZS	2497	177	P	V6	F	136	7.5	30	-	4360	1700	1300
2.0 Di Turbo	1994	101	D	S4	F	115	10.6	52	7	4360	1700	1230
75												
1.8	1795	120	P	S4	F	121	10.9	36	8	4747	1780	1390
2.0	1991	150	P	V6	F	130	10.2	30	10	4747	1780	1445
2.0 MG ZT	1991	160	P	V6	F	131	8.7	30	-	4747	1780	-
2.5	2497	175	P	V6	F	136	8.8	29	14	4747	1780	1445
2.5 MG ZT	2497	195	P	V6	F	142	7.8	29	-	4747	1780	1500
2.0 CDT	1951	116	P	S4	F	120	11.7	50	8	4747	1780	1485
MGF												
1.6	1588	112	P	S4	R	115	10.0	-	11	3910	1630	1060
1.8	1795	120	P	S4	R	120	9.0	38	12	3910	1630	1060
1.8 VVC	1795	145	P	S4	R	130	7.7	36	14	3910	1630	1070
1.8 VVC Trophy	1795	160	P	S4	R	140	7.0	-	-	3910	1630	-
MITSUBISHI												
Colt												
1.3	1299	75	P	S4	F	105	12.5	41	5	3900	1680	945
1.5	1468	92	P	S4	F	112	10.5	35	–	3900	1680	975
1.6	1597	103	P	S4	F	115	10.5	38	6	3900	1680	975
Lancer												
2.0 Turbo	1997	280	P	S4	4x4	150	-	–	–	4455	1770	1320
Carisma												
1.6	1597	103	P	S4	F	115	12.4	34	9	4475	1710	1180
1.8 GDi	1834	125	P	S4	F	124	10.4	40	12	4475	1710	1210
1.9 TD	1870	102	D	S4	F	118	11.9	52	-	4475	1710	1260
Galant												
2.0	1997	133	P	S4	F	124	10.5	34	-	4660	1740	1325
2.0 GDi	1997	145	P	S4	F	112	-	-	-	4660	1740	1290
2.4 GDi	2351	144	P	S4	F	130	10.0	35	-	4660	1740	1345
2.5	2498	161	P	V6	F	136	8.9	30	-	4660	1740	1335
3.0 Turbo	3000	280	P	V6	4x4	-	-	-	-	4660	1740	1480
Eclipse												
2.4	2351	149	P	S4	F	130	–	-	-	4385	1745	1320
3.0	2972	203	P	V6	F	136	–	-	-	4385	1745	1320
FTO												
1.8	1834	125	P	S4	F	124	–	26	-	4320	1735	1100
2.0	1999	170	P	V6	F	136	–	29	-	4320	1735	1150
2.0	1999	200	P	V6	F	143	–	29	-	4320	1735	1150
Space Star												
1.3	1299	82	P	S4	F	105	14.2	42	7	4030	1715	1160
1.6	1597	101	P	S4	F	112	-	40	8	4030	1715	1200
1.8 GDi	1834	122	P	S4	F	118	10.3	39	9	4030	1715	1230
1.9 TD	1870	102	D	S4	F	115	12.0	51	-	4030	1715	1250
Space Runner												
1.8 GDi	1834	150	P	S4	F	112	11.0	32	–	4290	1695	1380
2.0	1997	133	P	S4	F	115	11.0	30	–	4480	1740	1380
2.4 GDi	2351	165	P	S4	4x4	118	10.6	30	–	4280	1695	1325
Space Wagon												
2.0	-	-	P	S4	F	112	12.0	30	12	4600	1775	-
2.4 GDi	2351	147	P	S4	F	118	11.4	29	12	4600	1775	1510
3.0 GDi	2972	215	P	V6	4x4	112	-	-	-	4600	1775	1640
Space Gear												
2.0	1997	113	P	S4	R	99	–	24	–	4595	1695	1625
2.4	2351	128	P	S4	R	103	–	24	–	4595	1695	1660
3.0	2972	185	P	V6	R	105	–	23	–	4595	1695	2030
2.5 TD	2477	99	D	S4	R	92	–	26	–	4595	1695	1650
2.8 TD	2835	125	D	S4	R	–	–	–	–	4595	1695	2020
Pinin												
1.8	1834	120	P	S4	4x4	104	10.2	31	11	3975	1695	1300
2.0 GDi	1999	129	P	S4	4x4	105	10.8	30	11	3975	1695	1390
Shogun												
3.5 GDi	3497	203	P	V6	4x4	118	10.0	22	16	4280	1875	1915
3.2 DID	3197	165	D	S4	4x4	105	11.5	30	16	4280	1875	1975
Sport/Montero												
3.0	2972	170	P	V6	4x4	109	11.6	23	16	4620	1775	1855
2.5 TD	2477	100	D	S4	4x4	93	18.5	27	13	4620	1775	1865
MORGAN												
4/4	1796	114	P	S4	R	106	9.0	37	13	3890	1500	870
Plus 4 – 2.0	1994	136	P	S4	R	115	8.1	30	14	3960	1630	-
Plus 8												
4.0	3948	190	P	V8	R	130	5.0	22	16	3960	1630	940
4.6	4552	194	P	V8	R	-	-	21	–	3960	1630	975
Aero 8												
4.4V8	4398	286	P	V8	R	160	5.0	-	20	4090	1750	1000

Model	Engine – CC	Power – bhp	Fuel	Engine config.	Driven wheels	Top speed – mph	0–60 mph – secs	mpg – average	Insurance group	Length – mm	Width – mm	Weight – Kg
NISSAN												
Micra												
1.0	998	60	P	S4	F	93	15.5	47	3	3720	1585	835
1.4	1348	81	P	S4	F	105	11.9	46	4	3720	1585	865
1.5 Diesel	1527	57	D	S4	F	91	18.7	54	–	3720	1585	900
Almera												
1.5	1498	90	P	S4	F	107	13.8	43	4	4180	1706	1190
1.8	1769	114	P	S4	F	115	11.1	38	7	4180	1706	1205
2.2 Di	2184	110	D	S4	F	115	12.3	50	7	4180	1706	1305
Almera Tino												
1.8	1769	114	P	S4	F	107	12.7	36	5	4264	1758	1370
2.0	1998	136	P	S4	F	112	12.6	30	7	4264	1758	1435
2.0 Di	2184	114	D	S4	F	112	12.5	44	5	4264	1758	1480
Primera												
2.0	1998	150	P	S4	F	130	–	–	–	4565	1760	1300
2.5	2488	170	P	S4	F	136	–	–	–	4565	1760	1340
Skyline												
2.0	1998	155	P	S6	R	124	–	28	–	4705	1720	1360
2.5	2499	200	P	S6	R	130	–	25	–	4705	1720	1400
2.5 Turbo	2499	280	P	S6	R	143	–	25	–	4705	1720	1430
2.6 twin-turbo	2569	280	P	S6	4x4	155	5.2	–	20	4600	1785	1540
Maxima QX												
2.0 V6	1995	140	P	V6	F	125	11.3	31	12	4770	1770	1415
2.5 V6	2496	190	P	V6	F	130	–	28	–	4770	1770	1430
3.0 V6	2988	200	P	V6	F	143	8.2	26	13	4770	1770	1450
Silvia												
2.0	1998	165	P	S4	R	130	–	–	–	4440	1695	1200
2.0 Turbo	1998	200	P	S4	R	146	7.5	29	–	4440	1695	1260
Serena												
1.6	1597	97	P	S4	R	93	18.1	26	–	4315	1695	1250
2.0	1998	140	P	S4	R	105	12.2	27	–	4315	1695	1485
2.3 Diesel	2283	75	D	S4	R	84	26.5	27	10	4315	1695	1485
Terrano II												
2.4	2389	116	P	S4	4x4	99	13.7	23	12	4217	1755	1560
2.7 TD	2664	125	D	S4	4x4	96	15.7	29	12	4217	1735	1670
X-Trail												
2.0	1998	150	P	S4	4x4	118	–	–	–	4445	1765	1340
2.0 Turbo	1998	280	P	S4	4x4	136	–	–	–	4445	1765	1460
Patrol												
4.5	4479	200	P	S6	4x4	105	–	–	–	4440	1930	2210
2.8 TD	2826	129	D	S6	4x4	96	17.5	–	–	4440	1930	2070
3.0 Di	2953	158	D	S4	4x4	102	15.0	26	13	4440	1930	2200
4.2 TD	4169	160	D	S6	4x4	93	–	–	–	4440	1930	2320
NOBLE												
M10												
2.5	2500	168	P	V6	R	140	6.0	–	–	3860	1752	960
M12												
2.5	2500	310	P	V6	R	–	–	–	–	4089	1828	980
OLDSMOBILE												
Alero												
2.4	2392	152	P	S4	F	124	10.5	–	–	4740	1780	1370
3.4	3350	173	P	V6	F	124	9.2	–	–	4740	1780	1370
Intrigue												
3.5	3473	218	P	V6	F	136	–	–	–	4975	1870	1555
Aurora												
3.5	3473	218	P	V6	F	124	10.0	–	–	5060	1850	1645
4.0	3995	253	P	V8	F	134	8.2	–	–	5060	1850	1725
Silhouette												
3.4	3350	188	P	V6	F	120	11.0	–	–	5115	1835	1790
Bravada – 4.2	4157	273	P	S6	4x4	118	9.0	–	–	4870	1895	2100
Pagani												
Zonda C12	7010	550	P	V12	R	–	3.7	–	–	4345	2055	1250
PERODUA												
Nippa	847	37	P	S3	F	84	15.8	53	3	3345	1395	650
Kenari	989	56	P	S3	F	87	15.0	50	3	3460	1475	815
PEUGEOT												
106												
1.1	1124	60	P	S4	F	102	14.9	46	3	3678	1610	815
1.4	1361	75	P	S4	F	109	12.9	46	5	3678	1610	815
1.6 16v	1587	118	P	S4	F	127	8.7	35	13	3678	1610	950
1.5 D	1527	57	D	S4	F	98	18.5	54	3	3678	1610	875
206												
1.1	1124	60	P	S4	F	98	15.2	46	3	3835	1652	910
1.4	1361	75	P	S4	F	105	13.2	43	4	3835	1652	950
1.6	1587	109	P	S4	F	124	9.9	41	5	3835	1652	1025
2.0 16v	1997	135	P	S4	F	130	8.9	36	14	3835	1652	1050
1.9 D	1868	69	D	S4	F	100	16.1	50	4	3835	1652	1010
2.0 HDi	1997	90	D	S4	F	112	12.7	57	5	3835	1652	1110
307												
1.4	–	–	P	S4	F	104	14.6	42	4	4202	1746	–
1.6	1587	109	P	S4	F	118	11.6	39	6	4202	1746	1175
2.0	1997	136	P	S4	F	127	9.8	36	11	4202	1746	1200
1.4 HDi	–	–	D	S4	F	99	16.3	–	4	4202	1746	–
2.0 HDi	1997	90	D	S4	F	111	13.6	54	6	4202	1746	1245
2.0 HDi	1997	110	D	S4	F	119	10.9	–	9	4202	1746	–
406												
1.8	1749	116	P	S4	F	122	12.2	37	10	4598	1765	1315
2.0	1997	135	P	S4	F	129	10.8	34	13	4598	1765	1350
2.2	2231	158	P	S4	F	135	10.0	32	15	4598	1765	1370
3.0 V6	2946	207	P	V6	F	149	8.1	29	16	4598	1765	1455
2.0 HDi	1997	90	D	S4	F	110	14.5	50	9	4598	1765	1330
2.0 HDi	1997	110	D	S4	F	118	12.5	51	12	4598	1765	1410
2.2 HDi	2179	133	D	S4	F	127	11.0	44	14	4598	1765	1410
Coupe												
2.0	1997	135	P	S4	F	129	9.9	34	15	4602	1765	1385
3.0 V6	2946	207	P	V6	F	149	7.8	28	18	4602	1765	1458
2.2 HDi	2179	133	D	S4	F	128	10.9	44	15	4602	1765	1410
607												
2.0	–	–	P	S4	F	–	–	–	16	4871	1835	–
2.2	2231	158	P	S4	F	136	9.6	31	17	4871	1835	1455
3.0	2946	207	P	V6	F	149	8.1	29	18	4871	1835	1560
2.0 HDi	–	–	D	S4	F	–	–	–	–	4871	1835	–
2.2 HDi	2179	133	D	S4	F	127	10.6	42	16	4871	1835	1535
Partner												
1.4	1361	75	P	S4	F	93	14.6	39	5	4110	1720	1125
1.8	1762	90	P	S4	F	99	12.2	32	–	4110	1720	1170
1.9 D	1868	69	D	S4	F	88	16.3	43	6	4110	1720	1190
2.0 HDi	1997	90	D	S4	F	99	13.1	51	–	4110	1720	1280
806												
2.0	1998	136	P	S4	F	115	11.9	31	11	4454	1834	1525
2.0 HDi	1997	109	D	S4	F	109	15.8	42	11	4454	1834	1595
PONTIAC												
Grand Am												
2.4	2392	152	P	S4	F	118	9.0	31	–	4730	1790	1415
3.4	3350	173	P	V6	F	118	9.8	29	–	4730	1790	–
Grand Prix												
3.1	3135	178	P	V6	F	121	–	30	–	5015	1845	1550
3.8	3791	203	P	V6	F	124	–	30	–	5015	1845	1550
3.8 S'charged	3791	243	P	V6	F	140	8.5	28	–	5015	1845	1550
Bonneville												
3.8	3791	208	P	V6	F	124	–	29	–	5145	1890	1630
3.8 Supercharged	3791	243	P	V6	F	136	8.5	25	–	5145	1890	1660
Firebird												
3.8	3791	203	P	V6	R	124	–	29	–	4910	1890	1515
5.7	5665	314	P	V8	R	155	6.0	28	–	4910	1890	1565
Aztek – 3.4	3350	188	P	V6	F	112	–	26	–	4625	1870	1715
Montana – 3.4	3350	185	P	V6	F	118	–	26	–	4755	1830	1725
PORSCHE												
Boxster												
2.7	2687	220	P	F6	R	155	6.6	29	18	4315	1780	1260
3.2	3179	252	P	F6	R	162	5.9	26	19	4315	1780	1295
911												
3.4	3387	300	P	F6	R	174	5.4	24	20	4430	1765	1320
GT3	3600	360	P	F6	R	187	4.8	22	–	4430	1780	1350
3.6 Turbo	3600	420	P	F6	4X4	189	4.2	20	20	4430	1780	1540
Carrera GT												
5.5	5500	510	P	V10	R	205	4.0	–	–	4555	1915	1250
PROTON												
Satria												
1.3	1299	75	P	S4	F	102	13.6	35	9	3990	1698	960
1.5	1468	87	P	S4	F	107	12.1	34	13	3990	1698	965
1.6	1597	95	P	S4	F	112	11.3	34	13	3990	1698	960
1.8	1834	130	P	S4	F	125	7.8	33	16	3990	1698	1105
Wira												
1.3	1299	75	P	S4	F	107	13.6	35	9	4360	1690	960
1.5	1468	87	P	S4	F	107	12.1	34	11	4360	1690	965
1.6	1597	120	P	S4	F	112	10.9	35	12	4360	1690	960
1.8	1834	116	P	S4	F	119	10.4	32	14	4360	1690	1105
1.8	1834	140	P	S4	F	126	9.0	33	15	4220	1690	1105
2.0 Diesel	1998	68	D	S4	F	99	18.5	54	–	4360	1690	1125
2.0 TD	1998	82	D	S4	F	105	14.3	36	11	4360	1690	1125
Impian												
1.6	–	–	P	S4	F	110	12.0	42	15	4465	1740	–
RENAULT												
Twingo – 1.2	1149	60	P	S4	F	93	13.4	47	–	3430	1630	865
Clio												
1.2	1149	60	P	S4	F	99	15.0	46	–	3812	1639	880
1.4	1390	75	P	S4	F	105	12.1	42	–	3812	1639	940
1.4	1390	98	P	S4	F	115	10.5	43	–	3812	1639	980
1.6	1598	90	P	S4	F	112	10.6	39	–	3812	1639	965
1.6 16v	1598	107	P	S4	F	121	9.6	39	–	3812	1639	995
2.0 16v	1998	172	P	S4	F	136	7.3	36	–	3812	1639	1035
3.0	2946	226	P	V6	R	146	6.4	25	–	3812	1810	1335
1.5 dCi	–	–	D	S4	F	–	–	–	–	3812	1639	–
1.9 D	1870	64	D	S4	F	100	15.4	47	–	3812	1639	975
1.9 TD	1870	75	D	S4	F	108	12.8	54	–	3812	1639	1000
Kangoo												
1.2	1149	60	P	S4	F	87	17.2	41	–	3995	1663	1020
1.4	1390	75	P	S4	F	96	14.9	38	4	3995	1663	1065
1.9 D	1870	64	D	S4	F	90	19.5	45	4	3995	1663	1110
1.9 TD	1870	80	D	S4	F	99	14.1	50	–	3995	1663	1120
Megane												
1.4	1390	95	P	S4	F	114	11.8	41	4	4129	1699	1090
1.6	1598	107	P	S4	F	121	9.8	40	6	4129	1699	1095
1.8	1783	116	P	S4	F	122	9.5	37	–	4129	1699	1150
2.0 16v	1998	140	P	S4	F	132	8.6	38	11	3930	1700	1135
1.9 dTi	1870	80	D	S4	F	115	12.3	46	4	4129	1699	1180
1.9 dCi	1870	102	D	S4	F	118	11.5	54	5	4129	1699	1115
Megane Scenic												
1.4	1390	95	P	S4	F	107	12.9	40	5	4134	1719	1235
1.6	1598	107	P	S4	F	115	11.2	39	6	4134	1719	1250
1.8	1783	116	P	S4	F	117	10.9	36	–	4134	1719	1300
2.0	1998	140	P	S4	F	122	10.2	35	9	4134	1719	1290
1.9 Diesel	1870	64	D	S4	F	94	18.9	41	–	4134	1719	1275
1.9 dTi	1870	80	D	S4	F	101	15.7	50	–	4134	1719	1290
1.9 dCi	1870	102	D	S4	F	107	12.8	48	–	4134	1719	–
Laguna												
1.6	1598	107	P	S4	F	121	11.5	39	7	4579	2060	1290
1.8	1783	120	P	S4	F	125	10.8	38	8	4579	2060	1320
2.0 16v	1948	140	P	S4	F	130	–	–	–	4579	2060	1335
3.0	2946	207	P	V6	F	146	8.1	28	13	4579	2060	1480
1.9 dCi	1870	107	D	S4	F	124	10.7	51	9	4579	2060	1370
2.2 dCi	2188	135	D	S4	F	121	–	–	–	4579	2060	1485

Model	Engine – CC	Power – bhp	Fuel	Engine config.	Driven wheels	Top speed – mph	0–60 mph – secs	mpg – average	Insurance group	Length – mm	Width – mm	Weight – Kg
Avantime												
2.0 Turbo	-	-	P	S4	-	-	-	-	-	4642	1826	-
3.0	2946	210	P	V6	137	8.6	25	-	-	4642	1826	-
Espace												
2.0 16v	1998	140	P	S4	F	115	11.6	31	13	4517	1810	1490
3.0	2946	190	P	V6	F	126	10.6	24	14	4517	1810	1680
1.9 TD	1870	100	D	S4	F	104	15.0	43	-	4517	1810	1520
2.2 dCi	2188	115	D	S4	F	109	13.5	-	-	4517	1810	1630
2.2 dCi	2188	130	D	S4	F	113	12.4	40	13	4517	1810	1630
ROLLS-ROYCE												
Silver Seraph – 5.4	5379	326	P	V12	R	140	7.1	16	20	5390	1930	2400
Corniche – 6.8	6750	329	P	V8	R	140	8.5	15	20	5405	2058	2735
SAAB												
9-3												
2.0 Turbo	1985	150	P	S4	F	133	8.5	32	13	4629	1711	1320
2.0 Turbo	1985	185	P	S4	F	143	7.5	32	14	4629	1711	1380
2.0 Turbo	1985	205	P	S4	F	146	6.9	30	16	4629	1711	1380
2.0 Turbo	1985	230	P	S4	F	155	6.5	29	-	4629	1711	1320
2.2 TiD	2172	116	D	S4	F	124	10.9	46	10	4629	1711	1350
9-5												
2.0 Turbo	1985	150	P	S4	F	134	9.0	31	-	4805	1792	1485
2.0 Turbo	1985	190	P	S4	F	143	8.3	30	-	4805	1792	1485
2.3 Turbo	2290	185	P	S4	F	143	7.9	30	-	4805	1792	1510
2.3 Turbo	2290	250	P	S4	F	155	6.5	32	-	4805	1792	-
3.0 Turbo	2962	200	P	V6	F	146	8.5	25	-	4805	1792	1600
3.0 TiD	-	200	D	V6	F	133	8.9	38	-	4805	1792	-
SATURN												
S-Series												
1.9	1901	101	P	S4	F	93	10.5	-	-	4525	1685	1055
1.9 16v	1901	126	P	S4	F	99	9.0	-	-	4525	1685	1085
L-Series												
2.2	2198	139	P	S4	F	105	9.5	-	-	4835	1755	1335
3.0	2962	185	P	V6	F	115	8.2	-	-	4835	1755	1445
SEAT												
Arosa												
1.0	999	50	P	S4	F	94	17.7	49	2	3551	1639	880
1.4	1390	60	P	S4	F	99	14.2	46	3	3551	1639	900
1.4 16v	1390	100	P	S4	F	117	10.0	43	5	3551	1639	945
1.4 TDi	1422	75	D	S4	F	105	12.1	66	4	3551	1639	965
1.7D	1716	60	D	S4	F	97	16.6	64	-	3551	1639	960
Ibiza												
1.0	999	50	P	S4	F	90	19.4	44	-	3876	1640	945
1.4	1390	60	P	S4	F	97	15.1	43	4	3876	1640	955
1.4 16v	1390	75	P	S4	F	105	12.5	44	-	3876	1640	995
1.4 16v	1390	101	P	S4	F	117	10.7	42	-	3876	1640	1020
1.6	1595	101	P	S4	F	117	10.7	36	7	3876	1640	1040
1.8 Turbo	1781	156	P	S4	F	135	7.9	36	15	3876	1640	1120
1.8 Turbo	1781	180	P	S4	F	140	7.2	36	18	3876	1640	-
1.9 D	1896	64	D	S4	F	100	16.0	57	-	3876	1640	1040
1.9 TD	1896	90	D	S4	F	112	12.1	57	7	3876	1640	1050
1.9 TD	1896	110	D	S4	F	120	10.5	58	-	3876	1640	1125
Cordoba												
1.4	1390	60	P	S4	F	97	15.9	43	-	4165	1640	1020
1.4 16v	1390	75	P	S4	F	105	12.9	44	-	4165	1640	1040
1.6	1595	101	P	S4	F	117	11.0	36	-	4165	1640	1080
1.8 Turbo	1781	156	P	S4	F	135	8.0	78	-	4165	1640	1135
1.9 D	1896	68	D	S4	F	100	17.1	55	-	4165	1640	1110
1.9 TD	1896	90	D	S4	F	112	12.5	58	-	4165	1640	1140
1.9 TD	1896	110	D	S4	F	120	10.6	58	-	4165	1640	1155
Leon												
1.4	1390	75	P	S4	F	105	14.3	43	4	4184	1742	1136
1.6	1595	101	P	S4	F	119	10.9	41	6	4184	1742	1150
1.8	1781	125	P	S4	F	124	10.3	33	9	4184	1742	1220
1.8 Turbo	1781	180	P	S4	F	142	7.7	33	16	4184	1742	1245
2.8	2791	204	P	V6	4x4	146	7.3	26	-	4184	1742	1485
1.9 D	1896	68	D	S4	F	99	17.7	55	-	4184	1742	1195
1.9 TDi	1896	90	D	S4	F	112	12.7	55	6	4184	1742	1230
1.9 TDi 110	1896	110	D	S4	F	120	10.7	57	7	4184	1742	1240
1.9 TDi 150	1896	150	D	S4	F	133	8.9	53	-	4184	1742	1300
Toledo												
1.6	1595	101	P	S4	F	119	10.9	41	-	4439	1742	1150
1.8	1781	125	P	S4	F	124	10.5	34	7	4439	1742	1225
2.3	2324	170	P	S5	F	140	8.6	32	13	4439	1742	1310
1.9 TDi	1896	90	D	S4	F	112	13.0	55	-	4439	1742	1245
1.9 TDi 110	1896	110	D	S4	F	120	11.2	57	7	4439	1742	1270
1.9 TDi 150	1896	150	D	S4	F	133	8.9	53	-	4439	1742	1310
Alhambra												
1.8T	1781	150	P	S4	F	123	10.9	30	12	4617	1810	1670
2.0	1984	116	P	S4	F	110	15.2	30	11	4617	1810	1645
2.8 V6	2792	204	P	V6	F	135	9.9	27	16	4617	1810	1855
1.9 TDi	1896	90	D	S4	F	102	17.2	43	-	4617	1810	1675
1.9 TDi 115	1896	115	D	S4	F	112	13.7	44	12	4617	1810	1675
SKODA												
Fabia												
1.0	997	50	P	S4	F	91	21.6	42	-	3960	1645	1035
1.4	1397	68	P	S4	F	100	15.4	40	4	3960	1645	1065
1.4 16v	1390	75	P	S4	F	104	13.8	42	4	3960	1645	1060
1.4 16v	1390	100	P	S4	F	115	11.5	40	6	3960	1645	1065
2.0	1984	120	P	S4	F	121	9.9	36	8	3960	1645	1110
1.9 SDi	1896	64	D	S4	F	95	18.7	59	4	3960	1645	1125
1.9 TDi	1896	100	D	S4	F	115	11.5	58	-	3960	1645	1145
Octavia												
1.4	1397	60	P	S4	F	96	18.9	38	5	4510	1730	1175
1.4 16v	1397	75	P	S4	F	106	15.3	42	-	4510	1730	1175
1.6	1598	75	P	S4	F	105	14.7	37	-	4510	1730	1190
1.6	1595	101	P	S4	F	118	11.8	40	10	4510	1730	1190
1.8 Turbo	1781	150	P	S4	F	133	8.4	36	13	4510	1730	1260
1.8 Turbo	1781	180	P	S4	F	144	8.0	35	16	4510	1730	1260
2.0	1984	115	P	S4	F	122	10.8	35	10	4510	1730	1235
1.9 SDi	1896	68	D	S4	F	101	19.2	54	8	4510	1730	1255
1.9 TDi 90	1896	90	D	S4	F	113	13.2	57	9	4510	1730	1270
1.9 TDi 100	1896	100	D	S4	F	114	13.4	46	-	4510	1730	1270
1.9 TDi 110	1896	110	D	S4	F	118	11.1	57	11	4510	1730	1270
SUBARU												
Justy – 1.3	1298	85	P	S4	4x4	96	13.0	41	6	3745	1590	845
Pleo	700	46	P	S4	4x4	81	-	-	-	3395	1475	770
Impreza												
1.5	1493	97	P	F4	4x4	-	-	-	-	4350	1690	1115
1.6	1597	95	P	F4	4x4	109	12.8	32	-	4350	1690	1005
2.0	1994	125	P	F4	4x4	115	9.7	29	13	4350	1690	1215
2.0 Turbo	1994	218	P	F4	4x4	143	6.3	28	17	4350	1690	1295
2.0 Turbo	1994	280	P	F4	4x4	-	-	-	-	4350	1690	-
Legacy												
2.0	1994	125	P	F4	4x4	117	10.8	29	14	4595	1700	1370
2.0	1994	155	P	F4	4x4	127	9.3	29	-	4595	1700	1170
2.0 Turbo	1994	280	P	F4	4x4	155	6.8	22	-	4595	1700	1380
2.5	2457	155	P	F4	4x4	128	9.0	30	15	4595	1700	1315
3.0	2999	209	P	F4	4x4	130	8.9	27	-	4595	1700	1535
Forester												
2.0	1994	125	P	F4	4x4	110	11.4	31	11	4450	1735	1380
2.0 Turbo	1994	250	P	F4	4x4	123	7.7	29	17	4450	1735	1405
2.5	2457	150	P	F4	4x4	118	-	29	-	4450	1735	1780
SUZUKI												
Alto												
0.7	657	46	P	S3	F	78	-	51	-	3495	1495	630
0.7 Turbo	657	64	P	S3	F	93	-	43	-	3495	1495	630
1.0	-	-	P	S4	F	93	16.3	50	3	3495	1495	-
Ignis												
1.3	1328	83	P	S4	F	99	-	44	4	3615	1595	880
Wagon R												
1.0	996	70	P	S4	F	90	-	-	-	3510	1620	900
1.0 Turbo	996	100	P	S4	F	-	-	-	-	3510	1620	900
1.3	1298	76	P	S4	F	96	12.8	46	3	3510	1620	920
Swift												
1.0	993	53	P	S3	F	90	18.2	51	4	3745	1590	730
1.3	1299	85	P	S4	F	102	-	50	-	3745	1590	755
Baleno												
1.3	1299	86	P	S4	F	99	-	46	-	3900	1690	915
1.6	1590	96	P	S4	F	105	-	39	-	3900	1690	890
1.8	1840	121	P	S4	F	115	10.2	37	10	3900	1690	935
1.9 TD	1905	75	P	S4	F	99	-	41	-	3900	1690	1030
Liana												
1.5	1491	110	P	S4	F	105	11.2	49	6	4230	1690	1130
Jimny												
0.7	658	64	P	S3	4x4	78	-	-	-	3625	1600	930
1.3	1298	80	P	S4	4x4	87	16.0	34	7	3625	1600	1025
Grand Vitara												
1.6	1590	94	P	S4	4x4	93	-	35	12	3860	1700	1200
2.0	1995	128	P	S4	4x4	99	12.5	30	12	3860	1700	1260
2.5	2494	144	P	V6	4x4	102	11.5	27	13	3860	1700	1405
2.7	2737	173	P	V6	4x4	112	-	-	-	4665	1800	1625
2.0 TD	1998	87	D	S4	4x4	99	-	38	-	3860	1700	1200
2.0 TD	1998	110	D	S4	4x4	93	-	37	-	3860	1700	1400
TATA												
Indica												
1.4	1405	75	P	S4	F	93	15.0	32	-	3660	1645	930
1.4 D	1405	54	D	S4	F	87	17.0	38	-	3660	1645	930
Safari												
2.0 TD	1948	90	D	S4	4x4	90	19.0	30	10	4800	2100	1920
TOYOTA												
Yaris												
1.0	998	68	P	S4	F	97	12.0	50	2	3615	1660	880
1.3	1299	90	P	S4	F	109	10.7	47	4	3615	1660	-
1.5	1497	110	P	S4	F	112	9.0	41	7	3615	1690	930
Corolla												
1.3	1299	88	P	S4	F	105	13.0	-	-	4175	1695	1030
1.5	1497	110	P	S4	F	118	10.5	-	-	4175	1695	1070
1.8	1764	136	P	S4	F	124	10.0	-	-	4175	1695	1120
1.8	1796	190	P	S4	F	136	-	-	-	4175	1695	1150
2.2 TD	2184	79	D	S4	F	105	-	-	-	4175	1695	1140
Prius – 1.5	1497	72	P	S4	F	99	13.4	55	8	4315	1695	1250
Avensis												
1.6	1587	110	P	S4	F	121	11.3	40	8	4520	1710	1195
1.8	1794	127	P	S4	F	124	10.0	38	9	4520	1710	-
2.0	1998	149	P	S4	F	130	9.1	37	10	4520	1710	1245
2.0 D4-D	1995	110	D	S4	F	121	11.4	48	7	4520	1710	1320
Camry												
2.2	2164	131	P	S4	F	124	10.4	32	12	4765	1785	1385
3.0	2995	190	P	V6	F	136	9.0	24	14	4765	1785	1445
MR2												
1.8	1794	140	P	S4	R	130	7.9	38	13	3885	1695	960
Celica												
1.8	1794	140	P	S4	F	127	8.7	37	13	4355	1735	1170
1.8	1796	190	P	S4	F	140	7.4	34	15	4355	1735	1140
Previa												
2.4	2362	156	P	S4	R	115	10.9	30	12	4750	1790	1525
3.0	2995	220	P	V6	R	112	-	-	-	4750	1790	1710
2.0 D4-D	-	-	D	S4	R	109	13.8	39	11	4750	1790	-
RAV4												
1.8	1794	125	P	S4	4x4	109	12.2	38	9	3850	1735	1125
2.0	1998	150	P	S4	4x4	115	10.6	32	11	3850	1735	1220
2.0 D4-D	-	-	D	S4	4x4	-	-	-	-	3850	1735	-

Model	Engine – CC	Power – bhp	Fuel	Engine config.	Driven wheels	Top speed – mph	0–60 mph – secs	mpg – average	Insurance group	Length – mm	Width – mm	Weight – Kg
Landcruiser Colorado												
2.7	2694	152	P	S4	4x4	102	–	22	–	4750	1820	1855
3.4	3378	176	P	V6	4x4	112	10.4	20	15	4750	1820	1810
3.0 D4-D	2982	-	D	S4	4x4	106	12.1	30	15	4750	1820	1720
Landcruiser Amazon												
4.7	4664	235	P	V8	4x4	109	11.7	17	15	4890	1940	2465
4.2 TD	4164	131	D	S6	4x4	105	13.6	25	14	4890	1940	2620
4.2 TD	4164	250	D	S6	4x4	–	–	–	–	4890	1940	2620
TVR												
Chimaera												
4.5	4552	288	P	V8	R	160	4.7	22	20	4105	1865	1060
5.0	4997	320	P	V8	R	167	4.1	18	20	4105	1865	1060
Tuscan Speed												
4.0	3996	364	P	S6	R	181	4.2	-	20	4235	1810	1100
3.6	-	-	P	S6	R	-	-	-	20	4235	1810	-
Cerbera												
4.0	3966	355	P	V8	R	170	4.4	–	20	4280	1865	1100
4.2	4280	365	P	V8	R	180	4.2	15	20	4280	1865	1100
4.5	4475	426	P	V8	R	190	3.9	15	20	4280	1865	1100
VAUXHALL/OPEL												
Agila												
1.0	973	58	P	S3	F	88	18.0	45	2	3500	1620	940
1.2	1199	75	P	S4	F	96	13.5	43	3	3500	1620	955
Corsa												
1.0	973	58	P	S3	F	96	17.0	50	1	3817	1646	905
1.2	1199	75	P	S4	F	105	13.0	45	1	3817	1646	935
1.4	1389	90	P	S4	F	112	11.5	39	4	3817	1646	1000
1.8	1796	125	P	S4	F	125	9.0	36	9	3817	1646	1085
1.7 Di	1686	67	D	S4	F	100	14.5	60	3	3817	1646	1020
1.7 DTi	1686	75	D	S4	F	105	13.5	60	4	3817	1646	1040
Astra												
1.2	1199	75	P	S4	F	105	15.0	46	–	4111	1709	1035
1.4 16v	1389	90	P	S4	F	112	12.0	39	4	4111	1709	1090
1.6	1598	85	P	S4	F	112	13.0	40	4	4111	1709	1090
1.6 16v	1598	101	P	S4	F	117	11.5	40	5	4111	1709	1090
1.8	1796	125	P	S4	F	127	9.5	36	7	4111	1709	1140
2.0	1998	147	P	S4	F	133	9.0	34	-	4111	1709	1180
2.0 Turbo	1998	190	P	S4	F	151	7.5	32	15	4111	1709	1260
2.2	2198	144	P	S4	F	133	9.0	34	13	4111	1709	1180
1.7 DTi	1686	75	D	S4	F	105	14.5	59	4	4111	1709	1185
2.0 Di	1995	82	D	S4	F	109	14.5	42	-	4111	1709	1225
2.0 DTi	1995	100	D	S4	F	117	12.5	48	7	4111	1709	1225
Vectra												
1.6 16v	1598	101	P	S4	F	117	12.5	40	7	4495	1710	1245
1.8	1796	125	P	S4	F	129	10.5	37	9	4495	1710	1270
2.2	2198	147	P	S4	F	135	9.5	34	12	4495	1710	1315
2.6 V6	2597	170	P	V6	F	143	8.5	29	15	4495	1710	1350
2.0 DTi	1995	101	D	S4	F	121	13.0	50	8	4495	1710	1375
2.2 DTi	2171	125	D	S4	F	128	10.5	43	11	4495	1710	1375
Omega												
2.0i 16v	1998	136	P	S4	R	130	11.0	30	-	4898	1776	1460
2.2i 16v	2198	144	P	S4	R	130	10.5	29	13	4898	1776	1530
2.6 V6	2597	170	P	V6	R	142	9.5	27	14	4898	1776	1610
3.2 V6	3175	211	P	V6	R	149	9.0	24	16	4898	1776	1635
2.2 DTi	2171	125	D	S4	R	121	12.5	40	13	4898	1776	1595
2.5 TD	2498	131	D	S6	R	124	12.0	36	-	4898	1776	1600
VX220												
2.2	2198	147	P	S4	R	136	5.6	33	16	3790	1710	870
Zafira												
1.6	1598	101	P	S4	F	109	13.0	36	6	4317	1742	1320
1.8	1796	125	P	S4	F	117	11.5	33	8	4317	1742	1370
2.2	2198	147	P	S4	F	124	10.0	32	12	4317	1742	1400
2.0 DTi	1995	101	D	S4	F	109	14.0	43	5	4317	1742	1430
Frontera												
2.2	2198	136	P	S4	4x4	102	13.4	25	9	4658	1814	1660
3.2 V6	3165	205	P	V6	4x4	115	10.3	22	12	4658	1814	1780
2.2 DTi	2172	116	P	S4	4x4	96	13.9	31	9	4658	1814	1720
VOLKSWAGEN												
Lupo												
1.0	999	50	P	S4	F	94	17.7	49	2	3525	1639	885
1.4	1390	60	P	S4	F	99	14.3	46	-	3525	1639	910
1.4	1390	75	P	S4	F	107	12.0	46	3	3525	1639	920
1.4	1390	100	P	S4	F	117	10.0	43	6	3525	1639	945
1.6	1598	125	P	S4	F	127	8.3	40	11	3525	1639	980
1.2 TD	1196	61	P	S3	F	102	14.5	97	-	3525	1639	855
1.4 TDI	1422	75	P	S3	F	105	12.3	67	4	3525	1639	985
1.7 D	1716	60	P	S4	F	97	16.8	64	3	3525	1639	975
Polo												
1.0	999	50	P	S4	F	94	18.5	50	3	3715	1655	925
1.4 8v	1390	60	P	S4	F	99	14.5	46	7	3715	1655	925
1.4	1390	75	P	S4	F	107	12.3	46	7	3715	1655	960
1.4 16v	1390	101	P	S4	F	117	10.4	42	10	3715	1655	985
1.6 100	1598	100	P	S4	F	117	10.9	36	10	4135	1640	1090
1.6 125	1598	125	P	S4	F	127	8.7	40	12	3715	1655	1010
1.4 TDi	1422	75	D	S3	F	105	12.9	64	7	3715	1655	1035
1.9 SDi	1896	64	D	S4	F	99	15.9	59	6	3715	1655	985
1.9 TDI	1896	90	D	S4	F	112	12.5	57	7	4135	1640	1145
1.9 TDI	1896	110	D	S4	F	120	10.7	58	10	4135	1640	1160
Golf Mk 1												
1.3	1349	71	P	S4	F	94	12.8	31	-	3815	1610	–
1.6	1595	82	P	S4	F	–	–	–	–	3815	1610	–
Golf												
1.4	1390	75	P	S4	F	106	13.9	44	4	4150	1735	1100
1.6	1595	101	P	S4	F	115	12.7	35	5	4150	1735	1125
1.8 T	1781	150	P	S4	F	134	8.5	36	14	4150	1735	1210
2.0	1984	116	P	S4	F	121	10.5	36	10	4150	1735	1170
2.3 V5	2324	170	P	V5	F	139	8.2	32	15	4150	1735	1250
2.8 V6	2792	204	P	V6	4X4	146	7.1	26	17	4150	1735	1410
1.9 SDi	1896	68	D	S4	F	99	17.2	54	4	4150	1735	1170
1.9 TDI 90	1896	90	D	S4	F	112	12.4	58	6	4150	1735	1200
1.9 TDI 100	1896	100	D	S4	F	117	11.3	55	-	4150	1735	1215
1.9 TDI 115	1896	115	D	S4	F	121	10.3	55	10	4150	1735	1230
1.9 TDI 150	1896	150	D	S4	F	134	8.6	53	-	4150	1735	1265
Bora												
1.4	1390	75	P	S4	F	106	14.9	43	-	4376	1740	1165
1.6	1595	101	P	S4	F	115	12.8	35	5	4376	1740	1210
1.8 T	1781	150	P	S4	F	134	8.9	36	-	4376	1740	1300
2.0	1984	116	P	S4	F	121	11.0	35	8	4376	1740	1240
2.3 V5	2324	170	P	V5	F	138	8.5	32	16	4376	1740	1300
2.8 V6	2792	204	P	V6	4X4	146	7.4	26	-	4376	1740	1455
1.9 TDI	1896	90	D	S4	F	112	12.9	57	7	4376	1740	1275
1.9 TDI	1896	100	D	S4	F	117	12.1	55	-	4376	1740	1280
1.9 TDI	1896	110	D	S4	F	120	10.9	57	-	4376	1740	1280
1.9 TDI	1896	115	D	S4	F	120	10.8	55	9	4376	1740	1315
1.9 TDI	1896	150	D	S4	F	134	9.0	52	-	4376	1740	1330
Beetle												
1.6	1595	101	P	S4	F	110	11.7	38	9	4081	1724	1205
1.8 Turbo	1781	150	P	S4	F	126	9.0	35	-	4081	1724	1275
2.0	1984	116	P	S4	F	115	10.9	32	11	4081	1724	1230
2.3 V5	2324	170	P	V5	F	131	8.7	32	-	4081	1724	1325
1.9 TDI	1896	90	D	S4	F	104	14.4	43	-	4081	1724	1290
1.9 TDI	1896	100	D	S4	F	110	12.4	55	-	4081	1724	1290
Passat												
1.6	1595	101	P	S4	F	119	12.7	37	-	4675	1740	1310
1.8 Turbo	1781	150	P	S4	F	138	9.2	34	14	4675	1740	1375
2.0	1984	115	P	S4	F	124	11.2	34	8	4675	1740	1340
2.3 V5	2324	170	P	V5	F	141	9.1	31	16	4675	1740	1440
2.8	2771	193	P	V6	4x4	148	7.8	26	17	4675	1740	1545
1.9 TDI	1896	100	D	S4	F	118	12.4	52	12	4675	1740	1380
1.9 TDI 130	1896	130	D	S4	F	129	9.9	50	12	4675	1740	1320
2.5 TDI 150	2496	150	D	V6	F	136	9.6	41	15	4675	1740	1510
Sharan												
1.8 Turbo	1781	150	P	S4	F	123	10.9	30	11	4620	1810	1670
2.0	1984	115	P	S4	F	110	15.2	30	11	4620	1810	1645
2.8	2792	204	P	V6	F	135	9.9	27	15	4620	1810	1700
1.9 TDi	1896	90	D	S4	F	102	17.2	43	12	4620	1810	1660
1.9 TDi 115	1896	115	D	S4	F	112	13.7	73	12	4620	1810	1660
VOLKSWAGEN Brazil/Mexico												
Gol												
1.0	998	54	P	S4	F	91	18.4	40	–	3810	1650	940
1.0 16v	998	69	P	S4	F	100	14.3	-	-	3810	1650	905
1.6	1595	92	P	S4	F	110	11.8	41	-	3810	1650	980
1.8	1781	99	P	S4	F	112	11.3	39	-	3810	1650	990
2.0 8v	1984	111	P	S4	F	118	10.3	36	-	3810	1650	1010
2.0 16v	1984	145	P	S4	F	128	8.7	36	-	3810	1650	1115
Beetle – 1.6	1585	44	P	F4	R	77	27.2	37	–	4060	1550	820
VOLVO												
S40/V40												
1.6	1587	109	P	S4	F	118	12.0	36	8	4480	1720	1255
1.8	1783	122	P	S4	F	124	10.5	35	9	4480	1720	1255
1.8 GDi	1834	125	P	S4	F	124	10.5	41	10	4480	1720	1230
2.0 Turbo	1948	200	P	S4	F	146	7.3	32	16	4480	1720	1300
2.0	1948	136	P	S4	F	127	9.7	34	11	4480	1720	1280
2.0 Turbo	1948	165	P	S4	F	137	8.5	34	-	4480	1720	1210
1.9 TD	1870	102	D	S4	F	115	12.0	52	11	4480	1720	1295
1.9 TD	1870	115	D	S4	F	121	10.5	52	11	4480	1720	1295
S60												
2.0 T	1984	180	P	S5	F	130	8.8	31	14	4576	1804	1500
2.3 T	2319	250	P	S5	F	155	6.8	30	16	4576	1804	1470
2.4	2435	140	P	S5	F	130	10.2	34	14	4576	1804	1430
2.4	2435	170	P	S5	F	130	8.7	32	15	4576	1804	-
2.4 T	2435	200	P	S5	F	130	7.6	31	-	4576	1804	1460
2.4 D5	-	-	D	S5	F	-	-	-	-	4576	1804	1460
V70												
2.0 Turbo	1984	180	P	S5	F	130	9.1	-	-	4710	1804	1530
2.3 Turbo	2319	250	P	S5	F	155	7.1	30	16	4720	1824	1540
2.4	2435	140	P	S5	F	127	10.5	33	13	4720	1824	1485
2.4	2435	170	P	S5	F	130	9.0	32	13	4720	1824	1485
2.4 D5	-	-	D	S5	F	-	-	-	-	4720	1824	1570
C70												
2.0 Turbo	1948	163	P	S5	F	130	9.3	32	14	4720	1820	1460
2.3 Turbo	2319	240	P	S5	F	155	6.9	30	16	4720	1820	1450
2.4 Turbo	2435	193	P	S5	F	143	7.8	29	16	4720	1820	1450
S80												
2.0 Turbo 180	1984	180	P	S5	F	140	9.1	31	-	4820	1830	1490
2.4 140	2435	140	P	S5	F	127	10.5	33	14	4820	1830	1460
2.4 170	2435	170	P	S5	F	130	9.0	30	14	4820	1830	1460
2.4 200 T	2435	200	P	S5	F	143	7.9	30	-	4820	1830	1505
2.8 Turbo	2783	272	P	S6	F	155	7.2	25	16	4820	1830	1605
2.9	2922	200	P	S6	F	146	8.2	29	15	4820	1830	1540
2.5 D5	-	-	D	S5	F	-	-	-	-	4820	1830	1550
WESTFIELD												
900	0.9	-	P	-	R	128	4.1	-	-	3710	1625	-
1.3	1300	-	P	-	R	137	3.7	-	-	3710	1625	-
1.8	1796	115	P	S4	R	110	6.5	-	-	3710	1625	-
1.8 Sport	1796	140	P	S4	R	118	5.8	-	-	3710	1625	-
1.8 Speed Sport	1796	150	P	S4	R	130	5.3	-	-	3710	1625	-
1.8 FW400	1796	145	P	S4	R	135	4.0	-	-	3710	1625	-
1.8 FW400	1796	190	P	S4	R	140	3.5	-	-	3710	1625	-
4.0 V8	3951	200	P	V8	R	138	4.3	-	-	3710	1625	-

NEW CAR PRICES

These tables give the UK list prices of new cars as the Guide went to press in September 2001. Check with your dealer for changes that may have occurred subsequently.

AC

Cobra	
5.0 V8 CRS	£38,950
3.5 V8 212 S/C	£68,990
Roadster	
5.0 V8 Superblower	£79,950

ALFA ROMEO

147	
1.6 Twin Spark Turismo 3dr	£13,175
1.6 Twin Spark Lusso 3dr	£14,250
2.0 Twin Spark 3dr	£15,740
2.0 Twin Spark Selespeed 3dr	£17,340
1.6 Twin Spark Turismo 5dr	£13,675
1.6 Twin Spark Lusso 5dr	£14,750
2.0 Twin Spark 5dr	£16,240
2.0 Twin Spark Selespeed 5dr	£17,840
156	
1.6 Twin Spark Turismo 4dr	£14,520
1.6 Twin Spark Veloce 4dr	£15,320
1.6 Twin Spark Lusso 4dr	£15,525
1.8 Twin Spark Turismo 4dr	£16,060
1.8 Twin Spark Veloce 4dr	£16,860
1.8 Twin Spark Lusso 4dr	£17,065
2.0 Twin Spark Turismo 4dr	£17,445
2.0 Twin Spark Veloce 4dr	£18,245
2.0 Twin Spark Lusso 4dr	£18,450
2.0 TS Selespeed Turismo 4dr	£18,795
2.0 TS Selespeed Veloce 4dr	£19,395
2.5 V6 24v Turismo 4dr	£19,485
2.5 V6 24v Veloce 4dr	£20,285
2.5 V6 24v Lusso 4dr	£20,490
2.4 JTD Turismo 4dr	£17,685
2.4 JTD Veloce 4dr	£18,485
2.4 JTD Lusso 4dr	£18,690
1.6 Twin Spark Turismo Est	£15,620
1.6 Twin Spark Veloce Est	£16,420
1.6 Twin Spark Lusso Est	£16,625
1.8 Twin Spark Turismo Est	£17,160
1.8 Twin Spark Veloce Est	£17,960
1.8 Twin Spark Lusso Est	£18,165
2.0 Twin Spark Turismo Est	£18,545
2.0 Twin Spark Veloce Est	£19,345
2.0 Twin Spark Lusso Est	£19,550
2.0 TS S'speed TurismoEst	£19,895
2.0 TS S'speed Veloce Est	£20,495
2.5 V6 24v Turismo Est	£20,585
2.5 V6 24v Veloce Est	£21,385
2.5 V6 24v Lusso Est	£21,590
2.4 JTD Turismo Est	£18,785
2.4 JTD Veloce Est	£19,585
2.4 JTD Lusso Est	£20,385
166	
2.0 Twin Spark Turismo 4dr	£20,410
2.0 Twin Spark Lusso 4dr	£22,510
2.5 V6 Turismo 4dr	£23,685
2.5 V6 Lusso 4dr	£25,805
3.0 V6 Super Turismo 4dr	£25,575
3.0 V6 Super Lusso 4dr	£29,270
Spider/GTV	
Spider 2.0 Twin Spark	£20,110
Spider 2.0 TS Lusso	£22,305
Spider 3.0 V6 6-Speed	£26,340
GTV 2.0 Twin Spark	£19,715
GTV 2.0 TS Lusso	£20,655
GTV 3.0 V6 6-Speed	£25,240

ASTON MARTIN

DB7	
6.0 V12 Vantage Coupe	£94,500
6.0 V12 Vantage Volante	£101,950

AUDI

A2	
1.4 5dr	£13,095
1.4 SE 5dr	£15,045
1.4 TDi 5dr	£14,105
1.4 TDi SE 5dr	£16,055
A3	
1.6 3dr	£14,590
1.6 Sport 3dr	£15,890
1.6 SE 3dr	£16,300
1.8 3dr	£15,715
1.8 Sport 3dr	£17,015
1.8 SE 3dr	£17,425
1.8 T Sport 3dr	£18,355
1.8 T Sport quattro 3dr	£20,895
1.8 S3 quattro 3dr	£24,770
1.9 TDi 3dr	£15,440
1.9 TDi 110 3dr	£16,290
1.9 TDi SE 3dr	£17,150
1.9 TDi 110 Sport 3dr	£17,635
1.9 TDi 110 SE 3dr	£18,000
1.6 5dr	£15,210
1.6 Sport 5dr	£16,510
1.6 SE 5dr	£16,920
1.8 5dr	£16,335
1.8 Sport 5dr	£17,635
1.8 SE 5dr	£18,045
1.8 T Sport 5dr	£18,975
1.8 T Sport quattro 5dr	£21,515
1.9 TDi 5dr	£16,060
1.9 TDi 110 5dr	£16,910
1.9 TDi SE 5dr	£17,770
1.9 TDi 110 Sport 5dr	£18,255
1.9 TDi 110 SE 5dr	£18,620
A4	
2.0 4dr	£18,640
1.8 T 4dr	£19,810
2.0SE 4dr	£19,250
2.0Sport 4dr	£19,540
1.8 T SE 4dr	£20,420
1.8 T Sport 4dr	£20,710
1.8 T quattro 4dr	£21,210
1.8 T quattro SE 4dr	£21,820
1.8 T quattro Sport 4dr	£22,110
3.0 quattro 4dr	£24,840
3.0 quattro SE 4dr	£25,450
3.0 quattro Sport 4dr	£25,740
1.9 TDi 100 4dr	£18,705
1.9 TDi 100 SE 4dr	£19,315
1.9 TDi 130 4dr	£19,915
1.9 TDi 130 SE 4dr	£20,525
1.9 TDi 130 Sport 4dr	£20,815
2.5 TDi 180 quattro 4dr	£24,345
2.5 TDi 180 quattro SE 4dr	£24,955
2.5 TDi 180 quattro Sport 4dr	£25,245
A6	
2.0 4dr	£20,450
2.0 SE 4dr	£21,300
2.0 Sport 4dr	£21,200
1.8T 4dr	£21,750
1.8T SE 4dr	£22,600
1.8T Sport 4dr	£22,500
1.8T quattro 4dr	£23,150
1.8T quattro SE 4dr	£24,000
1.8T quattro Sport 4dr	£23,900
2.4 4dr	£22,550
2.4 SE 4dr	£23,400
2.4 Sport 4dr	£23,300
2.4 quattro 4dr	£23,950
2.4 quattro SE 4dr	£24,800
2.4 quattro Sport 4dr	£24,700
2.7T quattro SE 4dr	£31,100
2.7T quattro Sport 4dr	£31,650
3.0 quattro SE 4dr	£28,850
3.0 quattro Sport 4dr	£29,400
4.2 quattro SE 4dr	£38,600
4.2 quattro Sport 4dr	£39,150
4.2 quattro S6 4dr	£45,470
1.9 TDi 130 4dr	£21,725
1.9 TDi 130 SE 4dr	£22,575
1.9 TDi 130 Sport 4dr	£22,475
2.5 TDi 4dr	£24,105
2.5 TDi SE 4dr	£24,955
2.5 TDi Sport 4dr	£24,855
2.5 TDi 180 quattro SE 4dr	£27,555
2.5 TDi 180 quattro Sport 4dr	£28,105
Avant 2.0	£21,850
Avant 2.0 SE	£22,700
Avant 2.0 Sport	£22,600
Avant 1.8T	£23,150
Avant 1.8T SE	£24,000
Avant 1.8T Sport	£23,900
Avant 1.8T quattro	£24,250
Avant 1.8T quattro SE	£25,100
Avant 1.8T quattro Sport	£25,000
Avant 2.4	£23,950
Avant 2.4 SE	£24,800
Avant 2.4 Sport	£24,700
Avant 2.4 quattro	£25,050
Avant 2.4 quattro SE	£25,900
Avant 2.4 quattro Sport	£25,800
Avant 2.7T quattro SE	£32,200
Avant 2.7T quattro Sport	£32,750
Avant 3.0 quattro SE	£29,950
Avant 3.0 quattro Sport	£30,500
Avant 4.2 quattro SE	£39,700
Avant 4.2 quattro Sport	£40,250
Avant 4.2 quattro S6	£46,570
Avant 1.9 TDi 130	£23,125
Avant 1.9 TDi 130 SE	£23,975
Avant 1.9 TDi 130 Sport	£23,875
Avant 2.5 TDi	£25,505
Avant 2.5 TDi SE	£26,355
Avant 2.5 TDi Sport	£26,255
Avant 2.5 TDi 180 quattro SE	£28,655
Avant 2.5TDi 180 q'tro Sport	£29,205
A8	
2.8 quattro 4dr	£38,250
2.8 quattro Sport 4dr	£41,155
3.7 quattro 4dr	£43,795
3.7 quattro Sport 4dr	£46,195
4.2 quattro 4dr	£49,820
4.2 quattro Sport 4dr	£52,220
4.2 quattro Long 4dr	£54,330
4.2 S8 quattro 4dr	£54,760
TT	
1.8 quattro 180 bhp	£24,050
1.8 quattro 225 bhp	£26,750
1.8 quattro 180 bhp Conv	£26,300
1.8 quattro 225 bhp Conv	£29,000

BENTLEY

Arnage Red Label 6.75 4dr	£149,000
Continental R	£199,750
Continental T	£233,355
Azure	£230,890

BMW

3 Series Compact	
316ti 3dr	£16,265
316ti SE 3dr	£17,775
325ti SE 3dr	£22,640
3 Series	
316i 4dr	£17,570
316i SE 4dr	£18,800
318i 4dr	£18,900
318i SE 4dr	£20,130
320i SE 4dr	£22,370
325i SE 4dr	£23,650
325i Sport 4dr	£26,020
330i SE 4dr	£26,740
330i Sport 4dr	£28,830
320d 4dr	£20,545
320d SE 4dr	£21,775
330d SE 4dr	£26,735
330d Sport 4dr	£28,825
318i SE Touring	£20,990
320i SE Touring	£23,220
325i SE Touring	£24,500
325i Sport Touring	£26,870
330i SE Touring	£27,540
330i Sport Touring	£29,630
320d SE Touring	£22,635
330d SE Touring	£27,545
330d Sport Touring	£29,635
318Ci	£21,040
320Ci	£22,890
325Ci	£24,650
325Ci Sport	£26,930
330Ci	£27,540
330Ci Sport	£29,440
M3	£38,500
318Ci	£24,845
320Ci	£25,880
325Ci	£27,540
325Ci Sport	£29,820
330Ci	£30,440
330Ci Sport	£32,340
5 Series	
520i 4dr	£23,360
520i SE 4dr	£24,880
525i 4dr	£25,220
525i SE 4dr	£26,690
525i Sport 4dr	£29,480
530i SE 4dr	£29,395
530i Sport 4dr	£32,000
535i 4dr	£35,140
535i Sport 4dr	£37,610
540i 4dr	£39,950
540i Sport 4dr	£40,450
M5 4dr	£52,000
525d 4dr	£25,215
525d SE 4dr	£26,685
530d SE 4dr	£29,400
530d Sport 4dr	£32,005
520i Touring	£25,210
520i SE Touring	£26,850
525i Touring	£27,070
525i SE Touring	£28,490
525i Sport Touring	£231,180
530i SE Touring	£31,395
530i Sport Touring	£33,900
540i Touring	£41,950
540i Sport Touring	£42,500
525d Touring	£27,075
525d SE Touring	£28,495
530d SE Touring	£31,400
530d Sport Touring	£33,905
7 Series	
728i 4dr	£37,550
728i Sport 4dr	£39,950
735i 4dr	£44,940
735i Sport 4dr	£47,340
740i 4dr	£51,500
740i Sport 4dr	£52,360
740iL 4dr	£57,650
750i 4dr	£71,450
750i Sport 4dr	£71,970
750iL 4dr	£75,580
Z3/M Coupé	
Z3 1.9	£18,990
Z3 2.2	£21,840
Z3 2.2 Sport	£23,230
Z3 3.0	£26,930
Z3 3.0 Sport	£27,730
Z3 3.2M	£36,000
M Coupe 3.2	£36,000
X5	
3.0 5dr	£33,000
3.0 Sport 5dr	£34,900
4.4 V8 5dr	£44,000
4.4 V8 Sport 5dr	£44,670
3.0d 5dr	£33,145
3.0d Sport 5dr	£35,045
Z8	
5.0 V8	£80,000

BRISTOL

Blenheim 3	
5.9 V8	£139,825

CADILLAC

Seville	
4.6 V8 STS 4dr	£34,499

CATERHAM

Seven	
1.6 Classic	£13,245
1.8 Classic	£14,500
1.6 Roadsport 115bhp	£17,900
1.6 Roadsport Supersport	£18,900
1.8 Roadsport 122bhp	£18,900
1.8 Roadsport Supersport	£19,900
1.8 Roadsport VVC	£20,745
1.8 Roadsport VHPD	£23,400
1.6 Superlight Road	£21,200
1.8 Superlight Road 122bhp	£21,200
1.8 Superlight Road 140bhp	£22,200
1.8 Superlight Blackbird	£23,500
1.8 Superlight Road VHPD	£27,200
1.8 Superlight R500	£34,200

CHEVROLET

Camaro	
3.8 V6	£18,975
3.8 V6 Convertible	£22,500
5.7 Z28	£22,900
Blazer	
4.3 V6 LS 5dr	£23,100
4.3 V6 LT 5dr	£25,100
Corvette	
5.7 V8	£33,999
5.7 V8 Convertible	£37,999

CHRYSLER

Jeep Wrangler	
4.0 Sport 5dr	£15,725
4.0 60th Anniversary 5dr	£15995
4.0 Sahara 5dr	£18,350
Jeep Cherokee	
4.0 60th Anniversary 5dr	£18,995
4.0 Orvis 5dr	£21,995
2.5TD 5dr	£16,995
2.5TD 60th Anniversary 5dr	£18,995
2.5TD Orvis 5dr	£21,995
Jeep Grand Cherokee	
4.0 Limited 5dr	£27,995
4.7 V8 Limited 5dr	£30,995
3.1 TD 5dr	£27,995
Neon	
2.0 SE 4dr	£10,995
2.0 LX 4dr	£12,695
2.0 RT 4dr	£13,995
Sebring	
2.7 V6 LX	£22,995
PT Cruiser	
2.0 Classic 5dr	£14,995
2.0 Touring 5dr	£15,995
2.0 Limited 5dr	£17,195
Voyager	
2.4 SE	£18,495
2.4 LX	£20,995
2.5 CRD SE	£19,695
2.5 CRD LX	£22,195
3.3 LX	£23,495
3.3 Grand Voyager LX	£25,595
3.3 Grand Voyager Limited	£28,995
2.5 Grand Voyager LX CRD	£23,895
2.5 G' Voyager Limited CRD	£27,695
Viper	
8.0 GTS Coupe	£68,830

CITROEN

Saxo	
1.1 First 3dr	£5,940
1.1 Forte 3dr	£6,940
1.1 Desire 3dr	£7,440
1.4 Furio 3dr	£8,960
1.4 Desire 3dr	£8,980
1.6 VTR 3dr	£9,960
1.6 VTS 3dr	£11,795
1.5D Desire 3dr	£8,650
1.1 Forte 5dr	£7,240
1.1 Desire 5dr	£7,740
1.4 Desire 5dr	£9,280
1.5 D Desire 5dr	£8,950
Xsara	
1.4 L 5dr	£9,660
1.4 LX 5dr	£10,360
1.6-16v LX 5dr	£10,860
1.6-16v SX 5dr	£12,360
2.0-16v SX 5dr	£13,380
2.0 HDi L 5dr	£11,150
2.0 HDi LX 5dr	£11,850
2.0 HDi LX 110 5dr	£12,350
2.0 HDi SX 110 5dr	£13,850
1.4 L Est	£10,460
1.6-16v LX Est	£11,660
2.0 HDi L Est	£11,950
2.0 HDi LX Est	£12,650
2.0 HDi LX 110 Est	£13,150
1.6-16v VTR Coupe	£10,860
2.0-16v VTS Coupe	£16,395
C5	
1.8i 16v LX 5dr	£14,580
1.8i 16v SX 5dr	£15,580
2.0i 16v SX 5dr	£16,095
2.0i 16v Exclusive 5dr	£18,095
2.0i 16v Exclusive SE 5dr	£21,395
2.0i 16v HPi Exclusive 5dr	£17,580
2.0i 16v HPi Exclusive SE 5dr	£20,880
3.0i V6 Exclusive 5dr	£20,500
3.0i V6 Exclusive SE 5dr	£23,800
2.0 HDi 90bhp LX 5dr	£15,270
2.0 HDi LX 5dr	£16,050
2.0 HDi SX 5dr	£17,050
2.2 HDi SX 5dr	£18,690
2.2 HDi Exclusive 5dr	£19,890
2.2 HDi Exclusive SE 5dr	£23,190
1.8i 16v LX	£15,595
2.0i 16v SX	£17,095
2.0i 16v HPi Exclusive	£18,580
2.0i 16v HPi Exclusive SE	£21,880
3.0i V6 Exclusive	£21,500
3.0i V6 Exclusive SE	£24,800
2.0 HDi 90bhp LX	£16,270
2.0 HDi LX	£17,050
2.0 HDi SX	£18,050
2.2 HDi SX	£19,690
2.2 HDi Exclusive	£20,590
2.2 HDi Exclusive SE	£23,890
Berlingo Multispace	
1.4i Forte Est	£8,980
1.6i Forte Est	£9,480
1.9 D Forte Est	£9,245
Xsara Picasso	
1.6i LX 5dr	£12,780
1.6i SX 5dr	£13,480
1.8iSX 5dr	£13,795
2.0 HDi LX 5dr	£13,750
2.0 HDi SX 5dr	£14,450
Synergie	
2.0i LX	£17,670
2.0i SX	£19,520
2.0i Exclusive	£22,385
2.0 HDi LX	£18,965
2.0 HDi SX	£20,815
2.0 HDi Exclusive	£22,680

DAEWOO

Matiz	
800 Xtra 5dr	£5,995
800 SE 5dr	£6,595
800 SE Plus 5dr	£7,295
Lanos	
1.4S 3dr	£7,495
1.4Special Edition 3dr	£7,495
1.4 SE 3dr	£7,995
1.6 Special Edition 3dr	£8,995
1.6 SX 3dr	£9,495
1.4 S 5dr	£7,995
1.4 SE 5dr	£8,495
1.6 SX 5dr	£9,995
1.6 SX 4dr	£9,995
Nubira	
1.6 Special Edition 4dr	£9,995
1.6 SE 4dr	£10,995
2.0 CDX 4dr	£11,995
1.6 SE Est	£11,995
1.6 Special Edition Est	£10,995
2.0 CDX Est	£12,995
Leganza	
2.0 Special Edition 4dr	£12,495
2.0 SX 4dr	£12,495
2.0 CDX 4dr	£13,495
2.0 CDX-E 4dr	£14,995
Tacuma	
1.8 Xtra 5dr	£10,995
1.8 SE 5dr	£11,995
2.0 CDX 5dr	£12,995
Korando	
2.3 5dr	£15,995
2.9TDi 5dr	£16,995
Musso	
2.3 5dr	£17,995
2.9TDi 5dr	£18,995

DAIHATSU

Cuore	
1.0 3dr	£6,445
1.0 Plus 5dr	£7,345
Sirion	
1.0 E 5dr	£7,495
1.0 EL 5dr	£7,995
1.3 SL 5dr	£8,940
YRV	
1.3 Radical 5dr	£7,995
1.3 Radical2 5dr	£8,495
1.3 Base 5dr	£9,440
1.3 Premium 5dr	£10,440
1.3 4trak 5dr	£10,495
1.3 F-Speed 5dr	£11,460
Terios	
1.3 E 5dr	£9,980
1.3 EL 5dr	£10,980
1.3 SL 5dr	£12,980
Fourtrak Independent	
2.8 TDX Est 5dr	£19,000

FERRARI

360M	
360M	£103,068
360M Spider	£109,101
550M	
550M	£152,345
550M Barchetta	£172,358
456	
456 GT	£170,358

FIAT

Seicento	
1.1 S 3dr	£5,940
1.1 SX 3dr	£6,214
1.1 Sporting 3dr	£6,790
1.1 Michael Schumacher 3dr	£7,894
Punto	
1.2 Mia 3dr	£6,940
1.2 3dr	£7,522
1.2 Go 3dr	£7,851
1.2 ELX 3dr	£8,440
1.2 16v ELX 3dr	£9,240
1.2 16v Sporting 3dr	£10,740

1.2 16v Sporting Speedg' 3dr	£11,260
1.8 16v HGT 3dr	£12,505
1.8 16v HGT Abarth 3dr	£13,506
1.9 D 3dr	£8,033
1.9 JTD ELX 3dr	£9,500
1.2 5dr	£8,023
1.2 ELX 5dr	£8,940
1.2 16v ELX 5dr	£9,740
1.2 16v ELX Speedgear 5dr	£10,260
1.2 16v HLX 5dr	£10,740
1.9 D 5dr	£8,450
1.9 JTD ELX 5dr	£10,001
1.9 JTD HLX 5dr	£11,001
Bravo	
1.2 SX 3dr	£10,360
1.2 Formula 3dr	£10,717
1.6 SX 3dr	£10,880
1.6 HLX 3dr	£11,980
1.9 JTD 100 SX 3dr	£11,250
1.9 JTD 100 HLX 3dr	£12,349
Brava	
1.2 SX 5dr	£10,360
1.2 Formula 5dr	£10,717
1.6 SX 5dr	£10,880
1.6 ELX 5dr	£11,980
1.9 JTD 100 SX 5dr	£11,250
1.9 JTD 100 ELX 5dr	£12,349
Marea	
1.6 SX 4dr	£11,995
1.6 ELX 4dr	£13,538
2.0 ELX 4dr	£13,702
2.0 HLX 4dr	£15,305
1.9 JTD110 SX 4dr	£13,052
1.9 JTD110 ELX 4dr	£13,660
1.6 SX Weekend	£12,745
1.6 ELX Weekend	£14,287
2.0 ELX Weekend	£14,452
2.0 HLX Weekend	£16,055
1.9 JTD100 SX Weekend	£13,802
1.9 JTD100 ELX W'end	£14,409
Barchetta	
1.8	£13,815
Doblo	
1.2 SX	£8,695
1.9 D SX	£8,950
1.9 D ELX	£9,995
Multipla	
1.6 SX 5dr	£12,995
1.9 JTD SX 5dr	£13,990
1.6 ELX 5dr	£14,895
1.9 JTD ELX 5dr	£15,890
Ulysse	
2.0 S	£16,995
2.0 EL	£19,855
2.0 JTD S	£18,152
2.0 JTD EL	£20,905

FORD

Ka	
1.3 Ka 3dr	£6,960
1.3 Ka Collection 3dr	£8,060
1.3 Ka Sun Collection 3dr	£8,560
1.3 Ka Luxury 3dr	£9,560
Fiesta - old model	
1.3 Fun 3dr	£6,995
1.3 Encore 3dr	£7,260
1.3 Finesse 3dr	£7,660
1.3 Flight 3dr	£7,780
1.25-16v Zetec 3dr	£8,660
1.25-16v Freestyle 3dr	£8,760
1.25-16v LX 3dr	£9,060
1.25-16v Black 3dr	£9,995
1.6-16v Zetec-S 3dr	£10,980
1.8 TDdi Flight 3dr	£8,250
1.8 TDdi Freestyle 3dr	£9,250
1.3 Encore 5dr	£7,660
1.3 Finesse 5dr	£8,260
1.3 Flight 5dr	£8,380
1.25-16v Zetec 5dr	£9,260
1.25-16v Freestyle 5dr	£9,360
1.25-16v LX 5dr	£9,660
1.6-16v Ghia 5dr	£11,980
1.8 TDdi Encore 5dr	£8,350
1.8 TDdi Finesse 5dr	£8,750
1.8 TDdi Flight 5dr	£8,850
1.8 TDdi Freestyle 5dr	£9,850
1.8 TDdi LX 5dr	£10,150
Focus	
1.4i CL 3dr	£10,460
1.4i Zetec 3dr	£10,960
1.6i Zetec 3dr	£11,460
1.8i Zetec 3dr	£11,980
2.0i Zetec 3dr	£13,995
1.8 TDdi Zetec 3dr	£12,550
1.4i CL 5dr	£10,960
1.6i Zetec 5dr	£11,960
1.6i LX 5dr	£12,460
1.6iGhia 5dr	£12,960
1.8i Zetec 5dr	£12,480
1.8i LX 5dr	£12,980
1.8i Ghia 5dr	£13,480
2.0i Zetec 5dr	£14,495
2.0i Ghia 5dr	£14,495
1.8 TDdi CL 5dr	£12,550
1.8 TDdi Zetec 5dr	£13,050
1.8 TDdi LX 5dr	£13,550
1.8 TDdi Ghia 5dr	£14,050
1.6i LX 4dr	£12,460
1.8i LX 4dr	£12,980
1.8 TDdi LX 4dr	£13,550
1.6i Ghia 4dr	£12,960
1.8i Ghia 4dr	£13,480
2.0i Ghia 4dr	£14,495
1.8 TDdi Ghia 4dr	£14,050
1.6i Zetec Est	£12,710
1.6i LX Est	£13,210
1.8i Zetec Est	£13,230
1.8i LX Est	£13,730
1.8i Ghia Est	£14,230
2.0i Zetec Est	£15,245
2.0i GhiaEst	£15,245
1.8 TDdi CL Est	£13,300
1.8 TDdi Zetec Est	£13,800
1.8 TDdi LX Est	£14,300
1.8 TDdi Ghia Est	£14,800
Mondeo	
1.8i LX 4/5dr	£14,580
2.0i LX 4/5dr	£15,095
1.8i Zetec 4/5dr	£15,595
2.0i Zetec 4/5dr	£16,095
2.0i Ghia 4/5dr	£17,195
2.5 V6 Zetec-S 4/5dr	£19,095
2.0i Ghia X 4/5dr	£19,395
2.5 V6 Ghia X 4/5dr	£19,895
2.0 D LX 4/5dr	£16,070
2.0 D Zetec 4/5dr	£17,070
2.0 D Ghia 4/5dr	£18,170
2.0 D Ghia X 4/5dr	£20,370
1.8i LX Est	£15,595
2.0i LX Est	£16,095
1.8i Zetec Est	£16,595
2.0i Zetec Est	£17,095
2.0i Ghia Est	£18,195
2.5 V6 Zetec-S Est	£20,095
2.0i Ghia X Est	£20,395
2.5 V6 Ghia X Est	£20,895
2.0 D LX Est	£17,070
2.0 D Zetec Est	£18,070
2.0 D Ghia Est	£19,170
2.0 D Ghia X Est	£21,370
Puma	
1.6 16v	£12,280
1.7 16v	£12,980
1.7 16v Black	£13,980
Galaxy	
2.3 LX 7st	£18,245
2.3 Zetec 7st	£19,745
2.3 Ghia 7st	£21,245
2.8 Ghia 7st	£24,245
1.9 TD LX 7st	£18,740
1.9 TD 115 LX 7st	£19,740
1.9 TD 115 Zetec 7st	£21,240
1.9 TD 115 Ghia 7st	£22,740
Maverick	
2.0 5dr	£17,995
3.0 V6 5dr	£20,995
Explorer	
4.0 V6 5dr	£25,895

Holden (UK imports)

HSV	
Maloo GTS 4dr	£36,635
GTS 4dr	£40,635
GTS Grange 4dr	£43,635
GTS - R 4dr	£50,635

HONDA

Civic	
1.4 S 3dr	£10,795
1.6 S 3dr	£11,495
1.6 S E 3dr	£11,995
1.6 S E Sport 3dr	£12,995
2.0 Type-R 3dr	£15,995
1.4 S 5dr	£11,960
1.4 SE 5dr	£12,460
1.6 S 5dr	£12,460
1.6 SE 5dr	£12,960
1.6 SE Executive 5dr	£13,960
1.7	£13,995
Insight	
1.0	£17,000
Accord	
1.8i VTEC S 5dr	£14,645
1.8i VTEC Sport 5dr	£15,645
2.0i VTEC SE 5dr	£15,645
2.0i VTEC SE Executive 5dr	£17,645
2.3i VTEC Type-V 5dr	£19,645
1.8i VTEC S 4dr	£14,495
1.8i VTEC Sport 4dr	£15,495
2.0i VTEC SE 4dr	£15,995
2.0i VTEC SE Executive 4dr	£17,495
2.3i VTEC Type-V 4dr	£19,495
2.2i Type-R 4dr	£21,495
2.0i ES Coupe	£19,995
3.0i V6 Auto Coupe	£21,995
Stream	
1.7i VTEC SE	£16,395
2.0i VTEC SE Sport	£16,995
HR-V	
1.6i 4WD 5dr	£13,695
1.6i 4WD VTEC 5dr	£14,195
1.6i 4WD 5dr	£14,495
1.6i 4WD VTEC 5dr	£14,995
CR-V	
2.0i LS 5dr	£16,495
2.0i ES 5dr	£17,695
S2000	
2.0 Cabriolet	£25,995
Legend	
3.5 Saloon 4dr	£31,995
NSX	
3.2	£69,590
3.2-T	£73,090

HYUNDAI

Amica	
1.0 Si 5dr	£6,599
1.0 GSi 5dr	£7,599
Accent	
1.3 i 3dr	£6,999
1.3 Si 3dr	£7,799
1.5 MVi 3dr	£9,799
1.3 GSi 5dr	£8,299
1.5 CDX 5dr	£9,319
ELantra	
1.6 Si 5dr	£10,999
1.6 GSi 5dr	£12,199
2.0 CDX 5dr	£13,999
1.6 GSi 4dr	£12,199
2.0 CDX 4dr	£13,999
Coupe	
1.6	£12,879
1.6 SE	£14,279
2.0 SE	£16,299
Sonata	
2.0 GSi 4dr	£12,999
2.0 CDX 4dr	£14,499
2.5 V6 auto 4dr	£17,999
XG	
3.0 V6 4dr	£20,999
Trajet	
2.0 GSi	£15,499
2.7 V6	£19,999
2.0 TD GSi	£16,499
Santa Fe	
2.4 5dr	£15,999
2.7 V6 5dr	£17,999
2.0 TD 5dr	£16,999

ISUZU

Trooper	
3.5 V6 SWB 5dr	£17,950
3.5 V6 SWB Duty 5dr	£19,950
3.5 V6 SWB Citation 5dr	£22,500
3.0 TD SWB 5dr	£17,950
3.0 TD SWB Duty 5dr	£19,950
3.0 TD SWB Citation 5dr	£22,500
3.5 V6 LWB Duty 5dr	£21,750
3.5 V6 LWB Citation 5dr	£24,650
3.5 V6 LWB Insignia 5dr	£26,950
3.0 TD LWB 5dr	£20,500
3.0 TD LWB Duty 5dr	£21,750
3.0 TD LWB Citation 5dr	£24,650
3.0 TD LWB Insignia 5dr	£26,950

JAGUAR

X - Type	
2.5 V6 4dr	£22,000
2.5 V6 Sport 4dr	£24,000
2.5 V6 SE 4dr	£24,750
3.0 V6 Sport 4dr	£25,500
3.0 V6 SE 4dr	£26,250
S - Type	
3.0 V6 4dr	£26,700
3.0 V6 Sport 4dr	£30,600
3.0 V6 SE 4dr	£31,150
4.0 V8 4dr	£35,350
4.0 V8 Sport 4dr	£38,400
XJ8	
3.2 Sport 4dr	£35,950
4.0 4dr	£40,950
4.0 Sovereign 4dr	£43,950
4.0 Sovereign lwb 4dr	£44,450
4.0 XJR 4dr	£51,950
Daimler V8 4dr	£50,700
Daimler Super V8 4dr	£58,700
XK8	
XK8 4.0	£48,700
XKR 4.0	£56,700
XK8 4.0 Conv	£55,350
XKR 4.0 Conv	£63,350

KIA

Mentor	
1.6 L 4dr	£8,995
1.6 LX 4dr	£10,200
Shuma	
1.6 S 5dr	£8,495
1.6 SX 5dr	£9,995
Rio	
1.3 5dr	£5,995
1.3 L 5dr	£6,895
1.3 LX 5dr	£7,645
1.5 SE 5dr	£8,995
Carens	
1.8i 16v SX 5dr	£9,995
1.8i 16v GSX 5dr	£11,995
Magentis	
2.5 V6 LX 4dr	£12,995
2.5 V6 SE 4dr	£15,995
Sedona	
2.5 V6 S	£13,995
2.5 V6 SX	£15,995
2.5 V6 GSX	£16,995
2.5 V6 Exec	£18,495
2.9 TDi S	£13,995
2.9 TDi SX	£15,995
2.9 TDi GSX	£16,995
2.9 TDi Exec	£18,495
Sportage	
2.0 S 5dr	£12,995
2.0 SX 5dr	£13,995
2.0 GSX 5dr	£14,995

LAMBORGHINI

Diablo	
6.0 VT	£152,500

LAND ROVER

Defender	
2.5 TD5 5dr	£19,925
2.5 County TD5 5dr	£20,775
2.5 TD5 5dr	£22,654
2.5 County TD5 5dr	£23,565
Freelander	
1.8 Soft Back S 5dr	£15,995
1.8 Soft Back GS 5dr	£17,795
1.8 Soft Back ES 5dr	£19,695
2.5 V6 Soft Back GS 5dr	£21,595
2.5 V6 Soft Back ES 5dr	£23,595
1.8 Hard Back S 5dr	£15,995
1.8 Hard Back GS 5dr	£17,795
1.8 Hard Back ES 5dr	£19,695
2.5 V6 Hard Back GS 5dr	£21,595
2.5 V6 Hard Back ES 5dr	£23,595
2.0Td4 Soft Back S 5dr	£17,195
2.0Td4 Soft Back GS 5dr	£18,995
2.0Td4 Soft Back ES 5dr	£20,895
2.0Td4 Hard Back S 5dr	£17,995
2.0Td4 Hard Back GS 5dr	£19,795
2.0Td4 Hard Back ES 5dr	£21,695
1.8 S/Wagon S 5dr	£17,495
1.8 S/Wagon GS 5dr	£18,995
1.8 S/Wagon ES 5dr	£20,995
2.5 V6 S/Wagon GS 5dr	£22,595
2.5 V6 S/Wagon ES 5dr	£24,595
2.0Td4 S/Wagon S 5dr	£18,695
2.0Td4 S/Wagon GS 5dr	£20,195
2.0Td4 S/Wagon ES 5dr	£22,195
Discovery	
2.5 Td5 E 5dr	£21,995
2.5 Td5 S 5dr	£24,495
2.5 Td5 GS 5dr	£27,295
2.5 Td5 XS 5dr	£29,595
2.5 Td5 ES 5dr	£31,995
4.0 V8 GS 5dr	£27,295
4.0 V8 XS 5dr	£29,595
4.0 V8 ES 5dr	£31,995
Range Rover	
2.5 DT County 5dr	£36,995
2.5 DT HSE 5dr	£42,995
4.0 V8 County 5dr	£36,995
4.0 V8 HSE 5dr	£42,995
4.6 Vogue 5dr	£49,995

LEXUS

IS200	
2.0 4dr	£18,380
2.0 SE 4dr	£19,995
2.0 Sport 4dr	£20,970
3.0 4dr	£26,700
3.0 SportCross 4dr	£28,450
GS300/430	
3.0 S 4dr	£28,450
3.0 SE 4dr	£30,950
4.3 SE 4dr	£36,995
LS430	
4.3 V8 4dr	£49,950
SC430	
4.3 V8	£50,850
RX300	
3.0 5dr	£28,950
3.0 SE 5dr	£32,550

LOTUS

Elise	
1.8	£22,995
Esprit	
GT V8	£49,950
V8 SE	£59,950
V8 Sport	£64,750

MASERATI

3200 GT	
3.2 Turbo V8	£60,950
3.2 Turbo V8 Assetto Corsa	£65,950

MAZDA

Demio	
1.3 LXi 5dr	£7,995
1.3 GXi 5dr	£8,495
1.5 GSi 5dr	£9,495
323	
1.3 i 5dr	£9,995
1.3 LXi 5dr	£10,295
1.6 LXi 5dr	£10,995
1.6 GXi 5dr	£11,995
2.0 Sport 5dr	£13,995
2.0 Di Turbo 5dr	£12,495
Premacy	
1.8 GXi 5dr	£12,995
1.8 GSi 5dr	£14,495
2.0 TD GXi 5dr	£13,995
MPV	
2.0i	£17,495
626	
1.8 LXi 5dr	£12,495
1.8 GXi 5dr	£12,995
2.0 GXi 5dr	£13,495
2.0 GSi 5dr	£14,495
2.0 Sport 5dr	£14,995
2.0D GXi 5dr	£14,495
2.0 GXi 4dr	£13,495
2.0 Sport 4dr	£14,995
2.0 GXi Est	£14,495
2.0D GXi Est	£15,495
Tribute	
2.0 GXi 2WD 5dr	£15,995
2.0 GXi 4WD 5dr	£16,995
2.0 GSi 4WD 5dr	£17,995
3.0 V6 4WD 5dr	£21,495
MX-5	
1.6i	£14,995
1.8i	£15,495
1.8i Sport	£17,495

MCC

Smart	
Smart Pure 3dr	£5,700
Smart Pulse 3dr	£6,600
Smart Pulse Limited Edition 3dr	£6,995
Smart Passion 3dr	£7,200
Smart Passion Convertible	£9,360

MERCEDES-BENZ

A-Class	
A140 Classic 5dr	£13,025
A140 Eleg'/ Avant' 5dr	£14,825
A160 Classic 5dr	£14,175
A160 Eleg'/ Avant' 5dr	£15,975
A190 Eleg'/ Avant' 5dr	£16,925
A170 CDi Classic 5dr	£14,895
A170 CDi Eleg'Avant' 5dr	£16,695
Long wheelbase + £900	
C-Class	
C180 Classic 4dr	£21,140
C200K Classic 4dr	£22,640
C240 Classic 4dr	£24,540
C320 Eleg'/ Avant' 4dr	£30,700
C220 CDI Classic 4dr	£23,675
C270 CDI Classic 4dr	£25,255
C180 Classic	£22,090
C200K Classic	£23,590
C240 Classic	£25,490
C320 Eleg'/ Avant'	£31,650
C220 CDI Classic	£24,645
C270 CDI Classic	£26,215
C180	£20,290
C200K	£21,790
C230K	£23,250
C220 CDI	£22,825
Elegance, Avantgarde + £2000	
E-Class	
E200K Classic 4dr	£24,040
E240 Classic 4dr	£25,790
E280 Eleg'/Avatn' 4dr	£30,840
E320 Eleg'/Avatn' 4dr	£32,990
E430 Eleg'/Avatn' 4dr	£39,040
E55 AMG 4dr	£55,140
E220CDI Classic 4dr	£25,265
E320CDI Eleg'/Avatn' 4dr	£31,795
E200K Classic Est	£25,840
E240 Classic Est	£27,590
E280 Eleg'/Avatn' Est	£32,640
E320 Eleg'/Avatn' Est	£34,790
E430 Eleg'/Avatn' Est	£40,840
E55 AMG Est	£56,940
E320CDI Eleg'/Avatn' Est	£33,595
Elegance, Avantgarde + £2000	
S-Class	
S280 4dr	£41,540
S320 4dr	£46,690
S430 4dr	£54,040
S500 4dr	£57,740
S55 AMG 4dr	£76,140
S320L 4dr	£49,340
S430L 4dr	£56,690
S500L 4dr	£60,390
S600L 4dr	£78,440
S55 AMG L 4dr	£78,790
S320 CDI 4dr	£44,445
CLK	
200K Avan'/Elegance	£26,340
230K Avan'/Elegance	£28,290
320 Avan'/Elegance	£32,190
430 Avan'/Elegance	£40,590
55 AMG	£56,590
200K Avan'/Elegance conv	£29,940
230K Avan'/Eleg' conv	£31,890
320 Avan'/Eleg' conv	£35,790
430 Avan'/Eleg' conv	£44,190
CL Coupe	
CL500	£66,440
CL600	£81,940
CL55 AMG	£84,140
SLK	
200K	£24,790
230K	£28,240
320	£31,240
SL	
SL280	£50,340
SL320	£53,290
SL500	£65,340
V-Class	
V230 Trend/Fashion	£23,230
V230 Ambiente	£27,260
V280 Ambiente	£29,280
V220 CDI Trend/Fashion	£23,230
V220 CDI Ambiente	£27,260
M-Class	
ML320 5dr	£31,140
ML430 5dr	£39,240
ML55 AMG 5dr	£50,640
ML270 CDI 5dr	£28,395

MG ROVER

25	
1.1i-16v i 3dr	£7,995
1.4i-16v i 3dr	£8,460
1.1i-16v iE 3dr	£8,585
1.4i-16v Impression 3dr	£8,640
1.4i-16v iE 3dr	£9,050
1.4i-16v iL 3dr	£9,610
1.4i-16v 103 iL 3dr	£10,310
1.4i-16v 103 iS 3dr	£10,760
1.6i-16v iL 3dr	£11,345
1.6i-16v iS 3dr	£11,815
1.6i-16v iXL 3dr	£13,980
2.0TD iE 3dr	£10,660
2.0TD iL 3dr	£11,200
2.0TD iS 3dr	£11,650
1.1i-16v i 5dr	£8,495
1.4i-16v i 5dr	£8,960
1.1i-16v iE 5dr	£9,085
1.4i-16v Impression 5dr	£9,140
1.4i-16v iE 5dr	£9,550
1.4i-16v iL 5dr	£10,110
1.4i-16v 103 iL 5dr	£10,810
1.4i-16v 103 iS 5dr	£11,260
1.6i-16v iL 5dr	£11,865
1.6i-16v iS 5dr	£12,315
1.6i-16v iXL 5dr	£14,480
2.0TD iE 5dr	£11,160
2.0TD iL 5dr	£11,700
2.0TD iS 5dr	£12,150
45	
1.4-16v iE 5dr	£9,980
1.4-16v Impression 5dr	£11,480
1.4-16v iS 5dr	£11,480
1.4-16v iL 5dr	£11,980
1.4-16v Impression S 5dr	£12,080
1.6-16v Impression 5dr	£12,080
1.6-16v iS 5dr	£12,380
1.6-16v Impression S 5dr	£12,680
1.6-16v iL 5dr	£12,680
1.8-16v Impression 5dr	£12,695
1.6-16v iXS 5dr	£13,280
1.8-16v Impression S 5dr	£13,395
1.8-16v iXS 5dr	£13,780
1.8-16v iXL 5dr	£14,080
2.0 TD iE 5dr	£11,950
2.0 TD Impression 5dr	£12,450
2.0 TD iL 5dr	£12,950
2.0 TD Impression S 5dr	£13,050
2.0 TD iXL 5dr	£13,850
1.6-16v Classic 4dr	£13,180
1.6-16v Impression S 4dr	£13,980
1.6-16v Club 4dr	£14,080
1.8-16v Classic 4dr	£13,680
1.8-16v Impression S 4dr	£14,495
1.8-16v Club 4dr	£14,580
1.8-16v Connoisseur 4dr	£15,580
2.0 V6 Club Steptronic 4dr	£16,095
2.0 V6 Connoisseur Step 4dr	£17,095
2.0 TD Classic 4dr	£13,750
2.0 TD Impression S 4dr	£14,650
2.0 TD Club 4dr	£14,650
2.0 TD Connoisseur 4dr	£15,650
75	
1.8i Classic 4dr	£16,480
1.8i Classic SE 4dr	£16,980
1.8i Club 4dr	£17,580
1.8i Club SE 4dr	£17,880
1.8i Connoisseur 4dr	£18,880
1.8i Connoisseur SE 4dr	£20,280
2.0 V6 Classic 4dr	£17,895
2.0 V6 Classic SE 4dr	£18,395
2.0 V6 Club 4dr	£18,995
2.0 V6 Club SE 4dr	£19,295
2.0 V6 Connoisseur 4dr	£20,295
2.0 V6 Connoisseur SE 4dr	£21,695
2.5 V6 Classic 4dr	£19,295
2.5 V6 Classic SE 4dr	£19,795
2.5 V6 Club 4dr	£20,295
2.5 V6 Club SE 4dr	£20,595
2.5 V6 Connoisseur 4dr	£21,595
2.5 V6 Connoisseur SE 4dr	£22,995
2.0 CDT Classic 4dr	£17,570
2.0 CDT Classic SE 4dr	£18,170
2.0 CDT Club 4dr	£18,670
2.0 CDT Club SE 4dr	£18,970
2.0 CDT Connoisseur 4dr	£19,970
2.0 CDT Connoisseur SE 4dr	£21,370
1.8i Classic Est	£17,430
1.8i Classic SE Est	£17,930
1.8i Club Est	£18,530
1.8i Club SE Est	£18,830
1.8i Connoisseur Est	£19,830
1.8i Connoisseur SE Est	£21,230
2.0 V6 Club Est	£19,945
2.0 V6 Club SE Est	£20,245
2.0 V6 Connoisseur Est	£21,245
2.0 V6 Connoisseur SE Est	£22,645
2.5 V6 Club SE Est	£21,545
2.5 V6 Connoisseur Est	£22,545
2.5 V6 Connoisseur SE Est	£23,945
2.0 CDT Classic Est	£18,520
2.0 CDT Classic SE Est	£19,120
2.0 CDT Club Est	£19,620
2.0 CDT Club SE Est	£19,920
2.0 CDT Connoisseur Est	£20,920
2.0 CDT Connoisseur SE Est	£22,320

MGF

1.6i	£15,500
1.8i	£16,980
1.8i Stepspeed	£17,995
1.8i VVC	£19,495
1.8i Trophy 160 SE	£20,995

MGZR

ZR 105 3dr	£9,995
ZR+ 105 3dr	£11,595
ZR 120 3dr	£11,395
ZR+ 120 3dr	£12,995
ZR 120 Stepspeed 3dr	£12,295
ZR+ 120 Stepspeed 3dr	£13,895
ZRTurbo Diesel 3dr	£10,895
ZR+Turbo Diesel 3dr	£12,495
ZR 160 3dr	£14,345
ZR 105 5dr	£10,495
ZR+ 105 5dr	£12,095
ZR 120 5dr	£11,895
ZR+ 120 5dr	£13,495
ZR 120 Stepspeed 5dr	£12,795
ZR+ 120 Stepspeed 5dr	£14,395
ZRTurbo Diesel 5dr	£11,395
ZR+Turbo Diesel 5dr	£12,995
ZR 160 5dr	£14,845

MG ZS

ZS 120 3dr	£12,495
ZS+ 120 3dr	£13,495
ZS 120 Stepspeed 5dr	£13,495
ZS+ 120 Stepspeed 5dr	£14,495
ZS 180 5dr	£15,595
ZS 120 4dr	£13,295
ZS+ 120 4dr	£14,295
ZS 120 Stepspeed 4dr	£14,295
ZS+ 120 Stepspeed 4dr	£15,295
ZS 180 4dr	£16,395

MG ZT

ZT 160 4dr	£18,595
ZT+ 160 4dr	£19,195
ZT 190 4dr	£20,495
ZT+ 190 4dr	£21,095

MINI

Mini

1.6 One 3dr	£10,300
1.6 Cooper 3dr	£11,600

MITSUBISHI

Colt

1.3 GL 3dr	£7,960
1.3 Classic 3dr	£8,460
1.3 Equippe 3dr	£9,960
1.6 Equippe 3dr	£10,980
1.6 Elegance 3dr	£12,480

Carisma

1.6i 5dr	£11,180
1.6 Classic 5dr	£12,580
1.8 GDi Equippe 4/5dr	£12,995
1.8 GDi Mirage 5dr	£13,995
1.8 GDi Elegance 5dr	£15,960

Lancer

2.0Turbo EVO VI GSR 4dr	£30,995

Galant

2.0 Equippe 4dr	£15,995
2.0 Sport 4dr	£17,295
2.4 GDi Elegance 4dr	£17,695
2.5 V6 Sport 4dr	£18,995
2.5 V6 4dr	£21,595
2.5 VR4 4dr	£31,995
2.0 Equippe Est	£16,995
2.0 Sport Est	£18,295
2.5 V6 Sport Est	£19,995
2.5 V6 Est	£22,595
2.5 VR4 Est	£32,995

FTO

2.0 V6 GPX	£22,995

Space Star

1.3i Classic 5dr	£9,960
1.3i Mirage 5dr	£9,995
1.3i SE 5dr	£11,560
1.3i Equippe 5dr	£11,560
1.6i Mirage 5dr	£10,695
1.6i Equippe 5dr	£11,995
1.8 GDI SE 5dr	£12,980
1.8 GDI Equippe 5dr	£12,980
1.8 GDI Elegance 5dr	£13,980

Space Wagon

2.0 Classic 5dr	£16,995
2.4 GDi Equippe 5dr	£18,995
2.4 GDi Elegance 5dr	£21,995

Shogun Pinin

1.8 GDi Classic 5dr	£12,495
1.8 GDi Equippe 5dr	£13,495
1.8 GDi Elegance 5dr	£14,995
1.8 GDi Vivo 5dr	£15,995
2.0 Equippe 5dr	£15,995
2.0 Elegance 5dr	£16,995
2.0 Vivo 5dr	£18,495

Shogun Sport

2.5 TD Classic 5dr	£19,000
2.5 TD Equippe 5dr	£22,000
3.0 V6 Equippe 5dr	£22,995
3.0 V6 Elegance 5dr	£24,495

Shogun

3.2 TD DID Classic 5dr	£22,000
3.2 TD DID Equippe 5dr	£24,000
3.5 V6 GDi Equippe 5dr	£25,995
3.2 TD DID Classic 5dr	£27,000
3.2 TD DID Equippe 5dr	£29,000
3.5 V6 GDi Elegance 5dr	£33,995

MORGAN

4/4

1.8 2-seater	£21,590
1.8 4-seater	£25,996

Plus 4

2.0 2-seater	£26,114

Plus 8

3.9 2-seater	£31,948
4.6 2-seater	£34,639

Aero 8

4.4V8	£49,950

NISSAN

Micra

1.0 S 3dr	£7,250
1.0 Activ 3dr	£7,850
1.0 Sport 3dr	£8,050
1.0 SE 3dr	£8,550
1.4 S 3dr	£7,795
1.4 Activ 3dr	£8,395
1.4 SE 3dr	£9,095
1.4 Sport + 3dr	£9,495
1.4 SE + 3dr	£9,995
1.0 S 5dr	£7,750
1.0 Sport 5dr	£8,550
1.0 SE 5dr	£9,050
1.4 S 5dr	£8,295
1.4 Activ 5dr	£8,895
1.4 SE 5dr	£9,595
1.4 Sport + 5dr	£9,995
1.4 SE + 5dr	£10,495

Almera

1.5 Activ 3dr	£9,995
1.5 E 3dr	£9,615
1.5 S 3dr	£10,315
1.5 SE 3dr	£11,165
1.8 E 3dr	£11,200
1.8 S 3dr	£11,900
1.8 Sport 3dr	£11,885
1.8 Sport + 3dr	£13,085
1.8 SE 3dr	£11,835
2.2 Di SE 3dr	£12,725
2.2 Di Sport + 3dr	£13,975
1.5 Activ 5dr	£10,745
1.5 E 5dr	£10,365
1.5 S 5dr	£11,065
1.5 SE 5dr	£11,915
1.8 E 5dr	£11,950
1.8 S 5dr	£12,650
1.8 Sport 5dr	£12,635
1.8 Sport + 5dr	£13,835
1.8 SE 5dr	£12,585
1.8 SE + 5dr	£13,785
2.2 Di 5dr	£12,625
2.2 Di SE 5dr	£13,475
2.2 Di Sport + 5dr	£14,725
1.5 S 4dr	£11,065
1.8 S 4dr	£11,735
1.8 SE 4dr	£12,585
2.2 Di SE 4dr	£13,475

Almera Tino

1.8 S 5dr	£12,900
1.8 SE 5dr	£13,600
1.8 SE2 5dr	£14,100
1.8 SE+ 5dr	£14,800
2.0 S 5dr	£14,900
2.0 SE 5dr	£15,600
2.0 SE2 5dr	£16,100
2.0 SE+ 5dr	£16,800
2.2Di S 5dr	£13,895
2.2Di SE 5dr	£14,595
2.2Di SE2 5dr	£15,095
2.2Di SE+ 5dr	£15,795

Primera

1.6 E 5dr	£12,585
1.6 Activ 5dr	£12,980
1.6 S 5dr	£13,435
1.8 Activ 5dr	£13,480
1.8 4/5dr	£13,935
1.8 Sport 5dr	£15,085
1.8 SE 5dr	£15,735
2.0 S 5dr	£15,200
2.0 Sport 5dr	£15,400
2.0 Sport + 4/5dr	£16,500
2.0 SE 5dr	£16,050
2.0 SE + 5dr	£17,550
2.0 TD S 5dr	£14,245
2.0 SE Est	£14,835
1.8 SE Est	£16,635
2.0 Sport + Est	£17,400
2.0 SE + Est	£18,450
2.0 TD S Est	£15,155

Maxima QX

2.0 V6 SE 4dr	£20,700
2.0 V6 SE+ 4dr	£23,700
3.0 V6 SE+ 4dr	£25,900

Skyline

2.6 Twin Turbo	£54,000

Terrano II

2.4 S 5dr	£16,150
2.7 TDi SE 5dr	£16,955
2.7 TDi Sport 5dr	£18,955
2.4 S 5dr	£18,750
2.7 TDi S 5dr	£19,555
2.7 TDi SE 5dr	£21,555
2.7 TDi SE 5dr	£21,555
2.7 TDi SE + 5dr	£23,255

Patrol

3.0 Di SE 5dr	£23,355
3.0 Di SE + 5dr	£26055
3.0 Di SE 5dr	£26,855
3.0 Di SE + 5dr	£29,755

PERODUA

Nippa

850 EX 5dr	£4,624

Kenari

1.0 GX 5dr	£6,175

PEUGEOT

106

1.1 Independence 3dr	£6,495
1.1 Zest 3dr	£6,595
1.1 Zest 2 3dr	£7,595
1.4 Quiksilver 3dr	£9,445
1.6 GTi 3dr	£11,795
1.5D Zest 2 3dr	£8,195
1.1 Zest 2 5dr	£8,095
1.5D Zest 2 5dr	£8,695

206

1.1 Style 3dr	£7,940
1.1 Look 3dr	£8,695
1.1 LX 3dr	£8,940
1.4 LX 3dr	£9,390
1.4 GLX 3dr	£10,390
1.4 Quiksilver 3dr	£10,640
1.6 XSi 3dr	£11,660
2.0 GTi 3dr	£13,680
1.9D Style 3dr	£8,750
1.9D LX 3dr	£9,750
2.0 HDi ECO 3dr	£9,800
2.0 HDi LX 3dr	£10,800
2.0D Turbo HDi 3dr	£12,600
1.1 Style 5dr	£8,440
1.1 Look 5dr	£9,195
1.1 LX 5dr	£8,940
1.4 LX 5dr	£9,890
1.4 GLX 5dr	£10,890
1.6 GLX 5dr	£11,360
1.6 Roland Garros 5dr	£12,890
1.9D Style 5dr	£9,250
1.9D LX 5dr	£10,250
2.0 HDi ECO 5dr	£10,300
2.0 HDi LX 5dr	£11,300
2.0 HDi GLX 5dr	£12,300
1.6 CC convertible 5dr	£14,480
2.0 CC convertible	£15,995

306

1.4 L Est	£11,695
1.4 Meridian S Est	£11,595
1.6 Meridian SE Est	£12,195
1.8 Meridian SE Est	£12,495
1.9 D Meridian S Est	£12,095
2.0 HDi Meridian SE Est	£13,495

307

1.4 Style 3dr	£10,860
1.6 16v Style 3dr	£11,560
1.6 16v Rapier 3dr	£12,060
2.0 16v XSi 3dr	£15,060
1.4 HDi Style 3dr	£11,560
1.6 HDi Style 3dr	£12,460
2.0 HDi Rapier 3dr	£12,960
2.0 HDi Dturbo 110 3dr	£16,160
1.4 Style 5dr	£11,360
1.4 LX 5dr	£11,860
1.6 16v Style 5dr	£12,060
1.6 16v LX 5dr	£12,560
1.6 16v Rapier 5dr	£12,560
1.6 16v GLX 5dr	£13,660
2.0 16v GLX 5dr	£14,960
2.0 16v XSi 5dr	£15,560
1.4 HDi Style 5dr	£12,060
1.4 HDi LX 5dr	£12,560
2.0 HDi Style 5dr	£12,960
2.0 HDi LX 5dr	£13,460
2.0 HDi Rapier 5dr	£13,460
2.0 HDi GLX 5dr	£14,560
2.0 HDi GLX 110 5dr	£16,060
2.0 HDi Dturbo 110 5dr	£16,660

406

1.8 L 4dr	£13,480
1.8 LX 4dr	£14,580
1.8 GLX 4dr	£15,580
2.0 LX 4dr	£14,895
2.0 GLX 4dr	£15,895
2.0 GTX 4dr	£17,095
2.2 SRi 4dr	£17,245
2.0 Executive 4dr	£19,395
3.0 V6 GTX 4dr	£19,395
3.0 V6 4dr	£21,695
2.0 HDi L 90 4dr	£14,350
2.0 HDi LX 90 4dr	£15,450
2.0 HDi LX 110 4dr	£16,250
2.0 HDi GLX 90 4dr	£16,450
2.0 HDi GLX 110 4dr	£17,250
2.0 HDi GTX 110 4dr	£18,450
2.2 HDi GTX 136 4dr	£19,390
2.2 HDi Executive 110 4dr	£20,750
2.2 HDi Executive 136 4dr	£21,690
1.8 L Est	£14,445
2.0 LX Est	£15,595
2.0 GLX Est	£15,895
1.8 GLX Est	£16,955
2.0 GLX Est	£16,895
2.0 GTX Est	£18,095
2.2 SRi Est	£18,245
2.0 Executive Est	£20,395
3.0 V6 GTX Est	£20,395
3.0 V6 Est	£22,695
2.0 HDi L 90 Est	£15,370
2.0 HDi LX 90 Est	£16,470
2.0 HDi LX 110 Est	£17,250
2.0 HDi GLX 90 Est	£17,470
2.0 HDi GLX 110 Est	£18,250
2.0 HDi GTX 110 Est	£19,450
2.0 HDi GTX 136 Est	£20,390
2.0 HDi Executive 110 Est	£21,750
2.2 HDi Executive 136 Est	£22,690
2.0 Coupe	£19,995
2.0 Coupe SE	£22,695
2.2 HDi Coupe S	£22,295
2.2 HDi Coupe SE	£24,995
3.0 V6 SE Coupe	£25,995

607

2.0 4dr	£18,195
2.2 S 4dr	£19,795
2.0 SE 4dr	£20,395
2.2 SE 4dr	£21,695
3.0 S 4dr	£24,595
3.0 SE 4dr	£29,795
2.0 HDi 4dr	£19,395
2.0 HDi S 4dr	£20,995
2.0 HDi SE 4dr	£21,595
2.2 HDi SE 4dr	£22,895

Partner Combi

1.4	£9,095
1.9 D	£9,360

806

2.0 LX	£17,920
2.0 GLX	£18,750
2.0 GTX	£20,150
2.0 HDi LX	£19,415
2.0 HDi Quiksilver	£19,990
2.0 HDi GLX	£20,245
2.0 HDi GTX	£21,645

PORSCHE

Boxster

2.7	£31,450
3.2 S	£38,150

911

Carrera	£55,950
Carrera 4	£59,650
Turbo	£86,000
Carrera Cabriolet	£62,000
Carrera 4 Cabriolet	£65,750

PROTON

Satria

1.3 Li 3dr	£6,999
1.5 LXi 3dr	£7,999
1.5 Lux 3dr	£9,299
1.5 Sport 3dr	£9,299
1.6 Sprint 3dr	£10,299
1.8 GTi 3dr	£12,999

Wira

1.3 Li 5dr	£7,799
1.5 LXi 5dr	£8,799
1.5 Lux 5dr	£9,599
1.6 EXi 5dr	£9,599
1.6 LXi 5dr	£9,799
1.8 SRi 5dr	£12,399
2.0 TD 5dr	£10,799
1.3 Li 4dr	£7,499
1.5 LXi 4dr	£8,499
1.6 16v Style 4dr	£12,000
1.6 16v LX 4dr	£12,560
1.5 Lux 4dr	£9,299
1.6 EXi 4dr	£9,299
1.6 LXi 4dr	£9,499
1.8 Lux 4dr	£11,099

Impian

1.6 4dr	£12,000
1.6 X 4dr	£13,000

Coupe

1.8	£11,499
1.8 Evolution	£12,999

RENAULT

Clio

1.2 Authentique 3dr	£7,495
1.2 -16v Expression 3dr	£7,995
1.2 -16v Expression + 3dr	£8,495
1.2 -16v Dynamique 3dr	£8,495
1.4 -16v Privilege 3dr	£10,295
1.4 -16v Dynamique + 3dr	£10,295
1.6 -16v Dynamique + 3dr	£10,595
2.0 -16v 172 Sport 3dr	£15,495
3.0 V6 Sport 3dr	£25,995
1.5 dCi Expression 3dr	£8,695
1.5 dCi Dynamique 3dr	£9,195
1.2 Authentique 5dr	£7,995
1.2 -16v Expression 5dr	£8,495
1.2 -16v Expression + 5dr	£8,995
1.4 -16v Privilege 5dr	£10,795
1.6 -16v Privilege 5dr	£11,095
1.5 dCi Expression 5dr	£9,195

Kangoo

1.4 Authentique Est	£8,850
1.9 D Authentique Est	£9,250

Mégane

1.6 16v Authentique 5dr	£10,265
1.6 16v Authentique 5dr	£10,565
1.4 16v Expression 5dr	£10,865
1.4 16v Sport 5dr	£10,865
1.6 16v Expression 5dr	£11,165
1.6 16v Sport 5dr	£11,165
1.4-16v Expression + 5dr	£11,465
1.6 16v Dynamique 5dr	£11,665
1.6 16v Expression + 5dr	£11,765
1.6 16v Dynamique 5dr	£11,965
1.4 16v Privilege 5dr	£12,065
1.6 16v Privilege 5dr	£12,265
1.6 16v Privilege + 5dr	£12,365
1.6 16v Privilege 5dr	£12,565
1.6 16v Expression + 5dr	£12,665
1.4 16v Privilege + 5dr	£12,965
1.9 dTi Authentique 5dr	£10,955
1.9 dTi Expression 5dr	£11,555
1.9 dTi Sport 5dr	£11,555
1.9 dTi Expression + 5dr	£12,155
1.9 dCi Expression 5dr	£12,255
1.9 dCi Expression + 5dr	£12,855
1.9 dCi Dynamique 5dr	£13,055
1.9 dCi Privilege 5dr	£13,455
1.9 dCi Dynamique + 5dr	£13,655
1.9 dCi Privilege + 5dr	£14,055
1.4 16v Expression Classic 4dr	£10,865
1.6 16v Expression Classic 4dr	£11,165
1.6 16v Expression + Classic 4dr	£11,465
1.6 16v Expression + Classic 4dr	£11,765
1.4 16v Privilege Classic 4dr	£12,065
1.6 16v Privilege Classic 4dr	£12,365
1.4 16v Privilege+ Classic 4dr	£12,665
1.6 16v Privilege Classic 4dr	£12,965
1.9 dTi Expression Classic 4dr	£11,555
1.9 dTi Privilege+ Classic 4dr	£12,155
1.9 dCi Expression Classic 4dr	£12,255
1.9 dCi Expression+ Classic 4dr	£12,855
1.9 dCi Privilege Classic 4dr	£13,455
1.9 dCi Privilege+ Classic 4dr	£14,055
1.4 16v Expression Coupe	£10,665
1.6 16v Expression Coupe	£10,965
1.4 16v Dynamique Coupe	£11,865
1.6 16v Dynamique Coupe	£12,165
1.4 16v Dynamique+ Coupe	£12,465
1.6 16v Dynamique+ Coupe	£12,765
1.6 16v Privilege+ Coupe	£13,065
1.6 16v Privilege+ Coupe	£13,365
2.0 16v Dynamique Coupe	£13,685
2.0 16v Dynamique + Coupe	£14,285
1.6 16v Privilege + Coupe	£14,485
1.6 16v Expression Conv'	£14,665
1.6 16v Dynamique + Con'	£16,665
1.6 16v Privilege + Con'	£17,265
2.0 16v Dynamique + Conv'	£18,185
1.6 16v Privilege + Conv'	£18,785

Scenic

1.4 16v Authentique 5dr	£12,400
1.6 16v Authentique 5dr	£12,700
1.9 dTi 80 Authentique 5dr	£13,100
1.4 16v Expression 5dr	£13,000
1.6 16v Expression 5dr	£13,300
1.8 16v Expression 5dr	£13,700
1.9 dTi 80 Expression 5dr	£13,700
1.9 dCi 105 Expression 5dr	£14,400
Expression+ add £600	
1.6 16v Dynamic 5dr	£14,100
1.8 16v Dynamic 5dr	£14,500
2.0 16v Dynamic 5dr	£15,200
2.0 16v RX4 Expression 5dr	£16,500
1.9 dCi 105 Dynamic 5dr	£15,200
1.9 dCi RX4 Expression 5dr	£16,500
Dynamic+ add £600	
1.8 16v Privilege 5dr	£14,500
1.8 16v Privilege 5dr	£14,900
2.0 16v Privilege 5dr	£15,600
1.9 dCi 105 Privilege 5dr	£15,600
1.9 dCi RX4 Privilege 5dr	£17,700
Privilege+ add £600	
1.6 16v Privilege Monaco 5dr	£15,700
1.8 16v Privilege Monaco 5dr	£16,100
2.0 16v Privilege Monaco 5dr	£16,800
2.0 16v RX4 Priv' Monaco 5dr	£18,900
1.9 dCi 105 Priv' Monaco 5dr	£16,800
1.9 dCi RX4 Priv' Monaco 5dr	£18,900

Laguna

1.6-16v Authentique 5dr	£14,255
1.8-16v Authentique 5dr	£14,580
1.6-16v Expression 5dr	£14,905
1.8-16v Expression 5dr	£15,230
1.6-16v Dynamique 5dr	£15,255
1.8-16v Dynamique 5dr	£15,580
1.8-16v Privilege 5dr	£16,680
3.0 V6 Dynamique 5dr	£18,795
3.0 V6 Privilege 5dr	£19,895
3.0 V6 Initiale 5dr	£21,895
1.6-16v Authentique Est	£16,050
1.9 dCi Authentique Est	£16,700
2.0 16v Dynamique Est	£17,050
1.8-16v Dynamique Est	£16,580
1.8-16v Privilege Est	£17,680
3.0 V6 Dynamique Est	£19,795
3.0 V6 Privilege Est	£20,895
3.0 V6 Initiale Est	£22,895
1.9 dCi Dynamique Est	£18,070
1.9 dCi Privilege Est	£19,170

Espace

2.0 Authentique	£19,350
2.0 Expression	£21,350
2.0 Race	£22,350
2.0 Privilege	£24,850
3.0 V6 Privilege	£27,600
3.0 V6 Initiale	£30,600
2.2 Expression dCi	£21,255
2.2 Expression dCi	£23,255
2.2 Race dCi	£24,255
2.2 Privilege dCi	£25,755
Grand 2.0 Expression	£22,350
Grand 2.0 Race	£23,350
Grand 2.0 Privilege	£25,850
Grand 3.0 V6 Privilege	£28,600
Grand 3.0 V6 Initiale	£31,600
Grand 2.2 Expression dCi	£24,255
Grand 2.2 Race dCi	£25,255
Grand 2.2 Privilege dCi	£26,755

Avantime

2.0 Turbo Dynamique	£24,000
3.0 V6 Privilege	£27,000

ROLLS-ROYCE

Silver Seraph	£159,000
Last of Line	£169,000
Corniche	£250,000

SAAB

9-3

2.0t 3dr	£16,795
2.0t SE 3dr	£18,795
2.0T SE 3dr	£20,145
2.0 Aero 3dr	£25,295
2.2TiD 3dr	£15,995
2.2TiD SE 3dr	£17,995
2.0t 5dr	£17,295
2.0t SE 5dr	£19,295
2.0T SE 5dr	£20,645
2.0 Aero 5dr	£25,795
2.2TiD 5dr	£16,445
2.2TiD SE 5dr	£18,445
2.0t SE Convertible	£24,885
2.0t SE Design Convertible	£25,645
2.0T SE Convertible	£26,895
2.0T SE Design Convertible	£26,995
2.0 Aero Convertible	£31,995

9-5

2.0t Linear 4dr	£21,395
2.0t Arc 4dr	£23,595
2.0t Vector 4dr	£23,595
2.3t Linear 4dr	£22,595
2.3t Arc 4dr	£24,795
2.3 Vector 4dr	£24,795
2.3 Hot Aero 4dr	£27,695
3.0t Arc 4dr	£28,495
3.0t Vector 4dr	£28,495
3.0 V6 TiD Linear 4dr	£24,495
3.0 V6 TiD Arc 4dr	£26,395
3.0 V6 TiD Vector 4dr	£26,395
2.0t Linear	£22,595
2.0t Arc	£24,795
2.0t Vector	£24,795
2.3t Linear	£23,795
2.3t Arc	£25,995
2.3t Vector	£25,995
2.3 Hot Aero	£28,895
3.0t Arc	£29,695
3.0t Vector	£29,695
3.0 V6 TiD Linear	£25,695
3.0 V6 TiD Arc	£27,595
3.0 V6 TiD Vector	£27,595

SEAT

Arosa

1.0 3dr	£6,695
1.0 S 3dr	£7,295
1.4 S 3dr	£8,480
1.4 16v Sport 3dr	£9,960
1.4 TDi 3dr	£8,950

Ibiza

1.4 S 3dr	£7,960
1.6 Sport 3dr	£10,995
1.8 T Cupra 3dr	£12,995
1.8 T Cupra R 3dr	£17,990
1.4 S 5dr	£8,360
1.9 TDi S 5dr	£10,750

Leon

1.4-16v S 5dr	£9,960
1.6 S 5dr	£10,980
1.8 20v SE 5dr	£13,745
1.8 20v Turbo Cupra 5dr	£14,995
1.9 TDI S 90bhp 5dr	£12,250
1.9 TDI SE 110bhp 5dr	£14,650

Toledo

1.8 20v SE 4dr	£14,495
2.3 V5 4dr	£16,995
1.9 TDi SE 4dr	£15,450

Alhambra

2.0 S	£16,995
1.8 20v Turbo S	£18,195
1.8 20v Turbo SE	£20,495
2.8 V6 Sport	£24,395
1.9 TDi 115 S	£18,990
1.9 TDi 115 SE	£21,290

SKODA

Fabia

1.4 Classic 5dr	£7,685
1.4 Comfort 5dr	£9,485
1.4-16v 75bhp Classic 5dr	£9,200
1.4-16v Comfort 5dr	£10,485
1.4-16v 75bhp Comfort 5dr	£11,000
1.4-16v Elegance 5dr	£11,285
2.0-16v Elegance 5dr	£11,900
1.9 SDI Classic 5dr	£8,355
1.9 SDI Comfort 5dr	£10,155
1.9 TDI 100bhp Comfort 5dr	£11,125
1.9 TDI 100bhp Elegance 5dr	£12,055
1.4 Classic Est	£8,385
1.4-16v 75bhp Classic Est	£9,900
1.4 Comfort Est	£10,185